CORN Publication Series 3

Dépôt légal 4e trimestre 1999
D/1999/0095/75
ISBN 2-503-50963-0

MARRIAGE AND RURAL ECONOMY
WESTERN EUROPE SINCE 1400

Edited by Isabelle Devos
& Liam Kennedy

BREPOLS

CONTENTS

LIST OF CONTRIBUTORS

GEORGE ALTER	Population Institute, Indiana University, USA
MICHAEL ANDERSON	Department of Economic History, University of Edinburgh, UK
ISABELLE DEVOS	Department of Early Modern History, University of Ghent, B
THEO ENGELEN	Department of History, University of Nijmegen, NL
GEORG FERTIG	Institute for Comparative Urban History, University of Münster, D
FRANCOIS HENDRICKX	Department of History, University of Nijmegen, NL
LIAM KENNEDY	Department of Economic and Social History, The Queen's University of Belfast, UK
CHRISTER LUNDH	Department of Economic History, Lund University, S
JAN NELISSEN	Work and Organisation Research Centre, Brabant University, NL
MICHEL ORIS	Department of Social and Economic History, University of Liège, B
RICHARD SMITH	Cambridge Group for the History of Population and Social Structure, UK
SØLVI SOGNER	Department of History, University of Oslo, N
AD VAN DER WOUDE	Department of Agrarian History, Agricultural University Wageningen, NL
FRANS VAN POPPEL	Netherlands Interdisciplinary Demographic Institute, NL

LIST OF FIGURES

LIST OF TABLES

LIST OF APPENDICES

Editors preface

The theme of demographic change is of special interest to the CORN network of historians. Its focus is the comparative rural history in the North Sea area, from the medieval to contemporary times. In November 1995, when the CORN group originated, it was decided to include 'marriage and economic conditions' in its research programme. In so doing, it was recognized that for centuries, marriage behaviour has been a key area of life in terms of rural economy.

This book examines rural marriage patterns in the long run, relating these to changing economic conditions in the North Sea area, from circa 1400 to the present. Since Hajnal's pioneering publication in 1965, research on nuptiality has expanded greatly and remained almost exclusively the field of historical demography. Wrigley and Schofield's monumental study of English population history between the 16th and the 19th centuries which *inter alia* matched nuptiality to changes in economic opportunity, was a turning point for the study of family formation. The debate this work prompted is still continuing. The starting point was the belief that more long-run studies within a region or country, and, even more, comparative studies across countries, are necessary to grasp the nature of the connections between economy, marriage and population change. By examining different forms of rural economy such as peasant farming, capitalist farming, proto-industry and other systems of production with differing implications for marriage and family formation, demographic and economic mechanisms may emerge more clearly. This book presents the current state of research on the European Marriage Pattern in Ireland, Scotland, England, Belgium, the Netherlands, Germany and Scandinavia. Turning from description to explanation, a complex of interacting factors which regulated the formation of new households is identified and directions for further research are shown.

The present volume arose from a seminar organised by the CORN network held in Cambridge in September 1998. We are most grateful to the (Flemish) Fund for Scientific Research (FWO) for its generous provision of funds to enable scholars to travel from many different countries to attend this event. We also want to express our gratitude towards the participants who have produced versions of their papers for publication and other colleagues such as Mark Overton, Erik Thoen, Ad van der Woude, Eric Vanhaute and Jan Luiten van Zanden, who attended the conference and participated in the discussions. We have given the contributors the opportunity to revise and to incorporate comments from the animated discussions into their papers. The contributions represented here constitute an important body of work that will be of interest to all those engaged in the study of the European Marriage Pattern, its workings and its implications. The fruits of this collaborative venture should also lay the basis for further research, particularly of a comparative kind.

Isabelle Devos, Ghent
Liam Kennedy, Belfast

Introduction

Ad VAN DER WOUDE, Agricultural University Wageningen

As a non-believer in the value of horoscopes and astrology, I would say simply that 'it was in the air'. The outbreak of historical demography as a scientifically founded historical discipline was in the air in the 1950s and 1960s. The techniques of family reconstitution, the discovery of a European Marriage Pattern, the study of household and family in the past as an object of scientific analysis, all have to be considered to belong to the fundamentals of the discipline, which can be traced back to the years between 1953 and 1969 (Henry, 1953; Hajnal, 1969). We may perhaps even say that, along with later techniques such as inverse projection, they constitute the pillars on which the structure of historical demography has been constructed.

More than thirty years after Hajnal's path-breaking publication, CORN (Comparative Rural History of the North Sea Area) organized a conference in Cambridge in 1998 with a view to establishing the state of the art as regards the study of the Western European Marriage Pattern (WEMP) and to promote, if possible, new directions of research into this phenomenon. This volume contains the papers to the conference, revised in the light of intensive discussion among the participants. The contributions were drawn from Ireland, Scotland, England, Belgium, the Netherlands, Germany and Scandinavia.

Michael Anderson, himself a leading historical sociologist of the family since the 1970s (Anderson 1971) has contributed an overview of the conference findings. This is contained at the end of the volume. This short essay is in itself a valuable introduction to the major themes and issues associated with the WEMP. In particular, it deals with questions which go beyond the specifically regional or national situation and which have a more general significance.

An analysis of the chronological coverage of the chapters shows that nine out of the eleven contributors concerned themselves with the 19th century (or major part thereof), six with the 18th century, four with the 20th century and only one with the marriage pattern in the 16th and 17th centuries. In the light of these temporal preoccupations, one might add to Anderson's commentary a further impression of the Cambridge gathering. For the most part, the participants in the conference were primarily trying to explain the workings of a marriage system that was already firmly in place. True, there were national and regional variations, and change over time in the typical age at marriage and the proportions never married, but these variations were contained within what was a recognisably West European pattern. Steeply fluctuating economic circumstances did not alter this essential continuity.

But what of the birth of the pattern itself? In the opening chapter Richard Smith (Chapter 1) pushes his analysis back into the Middle Ages, when, at least in England, a 'modern' marriage system seems to have operated. Theo Engelen, appropriately enough in the final chapter of the volume, also touches on the remote origins of the WEMP, albeit indirectly, as he explores the forces making for the dissolution of the system itself, the resolution of which might allow us a greater understanding of the nature of the system and its remarkable endurance in time.

Two big questions follow from this, though they are really part of an agenda for the future. First, when, where and why did the WEMP originate? Second, where, when and why did it spread? Had it something to do with a worsening of the bargaining power of the individual worker in the later Middle Ages, provoking a so called 'industrious revolution' (as formulated by Jan de Vries, 1994) by which the family income was kept intact as much as possible? Had it anything to do with the need for the existence of a mobile and flexible workforce, that could be created by keeping young workers unmarried till their mid-twenties and even later? Or is there further insight to be gained from Richard Smith's suggestions that 'the period 1350–1450 and 1650–1750 (in England) share certain features in common with respect to their nuptiality patterns and survivorship levels'? Perhaps we need to look more closely at long swings of the secular trends, not only regionally but internationally as well.

In any case, in the 18th century the WEMP seems to have had its weakest development in the periphery of its territory of dissemination (Europe west of the line St Petersburg–Trieste), i.e. Ireland (Chapter 3) and eastern parts of Finland (Chapter 8). Did it not at an earlier time expand from a core region in western Europe to these remote fringes of western Europe? Or has the establishment of these patterns to be explained in a different way? It is at least possible, in case of Finland, for example, that in the early modern people the population of eastern Finland was composed of Lutheran Finns but also of Orthodox Slavic people.

But these are questions for the future. The organisers of the Cambridge conference, Erik Thoen, Liam Kennedy and Isabelle Devos, deserve our warm congratulations and gratitude. This has been an important initiative. Such international collaboration is one further step in discovering a European past which, in the case of marriage institutions and associated cultural forms, seems to have been far more united than we might have dared dream.

Bibliography

Henry, L. (1953) 'Une richesse démographique en friche: les registres paroissiaux', *Population*, 8, pp. 281–90.

Hajnal, J. (1965) 'European marriage patterns in perspective', in D.V. Glass and D.E.C. Eversley (eds), *Population in history*, London, pp. 101–43.

Laslett, P. and Wall, R. (eds) (1972) *Household and family in past time*, edition of papers read in a conference held in Cambridge in September 1969, Cambridge.

Anderson, M. (1971) *Family structure in nineteenth century Lancashire*, Cambridge.

Vries, J. de (1994) 'The Industrial Revolution and the Industrious Revolution', in *Journal of Economic History*, 54, pp. 249–70.

1 Relative prices, forms of agrarian labour and female marriage patterns in England, 1350–1800

Richard M. Smith, University of Cambridge

With the publication of Wrigley and Schofield's *Population History of England* in 1981, there appeared a set of fertility, mortality and nuptiality indices that have subsequently proved to be widely accepted as a statement about national trends from the 16th to the 19th centuries, although based upon the inflation of estimates derived from 404 parishes. These estimates were derived from aggregative analysis of counts of baptisms, burials and marriages in parish registers which formed the 'data' for calculating various demographic rates utilizing the technique of generalized inverse projection (as it has come to be termed). In a more recent publication new estimates have appeared from twenty-six parishes that have been generated using the technique of family reconstitution (Wrigley et al., 1997). These estimates tell a story of demographic change that is in many respects similar to that obtained from aggregative analysis, although there are some important refinements to the earlier account and access is now granted to data that could not be secured by use of inverse projection, a novel demographic accounting technique that was created in the early 1980s at the Cambridge Group for the History of Population and Social Structure. Certain relatively crude nuptiality measures were obtained from this aggregative analysis that can now be further refined with data derived from family reconstitution. In neither approach is it possible to deal effectively with regional patterns, although we are somewhat better informed about demographic trends and patterns to be found in certain 'types' of community distinguished by rather crudely defined economic characteristics. This handicap must be kept in mind in assessing many of the issues that are discussed below.

As Lesthaeghe (1980: 528) stated almost twenty years ago, 'the story of the nuptiality valve in western Europe before 1850 is well known' with a sizeable component of the female reproductive capacity underexploited or unexploited because of the late age of entry into, and a significant number of women remaining definitively out of marriage. It has frequently been asserted that this nuptiality pattern acted as a safety valve in the creation of demographic homeostasis responding as a dependent variable to shifts in mortality. In fact Lesthaeghe, in a paper that has achieved classical status, argues that 'the central force in demographic homeostasis is the force of mortality' (Lesthaeghe, 1980: 528). This particular conceptualization of homeostasis inclines us to see fertility marching to the tune played by mortality. If mortality is assumed to have been unstable, showing no detectable secular trend, *ipso facto* nuptiality as the principal 'driver' of fertility, would be expected to behave in a similar fashion. Indeed, it is this particular assessment of the relationship between nuptiality and life expectancy that might lead an analyst of the pre-19th century West European demographic system to feel that the role of nuptiality can easily be overstressed as a fundamental, indeed proximate, influence upon secular demographic trends.

Figure 1.1 Changes in English fertility, 1541–1901: quinquennial GRRs

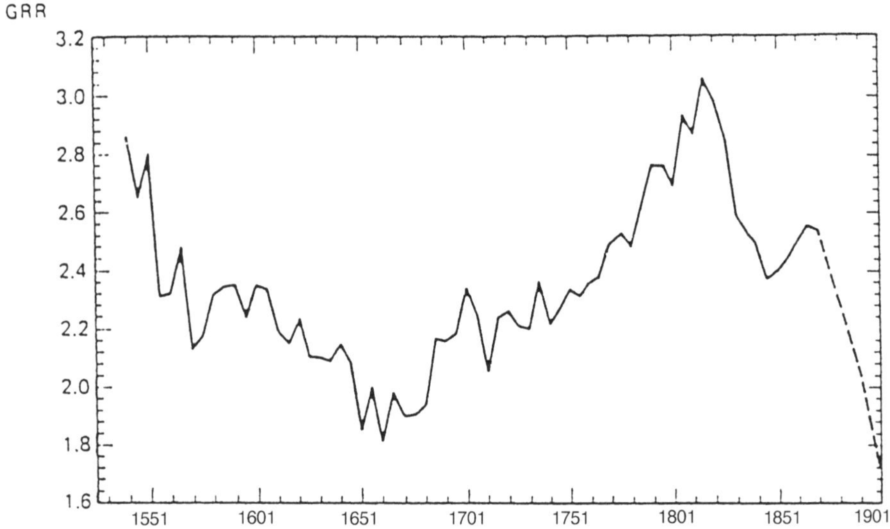

Empirical analysis of English demographic evidence from the period before 1800 requires us to revise this view. Nuptiality and associated fertility shifts appear in the main not to have operated primarily as a short-term equilibrating force reacting immediately and principally in the wake of mortality surges; rather, shifts in fertility and nuptiality took the form of long, often century-long, waves of growth and decline. From 1541 to 1871, the secular pattern in English fertility was relatively simple (see Figure 1.1). Fertility was high in the mid-16th century when the gross reproduction rate was about 2.8, then fell abruptly to about 2.4 and thereafter tended to fall further but only slowly and slightly, until it sagged suddenly to a nadir of about 1.8–1.9 in the last third of the 17th century. Thereafter there was recovery, although this was irregular and somewhat hesitant until the mid-18th century. After 1756 the rise of fertility accelerated noticeably, with the Gross Reproduction Rate (GRR) reaching a peak value of 3.1 in 1816. Throughout the whole fertility series there were very few marked short-term departures from the trend line, but rather a steady progression toward and between the two major turning points in the late 17th century and at the end of the second decade of the 19th century. The pattern of fertility shift is mirrored in very large part in the graph showing intrinsic growth rates. In this graph we cannot detect a regular cycle in which, for example, a constant growth rate (i.e., a tendency toward stationarity) was periodically interrupted by brief spells of abrupt population decline (see Figure 1.2). The mortality series as represented by expectation of life at birth, also suggests a cycle which, while less regular than that displayed by the GRR, reveals a lengthy deterioration through the 17th century followed by a recovery to late 16th levels by the early 19th century (see Figure 1.3). Rather than homeostasis, the pattern suggests that fertility behaviour may have been responding systematically to secular changes in its social, economic and biological milieu.

Figure 1.2 Compound annual growth rates of the population of England, 1541–1871

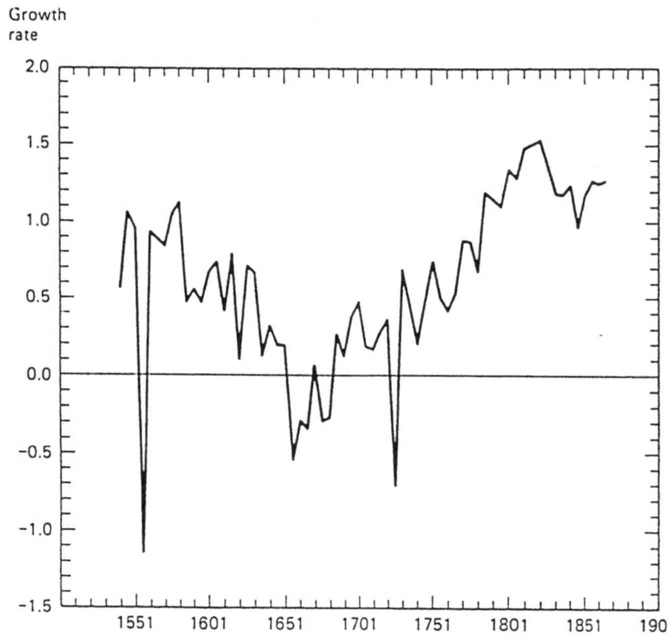

Figure 1.3 Changes in English mortality, 1541–1901: quinquennial e_0s

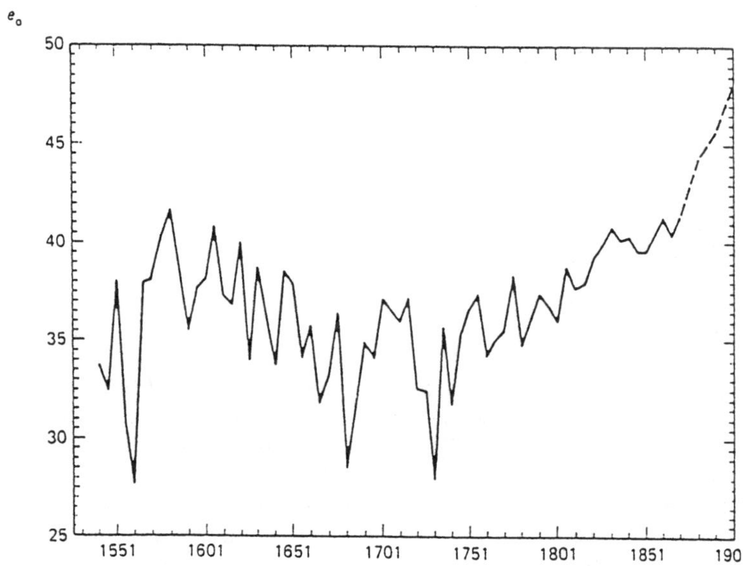

Wrigley and Schofield in their original publication of the data derived from the sample of 404 parishes, much influenced by the work of John Hajnal (1982), assumed that in England a household formation system prevailed in which entry into headship was concentrated into a fairly narrow age group. A crude rate of first marriage per thousand persons aged 15–34 (calculated somewhat arbitrarily by assuming that remarriage proportions were 30 per cent in 1541 and declined thereafter linearly) was thought to provide an approximate surrogate measure for the rate of new household creation per thousand persons (see Figure 1.4). The shape of the curve thereby created resembled very closely the shapes of the curves depicting the gross reproduction rate, falling steadily to a low point in the late 17th century and then rising steadily to a high plateau from 1771 to 1796.

Figure 1.4 Estimated crude first marriage rates (marriages per 1,000 persons aged 15–34) compared with gross reproduction rates (both twenty-five-year moving averages)

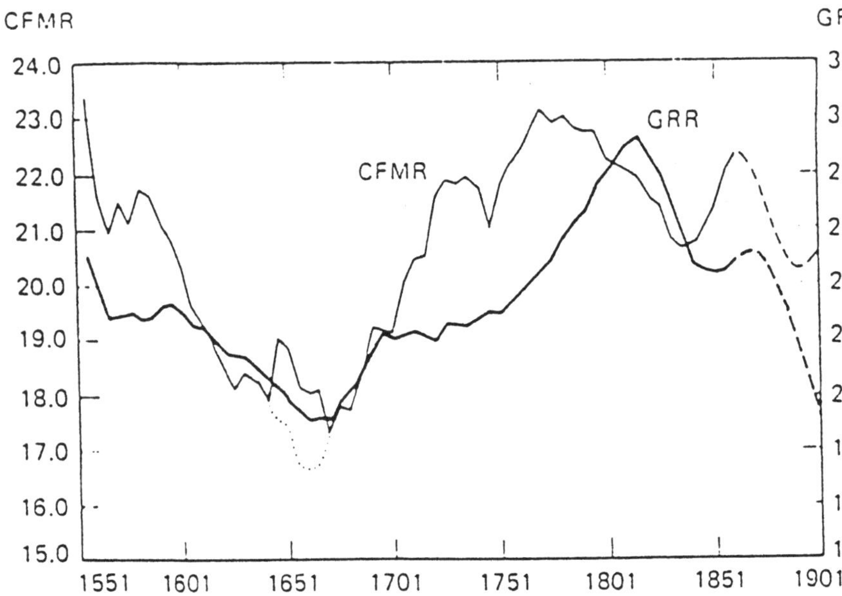

Perhaps the most remarkable evidence that emerged with the publication of Wrigley and Schofield's weighty work concerned the level of fertility and its associated marriage rate in the half century after 1650. The GRR remained below 2 for the whole period between 1651 and 1681 and did not exceed 2.18 before 1700. Life expectancy at birth in the century between the accession of Elizabeth I to the throne (1558) and the restoration (1660) passed from a mortality regime that had been unusually mild by the general standards of early modern Europe to one that was probably closer to the norm; expectation at birth fell from 40–41 years in the 1570s and 1580s to a low point in the 1680s when it was marginally below 30 years, before recovering for a while and then falling again in the 1720s.

Figure 1.5 Homeostasis on a demographic terrain map

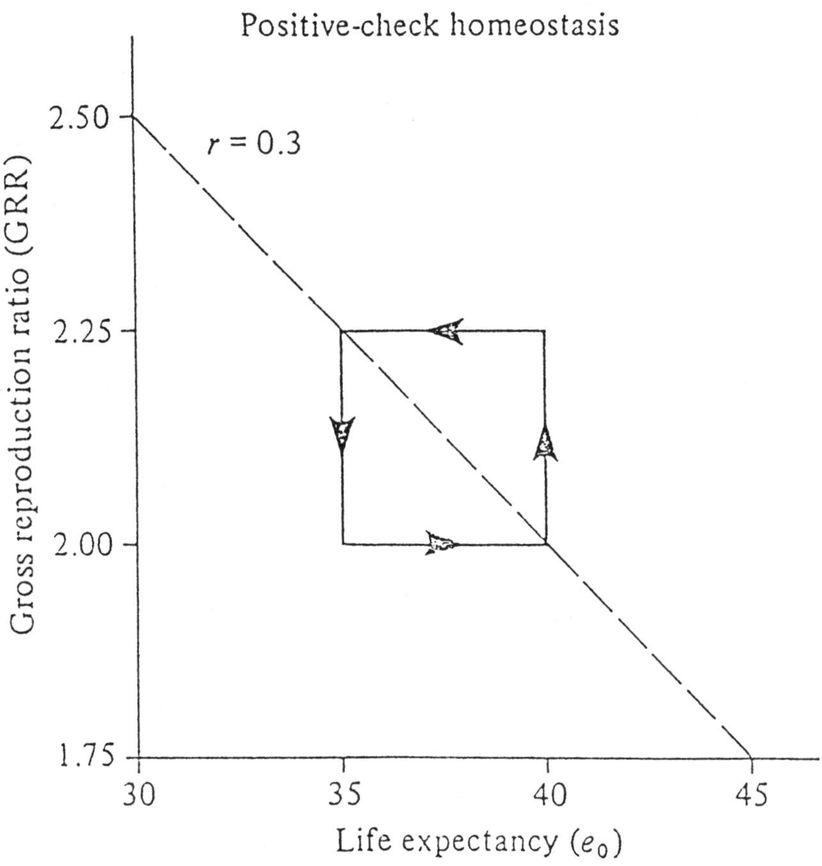

What is noteworthy throughout the 17th and the first half of the 18th centuries is that the effect of a decline in life expectancy was being compounded by a fall in fertility in such a way as to stifle demographic growth and to offer the possibility of actual demographic decline. This hardly seems compatible with what is sometimes described as 'preventive-check homeostasis'. The latter is a notion used by Jack Goldstone (1983) in a widely cited article to characterize the English demographic regime prior to 1750. Goldstone argues that the secular movements in fertility and mortality, when plotted on demographic terrain maps, display the characteristic 'clockwise signature' of a preventive-check homeostasis in which a rise in mortality lowers the intrinsic growth rate to be followed by a compensating increase in fertility to such an extent that the former growth rate is restored (see Figure 1.5).

The tendency of mortality to rise and fertility to fall in tandem or simultaneously might well strike a French historical demographer as somewhat odd. Based very largely on their findings in researching the demographic histories of Normandy and the Paris Basin over the same centuries, Pierre Chaunu (1974) and Jacques Dupâquier (1972, 1979), in particular, emphasize a demographic equilibrium that was continually re-establishing itself despite disturbances largely initiated by epidemics or exogenously driven mortality rises. The nuptiality valve opened and closed in response to mortality movements such that marriage age or marital incidence adjusted to compensate for the losses of lives that occurred. In his major demographic history of the Paris Basin in the Ancien Régime, Dupâquier appears to argue that over what he terms 'la Période Classique' (1670–1739) the number of households or hearths varied hardly at all. To explain this phenomenon, he draws upon the concept of an agricultural holding or craft workshop as fulfilling a function analogous to that of a territory in a bird population in which a new breeding pair is only allowed to establish itself once a nest is vacated. Dupâquier actually refers to this system as 'une sorte de purgatoire matrimonial rapellant les épreuves solidaires des jeunes oiseaux privés des nids par les adultes' (1972: 201). For Dupâquier, this was a purgatory that was often relieved in the short term as epidemics struck and provided those in society's subordinate positions with an opportunity to establish a new household. There is no doubt that throughout the late 17th and 18th centuries, rural French society seems to have displayed the attributes of the homeostatic regime *par excellence* with fertility declining as mortality, especially after 1740, improved.

This concept of a nuptiality valve which took its cue from shifts in mortality appears to have been singularly inappropriate as a conceptual device for considering England as a demographic entity in the 17th and 18th centuries. Of course, it is possible that certain groups who derived a livelihood in slow-growing sectors of the English economy or acquired wealth principally through inheritance of a fixed slot or niche may have displayed such behaviour, but were undetected in the aggregated behaviour patterns or were located in regions that were insufficiently large to make a noticeable impact on the national 'average' behaviour. There are, it must be acknowledged, some signs of a 'peasant' demographic system in the late 16th century when there was some compensatory fall in fertility as mortality declined from the severe levels that applied in the 1550s. In such a situation worries about slots into which younger sons and unemployed young adult males might be placed emerges as a concern among contemporary social commentators and describers of the social order as well as of those who were experimenting with early schemes for the relief of poverty and the containment of male vagrancy (Fisher, 1936; Beier, 1985).

Furthermore, it should not be assumed that in the 17th century the English displayed no compensatory shifts in their fertility through increased marriage frequencies in the wake of mortality surges. Indeed in this period before 1640, after a mortality crisis in which the death rate was 100 per cent above normal in the ensuing five years, marriages would have been 47 per cent above normal. But for the period from 1641 to

1745, comparable mortality surges would have stimulated only a 16 per cent increase in marriages in the following quinquenium (Wrigley and Schofield, 1981: 376). In the later 17th century, French marital responsiveness to short-term mortality changes was much more marked. Over the course of the 17th century, we therefore observe in England a marked decline in the responsiveness of marriages to stimuli from mortality surges. Such a development is viewed by some interpreters as indicative of a considerable drop in the incidence of remarriage and probably a lengthening of remarriage intervals. One might speculate, as do Ronald Lee and Roger Schofield (in Wrigley and Schofield, 1981: 376) that remarriage change, in part reflects a diminishing importance of landholdings as a basis for marriage and a drop in the demand for widows in possession of land as material conditions improved in the course of the century. Similar conditions have been documented over the course of the 14th century (Smith, 1983a, 1983b). It is likely too that the land-holding component of the rural population fell relative to the number of property-less or property-deficient labourers for whom property possession in widowhood was unlikely to have been a factor enhancing the remarriage chances of the widow who had been pre-deceased. This suggests that over the later 17th century, England apparently unlike France (or more specifically Northern France) came to possess a demographic climate in which marriage frequencies were relatively insensitive to changes in mortality in both the short and medium term. Later in this chapter, attention will be drawn to other influences that might have contributed to this shift in marital behaviour among the English population.

Up to this point in the discussion, little attention has been given to the obvious point that there are two aspects of nuptiality that impact upon fertility: the proportion of each birth cohort surviving into adulthood that proceeds to marry, and the mean age of marriage of those who do so. Recently it has been possible substantially to expand the information available on trends in marriage ages through the use of twenty-six parish-based family reconstitutions (Wrigley et al., 1997). However, we are not able, using the information in parish registers, to calculate the proportions never marrying. We can follow those who remain in observation, and all marriage age calculations concern those who are baptised/born in the parish and proceed to marry in that place. We cannot establish the marital status or age of those marrying from the remaining individuals who are born and do not die or marry in the parish. As Roger Schofield notes, 'if we suppose that we were to discover that the average age at marriage was the same at two different dates, then we would be wrong to say that the nuptiality of the population was the same at the two dates, because we are quite unaware of the proportion that was never married at either date' (Schofield, 1998: 2–3). Furthermore, in using family reconstitution to measure the age at marriage it is distinctly possible that we might derive estimates of average marriage that are too low (Ruggles, 1992). However, it seems that in England a very substantial amount of the mobility that took place occurred in association with life-cycle service in husbandry in rural society in which migration and marriage were part and parcel of the same process or event (Wrigley, 1994). (Desjardins has shown that in French Canada in the period 1680–1740, where the registers allow the subsequent histories of those who left their place of birth and later married elsewhere to be traced, the mean age of marriage differed by 0.3 years in the case of men, and was actually the same in the case of women (Desjardins, 1995).)

Figure 1.6 Mean age at first marriage, bachelor–spinster marriages, decennial data

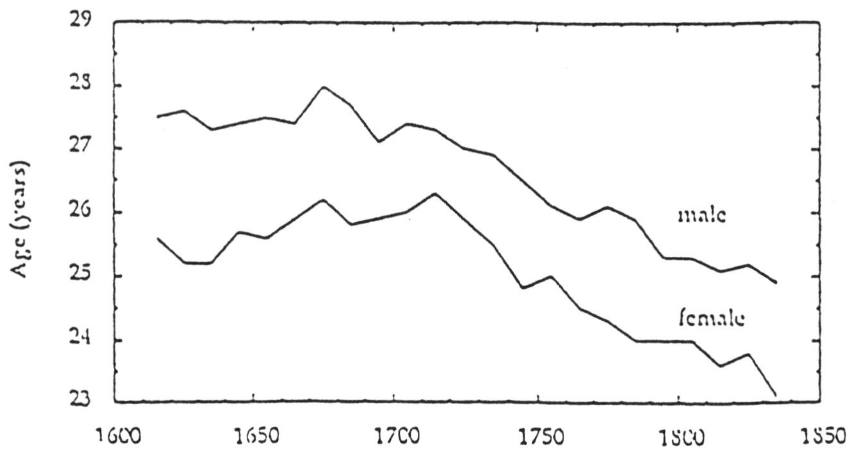

Figure 1.6 plots the decadal means concerned, beginning in 1610–9 and ending in 1830–7.[1] From the start of the period until the 1670s, the male mean age at marriage was practically stationary at about 27.5. In the 1680s it rose to 28.0, and then fell by three years to 24.9 by the 1830s. The female mean age at marriage rose slightly from 25.5 years in the 1610s to 26.3 years in the 1710s, and after that date it also fell until it reached 23.1 in the 1830s. So the period divides into two: before 1680 or 1720 in the case of women, there is practically no movement in the mean age at marriage, while during most of the 18th century the mean age fell by 3.2 years for both sexes. By the middle of the 18th century there was a very marked change in the proportion of men and women who began to be married much younger than in the previous six generations. By the end of the 18th century, 70 per cent of all spinsters who married bachelors had done so before their twenty-fifth birthday. Their grooms were scarcely less quick to marry; approaching 60 per cent of them had done so by the same birthday. At the other end of the distribution, fewer than 10 per cent of the brides married above the age of 30 in the later period, compared with 18 per cent in the earlier period, while for grooms the comparable percentages were 15 and 25 (Wrigley et al., 1997: 144).

[1] The marriage data were 'spliced' at each end of the data period to take account of the compositional changes as parishes pass out of observation (Wrigley et al., 1997: 129–32).

The distribution of the age gap between grooms and brides showed the same pattern. While the median difference between grooms' and brides' ages scarcely changed between 1600-1729 and 1750-1837 at 1.6 and 1.5 years, the proportion which fell between +/–4 years rose from 58.5 per cent to 69.8 per cent. Although the age gap appears basically stable, more couples after 1750 than before married a partner who was neither five years older or younger than themselves (Wrigley et al., 1997: 172). While the downward trend in marriage age after 1720 appears to have been notably uniform across all twenty-six parishes, it might, of course, have been more pronounced in some kinds of parish than others. English registers give almost no information on the occupation of individuals, so to test this possibility, and to see if there was any occupational continuum in marriage age, Wrigley et al. divided the parishes into four groups, depending on the predominant occupation of the male labour force at the earliest census for which economic attributes of individual communities can be assessed. Eight agricultural parishes were distinguished in the sample, where 60 per cent or more of the labour force were so engaged; five 'retail', trade and handicrafts' parishes, where 40 per cent or more were so engaged; three 'manufacturing' parishes, where 30 per cent or more were so engaged; and the rest (ten parishes) were deemed to be 'mixed' economies.[2]

[2] The criteria for the first three groups are such that no parish qualified under more than one head.

Figure 1.7 **Mean age at first marriage in the twenty-six reconstitution parishes: bachelor-spinster marriages (years)**

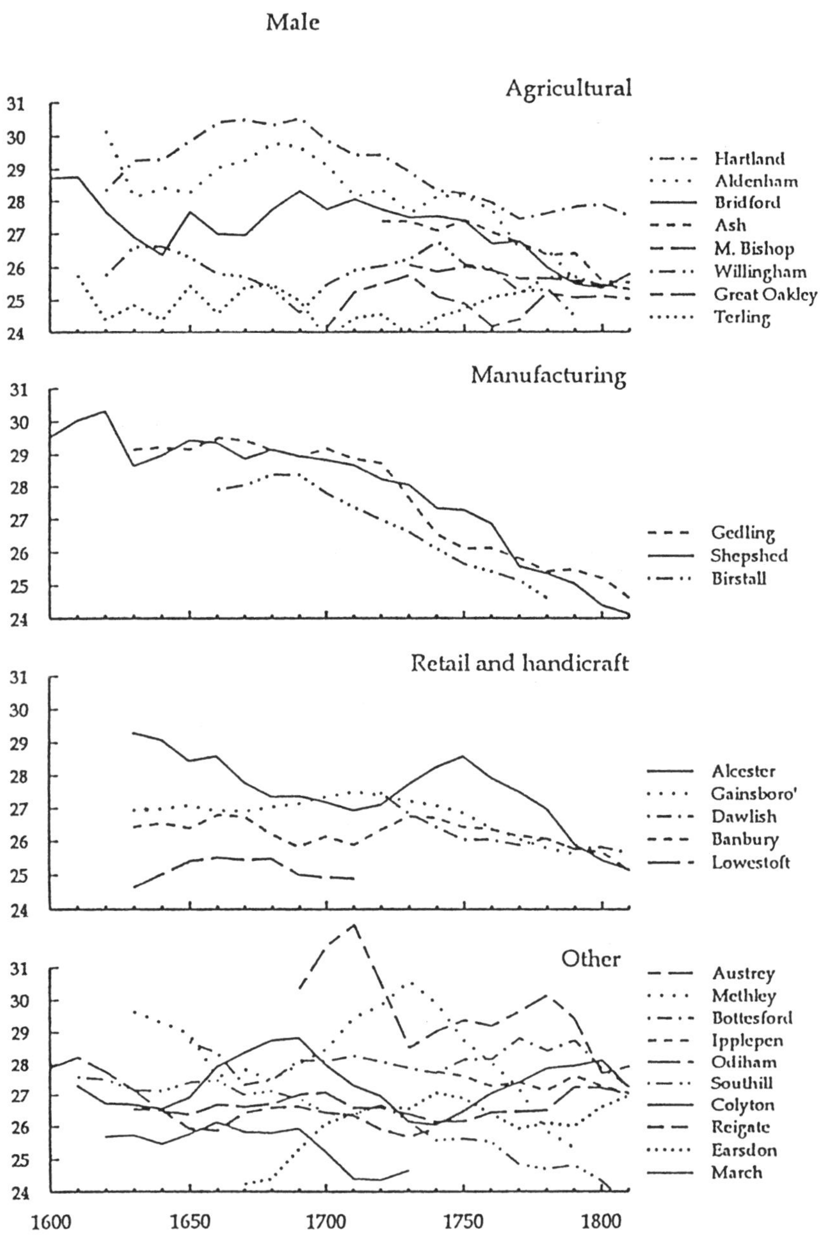

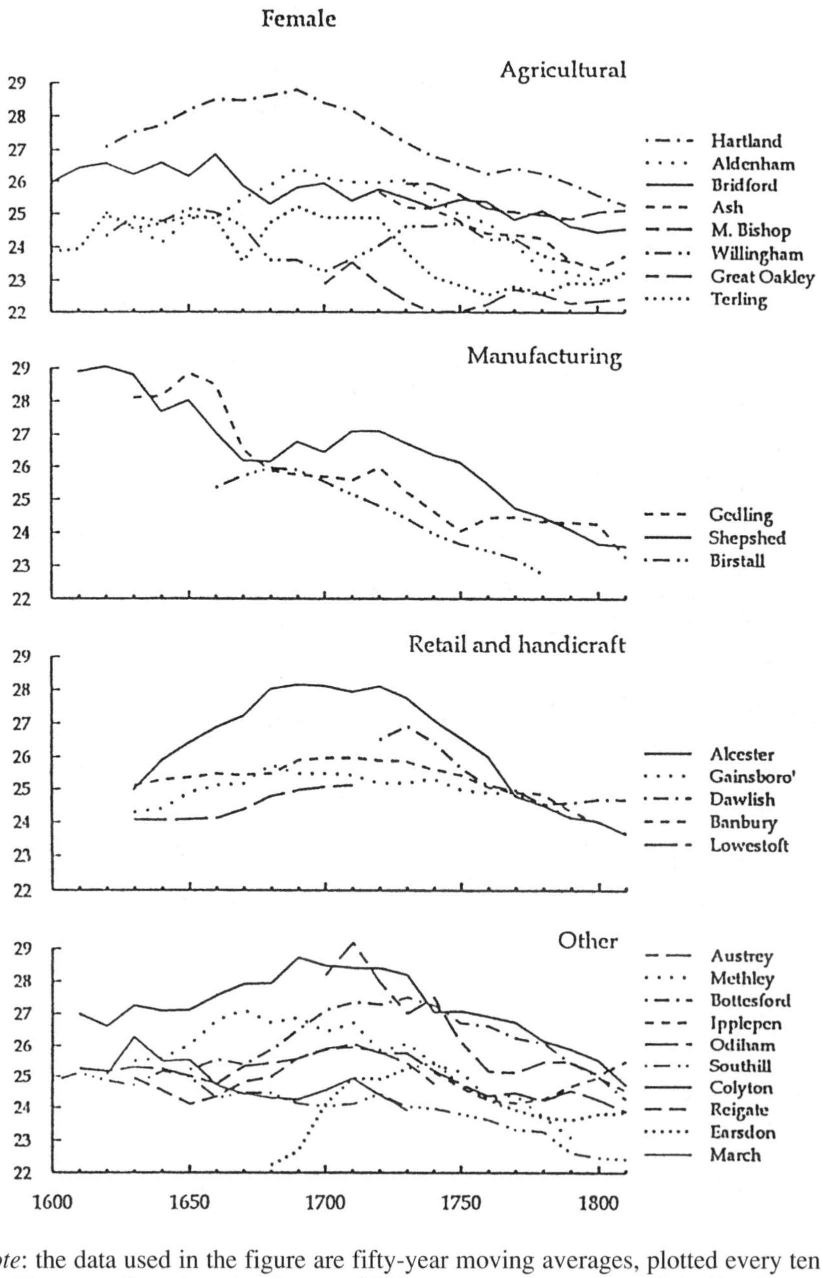

Note: the data used in the figure are fifty-year moving averages, plotted every ten years. Thus a reading plotted at the year 1650 represents the average of the five decennial figures for the decades 1630–9 to 1670–9.

Figure 1.7 presents the data in the form of fifty-year centred moving averages of the mean age of brides and grooms in bachelor/spinster marriages in each of the parishes, though it should always be remembered that in some small parishes the number of ages at marriage, even over a fifty-year period, might have been very small and the possibility for random fluctuation not inconsiderable. In the agricultural group, perhaps the most striking feature is the convergence towards a low age at marriage at the end of the parish register period, a feature especially marked among males. In the early 19th century every parish, except Hartland, lay within the range 25–27 years for male age at marriage. This feature stands in vivid contrast with the situation one hundred years earlier, when there was a wide spread of mean ages. The tendency for female marriage ages to converge over the 18th century is less pronounced in the agricultural parishes, nor is the division into high and low marriage age groups in the 17th century so clear-cut.

The manufacturing parishes are few in number, and the pattern of change is simple. Before the advent of large-scale employment of a proto-industrial type, all three parishes were late marrying. Marriage age plunged in the course of the 18th century, though by the early 19th century, when the fall was bottoming out, age at marriage was only slightly lower than in the other groups. The three display great uniformity, but the small number of parishes precludes confident generalizations. The retail trade and handicraft group also witnessed a significant fall in the age at marriage during the 18th century. As in the case of the agricultural parishes, there was a marked convergence of lines on the graph towards the end of the period, leaving little difference between the parishes by 1800. The 'other' or 'mixed' group, as might be expected from a miscellaneous set of parishes, display a fairly wide spread of average ages at marriage. However, there is once again evidence of falling marriage age and of convergence during the 18th century, more marked in the case of women than of men.

It has already been emphasized that for these individual parishes, we know nothing concerning the second element in nuptiality: the proportion of men and women who died celibate. But we do know the mean age of marriage of women – certainly retrievable from family reconstitutions and the legitimate fertility rate – obtainable from aggregative analysis and inverse projection. The logic of the estimation of the unknown proportion never married (at age 40–44) from the two 'known' parameters was first established by David Weir (1984) and then further refined by Roger Schofield (1985). Schofield's estimates are shown in Figure 1.8.

Figure 1.8 Celibacy and age at marriage in English cohort fertility

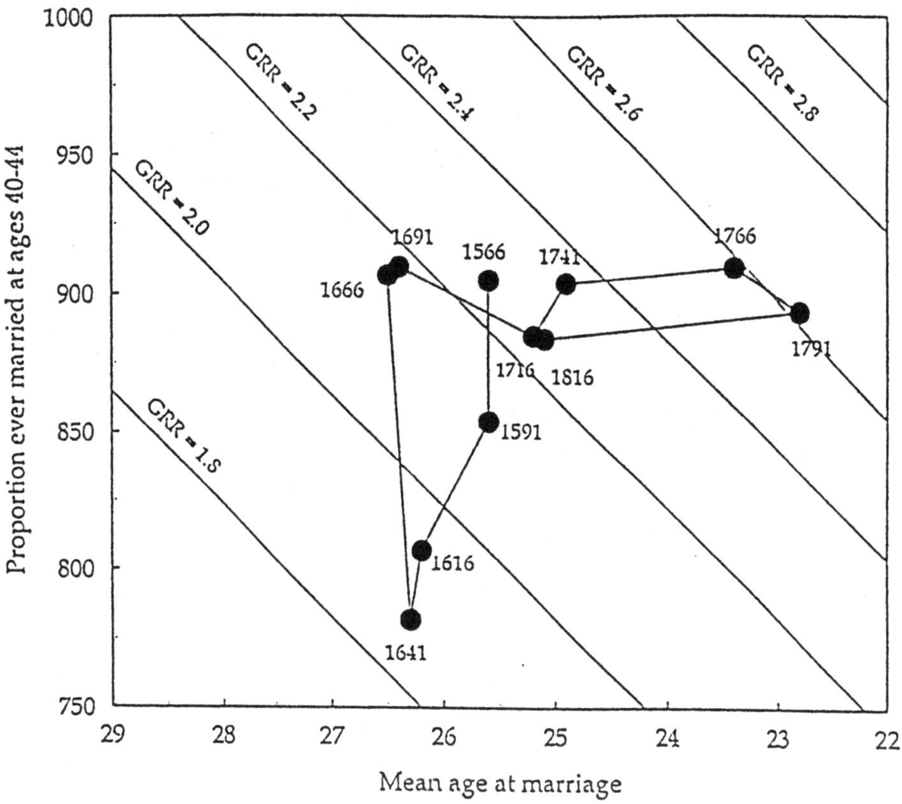

Note: Points refer to data for twenty-five-year birth cohorts and are plotted against the mid-year of the cohort. Add twenty-five years to obtain the centred twenty-five-year time period of marriage.

Figure 1.8 is based on the mean of first marriage ages of women in the full set of twenty-six parishes. It was ingeniously scaled by Weir so that inferences about the relative importance of changes in the proportions ever married, and the mean age at marriage, could be drawn directly from it. A movement of one centimetre vertically (in the proportion ever married) has the same impact on the diagonal line representing fertility (GRR) as a movement of one centimetre horizontally (in the mean age of marriage). From the figure, it is quite evident that while both aspects of nuptiality changed over time, amongst those born before 1691 (and thus marrying before 1704), changes in the proportion ever marrying had a much greater impact on fertility than did changes in the age at marriage. Women went from 10 per cent celibate in the birth cohort of 1566 to 22 per cent celibate in the birth cohort of 1641, and back to 10 per cent in the birth cohort of 1661; a rise that was not sustained, as the proportions never marrying drifted back to 12 per cent, a level at which they stayed for the majority of 18th century birth cohorts. For those marrying later in the period, fertility changed because of a sharp fall, then rise, of 3.6 years in the age at marriage; the fall, it is important to note, had been largely achieved by 1790.

In the remainder of this chapter, discussion of these shifts in marital behaviour will be placed within a broader assessment of female labour force participation, largely but far from exclusively within the rural economy. Initially the focus will be upon the 18th century, when evidence is relatively more abundant and reliable. Thereafter the discussion takes the form of a review of those relatively lengthy periods of English demographic history that were distinguished by population decline or stagnation within the preceding four centuries. The analysis proceeds in a manner which may initially seem eccentric, but which is intended to redress a balance in a debate about marriage which has been focused very heavily on male well-being as reflected in male wage rates.

In studying female labour force participation in the 18th century, it should be noted that population growth was for the most part concentrated in the period of rising marriage rates after 1750 when population totals expanded from 6 million to 8 million after a century in which demographic stagnation and actual decline had been a dominant feature. It is clear, given rates of urban growth, that the agricultural population grew at a rate somewhat lower than the total population, although there was an absolute expansion in the rural workforce in all regions (Wrigley, 1987). Research into servants in husbandry, their wages and seasonal unemployment reveals some striking changes in female participation in agricultural work and the rural economy more broadly defined (Kussmaul, 1981; Snell, 1985). Because unmarried females were almost as likely as unmarried males to be found in the farm servant population, a decline in that population would doubtless have had both implications for female employment and possibly marriage behaviour in those rural economies. The decline in service is reflected in a fall in the proportion of hirings for contract periods of two years and over, and also in a reduction of marriages at or immediately after Michaelmas (October), the end of the hiring year in southeast England, when servants would be most likely to leave service to begin married life. It has been argued that the high level of servant keeping from the end of the 17th century through to a peak in 1740 coincided with a period in which price changes favoured pastoral products over grain, with a shift to farming techniques that seem to have placed greater emphasis on livestock husbandry. In a period in which daily wage rates were relatively high, it would have been in the interests of employers to pay their labour in the form of bed and board. Furthermore, falling prices served to diminish the liquidity of farmers who, under such conditions, would prefer to pay their labour by the year. Perhaps a most important factor bearing upon levels of female employment was that the shift to livestock husbandry increased the demand for female labour, which had traditionally been associated with both the care of animals and the processing of their by-products such as butter and cheese. While livestock prices remained more buoyant than those for grain the retention by farmers of a servant labour force employed on an annual contract reflected the more evenly spread demand for labour over the year, a demand pattern that distinguished pastoral from arable farming.

After 1750, as prices began to rise and the terms of trade between pastoral and arable pursuits shifted most definitely in favour of the grain producer, farmers moved towards hiring practices that favoured the employment of male labourers hired by the day who were paid in wages rather than in kind. This shift in payment may have had the effect of forcing prices up, because wage labour was obliged to purchase grain-based foodstuffs in the market. The shift towards grain farming with its highly seasonal work regime also undermined the value to the farmer of the live-in servant, especially the live-in female servant whose work would have been more heavily directed towards animal husbandry. The growth in farm size in an agrarian economy that was distinguished by seasonal work peaks exposed 'the great difficulty of finding constant employment for a large staff of farm hands all the year round' (Hobsbawm and Rudé, 1969: 25).

In the areas of mixed husbandry of the 17th century, the keeping of servants had been an important contribution to maintaining the labour needs of the farm household economy, enabling small tenants or owner-occupiers to realize an optimum labour force without altering the size of the farm itself as the family labour force passed through its developmental cycle. It is perhaps of great significance that in 1851 the census returns reveal that the western and northern farming regions of England had small ratios of labour to farmer indicative of the overwhelming importance in these areas of small, primarily pastoral farms (Snell, 1986: 46–7). These were the counties in which servants were still an important component of the farm labour force. These also were the counties in which female live-in servants and female outdoor workers were to be found at their highest levels, and they were also areas in which female wages were relatively 'high'. It is perhaps noteworthy that they were also, in the main, areas with relatively low values of I_m (a fertility-weighted index of marriage proportions) in the mid-19th century censuses.

In the late 17th and 18th centuries, farm service was a relatively common existence for young adults between the ages of 15 and 25 or 30 (Smith, 1981). This life-cycle specific form of employment declined dramatically for both sexes, but especially for females, although it remained, as we noted above, more buoyant in the north and west (Kussmaul, 1981). Such developments are mirrored in another body of evidence bearing upon seasonal unemployment in rural areas. A striking pattern emerges from the analysis of rural settlement examinations taken under the Settlement Act of 1662, carried out, it is generally supposed, to identify the parish of settlement of those seeking poor relief by JPs, whose responsibility it was to determine such geographical affiliations. Keith Snell (1981), in an interpretation not without its detractors, claims that this evidence provides the exact date at which the examinant came to require parish-rate funded assistance from the local overseer of the poor.

While such evidence can reveal little about the relative size of the male and female work forces in the period or the total numbers seasonally unemployed, it is highly suggestive when used alongside the evidence bearing upon servant employment. In the predominantly grain-growing counties of southern and eastern, England males displayed a distinctive pattern of seasonal unemployment throughout the 18th century: employment for them was high during the harvest and low during the winter months.

Women, by contrast, showed a marked change in their seasonality of employment over the same period. From 1690 to 1750 the pattern for women was very similar to that for men, but after 1750 there was a rise in female harvest-time unemployment and a slight fall in springtime unemployment, suggesting that they were becoming distinguishable from males and, in particular, less involved in harvest work. As Snell notes in commenting on these developments, there was a move 'from an environment with a relatively high degree of sexually shared labour, in which gender differences appear to have been a matter of indifference to employers…to a situation indicating an unprecedented sexual specialization of work' (Snell, 1985: 22). What is more, the shift was linked with a marked tendency for male and female wages to move in diametrically different directions after about 1750. In the grain-growing areas of the south and east of England, female real wages moved down while male real wages held steady or shifted up very marginally. However, the patterns in the pastoral areas of the west were very different. In those regions, no downward movement in female real wages can be detected, for they became progressively more specialized in pastoral farming with an attendant increase in the relative demand for female labour (Kussmaul, 1985). In the east and south, the continued rise in wheat prices saw an expansion in the arable acreage with a greater emphasis upon male harvest labour and a change in harvest technology.

If this was associated, as is claimed, with more calculating behaviour on the part of capitalist farmers who, desiring to shorten the harvest period to catch the early-season grain price peak, used threshing machines and shifted away from the sickle to scythe after 1790, this too would have intensified the sexual division of labour (Collins, 1969; Roberts, 1979). There is very little evidence to suggest that women had ever used the scythe, but much to indicate their widespread employment of the sickle. The displacement of women from agricultural employment was certainly enabled by a labour market which was becoming increasingly seasonal and oversupplied for most of the year as a consequence of the supremacy of grain production in the agrarian regime. Male vulnerability to unemployment may have increased their 'claim' to work, while farmers anxious to minimize rising familial dependence upon rate-financed poor relief may have given them, as the principal breadwinner, preference over females in their labour hiring. In fact, poor relief in the east and south, while rising steadily, was going disproportionately to males. From a situation in the early 18th century when pensioners or 'collectioners' composed three females for every male, by 1800 the sex balance of beneficiaries was closer to unity. Women of all age groups fared less well with increasing numbers of elderly females incarcerated in workhouses (Smith, 1998; Williams, 1998; also see Sharpe, 1996: 134–38). However, younger widows and unmarried females were the group most seriously affected by the decline in outdoor relief allocations. What is striking is that the net effect of these developments by the late 18th century was an overall drop in familial or household incomes as male wages ultimately fell or failed to make up for the loss of female earnings and welfare benefits.

In such developments as those that occurred at the end of the 18th century in England, we have strong evidence supportive of one thesis that sees the growth of the plough, responding to the stimulus of population growth, as fundamentally hostile to female labour prospects. Such a development is, of course, a central tenet of the 'Boserup thesis', bearing upon female work in agrarian societies. Boserup begins her discussion of what is often termed 'agricultural intensification' by proposing that population pressure causes shortening of the fallow and also the more frequent use of the plough per unit of time and per unit of land (Boserup, 1965, 1970). The plough is supposed to bring about increased male employment because it increases the number of hired labourers, who tend to be males, partly because it is usual for men to do the ploughing and partly because of the heavy demands on physical strength and preferences for employing younger adult males in the short periods of intensive activity in spring summer and early autumn.

It seems that developments in the agrarian economy of the arable farming areas of late 18th-century England may have disturbed the functioning of the 'family economy' which had, prior to the subjection of large acreages in that period to parliamentary enclosure, possessed greater access to the common, less dependence upon wage labour and operated with a more equitable sexual division of labour (Humphries, 1990; for a reconsideration of the arguments, see Shaw-Taylor, 1999). When viewed against a background of deteriorating life expectancies for older female child and young adult female mortality, late 18th-century developments provide strong evidence for the case that rural capitalism was damaging to female employment opportunities and their status *vis-à-vis* males (Wrigley et al., 1997: 298–307; Johnson and Nicholas, 1997; Johansson, 1991).

Such a view is buttressed by another development that occurred over the course of the 18th century. Snell (1985, chap. 6) has analysed a substantial body of evidence bearing upon the apprenticeship of women, both in rural and urban contexts. He makes particularly heavy use of the evidence relating to parish or charity-funded apprenticeships concerning younger persons from the lowest social classes who were generally either orphans under parish care, or whose families were too poor to pay the premiums. In the late 17th and early 18th century, his samples suggest that over one-third of such apprenticeships were allocated to girls who were placed in fifty-one different trades, compared with a range of trades that numbered only forty-six for apprenticed boys. Furthermore, many girls were apprenticed to the trade which their father pursued, and the premium paid in these cases differed little for that paid for boys. However, by the early 19th century there had been a dramatic decline in the number of females apprenticed through such routes and women who entered this institution were restricted to a far narrower range of trades.[3] Snell makes much of the appearance in the early 18th-century settlement examinations of single apprenticed women who had never been married, renting properties with a value in excess of £10 per

[3] Of course, this was part of a general decline in pauper apprenticeship in the last two decades of the 18th century. Earlier such apprenticeships had functioned as a valuable 'training' facility for both young men and women. The retreat of the Old Poor Law in response to spiralling costs after 1780 led to a decline in the willingness of parishes to invest in young persons in this way. An excellent discussion of these issues from the perspective of human capital theory is to be found in Humphries (forthcoming).

annum from which they independently practised trades. Others pursued the same craft in a household economy with husbands who had likewise been apprenticed in the same trade, thereby suggesting the possibility of a mutual or reciprocally balanced relation between spouses in such enterprises (Snell, 1985: 305).

The decline in agricultural work or crafts that derived from a formal apprenticeship for women in rural areas in the late 18th century should not necessarily give rise to the view that employment opportunities for females in such areas declined *in toto*. Historians such as David Levine would argue that the growth of labour demands in association with proto-industrialization had important effects upon the family economy and female work prospects. The industries most prominently implicated in these developments needed cheap and easily expanded supplies of labour from women and children in particular. Roger Schofield believes that this must be a factor responsible for the declining female marriage age in communities intensely involved in such manufactures, although he adds the important requirement that demand for such labour must hold up, particularly against the increasingly inflationary background of growing population. That this demand is not just to be viewed as driven by overseas or foreign markets but by a consumption-led shift in demand patterns within even the households of the modestly situated is a view that has become increasingly associated with Jan de Vries. De Vries has yet to relate his ideas to their possible implications for female marriage behaviour, although he sees the late 17th and early 18th centuries as a phase distinguished by a growing female authority in the decision-making processes within households as well as stimulating an increasingly specialized allocation of household labour time.

It should be noted that the classical proto-industrial model as developed by Levine and Medick regarded the female contribution to agriculture as minimal before the arrival of proto-industry. Such a view is problematic in the case of England where marked sexual division of labour in the late 17th and early 18th century is hard to find. However, a key issue yet to be satisfactorily studied is whether the growth of handicraft production in the 18th century was sufficiently great in its impact to counteract the loss of female employment in agriculture and other traditional crafts. Maxine Berg believes that it is too soon to accord the title of victor to any of the protagonists in this debate; she sees developments as highly variable between industries and parts of the country. She argues that the expanding putting-out trades were predominantly employers of women who did not require formal apprenticeships which made female entry into them easier. However, it may be that the decline in agricultural work opportunities in some areas had created substantial numbers of married women for work in these industries at below subsistence wages. As Berg put it 'the expansion of unregulated domestic industries may have enhanced women's employment opportunities, but there is little evidence that they enhanced their job status or wages' (Berg, 1987: 76). Hand spinning was the archetypal form of female employment in rural areas in the 18th century, and women who pursued that activity were among the lowest paid of workers. It is perhaps revealing that two unusually detailed village listings from the 1790s relating to Cardington in Bedfordshire and Corfe Castle in Dorset show high female participation in the labour force (Saito, 1979: 22–23). Snell, too, is aware of this home-based work in spinning, lace-making and straw-plaiting, but stresses that they were low-paid tasks and were incapable of averting the relative decline of household incomes, particularly in the grain-growing areas where total household incomes were failing to keep abreast of the inflationary forces driven by both population growth and the demands placed on the economy by war with France (Snell, 1985).

Indeed, work on occupational change over the late 18th and early 19th centuries suggests the numbers of workers in putting-out trades should not be exaggerated. Such trades were located in the broader category of 'manufacturing; in the 1831 census, the category as a whole accounted for only 10.4 per cent of the male work force. Although a larger proportion would doubtless apply to the female proportions employed in these trades, the most striking feature of male employment was the very great place reserved for retail trade and handicrafts whose five largest individual occupations were in declining order of size, blacksmiths, masons, butchers, bricklayers and bakers (Wrigley, 1986). Such occupations were disproportionately staffed by small masters, and they have rarely been regarded by scholars whose interests relate to proto-industry as contexts within which female labour was especially prominent.

The consequences for nuptiality patterns arising from the shrinking opportunities for single women, whether the decline was in agricultural service, day-labouring, spinning, or in trades for which an apprenticeship was served, are intriguing. When Wrigley and Schofield published their path-breaking study of English population history, special attention attached to the period from 1750 through to 1830 when marriage rates and fertility appeared to be rising against a background of stagnant and probably falling real wages. Much effort has been expended in reflecting on this feature, and Wrigley and Schofield appear to have moved back from their explanation offered in the earliest edition for a lagged relationship between trends in the later edition published in 1989.

It is also important to realize that in the 1981 edition of Wrigley and Schofield's study the relative importance of age at first marriage and proportions never marrying in influencing the overall marriage rate had not been effectively resolved. The biggest influence after 1750, as we have seen, influencing fertility was the decline in female marriage age, with some smaller influences stemming from proportions ever-marrying and illegitimacy. More recent work points to a slow rise in marital fertility, recently argued by Wrigley to have been in effect a mortality decline associated with falling still birth rates (Wrigley, 1998). It would seem that in most of these components determining the GRR, some consideration must be given to the impact of the growing and shrinking levels of female labour force participation, particularly the participation of unmarried females.

There must surely be some reason to suppose, as Levine has so powerfully claimed, that proto-industry, however restricted geographically and in its aggregate scale of growth, provided a new and effective framework for a family-wage or earnings economy. In so far as the household was the unit of production, individuals involved in these industries and initiating marriages might have been disposed to take a more optimistic view of prospective family earnings than would be the case with those in general labouring.

However, in the south and east of England, the arable farming areas *par excellence*, a potent influence derived from the changing pattern of demand for agricultural labour. As we have seen, the changing ratio of food prices and nominal wage rates induced a shift in employer preferences away from servants in husbandry of both sexes hired on annual contracts, which as a category of labour had earlier grown in importance, as it had become increasingly expensive to feed living-out male labour hired by the day. The population growth that intensified in the last half of the 18th century led to increasing allocation of agricultural work at all seasons to males, thereby making it more difficult for households to secure a dual-income family involving both husband and wife in agricultural work.[4] For unmarried females, the deteriorating prospects were even greater. Under such circumstances there were for women, in particular, good reasons for marrying younger as a defence against the unemployment and under-employment which were increasingly their lot. Whether the growth in both pre-nuptial pregnancy rates and illegitimacy ratios that move in tandem during this period is to be regarded as an accompaniment of this desire to seek the protection of marriage is difficult to establish.[5] Certainly the Old Poor Law did little to discourage practices by its reduction in relief allocations to single women and by preferencing married males through the linking of welfare payments to food prices and the size of families. This is not to subscribe to a crude Malthusian explanation for female marriage age declines. The argument that family allowances, which were given relatively frequently after 1795, carried a considerable fall in marriage age by taking away disincentives to marriage have to be treated sceptically. First, much of the decline in marriage age had taken place prior to the adoption of such practices in the late 1790s. Furthermore, in those parishes which adopted this mode of relief the practice was used sparingly and frequently abandoned once the crises associated with sharp bread price rises had abated (Williams, 1998). Family allowances may be most appropriately seen as a welfare response to the relatively high rates of population growth brought about in part by the falling marriage ages occurring from the mid-18th century through to *c*.1790. In so far as falling incomes and eventually falling male wages were associated with declining female employment opportunities in agricultural work, the contradictory trends in real wages and fertility in the later 18th century are far from confusing, especially if the notion of a lagged relationship between economy and fertility is jettisoned. Such a view only retains some plausibility if an orthodox Malthusian argument, which sees marriage rates as a function of the male (breadwinner) wage

---

[4] Ample evidence for such restricted contributions by women is to be found in Davies (1797, 131–87) and Eden (1797, vol. III: 331–50). See also Sokoll (1991: 34–58).An excellent analysis of a late 18th-century listing of inhabitants for Corfe Castle, Dorset shows how wide the earnings differential was between men and women and why females at that juncture were entirely rational in their desire to seek marriage as a means of mitigating the consequence of their earnings disadvantage as spinsters in the labour market. See Wall (1994a: 312–35).

[5] Age at first marriage stays remarkably close to the age of unmarried motherhood over the course of the eighteenth century with both moving in tandem to a low point at the turn of the century. Likewise, prenuptial pregnancy is heavily associated with young brides to the extent that by 1800 about one half of first births were conceived extra-maritally.

and the groom as the principal marriage decision maker, is narrowly applied to the problem.

While the centuries before 1700 have not been the subject of such intensive research, there are components within the argument that has been applied to the 18th and early 19th centuries which may also have some bearing upon developments. Fertility changes, driven primarily by shifts in the proportions ever marrying, seems to have had a noteworthy impact upon the intrinsic growth rate. We have already noted the tendency for fertility and mortality to decline and rise respectively in tandem over the 17th century. These trends were such that population growth slowed markedly, aided by high levels of out-migration to Ireland, the American Middle Atlantic colonies and the Caribbean, which helped bring about absolute population loss at the national level.

Against the background of low fertility, which saw the average English female between the ages of 15 and 49 giving birth to fewer than four offspring, the degree of female labour force participation, which Snell documents as being high in the late 17th century, is suggestive. The rise in male wages that is generally viewed as characteristic of all sectors of the late 17th and early 18th century English economy does not appear to have engendered a rush into marriage on the part of English women. In fact for the 1641 birth cohort, whose females married on average at 26.5 years, almost 20 per cent remained outside of marriage altogether and while male real wages rose by 30 per cent between 1660 and 1691, the proportions never-marrying fell by only 2 or 3 percentage points. We are perhaps offered some explanation for this sluggishness by the substantial growth in agricultural service that grew in importance well into the third decade of the 18th century as farmers strove to employ a live-in labour force. Indeed, the demographic conditions of labour shortage that were the object of considerable complaint and anxiety by contemporaries were being exacerbated by a string of developments that were likely to have increased the demand for female labour. Between 1656 and 1686 the English population, if we employ Wrigley and Schofield's estimates, fell from 5.28 to 4.86 million, a fall of 416,000, and of this decline about 58 per cent could be explained by net emigration. The bulk of the emigrants went to the Middle Atlantic Colonies of Maryland and Virginia, where for every one female immigrant there were three or four males who were primarily in the age groups 15–30. Such patterns of migration no doubt help to explain why the sex ratio of those dying in England in 1700 indicates that there were only 98.2 males for every 100 females, whereas the sex ratio at baptism was 104.5 males for every 100 females. It also helps to explain why marriages by couples of English stock in Virginia and Maryland almost invariably involved brides whose ages were well below twenty years of age (Souden, 1984, 1987). In England during this period, a quickening of the pace of urban growth in the 17th century was fuelled disproportionately by the movement of unmarried women from countryside to town. Such movements most likely exacerbated a labour shortage, particularly for female servants in rural economies that increasingly contained substantial livestock husbandry, as the ratio of pastoral product prices moved favourably relative to those of grain. Against such a background, it is perhaps easy to accept the surprisingly narrow gap between female and male wages that were paid to agricultural servants at this period.

We have already considered the relatively large numbers of females who were found to be among parish apprentices of the late 17th and early 18th centuries and the wide range of trades in which they had been placed. How far we can see the low pre-nuptial pregnancy and illegitimacy levels of this period as further evidence of a young adult female population that experienced substantially diminished marital desires is a subject worthy of far more consideration than it has to date received. Once again, there are grounds for supposing that an interpretation that rests solely or largely upon the remuneration of young adult male workers will fail to detect the possible implications of these developments for the feasibility of a non-married existence for females. We have already shown how the short-term responsiveness of the totals of English marriages to price and mortality movements drops in this period. Part of this declining responsiveness to mortality, as we noted, resulted from a fall in remarriage propensities and a probable lengthening of the remarriage interval (Schofield and Wrigley, 1981). The decline in the number of landed holdings as average farm size rose and the decline in the demand for widow smallholders as other economic opportunities burgeoned may have some role to play in these changes. However, these interpretations are based for the most part upon a view of marriage in which women are viewed as passive reactors to males, who are regarded as taking the initiative in the marriage decision. We might tentatively entertain the possibility that a widening choice set for women in the late 17th century offered alternatives to marriage both for those contemplating it for the first time or from the position of a widow. In this connection, the growth of welfare facilities after 1640 for women is a striking feature of the overseers' account books (Wales, 1984; Smith, 1996: 38–39). Of course, much of this relief, distributed at what were increasingly generous rates, may have been necessitated by the declining remarriage rates as elderly women themselves without the assistance of kin came to require the support of the collectivity in later life. However, it is equally possible that an increasing awareness of available poor relief may have reduced the risk of a life without a husband, whether as spinster or widow, just as after 1780 the knowledge that welfare was more readily available if one were married may have served to increase the attractiveness of the marital state in a world in which the range of options for women had narrowed considerably. Such support for the elderly may also have made it significantly easier for young adults to leave their natal hearths in search of relatively well paid employment in London, other urban centres and the colonies. Such geographical redistributions of young adults may well have significantly disturbed marriage markets, thereby reducing the collective marriage chances of those in such age groups.

It should be noted that some historians have used poor relief in a different sense to account for the declining proportions ever-married in the 17th century (Hindle, 1998). They argue that the poor was prohibited from marriage by the 'better sorts' of parish vestries and poor-law officers in their attempts to reign back expenditure on poor relief, an expenditure which was beginning to grow, particularly in the south and east, from the 1630s. Far from seeing non-marriage as a product of a widening choice set, the emphasis of such historians is on what are regarded as substantially reduced freedoms for those of marriage age. This is an interesting argument, although based on a very thin veneer of evidence and literally a couple of handfuls of references to such actions, not all of which are unambiguously efforts to thwart marriage.

Furthermore, such references to practices are to be found at dates distributed from the late 16th to the late 17th centuries which are far from being closely associated with the period of particularly low marital incidence and rising poor law expenditure after 1640, when the proportions never marrying rise to such striking levels

At the root of the argument developed in this chapter are a set of demographic processes that served to reduce the supply of labour, to which the response was increasing substitution of females for males in the labour market when male wages were high and vice versa. It is premised on the existence of a relatively muted degree of sex segmentation and a set of societal reactions and institutions facilitating that substitution. In considering such an argument, it is in no sense intended to deny the existence of intransigently gendered labour markets, nor is it presumed to suggest that women made any fundamental long-term inroads into higher status, more highly paid levels of the labour market. However, some degree of skill enhancement or narrowing of the skill differential between the sexes may have been involved in the process, for it is in the post-Civil War era that levels of female literacy rose relative to males; a development that certainly seems to have been sharply reversed in the late 18th century (Cressy, 1980; Schofield, 1981).

It is of course hard to resist the temptation to deploy similar arguments in the 14th and 15th centuries in England when population had fallen in a far more extreme fashion than occurred in the late 17th century. We have stressed the lack of the classic form of homeostasis throughout much of the early modern period as a distinctive feature of the English demographic regime. In what sense are there grounds for supposing that a rise in mortality induced an associated fall in fertility against the background of rising real incomes, and presumably objectively easier conditions for marriage and household formation after 1350? Medievalists have not failed to consider this issue, but, overinfluenced by starkly Malthusian sensitivities, they have generally concluded that a retreat from or reluctance to enter marriage in periods of rising living standards appears to 'turn logic on its head'. Such a reaction is perfectly understandable given certain powerful a priori expectations that are to be found in Malthusian formulations regarding the operation of the preventive check. Some have finessed the problem by supposing that changes in fertility induced by a nuptiality shift could not have driven up population growth rates because fertility was already at a maximum since women married at or close to puberty, so there was no slack that could be taken up by a significant proportion generating a fertility rise through a shift upwards in marital proportions or a fall in ages of first marriage. Such a view would be perfectly compatible with the ideas of Hajnal, as first presented in 1965. In his classic essay, which no serious discussion of pre-industrial European marriage behaviour can ignore, Hajnal concluded that because he found that on average 60 to 70 percent of women aged 14 were listed as married on a set of poll tax returns from 1377, a non-European marriage pattern was firmly in place. Subsequently these views of the evidence in the poll taxes have been subject to major revisions, as fuller account is taken of their biases, especially the substantial under-recording of women who were unmarried. Rarely do the lists have sex ratios lower than 110. It would seem that spinsters and widows were not taxed for reasons of their economic status. Furthermore young adult females may have been easier to hide from the tax collector's net since, unlike males, they were not obliged to be sworn into tithing at the age of 12. When such distortions as these are taken into account, it would seem improbable that female proportions currently married could have exceeded 60 per cent, suggesting a level of marital incidence that is fully compatible with the European type in late 14th-century England. As Hajnal has also emphasized, the importance of service-in-husbandry for young adults of both sexes in the age range 15–25 or 15–30 was another distinguishing attribute of so-called European marriage regimes. Special attention therefore attaches to the position of servants in the poll tax lists. Servants were also a category that were at high risk for omission from such lists. In the returns that survive for substantial tracts of rural England – Rutland, Shropshire, Nottinghamshire and Northumberland – over 17 per cent of households are listed as containing them. While this must be regarded as a minimum figure because of evasion, this is a remarkably similar proportion to that found in the late 17th century. In the towns, as in the early modern era, even more households possessed servants (30 per cent) and a higher proportion of those servants were unmarried females. In fact, like the towns of late 17th-century England, late 14th-century urban populations were characterized by significant female surplus, frequently suggesting 100 females above the age of 14 or 15 for every 90 or 85 males. Such patterns were unlikely to have arisen unless there had been significant flows of women from rural to urban areas (Smith, 1997). Work by Goldberg (1992) on the role of women in later 14th and early 15th century urban economies suggests that unmarried women were to be found in a wide range of crafts and in many instances co-residing in households made up solely of spinsters. He interprets these trends as fully compatible with labour shortages that had been partially overcome by substantial substitution of unmarried females for males in the high-labour-cost urban areas.

Developments in the countryside are harder to follow, and this is a subject in grave need of fuller investigations. Judith Bennett (1987), the leading historian of medieval English women, has disputed the notion of an intensification of female involvement in the rural economy in the context of demographic retrenchment and adheres to the view that any increase that this sex might display in their involvement in work outside the household should be interpreted as a devaluation in their economic role. The evidence on this issue, as it has been presented with respect to the Northamptonshire manor of Brigstock before 1348, is certainly capable of alternative interpretations. The population of this manor declined noticeably in the half-century before 1350, which Bennett regards as an indication of general economic deterioration. In that changing environment, women, she argues, began to participate more actively in what she terms the 'public economy' to distinguish it from the household; she documents a growth in female participation in the baking trades to such an extent that they moved from a position in which they were responsible for 20 per cent of the fines paid for Infraction of the Bread Assize to one where they paid 80 per cent of the fines; women also increased their involvement in the land market on the basis of the frequency with which they are identified in registered land transactions in the manor court. As a consequence of this greater public exposure, as revealed in Bennett's reading of the proceedings of the local manorial court, there was an increased liability to criminal action and victimization. Of particular interest is that women came increasingly to use non-familial guarantors or pledges in the manor court.

Bennett emphasizes in her interpretation the centrality of the household in determining the personal circumstances of peasant women. She argues that peasant women were seldom to be found as independent workers; in good times, householders could afford to remove their daughters and wives from public activities, but bad times brought these women into public life as they sought to bring extra cash into households as they took over or supplemented the public functions of fathers and husbands dead from disease or famine.

Apart from failing in this interpretation to consider external demands for female labour, some confusion enters into the discussion which requires a clearer specification of the changing activities of married women, widows and unmarried daughters. These distinctions are important because much of the recent discussion of a possible growing role for women in the later 14th century is concerned with the activities of unmarried women. Furthermore, Simon Penn (1987), in his very valuable assessment of infractions of the post-Black Death labour laws, draws attention to the substantial numbers of women who appear among those indicted. One in four of those indicted were women, which is a very similar figure to that discovered by Poos (1983) in his analysis of the 1352 Essex Estreat of Statute of Labourer' offenders' fines. The latter source contains the names of 7,056 persons, of whom approximately 20 per cent were female. Penn is particularly interested in the case of women harvest workers, and is especially impressed by the similarity of wages paid to women and men for this work in the late 14th century. A large number of those women were presented alone, and by implication are thought to have been single and most likely free of familial obligations.

Poos' analysis of the Essex evidence is even more suggestive. He notes the particularly high incidence of fines and numbers of persons fined for receipt of excess wages in the eastern and southeastern parts of Essex, which were marshland areas distinguished by large-scale pastoral farming in the form of sheep farms or wicks. This same area we know in the 16th and 17th centuries to have been afflicted by recurrent disease outbreaks in the form of malaria, and to have suffered from endemic labour shortages and high wages. Here, the late 14th-century rural employers of labour were clearly seeking a resident live-in servant population, although Poos unfortunately did not consider the gender composition of the offenders against the Statute in this area.[6]

Obviously there is a dearth of detail on labour force participation of women with particular reference to their marital status in late medieval England, and a discussion of the kind undertaken in this paper must remain highly partial and incomplete. As a guiding light to this research which is so badly needed, it may be useful to keep in

[6] It is interesting to note that this area of south Essex with its endemically high mortality may have provided a context favourable for female employment even in the late eighteenth century. For favourable treatment of women in this area in the late 18th century by farmers and poor-law officers, see Sharpe (1996: 137).

mind a comment by Perroy when he contrasted the situation in 15th century France and England. He wrote that 'in England, the demographic contraction was more accentuated than the fall in production; therefore wages rose. In France, the economic disruption due to wars and other as yet unknown factors was so complete as to limit production faster than population' (Perroy, 1995: 260). He might have made a similar comment about Tuscany, that exceptionally well-documented area of late medieval Europe in respect of its demography and economy. There, a very distinctive marriage pattern is detectable in the 15th century, in which women became brides around 17 or 18 years and very few remained outside of marriage altogether. Few also entered into service, and barely any were to be found in rural areas or the sizeable urban centres in that state between the ages of 15 and 30. It seems that in early and mid-15th century Tuscany, in the wake of population declines over the late 14th century, marriage ages had fallen and marital incidence approached a maximum. The notable substitution of unmarried women for a deficient male element in the labour force is not a readily detectable feature of this area. It is striking that this area, like many other areas of southern Europe, return to their pre-plague population totals over the course of the 16th century. This was a development which, when viewed from an English vantage point, was not achieved until the 18th century; and it was certainly the case that even by 1650, the English population was well below its early 14th-century maximum. It is a matter of some importance to know more about these demographic trends as they affected other parts of northern Europe, since it might be supposed that this region may have also seen comparable opportunities for substantial substitution of females for males in social structures and labour markets that were far less segmented than those which discouraged high labour force participation rates of unmarried women in much of southern Europe.

There remains no reason why certain of the ideas of Malthus cannot still be retained in these discussions. We frequently fail to note that Malthus himself was convinced in his *Essay* of what he termed 'long oscillations', rather than instantaneous adjustments between resources and numbers ensuring a rapid return to equilibrium, in which quite long periods of disequilibrium could prevail in which it might be supposed fertility and mortality did not adjust homeostatically (Malthus, 1992: 25–27). There are suggestions that the periods 1350–1450 and 1650–1750 in England share certain features in common with respect to their nuptiality patterns and survivorship levels. These parameters were positively rather than inversely related. In this, they share a structural feature with the period *c.*1750–1830, although at the later date the consequences for demographic growth rates were very different.

Bibliography

Beier, A.L. (1985) *Masterless men: The vagrancy problem in England 1560–1640*, London.

Bennett, J.M. (1987) *Women in the medieval English countryside: gender and household in Brigstock before the Plague*, Oxford.

Berg, M. (1987), 'Women's work, mechanization and the early phases of industrialisation in England', in P. Joyce (ed.), *The historical meaning of work*, Cambridge, pp,64-98.

Boserup, E. (1965) *The conditions of agricultural growth: the economics of agrarian change under population pressure*, London.

Boserup, E. (1970) *Women's role in economic development*, New York.

Chaunu, P. (1974) 'Démographie historique et système de civilisation', *Mélanges de l'école française de Rome. Moyen Age, Temps Modernes*, 86, pp. 301–21.

Collins, E.J.T. (1969) 'Harvest technology and labour supply in Britain, 1790–1880', *Economic History Review*, 22, pp. 453–73.

Cressy, D. (1980) *Literacy and the social order: reading and writing in Tudor and Stuart England*, Cambridge.

Davies, D. (1797) *The case of the labourers in husbandry stated and considered*, Bath.

Desjardins, B. (1995) 'Bias in age at marriage in family reconstitutions: evidence from French-Canadian data', *Population Studies*, 49, pp. 165–69.

Dupâquier, J. (1972) 'De l'animal à l'homme: le mécanisme autorégulateur des populations traditionelles', *Revue de l'Institut de Sociologie*, 11, pp. 177–209.

Dupâquier, J. (1979) *La population rurale du bassin parisien à l'époque de Louis XIV*, Paris.

Eden,, F.M. (1797) *The state of the poor*, repr. London, 1966.

Fisher, F.J. (1936) 'The state of England, 1600 by Sir Thomas Wilson', *Camden Society*, 3rd ser., 52, pp. 23–24.

Goldberg, P.J.P. (1992) *Women, work and the life-cycle: women and work in York and Yorkshire c. 1300–1520*, Oxford.

Goldstone, J.A. (1986) 'The demographic revolution in England: a re-examination', *Population Studies*, 49, pp. 5–33.

Hajnal, J. (1982) 'Two kinds of pre-industrial household formation systems', *Population and Development Review*, 8, pp. 449–84.

Hindle, S. (1998) 'The problem of pauper marriage in seventeenth-century England', *Transactions of the Royal Historical Society*, 6th ser., 8, pp. 71–89.

Hobsbawm, E.J. and Rudé, G. (1969) *Captain Swing*, Harmondsworth.

Humphries, J. (1990) 'Enclosures, common rights and women: the proletarianization of families in the late eighteenth and early nineteenth centuries', *Journal of Economic History*, 50, pp. 17–42.

Humphries, J. (forthcoming) 'English apprenticeship: a neglected factor in the first Industrial Revolution', in P. David, P. Solar and M. Thomas (eds), E*conomic challenges of the 21st century in historical perspective,* London.

Johansson, S.R. (1991) 'Welfare, mortality and gender: continuity and change in explanations for male/female mortality differences over three centuries', *Continuity and Change*, 6, pp. 135–77.

Johnson, P. and Nicholas, S. (1997) 'Health and welfare of women in the United Kingdom, 1785–1920', in R.H. Steckel and R. Floud (eds), *Health and welfare during industrialization*, Chicago, pp. 209–32.

Kussmaul, A. (1981) *Servants in husbandry in early modern England*, Cambridge.

Kussmaul, A. (1985) 'Agrarian change in seventeenth-century England: the economic historian as palaeontologist', *Journal of Economic History*, 45, pp. 1–30.

Lesthaeghe, R. (1980) 'On the social control of human reproduction', *Population and Development Review*, 6, pp. 527-48.

Malthus, T.R. (1992) *An essay on the principle of population*, repr. Cambridge, 1992.

Penn, S.A.C. (1987) 'Female wage-earners in late fourteenth-century England', *Agricultural History Review*, 35, pp. 1–14.

Perroy, E. (1955) 'Wage labour in France in the later Middle Ages', *Economic History Review*, 8, pp. 232-39.

Poos, L.R. (1983) 'The social context of the Statute of Labourers' enforcement', *Law and History Review*, 1, pp. 27–52.

Poos, L.R. (1991) *A rural society after the Black Death: Essex 1350–1525*, Cambridge.

Roberts, M. (1979) 'Sickles and scythes: women's work and men's work at harvest time', *History Workshop*, 7, pp. 246–69.

Ruggles, S. (1992) 'Migration, mortality and marriage: correcting sources of bias in English family reconstitution', *Population Studies*, 46, pp. 507–22.

Saito, O. (1979) 'Who worked when: life-time profiles of labour force participation in Cardington and Corfe Castle in the late eighteenth century', *Local Population Studies*, 22, pp. 22–23.

Schofield, R. (1981) 'Dimensions of literacy 1750–1850', in H.J. Graff (ed.), *Literacy and social development in the West*, Cambridge, pp. 206–11.

Schofield, R. (1985) 'English marriage patterns revisited', *Journal of Family History*, 10, pp. 2–20.

Schofield, R. (1998) 'English marriage patterns revisited: once more', paper presented at the International Economic History Conference, Madrid, August.

Schofield, R. and Wrigley, E.A. (1981) 'Remarriage intervals and the effect of marriage on fertility', in J. Dupâquier et al. (eds), *Marriage and remarriage in populations of the past*, London, pp. 211–27.

Sharpe, P. (1996) *Adapting to capitalism: working women in the English economy 1700–1850*, London.

Shaw-Taylor, L. (1999) 'Proletarianisation, parliamentary enclosure and the household economy of the labouring poor 1750–1850', unpublished Ph.D. thesis, University of Cambridge.

Smith, R.M. (1981) 'Fertility, economy and household formation in England over three centuries', *Population and Development Review*, 7, pp. 595–622.

Smith, R.M. (1983a) 'Hypothèses sur la nuptialité en Angleterre aux XIIIe–XIVe siècles', in *Annales, Economies, Sociétés, Civilisations*, 38, pp. 107–136.

Smith, R.M. (1983b) 'Some thoughts on "hereditary" and "proprietary" rights in land under customary law in thirteenth and early fourteenth century England', *Law and History Review*, 1, pp. 95–128.

Smith, R.M. (1996) 'Charity, self-interest and welfare: reflections from demographic and family history', in M. Daunton (ed.), *Charity, self-interest and welfare: self-interest and welfare in the English past*, London, pp. 23-51.

Smith, R.M. (1997) 'Geographical diversity in the resort to marriage in late medieval Europe: work, reputation and unmarried females in the household formation systems of northern and southern Europe', in P.J.P. Goldberg (ed.), *Women in medieval English society*, Stroud, pp. 25–43.

Smith, R.M. (1998) 'Ageing and well-being in early modern England: pension trends and gender preferences under the English Old Poor Law c. 1650–1800', in P. Johnson and P. Thane (eds), *Old age from antiquity to post-modernity*, London, pp. 64–95.

Snell, K. (1981) 'Agricultural seasonal unemployment, the standard of living and women's work 1690–1860', *Economic History Review*, 34, pp. 407–37.

Sokoll, T. 'Early attempts at accounting the unaccountable: Davies' and Eden's budgets of agricultural labouring families in late eighteenth-century England', in T. Pierenkemper (ed.), *Zur ökonomik des privaten haushalts. Haushaltsrechnungen als quellen historischer wirtschafts- und sozialforschung*, Frankfurt, pp. 34–58.

Souden, D. (1984) 'English indentured servants and the trans-Atlantic colonial economy', in S. Marks and P. Richardson (eds), *International labour migration in historical perspective*, London, pp. 19–33.

Souden, D. (1987) 'East, west–home's best? Regional patterns of migration in early modern England', in P. Clark and D. Souden (eds), *Migration and society in early modern England*, London, pp. 292–332.

Wales, T. (1984) 'Poverty, poor relief and the life-cycle: some evidence from seventeenth-century Norfolk', in R.M. Smith (ed.), *Land, kinship and life-cycle*, Cambridge, pp. 351–404.

Wall, R. (1994a) 'Some implications of the earnings, income and expenditure patterns of married women in populations in the past', in J. Henderson and R. Wall (eds.), *Poor women and children in the European past*, London, pp. 312–35.

Wall, R. (1994b) 'The household: demographic and economic change in England 1650-1970', in R. Wall (ed.) *Family forms in historic Europe*, Cambridge.

Weir, D. (1984) 'Rather late than never: celibacy and age at marriage in English cohort fertility, 1541–1871', *Journal of Family History*, 9, pp. 340–54.

Williams, S. (1998) 'Poor relief, welfare and medical provision in Bedfordshire: the social. economic and demographic context c. 1770–1834', unpublished Ph.D. thesis, University of Cambridge.

Wrigley, E.A. (1986) 'Men on the land and men in the countryside: employment in agriculture in early nineteenth-century England', in L. Bonfield, R.M. Smith and K. Wrightson (eds), *The world we have gained: histories of population and social structure*, Oxford, pp. 295–336.

Wrigley, E.A. (1987) *People, cities and wealth: The transformation of traditional society*, Oxford.

Wrigley, E.A. (1994) 'The effect of migration on the estimation of marriage age in family reconstitution studies', *Population Studies*, 48, pp. 81–97.

Wrigley, E.A. (1998) 'Explaining the rise in marital fertility in England in the "long" eighteenth century', *Economic History Review*, 51, pp. 435–64.

Wrigley, E.A. and Schofield,, R.S. (1981) *The population history of England 1541–1871*, London.

Wrigley, E.A., Davies, R.S., Oeppen, J.E. and Schofield, R.S. (1997) *English population history from family reconstitution, 1580–1837*, Cambridge.

2 Why was Scottish nuptiality so depressed for so long?

Michael ANDERSON, University of Edinburgh

I. Introduction

Although united with England and Wales in a single Kingdom in 1707, Scotland has remained in many ways, culturally and for internal government purposes, a separate state right through to the 20th century. In economic terms, while Scotland shared much of England's industrial development and rapid urbanization, nevertheless, in every decade for which records exist, net emigration both to other parts of Great Britain and overseas was always well above the English level. As a result, although there were only small differences at most dates in natural increase of population north and south of the border, Scottish actual increase was always below that of England. In some parts of the country, absolute population decline was already apparent in the later 18th century, and after the mid-19th century, numbers fell steadily across most rural districts (Flinn et al., 1977; Gray, 1957; Anderson and Morse, 1993; Anderson, 1996).

Rural Scotland, however, was far from homogeneous. In particular, there were major contrasts between the advanced large-scale commercial farming of much of the south-east, the more modest scale, dairy-focused pastoral activities of the south-west, the mixed farming and cattle rearing regime of much of the north-east and, especially, the agrarian system of the highlands and islands, where an often marginal pluri-active and mixed economy was first encouraged and then attacked by changing landlord attitudes to the exploitation of their estates (Gray, 1957, 1973; Smout, 1973, 1986).[1] This wide variety of legal, cultural, economic and agrarian variations in turn impacted on the operation of the household economies of the mass of the rural population, and especially on the majority who were still directly or indirectly dependent on agricultural activity. One key variable was the circumstances under which new households were formed, and thus under which marriage occurred.

In an ideal world, these major contrasts, both compared with England and between different parts of the country, should make Scotland an ideal laboratory to explore comparatively the relationship of marriage to differing forms of rural economy on the one hand and wider economic, cultural and legal factors on the other. Unfortunately, Scottish sources are difficult to use for study of marriage behaviour before the introduction of civil registration in 1855. While parish registers are now proving more tractable and

[1] Orkney and, especially, Shetland were different again and are excluded from this paper. They merit similar consideration in their own account, althouth the often heavy temporary absence of men (and particularly single men) at sea makes census-based analysis rather suspect.

reliable than Flinn and his colleagues suggested (Flinn et al., 1977: 271–74; Blaikie 1993), it remains the case that full-scale family reconstitution is rarely possible. Even when registers survive and are of reasonable quality for the study of mortality, the recording of marriages is frequently problematic, because marriage had no special sacramental status in the Church of Scotland. With the authorities primarily concerned to maintain chastity among the unmarried, the key interest was often in maintaining records of the proclamation of banns – often declared in two parishes – or of the payment of caution money in respect of good behaviour, rather than in maintaining a comprehensive register of marriages themselves. High rates of population turnover and limited numbers of names simply make the difficulties worse. An additional problem in some areas was the practice whereby couples went to a neighbouring town to make an 'irregular marriage', in order to escape restrictions imposed locally by the church or by parents, or simply to avoid the public rituals of 'regular' marriage.

The fragmentation of the Church of Scotland in the 1840s exacerbated these problems, and this, together with growing concern about public health in the cities, was a key impulse to the creation of a national system of vital registration in 1855. For the population historian, this produced a transformation in available source material, both through the comprehensive retention of individual-level registration documentation, and from the publication of a growing mass of detailed statistical summaries in the decennial censuses and in the Detailed Annual Reports of the Registrar-General for Scotland.[2]

II. The national level: Scotland in a United Kingdom context

From the 1850s to the early 1970s, Scotland's marriage patterns are clearly differentiated from those of England and Wales. Figure 2.2 uses population census data to show the national contrasts in numbers of women never married per 1,000 population, for a selection of age groups and covering a period from 1861 to 1991 (see also Table 2.1).

Although the broad trends are similar between the two countries, clear differences in proportions married are apparent right across the age ranges until well after the Second World War. Typically, throughout this period, some 6–7 per cent more of the female population remained never married at all age groups in Scotland compared with south of the border, though the gap narrowed for women in their early twenties in the later 19th century and at all other ages after 1951. It finally disappeared in the 1970s, as marriage rates declined everywhere. Similar differences in proportions married are also observable for men (Figure 2.1), though the gaps tend to be rather smaller except at ages 25–29. Particularly notable is the fact that, while the proportion of women never married in 1851 at ages 45–49 was, at 209 per 1,000 population, 66 per cent higher in Scotland than in England and Wales, the male figure of 152 per 1,000 was only 26 per cent above the England/Wales figure.

---

[2] More detail can be found in Flinn et al. (1977: part 2) and Anderson and Morse (1993).

Figure 2.1 Percentages of males never married by age group, Scotland and England/Wales, 1851-1991

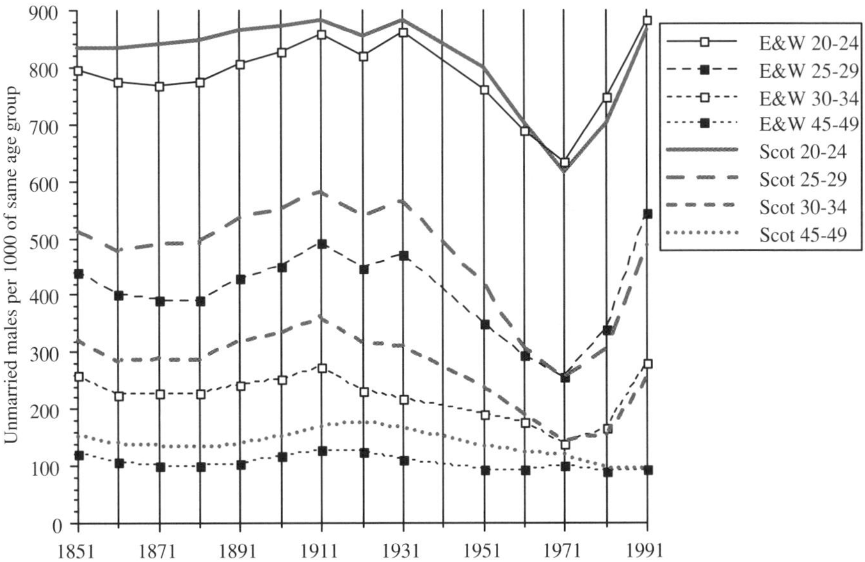

Figure 2.2 Percentage of females never married by age group, Scotland and England/Wales, 1851–1991

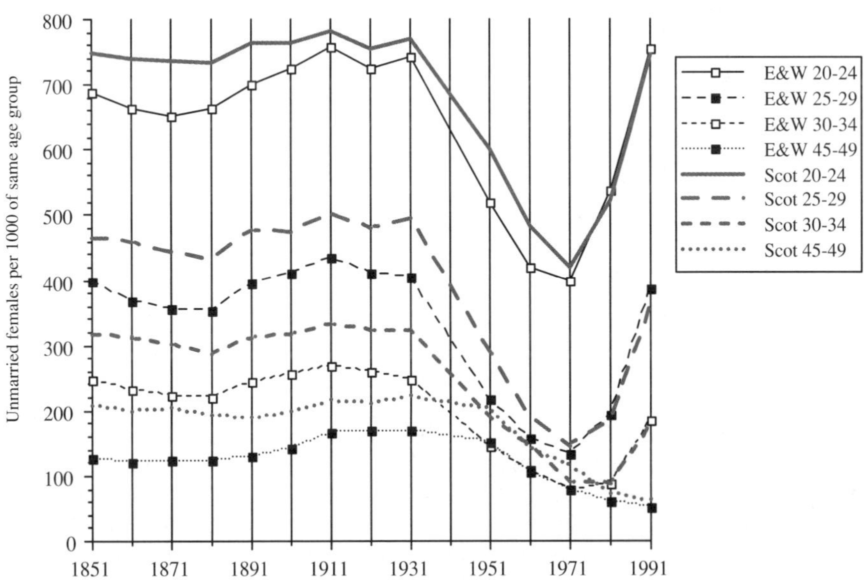

Differences between Scotland and England and Wales were pervasive, and seem to have been longstanding. Figure 2.3 plots data at county level for the two countries for those aged 20–24 and 45–49 in 1861. In the younger age group, where almost universally in both countries a larger proportion of women than of men had married, only a few counties in Scotland (all of them in the industrial and mining regions of the Central Belt) had proportions unmarried that lay below those of almost any English county. In the older age group, compared with England, almost every Scottish county was distinguished both by a tendency to have rather more men never married at ages 45–49, and, above all, by an almost universal pattern whereby significantly more women had never married compared with their age peers south of the border.

Figure 2.3 Percentage of men and women never married at ages 20–24 and 45–49, Scottish and English counties, 1861

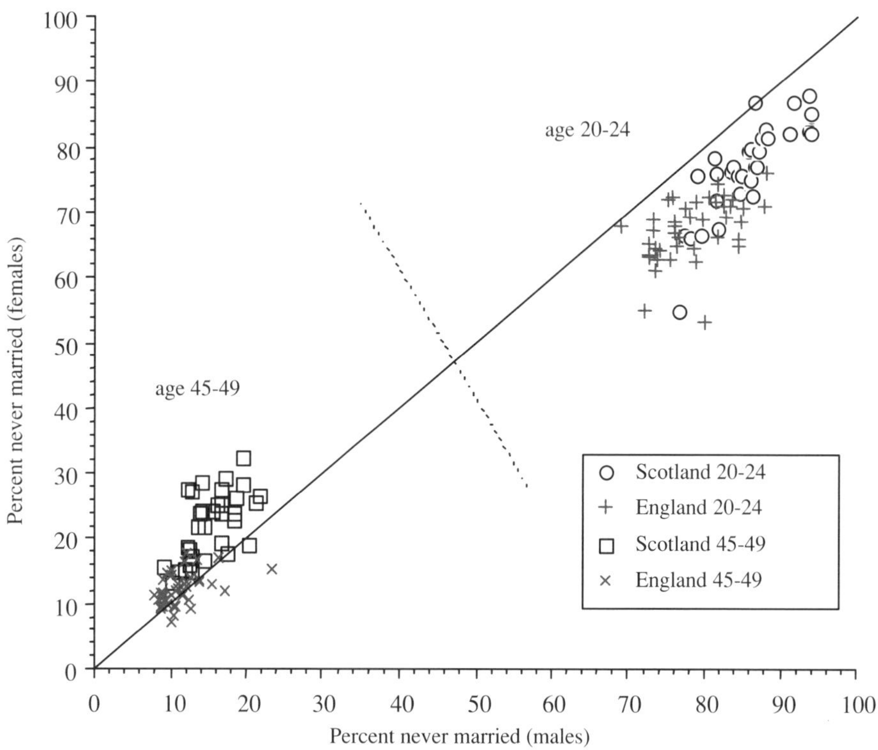

Given that it is not possible to reverse the status of being 'never married', and on the basis of what seems a reasonable assumption that there was no significant differential survival into old age north and south of the border by marital status, Figure 2.4, which plots data for men and women aged 75–84, strongly suggests that the Scottish–English contrast was not simply the result of the marked economic and agrarian transformation of the second quarter of the 19th century, but was of much more long-standing significance.

Figure 2.4 Percentage of men and women never married at ages 75–84, Scottish and English counties, 1851

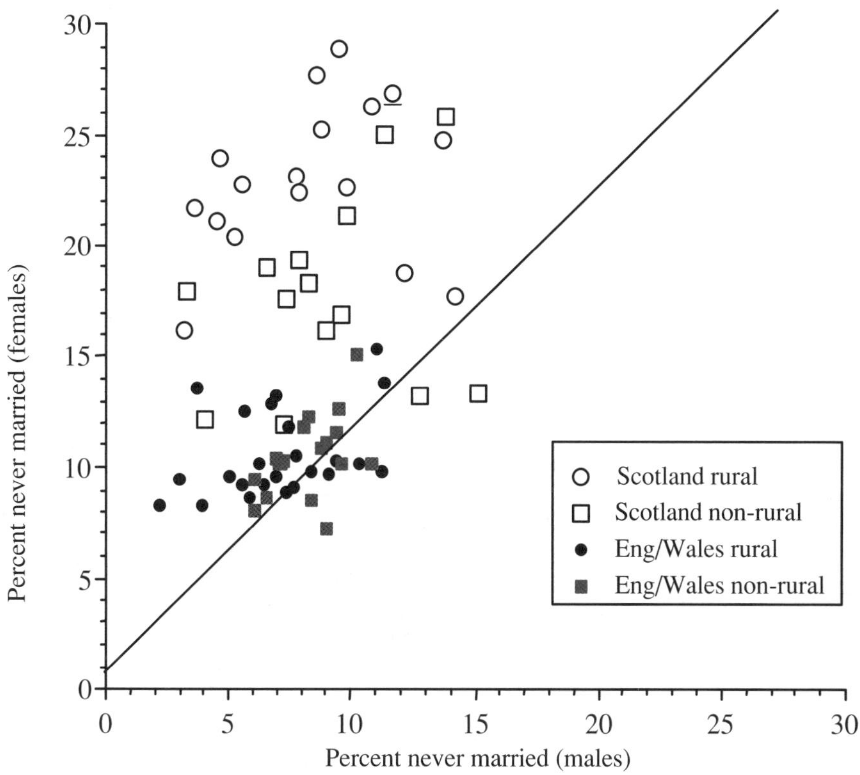

Women aged 75–84 in 1851 would have been in the prime marrying ages in the early years of the century and would have been aged 45–54 in 1821; later in the century, at least, very few women seem to have married for the first time after the age of 45, and even for men the figure was only a few per cent. The male plots in Figure 2.4 show only modest excess permanent celibacy for Scotland, but, compared with the pattern for English counties (which roughly matches the national estimate for the later 18th century inferred by Schofield (1985: 10) from family reconstitution and back projection), women were far more likely to be unmarried in old age in almost every part of Scotland, and were dramatically likely to be so in many counties, particularly the more rural ones.[3]

[3] The three highest 'non-rural' Scottish counties in Figure 2.4 are Roxburgh and Selkirk (with their high proportions in textiles and highly skewed sex ratios) and Aberdeenshire (where the city of Aberdeen, although of significant size, comprised only about a third of the population of the county in a region where 'rural' nuptiality was elsewhere very low).

These data provide a rather contrasting picture to that obtained from other sources for the pre-1855 period. Information gleaned by Flinn et al. (1977: 282) for fourteen parishes from the *Statistical Account* of the 1790s, superficially implies that a mean of only about 15 per cent of women aged 40 and over (with a few cases of 45 and over, or 50 and over) remained unmarried at the time of their deaths. There is, however, wide variation between different parishes, and the data include some figures which seem implausibly low, notably the 2.7 per cent and 3.2 per cent for two parishes in Perthshire. Similar data for eleven parishes for the mid-18th century, also cited by Flinn et al. (1977: 280), for women dying at age 50 or over, produce markedly higher figures never married, with a mean of 19 per cent and with six figures of 25 per cent or more. On the other hand, Houston (1989: 65) notes that only 11 per cent of female deponents aged 50 and over at the High Court of Justiciary between 1660 and 1770 were never married, though he believes that this may be an underestimate since unmarried women may have experienced higher mortality; such a view would not, however, be consistent with the data for 1851 cited above. Alternatively, the deponents may have been a more skewed sample than he suggests; certainly the Court dealt mainly with lowland cases, but there may have been other factors also.

While it is possible that proportions marrying had fallen over the first half of the 18th century, then risen after 1755, but had already started to fall again by the 1790s, it seems more plausible to suggest that nuptiality at least in many parts of Scotland was highly depressed even in the second half of the 18th and the early part of the 19th century, but that it was locally and regionally so highly variable that any firm estimates before 1800 are of dubious validity. Figure 2.5 plots available data on age at first marriage in bachelor–spinster marriages in England until 1837, England and Wales from 1837, and Scotland from 1855 (see also Table 2.2).[4]

[4] Sources are as follows: England pre-1837: Wrigley et al. (1981) (for marriages at age <50). England and Wales post-1837: Registrar General for England and Wales; Scotland post-1855: Registrar General for Scotland (5/10 year means up to 1905).

Figure 2.5 Mean ages at marriage (bachelor–spinster marriages), 1700–1995 (Scotland and England/Wales)

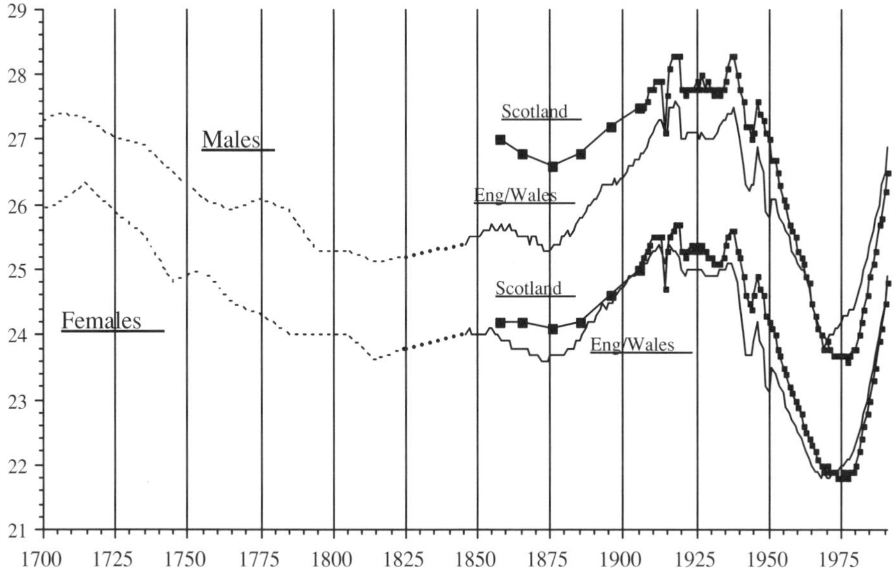

All data before the last quarter of the 19th century are derived from incomplete enumeration, but the trends are probably reasonably robust. The English data, which until 1837 come from mostly rural family reconstitution, show the mean ages at marriage falling steadily and markedly over the 18th century, rising modestly into the 1850s, and then, by now based on increasingly comprehensive national data, falling to a low point in the early 1870s, and then rising steeply thereafter. Marriage ages for both sexes then dipped dramatically after World War Two, before the recent rise which is partly linked to increased cohabitation. The Scottish data after 1855 follow the English quite closely, showing modestly higher mean ages for women until the early 1970s. The age difference for men is much larger, narrowing after the Second World War and again falling below the English/Welsh figures in the early 1970s.

For the period before 1855, Scottish data on age at marriage are highly fragmentary or inferential. Inferentially, and assuming constant proportions married, estimates of the crude birth rate suggest little change between 1755 and the 1790s or between the 1790s and 1855.[5] This might imply that the age at first marriage remained

[5] Flinn et al. (1977: 329–31), who is followed by Houston (1989: 19), used retrospective data for women who died in 1855 to argue for little change over the early nineteenth century, but failed to consider the implication of differential survival of younger and older brides; his conclusions are thus unreliable.

unchanged in Scotland over this period, and in support of this case, Tyson has suggested that proto-industrialization, seen as a key factor by Goldstone in encouraging a rise in younger marriages in England, played a much less significant role in most of rural Scotland because its main impact north of the border was on female employment, while men's marriage chances continued to depend on what was happening in agriculture. Here, as we shall see below, opportunities remained in many areas very limited.[6]

On the other hand, it should be noted that an unchanged mean age at first marriage in Scotland between the 1750s and 1855 would imply that the Scottish mean marriage age for women in bachelor–spinster marriages in the mid-18th century would have been at least six months *younger* than in England. This might, against a longer time perspective, seem implausible. Some fragmentary figures do exist from a number of partial family reconstitutions or other similar exercises (Flinn, et al. 1977: 276, 279; Houston, 1992: 127), and from Houston's work on depositions (Houston, 1989: 65). Most of these estimates imply, for southern Scotland, that the mean age at marriage for women was rather higher in the second half of the 18th century than in the first two-thirds of the 19th, which might well, therefore, suggest some parallels with the situation in England.[7] However, there is a major exception in the coastal areas of the Highlands, the Hebrides and the Northern Isles, where contemporary comment almost universally implies early marriage for women in the 1790s, although with rising marriage ages from the 1820s. The implications of this suggestion are returned to below.[8]

Finally, at the aggregate national level, we may consider the wider consequences of these low levels of nuptiality. Table 2.3 shows I_m and sex ratio values for Scotland and England and Wales for 1841–1961, while Figure 2.6 sets Scotland's I_m for 1911 in the context of other western European countries at around the same date (Coale and Watkins, 1986). The figure for Scotland is below that for all the other countries shown except for Iceland and Ireland. No figure is available for Sweden or Norway for *c*.1910, but their *c*.1900 figures are .411 and .420 respectively, compared with a Scottish figure for 1901 of .425. In this, as in a number of aspects of her demography, Scotland looks more like Norway or Sweden than England and Wales.

---

[6] R.E. Tyson, personal communicaton. relating to Chap. 5 of a new Scottish Population History, to be edited by E. Graham, M. Anderson and C. W. J. Withers; Goldstone (1986).
[7] But this was not the case in Rothiemay in Banffshire, where marriage ages were higher in 1801–50 than in 1750–1800 (Blaikie, 1993).
[8] Contemporary comment is widespread in Sinclair (1975–83) and elsewhere (Flinn et al., 1977).

Figure 2.6 Nuptiality and fertility indicators, selected countries of Europe, c.1910

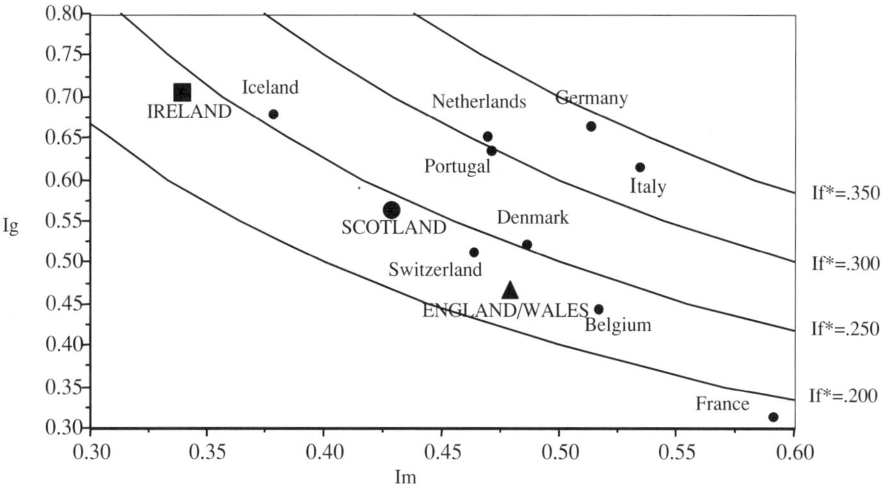

In fact, however, in 1911 as throughout our period, the depressing impact of low nuptiality on fertility north of the border was offset by the fact that Scotland had higher marital fertility than England and Wales. The result, as Figure 2.6 shows, was that overall fertility in Scotland was actually higher in 1911 than in England and Wales (Scottish I_f was .260 compared with a figure of .234 for England and Wales). And, as the tables presented at the end of the chapter show, the same was true for much of the period covered here. As a result, since mortality levels nationally were also very similar in the two countries, the fact that at a national level Scotland's population grew more slowly throughout our period compared with that of England and Wales was almost entirely the result of Scotland's markedly higher rates of emigration (Anderson and Morse, 1993).[9]

III. Regional differences

Regionally, however, the position seems to have been rather different, with marriage patterns in Scotland highly variable from at least the later 18th century right through to the later 20th century. Some elements of this regional diversity across the

---

[9] Fifty years earlier, Scotland's I_m had been above the levels of the Netherlands, Belgium and Switzerland, but, in the meantime the Scottish figure had fallen while those for most other countries had tended, with the onset of fertility decline, to rise. In 1861, Scottish I_g was much higher than the English level, but, even so, Scotland's much lower nuptiality meant that English I_f* was actually higher.

whole of Scotland up to 1911 have been explored in earlier work (Anderson and Morse, 1993; Anderson, 1996, 1999). Here the focus is on a smaller number of predominantly rural counties, divided into five groups, in each of which the rural household economy was to a considerable extent founded on a rather different underlying agrarian system. More detail on each of these systems will be explored later as part of the discussion. Rates of population change for each of these counties is given in Table 2.4, and mean ages at marriage in Table 2.5.

Table 2.6 shows changes in the proportions of men and women living in the different rural counties who remained unmarried at ages 45–54 in, respectively, 1851, 1911, 1931 and 1961. Overall, the proportion of women never married at these ages mostly lay somewhere between one-fifth and three-tenths throughout the period from 1851 to 1911. After the Second World War, by contrast, there was a dramatic change, so that by 1961 in only two counties was the figure in excess of 20 per cent. The picture for men was very different. In 1851, in only one county (Perth) did the proportion unmarried at ages 45–54 exceed one-fifth, and, of the four 'Crofting Counties', only in Argyll was it in excess of 17 per cent. Over the second half of the 19th century, however, there was a very marked decline in male nuptiality in all the 'Crofting Counties' and also in parts of what is here called the 'Highland Fringe'. By 1911, Sutherland, Inverness and Argyll all had more than a quarter of men unmarried at ages 45–54, and although Argyll fell back significantly by 1931, Sutherland, Inverness and Ross and Cromarty retained very high proportions of celibates into the inter–war period. The post–war years saw a modest fall in almost all counties, but particularly dramatically in the far north of the country. Nevertheless, other than in Argyll, both within a Scottish national and in a UK context, even in the 1960s, very high proportions of men remained unmarried at age 50 in the 'Crofting Counties' and also in Caithness.

The impact of these marriage patterns on potential fertility is illustrated in Table 2.7, which shows the changes in I_m for this same group of counties between 1861 and 1961, with the addition, for comparison, of data for a group of counties from the industrial and commercial Scottish 'Central Belt'. Throughout the period, nuptiality remained low in almost all rural counties compared with the Central Belt, but it was especially depressed in some of the Crofting Counties and notably in Sutherland where, between 1861 and 1931, only about a third of women's potential fertility was available for conception within marriage. Indeed, Sutherland's 1871 I_m of .285 appears to be among the very lowest figure for any 'province' for which data were recorded in the European Fertility Project (Coale and Watkins, 1986).[10] The lowest figure for 1871 for Ireland was .340 for Kilkenny, while the lowest for England were .451 for Sussex (presumably largely a result of high levels of middle class domestic service) and .452 for Cornwall. In 1881, when Scottish figures can be calculated for the first

[10] The lowest I_m values of all seem to be for several provinces in Switzerland for 1860, but the marked changes recorded by 1870 must cast some doubt on the reliability of the 1860 figures.

time at parish level, roughly half the parishes in the Scottish highlands and islands had I_m values below .333, and in less than a dozen in any part of the highlands or highland fringe (outside of Perthshire) did I_m exceed .400 (see Figure 2.7).[11] Even in 1961, most of the 'Crofting Counties' still had I_m values significantly below the Scottish average. Yet, if we believe contemporary comment, these were the areas with the youngest marriage in Scotland in the later 18th century, and they were certainly areas in some parts of which population growth was exceptionally fast at that time (Anderson, 1999).

Figure 2.7 I_m, Scotland, 1881

[11] For maps for other dates, see Anderson and Morse (1993).

Other parts of rural Scotland also showed some tendency to depressed nuptiality in the later 19th and early 20th centuries, although, as Table 2.7 and Figure 2.7 show, this was less the case in much of the northeast (where there had been a modest rise between 1851 and 1881 in particular) and also in East Lothian (though here the highest nuptiality was in what became heavily mining-dominated parishes in the extreme west of the county). By 1931, nuptiality in the northeast, the southeast and the southwest was approaching Central Belt levels, and after the Second World War, nuptiality as measured by I_m increased everywhere as age at marriage fell and proportions marrying increased. Indeed, in only three counties (all in the Central Belt) did I_m rise by less than 0.20, but the rises tended to be largest in areas where marriage levels had previously been especially depressed, and by 1961 it was only the Crofting Counties which stood out as continuing rural areas of lower nuptiality.

Finally, it may be noted that similar differences and trends can be observed if we focus not on proportions never marrying but on age at marriage (unfortunately, data relate to all marriages rather than first marriages, but clear patterns still emerge). Table 2.8 shows estimates of the median age at marriage for men and women in 1860–62 and 1910–11. In nearly every rural county the median age at marriage for men was significantly above that for women, and the median age tended to be somewhat higher in the years around 1911 than around 1861. In both periods the medians were higher in the Crofting Counties and the Highland Fringe. Rises were particularly marked between the two periods in Sutherland, Ross and Inverness, and for women in Argyll, Berwick and in Moray.

For 1930–32 and 1960–62, data on average marriage ages are available for counties excluding the cities and larger towns. At the upper extreme in 1930–32, in Ross and Cromarty the mean age at marriage for men was 34.1 and for women was 29.4. Among the 'rural' counties under consideration here, the highest six positions in the rank order for both men and women were Crofting or Highland Fringe counties. In 1930–32, only four rural counties (Banff and Kincardine, both heavily involved in fishing, East Lothian, with its significant coal mining sector, and Wigtown) were below the Scottish national mean of 29.3 for men and 26.3 for women. Thirty years later, the position was very different, though again the six highest rank order ages at marriage were in the Crofting and Highland Fringe areas (this time, Nairn was the exception). The highest means for 1960–62 were in Inverness (30.1 for males, 25.7 for women). But, by now, ten of the 'rural' counties (including all in the northeast, southeast and southwest) had female marriage ages below the national mean, as did seven of the counties for men. The largest falls over the thirty-year period were in Ross and Cromarty (4.9 years for men, 4.6 years for women). While some differences still remained, by the early 1960s rural marriage patterns over most of the country were no longer dramatically different from the national norm. In part this was because the major processes of structural readjustment to be outlined below had largely been worked through, but it was also because the proportion of the populations of most counties dependent on the agricultural economy was by then very much reduced.

In terms of the wider consequences of Scotland's nuptiality, we noted earlier that there seems to have been no direct impact of low nuptiality on national population growth, since, compared with England, it was to a great extent offset by higher marital fertility. The same combination of low nuptiality and high marital fertility was found in the Crofting Counties, but nuptiality in these areas was so low that depression of levels of overall fertility nevertheless occurred.[12] In the extreme case of Sutherland in 1871, a high I_g of .782 combined with the a low I_m of .285 to produce an I_f value of just .239 (illegitimacy was negligible: I_h was only .022). I_f was also below .300 in Ross and Cromarty and Inverness. Even on Teitlebaum's figures, where fertility is almost certainly underestimated, no Irish county had an 1871 I_f value of below .240.

Figure 2.8 Natural increase by net migration, mean per cent change per decade, 1861–1911

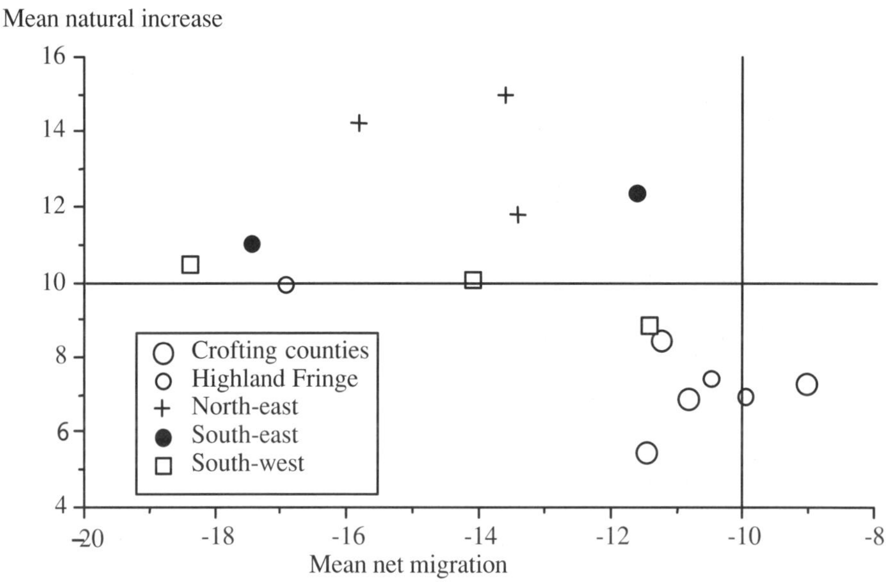

[12] For more detailed graphs, see Anderson and Morse (1993: 6).

The result of these extremely low levels of Scottish rural fertility in the period 1861–1911 can be seen in Figure 2.8. This shows the relationship between net migration and natural increase for selected rural counties of Scotland and confirms what has been demonstrated elsewhere: that, in comparative terms within Scotland, the Crofting Counties, where populations were generally in modest decline, were dominated by a regime of very low natural increase but only modest out-migration, while the counties in the northeast, where population was growing the most rapidly, had much higher natural increase but also much higher rates of out-migration. The southwest and southeast occupied an intermediate position. Also, the main difference in natural increase between the northwest and the northeast was not in mortality (which was moderate in all areas) nor in marital fertility, which was, relative to most of the rest of the country, high in both areas. The key difference between the demography of the northeast and of the northwest was in their nuptiality, which, as we have seen above, was relatively high and actually rising somewhat in the northeast between 1861 and 1911, while it was low and falling in the northwest.[13]

IV. Why was Scottish rural nuptiality so low?

In answering this question it will be helpful to differentiate between the 'Crofting Counties' and much of the 'Highland Fringe' on the one hand and other areas of rural Scotland on the other (though some of the factors which were crucial for the latter groups of counties also apply to parts of the population in the northwest). Nevertheless, two key differences distinguished all of rural Scotland to some extent from most of England and Wales: the organizational and institutional arrangements relating to the hiring and housing of agricultural labour, and the rules governing access to Poor Relief.

In many ways, constraints on marriage were most directly observable in the southeast. Here, from the 1760s, landlords began a process of consolidation and 'improvement' of their lands, compelling the much reduced number of tenants to accept longer leases and new forms of mixed husbandry which produced a strong year-round demand for paid labour of both sexes, but particularly for significant numbers of skilled ploughmen. There was also some need for seasonal field labour, much of which was provided by women. To meet these needs, farmers focused recruitment on highly skilled and married 'farm servants', employed on six-month or yearly hire, and mostly housed on the farm so as to be near to their animals. Most farmers also employed some young single workers of both sexes, who were again housed on the farm, some of them being the children of the labourers. In this new environment, labour demand was highly controlled, there were few villages on the English model, and very little housing was not under the control of employers.[14]

---

[13] For more detailed discussion of these issues, see Anderson and Morse (1993), Anderson (1996) and Anderson (1998).
[14] The developments outlined in this and the following paragraphs are concisely reviewed in, for example, Smout (1973: chaps 5–6, 12–14); Gray (1957, 1973); Orr (1984).

This system provided a strong incentive for farmers to try to recruit families who could match their precise set of labour requirements, and an equally strong incentive for labourers to seek work on farms which could offer the employment that their own family was able to supply. As a result, both single and married farm workers regularly moved from farm to farm as they sought a better house or a better employer or, for the married or those about to marry, a situation which offered appropriate work opportunities for a wife or their children. Other rural workers also moved in response to new or declining opportunities for employment. However, over the century after 1840, new technologies and changing markets for arable products meant that labour demand fell away, except in areas as in the far west of East Lothian, where mining, fishing and market gardening combined to sustain population growth and, for many, to provide new opportunities for marriage.

In this system, some men and women left the area altogether each year, as opportunities for employment disappeared or, increasingly over time, as better opportunities were perceived elsewhere (Smout, 1986: 60–61). Others stayed, and most of these at some point in their lives saw an opportunity which appeared to offer a secure enough niche in the local economy to contemplate establishing a household of their own; for a large group of farm workers in the southeast, this would only first come when they were offered a plough team of their own and the house that went with their new status. The need to wait for this defining life-cycle moment resulted from two crucial differences of Scottish as opposed to English rural life. In England, in many parishes, some housing could frequently be obtained through what was effectively an open market, so a couple could make their own decision as to when to establish a household of their own. Indeed, under the English day-labour system there was no necessary connection between employment, housing and marriage; if a man could not get work, he would not automatically have to move house, as long as there was some way in which he could continue to support his family. In most lowland Scottish communities, by contrast, there was an almost total absence of housing which either did not go with one's job or which was not under the control of a landlord or substantial tenant. As a result, in most parishes, a man who failed to get hired normally just had to move on. This was linked to a second factor which also encouraged much more caution in approaching marriage in rural Scotland than in England and Wales. In England, if a married man became unemployed, he and his family were entitled to poor relief, and could often obtain it for a time at least without moving to his parish of settlement. In Scotland, by contrast, the Poor Law made at best only small transitory payments to any able-bodied person. The risk of marrying 'improvidently' in Scotland was therefore far greater than south of the border.[15]

---

[15] The contrast between the English and the Scottish Poor law did not escape the attention of Malthus (1986: 273). The population impact of increases or reductions in the provision of housing is extensively cited in comments on population change collected as part of the 1811 census comments (British Library, Additional Manuscripts, 6897; for more details, see Flinn et al. (1977: Part 2). For further discussion, see Anderson and Morse (1993). This interpretation owes much to Devine (1988: 45–47).

In areas of the lowlands outside the southeast, the same principles of limited supply of free market housing and a restricted Poor Law applied, but the different underlying agrarian systems placed rather different constraints on marriage and on migration. In the southwest, pasture was dominant, with many small family farms producing liquid milk or cheese for the expanding urban markets, and with additional dairy girls the main requirement for year-round supplementary labour, although some additional male labour, increasingly provided by Irish migrants, was needed at harvest time. As a result, by the mid-19th century marriage opportunities were limited already in this area, and they continued to be so, especially in Wigtown where, reacting at least in part to rapid growth in the later 18th and early 19th centuries, population fell by nearly a quarter between 1851 and 1911 and employment in agriculture, at least at the spring census dates, was reduced by 39 per cent (Campbell, 1984; Gray, 1973).

In much of the northeast, the rural economy focused on rearing beef cattle, and, though there was some demand for ploughmen, there was less for supplementary female labour. As a result, more of the farm labour consisted of unmarried men, most of whom were housed in communal space around the farm. However, in this area, for much of the earlier part of the century, there were opportunities for reclaiming new farmland from the hills, and small tenancies were let out to couples who would pioneer this process (Carter 1984; Gray, 1973, 1984). There were also in these northeastern counties rapidly expanding opportunities in fishing, and it was this that primarily produced some dynamism in the county-level figures for population growth and nuptiality, as declining opportunities in agriculture (as the internal frontier closed) were more than offset between 1851 and 1911 at a county level by rises in numbers employed in fisheries.

The situation in the north and northwest was very different indeed, especially in the islands (other than for a while in Lewis) and in the western mainland, where from the later 18th century a small-scale mixed peasant economy was gradually changed by the widespread introduction of sheep husbandry. Most of the former tenants were moved elsewhere, particularly to coastal areas, where the landlords believed they could be sustained by a mixture of small-scale farming, fishing and other non-agricultural activities. Particularly important among the non-agricultural activities during the Napoleonic Wars, when the price of potash was extremely favourable, was landlord action to exploit their coastlines for the collection and burning of seaweed (kelp); indeed, many landowners actively encouraged the establishment of new households to provide labour for this task. However, dramatic fall of kelp prices after 1820, increasing unpredictability of the fishing, collapse of other manufacturing ventures and almost total failure of the staple potato crop in the 1840s all challenged the basis of this economy. As a result, landlords increasingly sought to restrict access to the many smaller parcels of land, which had never in many cases been able or designed to provide a total subsistence for a family.

This produced a response which was inevitably of long duration. As we have seen, many landowners had deliberately destroyed the older mixed peasant economy with its own strong elements of self-regulation. In its place they had reorganized settlement in ways which tolerated or even encouraged subdivision of tenancies and establishment of new households, so as to increase revenue from non-farming activities on their estates and turn their people into part-time agriculturalists forced to supplement their resources by other forms of income-generating activity.[16] In this they were only too successful, for it was the expanding number of families, with high levels of male marriage and, probably, somewhat lower ages at marriage for women which underlay most of the rapid population growth in these regions before 1840. But when the basis of this economy was destroyed, the whole system went into a crisis which could only be resolved when the number of households contracted to just those capable of supporting a family under the new economic conditions. However, in a situation where there was no welfare fall-back for the able-bodied, permanently giving up the ultimate minimal insurance of a house and a holding was itself a risky step.[17] As a result, demographic readjustment was inevitably slow since, after the crisis of the 1840s, most landowners (outside Lewis, where population continued to rise (Anderson and Morse, 1993; Smout, 1986: 70-71)), pressed strongly for consolidation and population reduction whenever the opportunity arose. In this situation, marriage chances were inevitably highly restricted, in some areas right through into the interwar years.

However, a second line of argument is also highly relevant here. The proportion of any area's population which is married at any age is not just the result of opportunities to establish a new and independent household. In a country such as Scotland, where high levels of temporary and permanent migration away from constrained opportunities and towards expanding ones was a long-standing feature of the society, the numbers of adults living in an area in a never-married state crucially reflect the balance between the availability of economic and residential opportunities for the unmarried in the area on the one hand, and opportunities available outside it on the other. As a result, the numbers both of never-married and married residents are the net residues of complex interactions between external pull and internal retention processes. And, crucially, it can often be the case that rather different economic and residential niches are available to the single as opposed to the married. Moreover, as Guinnane (1990) has nicely shown in the Irish context, where a choice existed, we should not necessarily assume that marriage, especially for women, would always or even normally be the preferred state.

The scale of net out-migration from many parts of Scotland in the 19th century makes this point particularly significant. For example, in the extreme case of Wigtown, age cohort depletion analysis suggests a net loss between 1861 and 1871 of about 40 per cent of men who were aged 15–24 at the earlier date and roughly 33 per cent of women. In Argyll, of every 100 males aged 5–14 in 1841, over the next forty years

[16] This argument is well developed in Devine (1994: chap. 3).

[17] The point that highlanders might quite logically have this kind of 'security-preference' is elaborated by Smout (1986: 67), who also argues for a strong cultural sense of status through landholding and felt obligations laid on paternalistic landlords to ensure its continuation (on which see also Devine, 1988: 40ff).

at least the equivalent of 28 would have died[18] and 48 would have outmigrated, leaving just 24 of the original cohort, or one-third of the survivors, in the county. Of this 24, now aged 45–54, roughly five would never have married. The comparable figures for women were 25 dead, 46 out-migrated, 29 remaining, of whom seven remained unmarried. For Wigtown, by the same process, only 28 men and 37 women would have remained after 40 years of an original 100 people of each sex, with four men and 10 women never married.

Under these circumstances, the factors that allowed or encouraged single men and women either to leave or to remain could have a crucial impact on nuptiality rates. This topic has been further explored elsewhere (Anderson 1998), but as illustration of the effect, Figures 2.9 and 2.10, and the more detailed data in Table 2.9, show rough estimates[19] of the net cohort depletion rates between 1861 and 1881 of men and women aged 15–19 in 1861, with those lost from the area subdivided into estimated numbers who would have died had they stayed in the area and numbers of net out-migrants, and with those staying subdivided into ever-married and never-married.

Figure 2.9 Twenty-year outcomes for cohorts aged 15–19 and resident in 1861, percentage, men

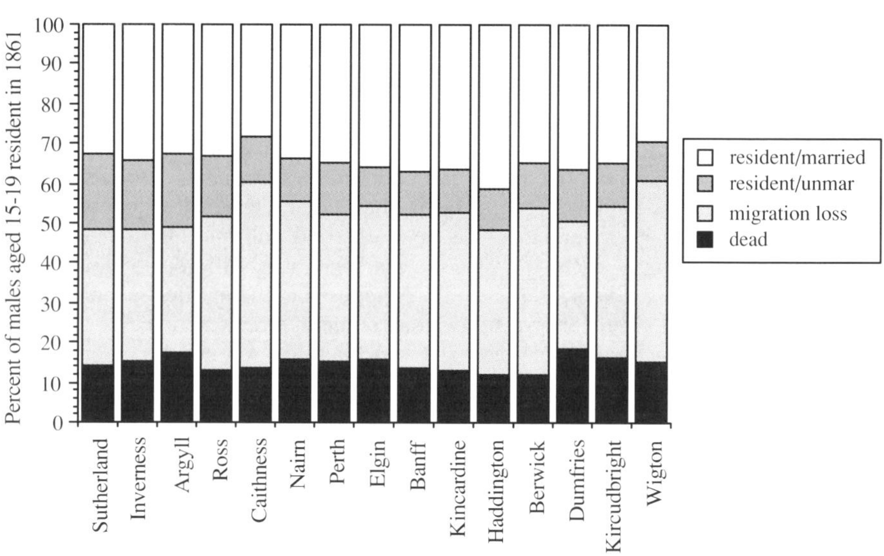

[18] See note 19 below.
[19] The migration figures are net flows, and this can be somewhat misleading in counties like Haddington where many young women seem to have left home to go to service in the towns, being replaced as farm workers by Highland temporary migrants. The mortality rates are based on figures for the county concerned for 1861–71. In as far as some migrants went to the towns their actual mortality would have been higher, and some of those shown as dead would have died after leaving the rural community. The partitioning of the 'leavers' between mortality and migration is therefore only indicative.

Comparisons, in Figure 2.9, between Sutherland, Inverness or Argyll on the one hand, and Wigtown, Perth or Caithness on the other, show how misleading it can be to analyse celibacy levels simply in terms of those remaining in the community. The latter three counties had among the lowest proportions of resident men never married, but they also had the lowest proportions of the original cohorts remaining as married in the community. By 1881, these were clearly areas which had offered few opportunities at home of *any* kind, for married or for unmarried men. The three core Crofting Counties, by contrast, had very high proportions of their residents as celibates, but the numbers of the original cohorts remaining and married were not dramatically lower than elsewhere. Rather, these crofting areas presented substantial opportunities for unmarried men to stay assisting on small crofts or with animals, working as second hands on boats or on the roads, activities that supported a single man but did not provide the basis for starting a family on a holding of one's own, even supposing that such a holding could have been made available. Some of these groups also engaged in seasonal migration to the lowlands, especially for harvest, returning to the family crofts for the winter; some were often still present at the spring census.[20] The inter-county differences for women (Figure 2.10), are less marked, mainly because out-migration levels were lower and celibacy rates at ages 35–39 everywhere quite high. Nevertheless, note for example how, while the proportion of those who stayed who remained unmarried was very different in Wigtown compared with Haddington, almost the same proportion of the original cohort (in net terms) had stayed and were still unmarried. In Haddington, there were many opportunities for married women, and some for single ones, even if many came from outside while local girls left for the cities. In Wigtown, opportunities in general were lacking, and were especially limited for married women.

By the later 19th century, therefore, delayed marriage or permanent celibacy had become a characteristic feature of the Crofting Counties, especially for men, as opportunities to establish new households contracted rapidly. However, the availability of economic niches for unmarried adults in fact produced relatively low rates of net outflow, which in turn meant that (except for women in Sutherland) as a proportion of those who had survived to young adulthood, numbers able to stay in the community and marry were not markedly lower than elsewhere (and this is true even in spite of significant levels of temporary out-migration which would raise the true 'resident' figures further). Elsewhere, wider structural changes had rather different effects, as growing opportunities in the towns and overseas combined with contracting employment opportunities in the home area for both single and married people. Looking over a rather longer period (see Table 2.9), in the most extreme case, Wigtown, a shift from 7.4 per cent population growth between 1841 and 1861 to 8.3 per cent population loss between 1861 and 1881 saw almost no

[20] In this context, it is worth noting the substantial amounts of crofting land made potentially available but never taken up and the fact that population in much of the northwest fell faster after access to crofting lands was secured following the Crofters' Holdings Act of 1886 than before (Smout, 1986: chap. 3).

Figure 2.10 Twenty-year outcomes for cohorts, aged 15–19 and resident in 1861, percentage, women

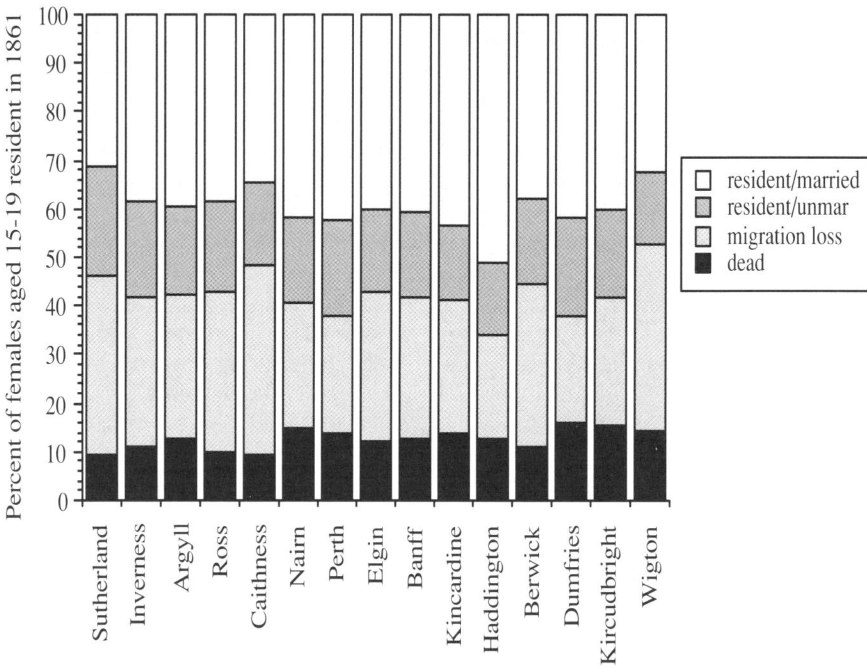

change in the percentage of resident men married at ages 35–39 (75.7 per cent in 1861, 75.8 per cent in 1881) and the proportion of resident women who were married remained constant at 68.5 per cent. However, the proportion of men dying or out-migrating in the twenty year period rose from 46.4 per cent between 1841 and 1861 to 61.1 per cent between 1861 and 1881; for women the rise was from 40.6 per cent to 52.8 per cent. This strongly suggests a situation where, in a relatively unchanging social structure, the balance of niches between married and unmarried people remained almost unchanged, while the number of opportunities fell markedly. A rather similar pattern can be observed in the northeast, where natural increase was extremely high, in great part because of high nuptiality, and a shift from rapid positive growth between 1841–1861 to almost no growth between 1861–1881 was associated with a marked increase in the proportion of the cohort which out-migrated for both sexes, while the proportion of the men who remained who were able to marry by age group 35–39 actually increased in Elgin and Banff.[21]

This discussion leads neatly into a final set of considerations. To what extent was Scottish nuptiality affected by the sex ratio of the population, either nationally or locally? Much higher rates of male than female out-migration have meant that, for more than two centuries, almost all parts of Scotland have had more women than men in the marriageable age groups. When the census first recorded age information in 1821, the national sex ratio at ages 20–29 was 799 men per thousand women in Scotland and 905 in England. In Scotland's eighteen most rural counties, the ratio was 789, while in England's twenty-two most rural counties it was 896. By 1841 the rural discrepancies were somewhat larger, with the sex ratio for the Scottish counties at ages 20–29 down to 767. In 1861, after the massive outflow of the 1850s, the sex ratio at ages 20-29 was at 798, the rather more reliable figure for the age group 25–34 being 768 (but in the southwestern counties a mere 746).

Figure 2.11 plots the national sex ratios for England and Wales and Scotland at ages 25–34 against the proportions never married at these age groups for males and females, at each census from 1851 to 1931. For England and Wales, no clear marriage squeeze effect can be discerned. For Scotland, it is indeed the case that the very low sex ratio of 1861 corresponds to the highest male proportion married: but that year also had among the highest female proportions, and for women across all years, no pattern emerges.[22]

---

[21] Fuller discussion is in Anderson (1999). There is, however, a further complication in this case, since the expansion in the scale of the fishing fleet in Banff in particular in this period may simply mean that a higher proportion of formally resident males were in fact absent at the census date, with single men being disproportionately involved.

[22] R^2 for Scottish males is .484, which at least is in the right direction, but for females it is .077 and in the wrong direction for the marriage squeeze hypothesis.

Figure 2.11 Sex ratio at ages 25–34 and proportions never married at ages 25–34, Scotland and England/Wales, decadal census counts, 1851–1931

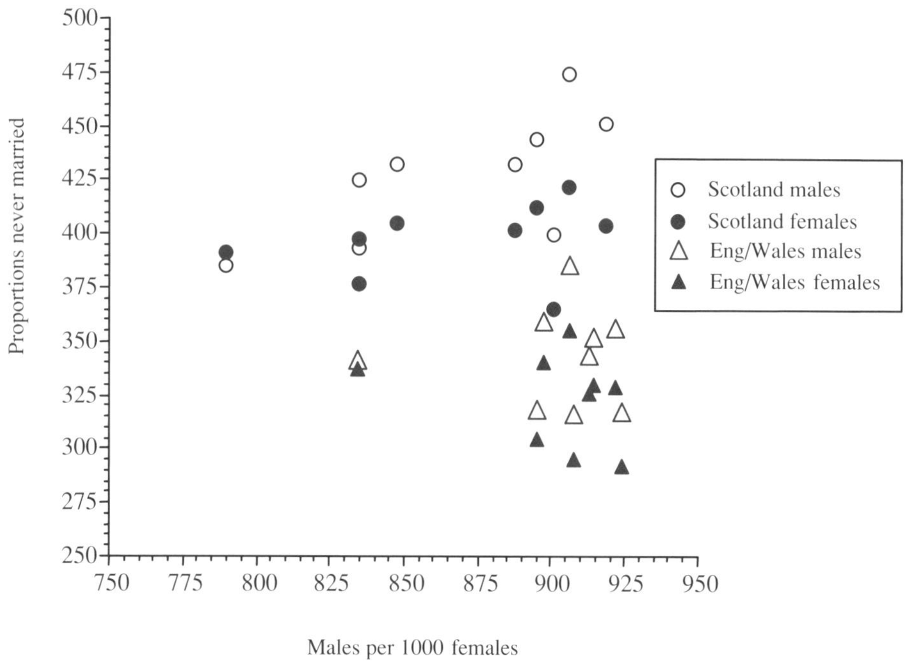

Figure 2.12 Percentage never married by sex ratio, males and females aged 25–34, 1851

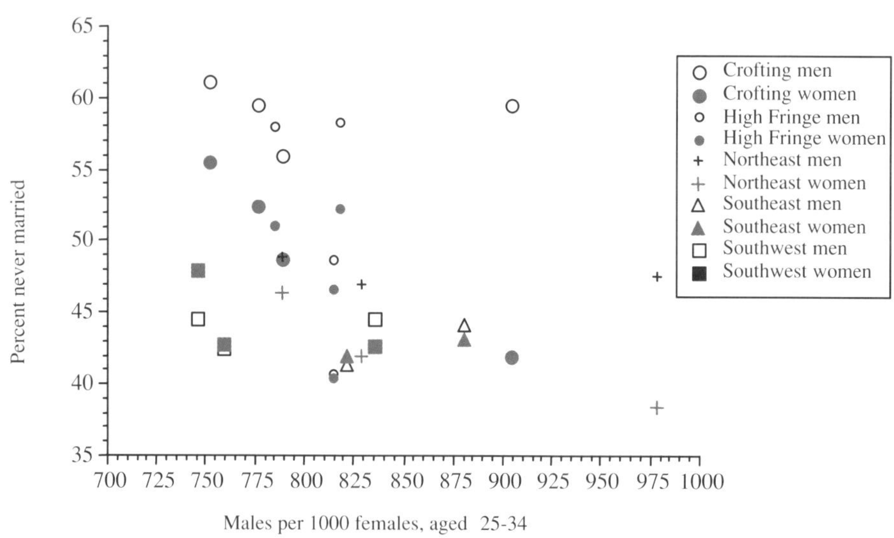

Figure 2.13 Percentage never married by sex ratio, males and females aged 45–54, 1851

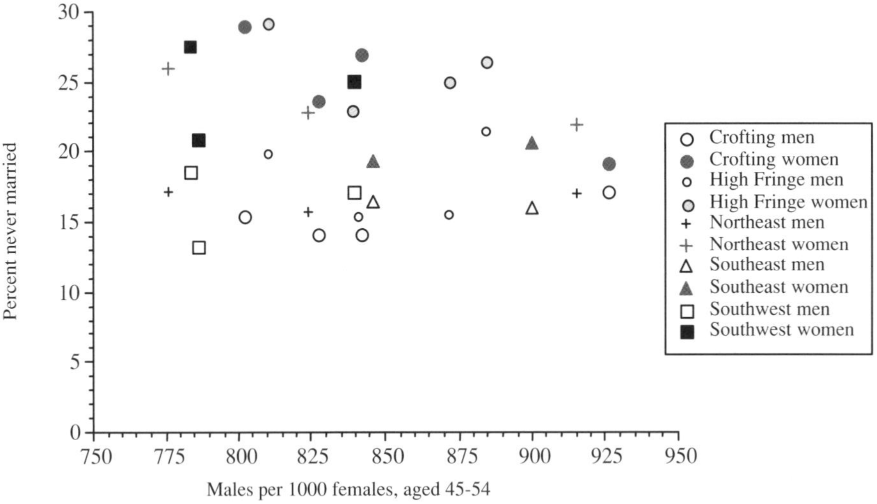

In the same way, the most striking feature of Figure 2.12, which shows the same statistics by rural county for Scotland for 1851, is the fact that high proportions never married are to be found for men and women in areas where the sex ratio is lowest. Indeed, the figures for ages 45–54 shown in Figure 2.13 produce, if anything, an effect for both sexes which is quite the opposite of that predicted by a marriage squeeze hypothesis.

A similar absence of any clear marriage squeeze effect can be observed in Figure 2.14, which shows median ages at marriage for men and women in rural counties 1890–92 against the sex ratio at ages 25–34. Indeed, what is clearest about these data is the strong correlation between the marriage ages of men and of women (Figure 2.15). While the correlation coefficients (R^2 between sex ratio and median marriage ages are (in the predicted direction) .601 for men, they are .465 (against the predicted direction) for women and the coefficient for the relationship between male and female median marriage ages (which the marriage squeeze hypothesis would expect to be negative) is highly positive at .905.

Figure 2.14 Median age at marriage by sex ratio, males and females ages 25–34, 1891

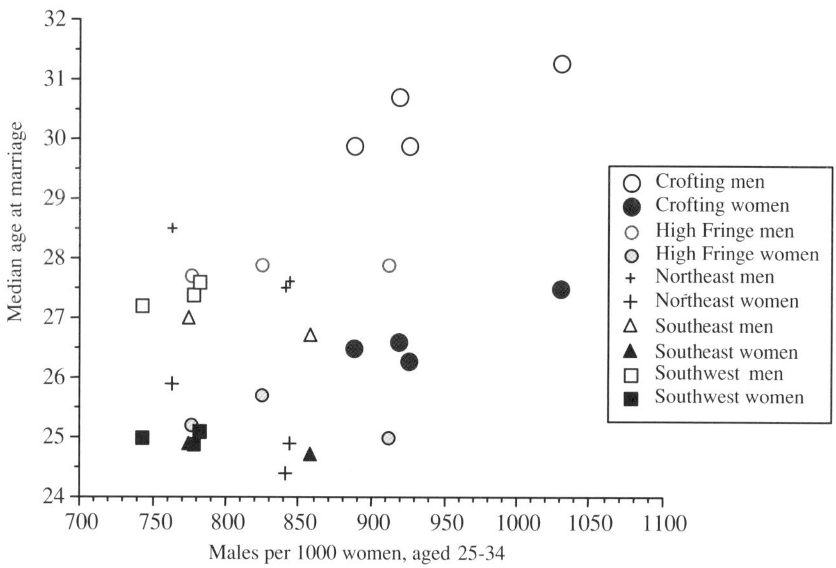

Figure 2.15 Female by male median age at marriage, 1891

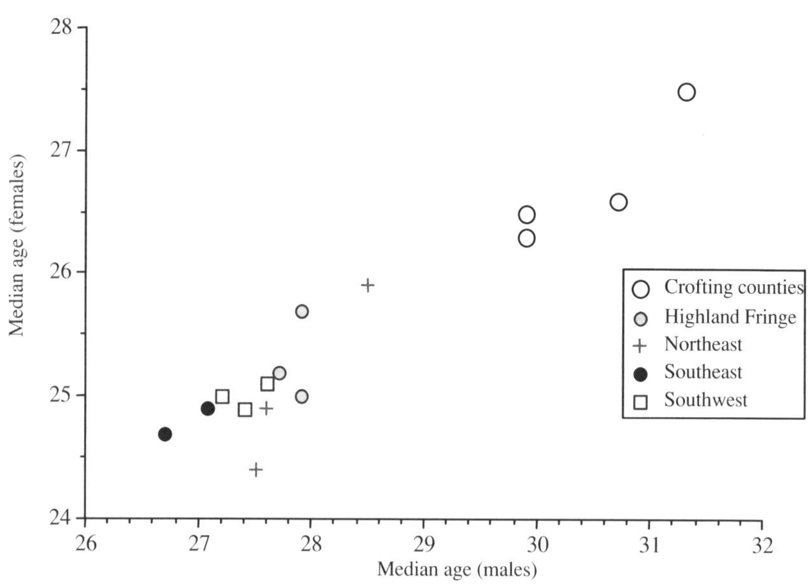

A great deal of further work, both at county (Anderson and Morse 1993; Anderson 1996) and parish[23] levels, has similarly failed to establish any clear signs of a marriage squeeze process influencing rural nuptiality (and especially female nuptiality) in most of rural Scotland at any time in the 19th or early 20th centuries. This in many ways is not surprising. A marriage squeeze might indeed occur in situations where the number of unmarried persons of one sex fell to very low levels while the numbers of the other sex still looking to get married remained high. However, this was not the case in Scotland, where there were typically large numbers of single people of both sexes throughout all the marriageable age groups. Marriage for both sexes was thus much more constrained by lack of housing and employment opportunities than by lack of potential spouses. Moreover, in a society with high rates of population mobility in and out of the community (and indeed of the country as a whole), the numbers of resident single people of each sex is not an arbitrary or chance phenomenon. Rather, it is crucially determined by the availability of housing and employment opportunities, many of which, in pre-20th century Scotland, were precisely controlled by the needs of the local economy. Under these circumstances, the availability of potential marriage partners is almost totally irrelevant.

[23] Sydney (1997) has investigated for Ross, Sutherland, Berwick and Peebles the possibility that the absence of correlation at county level was due to the county being larger in area than the local marriage market, with the result that aggregate county figures might conceal marked differences in sex ratios and associated marriage opportunities at parish level. However, in her research, no clear connections emerged at parish level, thus further supporting the view that marriage squeeze is not the principal factor behind Scotland's low rural nuptiality.

Table 2.1 **Numbers of men and women never married, per 1,000 living, by age group, Scotland and England/Wales, 1851–1991**

MALES

Year	20–24	20–24	25–29	25–29	30–34	30–34	45–49	45–49
	Eng/Wales	Scotland	Eng/Wales	Scotland	Eng/Wales	Scotland	Eng/Wales	Scotland
1851	797	834	441	513	259	322	121	152
1861	775	833	402	477	226	283	108	138
1871	767	842	392	487	230	286	99	134
1881	777	848	392	493	229	287	99	130
1891	806	866	429	536	244	318	104	137
1901	826	874	450	550	254	334	116	152
1911	857	884	492	582	272	360	127	169
1921	722	854	446	538	231	316	124	176
1931	861	882	471	564	218	307	110	165
1951	762	800	349	418	190	240	95	135
1961	690	704	294	308	175	189	95	124
1971	632	616	257	251	138	142	99	117
1981	748	702	338	306	166	155	89	96
1991	883	864	542	487	281	249	92	96

FEMALES

Year	20–24	20–24	25–29	25–29	30–34	30–34	45–49	45–49
	Eng/Wales	Scotland	Eng/Wales	Scotland	Eng/Wales	Scotland	Eng/Wales	Scotland
1851	687	748	398	466	249	316	126	209
1861	664	741	368	460	232	311	122	199
1871	652	738	356	443	224	301	124	202
1881	665	735	353	431	221	288	123	194
1891	701	764	394	478	245	312	129	188
1901	726	764	410	475	257	318	143	197
1911	757	782	434	502	270	333	165	213
1921	726	754	410	480	260	322	168	211
1931	742	771	406	495	249	324	168	219
1951	518	602	217	290	146	190	152	203
1961	420	482	157	190	109	144	105	142
1971	397	420	133	146	78	92	78	114
1981	537	523	192	185	87	89	59	73
1991	755	745	386	355	183	174	51	60

Source: Censuses of Population

Table 2.2 Mean ages at first marriage (bachelor–spinster marriages), Scotland and England/Wales, 1855–1990

	Males Scotland	Males Eng/Wales	Females Scotland	Females Eng/Wales
1855–1860	26.8	25.6	24.2	24.0
1861–1870	26.6	25.5	24.2	23.8
1871–1880	26.4	25.4	24.1	23.7
1881–1890	26.6	25.8	24.2	24.0
1891–1900	27.0	26.3	24.6	24.5
1901–1910	27.4	26.8	25.0	25.0
1911–1920	27.9	27.3	25.4	25.3
1921–1930	27.8	27.1	25.3	25.0
1931–1940	28.0	27.2	25.3	24.9
1941–1950	27.3	26.4	24.6	23.7
1951–1960	26.0	25.6	23.5	23.0
1961–1970	24.5	24.5	22.3	22.0
1971–1980	23.7	24.2	21.9	22.0
1981–1990	25.0	25.5	23.2	23.4

Source: Annual Reports of the Registrars-General

Table 2.3 Sex ratios and I_m, Scotland and England/Wales, 1841-1961

	Sex ratio Scotland	Sex ratio Eng/Wales	I_m Scotland	I_m Eng/Wales
1841	830	923		
1851	835	922	0.410	0.483
1861	789	895	0.422	0.502
1871	834	908	0.432	0.509
1881	901	924	0.438	0.501
1891	887	913	0.420	0.477
1901	918	898	0.425	0.476
1911	905	906	0.428	0.479
1921	847	835	0.433	0.489
1931	895	914	0.441	0.503
1951	948	975		
1961	965	1030	0.656	0.699

Source: Censuses of Population; Coale and Watkins (1986)

Table 2.4 Population change, Scottish rural counties, 1755–1901

	1755–1801	1801–1821	1821–1841	1841–1861	1861–1881	1881–1901
Crofting Counties						
Sutherland	11.6	3.1	4.0	1.9	-7.4	-8.3
Inverness	22.0	23.8	8.7	-9.1	1.8	-0.4
Argyll	22.6	19.7	0.1	-18.6	-3.5	-3.7
Ross	17.1	22.1	14.4	3.5	-3.5	-2.7
Highland Fringe						
Caithness	1.8	29.1	24.5	13.1	-5.5	-12.9
Nairn	46.2	11.4	-0.6	9.2	3.9	-11.1
Perth	4.6	10.1	-0.6	-2.9	-3.4	-4.4
Northeast						
Elgin	-9.3	13.1	11.5	21.9	2.6	2.3
Banff	-3.3	17.3	13.8	19.2	5.9	-2.0
Kincardine	14.3	10.5	13.6	4.2	0.0	18.7
Southeast						
Haddington	0.9	17.1	2.2	4.9	2.3	0.4
Berwick	25.9	10.5	3.2	6.3	-3.3	-12.9
Southwest						
Dumfries	37.3	29.8	2.8	4.2	0.3	-4.7
Kirkcudbright	37.8	33.2	5.7	3.3	-0.9	-6.5
Wigtown	39.2	45.0	17.9	7.4	-8.3	-15.3

Table 2.5 Mean ages at marriage, Scottish rural counties, 1860–62 to 1960–62

	1861 Males	1881 Males	1911 Males	1931 Males	1961 Males	1861 Females	1881 Females	1911 Females	1931 Females	1961 Females
Crofting Counties										
Sutherland	31.8	32.6	34.7	33.3	28.7	27.0	28.1	30.2	28.3	25.1
Ross	30.9	31.4	32.8	34.0	29.2	26.2	26.6	26.7	29.5	24.8
Inverness	31.3	31.8	33.3	32.2	30.1	26.5	26.9	28.6	28.0	25.7
Argyll	31.5	31.2	31.8	31.9	29.3	26.2	26.9	28.3	28.0	25.5
Highland Fringe										
Caithness	29.8	29.9	31.3	29.9	27.9	26.5	26.8	27.1	26.4	24.6
Nairn	31.4	29.9	32.0	30.9	27.2	28.6	26.2	27.6	27.3	23.9
Perth	29.2	29.5	30.5	30.6	28.0	26.2	26.6	27.7	26.2	24.7
Northeast										
Elgin	29.3	29.7	31.2	29.9	27.0	26.2	26.2	28.0	26.8	24.1
Banff	29.1	29.1	29.4	28.9	27.0	25.9	26.0	26.5	25.8	23.9
Kincardine	28.8	29.2	29.6	29.1	26.7	25.3	26.0	26.7	25.9	24.1
Southeast										
Haddington	28.6	28.2	28.1	28.0	26.7	26.3	25.8	26.0	25.7	24.1
Berwick	28.8	29.0	30.0	29.7	27.0	26.2	26.4	27.6	27.0	24.1
Southwest										
Dumfries	29.0	29.2	30.3	30.3	25.3	26.2	26.9	27.6	27.0	22.0
Kirkcudbright	29.3	29.3	30.4	30.0	27.3	26.1	26.4	27.6	28.1	24.0
Wigtown	29.1	28.6	29.8	26.8	27.1	25.9	26.1	27.0	25.5	23.9

Source: Censuses of Population. The figures for 1861–1931 are from tables prepared by Flinn et al. for *Scottish Population*. Due to boundary changes, the figures for 1911 are for 1910-1911 only.

Table 2. 6 Percentage of men and women never married at ages 45–54, Scottish rural counties, 1851–1961

	Males				Females			
	1851	1911	1931	1961	1851	1911	1931	1961
Crofting Counties								
Inverness	14.2	27.3	28.4	20.7	26.9	29.3	28.0	18.7
Argyll	17.1	29.3	15.7	12.2	19.2	30.4	28.3	18.1
Ross	14.1	23.9	24.8	22.5	23.6	28.1	26.2	22.0
Sutherland	15.4	28.4	31.5	20.0	29.0	28.3	27.7	17.8
Highland Fringe								
Perth	21.5	19.7	19.8	12.4	26.6	29.8	29.0	16.5
Nairn	19.9	21.6	19.4	12.5	29.4	28.2	25.9	15.4
Caithness	15.6	23.4	19.8	18.9	25.1	28.0	28.3	15.9
Northeast								
Kincardine	17.0	15.4	14.9	12.2	21.9	21.4	22.7	16.5
Banff	15.7	15.7	14.8	15.2	22.8	22.2	18.4	17.7
Elgin	17.1	17.8	16.6	14.4	26.0	25.9	25.3	15.4
Southeast								
Berwick	16.0	17.3	16.8	15.5	20.6	28.4	25.6	15.0
Haddington	16.5	16.7	14.5	12.1	19.3	21.1	19.9	13.6
Southwest								
Dumfries	17.2	19.5	16.9	13.4	25.1	27.5	26.0	15.7
Kirkcudbright	18.6	17.2	19.6	13.9	27.6	27.7	25.3	15.4
Wigtown	13.2	20.3	17.4	14.3	20.9	28.8	25.2	16.2

Table 2.7 I_m, Scottish rural counties, 1851–1961

	1851	1881	1911	1931	1961
Crofting Counties					
Sutherland	0.308	0.318	0.319	0.353	0.649
Ross	0.353	0.339	0.321	0.329	0.600
Inverness	0.330	0.340	0.327	0.370	0.608
Argyll	0.394	0.363	0.327	0.358	0.604
Highland Fringe					
Caithness	0.324	0.356	0.364	0.412	0.706
Nairn	0.332	0.390	0.325	0.368	0.655
Perth	0.374	0.371	0.357	0.395	0.634
Northeast					
Elgin	0.359	0.374	0.373	0.428	0.701
Banff	0.393	0.406	0.423	0.454	0.659
Kincardine	0.424	0.423	0.451	0.454	0.659
Southeast					
Haddington	0.391	0.414	0.438	0.453	0.671
Berwick	0.390	0.368	0.373	0.443	0.673
Southwest					
Dumfries	0.399	0.372	0.377	0.439	0.679
Kirkcudbright	0.364	0.382	0.363	0.432	0.680
Wigtown	0.382	0.373	0.380	0.434	0.659
Central Belt					
Angus	0.397	0.402	0.385	0.417	0.676
Fife	0.437	0.425	0.482	0.489	0.701
Clackmannan	0.486	0.421	0.382	0.448	0.722
Stirling	0.445	0.511	0.498	0.476	0.667
Dunbarton	0.427	0.439	0.457	0.440	0.674
Renfrew	0.426	0.452	0.424	0.433	0.666
Ayr	0.471	0.480	0.433	0.449	0.676
Lanark	0.454	0.505	0.471	0.461	0.644
Linlithgow	0.488	0.566	0.573	0.515	0.678

Source: 1881–1961: Coale and Watkins (1986); 1851: Census of Population.

Table 2.8 Median ages at marriage, 1860–62 and 1910–11, and sex ratios at ages 25–34, 1861 and 1911, Scottish rural counties

	Sex ratio at ages 25–34		Median ages at marriage			
	1861	1911	1860–62 Males	1910–11 Males	1860–62 Females	1910–11 Females
Crofting Counties						
Sutherland	723	998	30.0	32.2	26.1	28.7
Ross	746	1113	29.0	31.4	25.0	27.7
Inverness	760	892	29.3	31.5	25.4	27.3
Argyll	874	1063	29.5	30.1	25.3	27.2
Highland Fringe						
Caithness	759	790	27.6	28.5	25.4	25.0
Nairn	793	782	28.6	30.0	27.5	26.5
Perth	757	785	27.1	28.7	24.7	26.5
Northeast						
Elgin	778	816	27.3	28.9	24.7	26.2
Banff	735	853	26.8	27.6	24.2	25.0
Kincardine	829	749	27.0	27.4	23.8	24.8
Southeast						
Haddington	770	970	26.1	26.9	24.6	24.6
Berwick	768	846	26.5	28.3	24.4	26.2
Southwest						
Dumfries	782	857	26.6	28.4	24.6	26.1
Kirkcudbright	704	793	26.8	28.7	24.3	26.4
Wigtown	720	796	26.5	27.8	24.0	25.5

Table 2.9 Twenty-year marriage and migration/mortality outcomes for cohorts aged 15–19, Scottish rural counties, 1841 and 1861

	Pop change		Outcomes for males						Outcomes for females						% married at ages 35-39			
			Married		Unmarried		Disappeared		Married		Unmarried		Disappeared		Males		Females	
	41–<61	61–>81	41–<61	61–>81	41–<61	61–>81	41–<61	61–>81	41–<61	61–>81	41–<61	61–>81	41–<61	61–>81	1861	1881	1861	1881
Crofting Counties																		
Sutherland	1.9	-7.4	35.0	32.6	16.0	19.4	49.0	48.1	37.4	31.1	25.5	23.0	37.1	45.9	68.7	62.7	59.5	57.5
Inverness	-9.1	1.8	29.7	34.4	12.2	17.0	58.2	48.6	32.8	38.4	17.3	19.7	49.9	41.8	70.9	66.9	65.4	66.0
Argyll	-18.6	-3.5	27.3	32.8	12.3	18.3	60.3	48.9	37.7	39.4	14.2	18.5	48.0	42.2	68.9	64.1	72.7	68.0
Ross	3.5	-3.5	40.0	33.1	14.3	15.1	45.7	51.9	42.1	38.7	19.7	18.6	38.2	42.8	73.6	68.7	68.2	67.6
Highland Fringe																		
Caithness	13.1	-5.5	37.0	28.1	12.9	11.6	50.1	60.3	41.1	34.6	21.2	17.1	37.7	48.3	74.2	70.8	65.9	66.9
Nairn	9.2	3.9	33.0	33.9	16.8	10.6	50.2	55.6	41.8	41.4	20.8	17.6	37.4	40.9	66.3	76.1	66.8	70.1
Perth	-2.9	-3.4	32.2	27.2	11.4	8.1	56.4	64.7	41.7	32.1	15.4	14.8	42.9	53.1	73.9	76.9	73.1	68.4
Northeast																		
Elgin	21.9	2.6	45.6	36.0	13.0	9.7	41.4	54.3	52.2	40.1	22.1	17.1	25.8	42.8	77.8	78.8	70.2	70.0
Banff	19.2	5.9	43.8	37.2	13.5	10.8	42.7	52.1	46.8	40.9	18.8	17.4	34.4	41.8	76.3	77.6	71.4	70.2
Kincardine	4.2	0.0	41.3	36.5	12.0	10.8	46.7	52.7	45.4	43.2	16.6	15.8	38.0	41.0	77.4	77.1	73.2	73.1
Southeast																		
Haddington	4.9	2.3	39.7	41.4	9.3	10.3	51.0	48.2	45.6	51.0	17.0	15.2	37.4	33.9	81.0	80.0	72.8	77.0
Berwick	6.3	-3.3	38.1	34.6	10.7	11.4	51.2	54.0	43.1	38.1	17.2	17.3	39.7	44.6	78.0	75.2	71.6	68.8
Southwest																		
Dumfries	4.2	0.3	39.2	36.4	12.5	13.1	48.3	50.5	40.9	42.1	19.1	19.9	40.0	38.1	75.7	73.5	68.1	68.0
Kirkcudb't	3.3	-0.9	40.9	34.8	11.7	10.9	47.3	54.3	36.2	40.2	17.8	18.0	46.0	41.8	77.8	76.1	67.1	69.1
Wigtown	7.4	-8.3	40.6	29.5	13.1	9.4	46.4	61.1	40.8	32.4	18.7	14.9	40.6	52.8	75.7	75.8	68.5	68.5

Note: For more discussion, see Anderson (1999) from which this table is derived.

Bibliography

Anderson, M. (1996) 'Migration and nuptiality as interacting regulators of Scottish population growth, 1855–1914', in A. Bideau (ed.), *Les systèmes démographiques du passé*, Lyon, pp. 141–160.

Anderson, M. (1999) 'Population growth and population regulation in nineteenth century rural Scotland', in T. Bengtsson and O. Saito (eds), *Population and economy: from hunger to modern economic growth*, Oxford.

Anderson, M. and Morse, D.J. (1993) 'High fertility, high emigration, low nuptiality: Scotland's demographic experience, 1861–1911', *Population Studies*, 47, pp. 319–343.

Blaikie, A. (1993) *Illegitimacy, sex and society: Northeast Scotland, 1750–1900*, Oxford.

Campbell, R.H. (1984) 'Agricultural labour in the south-west', in T.M. Devine (ed.), *Farm servants and labour in lowland Scotland, 1770–1914*, Edinburgh, pp. 55–70.

Carter, I. (1984) *Farm life in Northeast Scotland 1840–1914*, Edinburgh.

Coale, A.J. and Watkins, S.C. (eds) (1986) *The decline of fertility in Europe*, Princeton.

Devine, T.M. (1988) 'Urbanisation', in T.M. Devine and R.M. Mitchison (eds), *People and society in Scotland,1760–1830*, Edinburgh, pp. 27–52.

Devine, T.M. (1994) *Clanship to crofters' war*, Manchester.

Flinn, M.W. et al. (1977) *Scottish population history from the seventeenth century to the 1930s*, Cambridge.

Goldstone, J.A. (1986) 'The demographic revolution in England: a re-examination', *Population Studies*, 50, pp. 5–33.

Gray, M. (1957) *The Highland economy, 1750–1850*, Edinburgh.

Gray, M. (1973) 'Scottish emigration: the social impact of agrarian change in the rural lowlands, 1775–1875', *Perspectives on American History*, 7, pp. 95–174.

Gray, M. (1984) 'Farm workers in north-east Scotland', in T.M. Devine (ed.), *Farm servants and labour in lowland Scotland, 1770–1914*, Edinburgh, pp. 10–28.

Guinnane, T. (1990) 'Coming of age in rural Ireland at the turn of the century', *Continuity and Change*, 5, pp. 443–72.

Houston, R.A. (1989) 'The demographic regime, 1760–1830', in T.M. Devine and R.M. Mitchison (eds), *People and society in Scotland, 1760–1830*, Edinburgh, pp. 9–26.

Houston, R.A. (1989) 'Age of marriage of Scottish women *c.*1660–1770', *Local Population Studies*, 43, pp. 65–66.

Houston, R.A. (1992) *The population history of Britain and Ireland, 1500–1750*, London.

Malthus, T.R. (1986) *An essay on the principle of population*, repr. London.

Orr, A. (1984) 'Farm servants and farm labour in the Forth Valley and south-east lowlands' in T. M. Devine (ed.), *Farm servants and labour in lowland Scotland, 1770–1914*, Edinburgh, pp. 29–54.

Schofield, R.S. (1985) 'English marriage patterns revisited', *Journal of Family History*, 10, pp. 2–20.

Sinclair, Sir John (ed.) (1975–83) *The Statistical Account of Scotland, 1791–1799*, Wakefield.

Smout, T.C. (1973) *A history of the Scottish people 1560–1830*, Glasgow.

Smout, T.C. (1986) *A century of the Scottish people 1830–1950*, Glasgow.

Sydney, M. (1997) '"The spinster problem"?: a study investigating the relationship between migration, the sex ratio and nuptiality in late nineteenth century Scotland', MA dissertation, Department of Economic and Social History, University of Edinburgh.

Wrigley, E.A. and Schofield, R.S. (1981) *The population history of England, 1541–1871*, London.

3 Marriage and economic conditions at the West European periphery: Ireland, 1600–2000

Liam KENNEDY, The Queen's University of Belfast

I. Introduction

Ireland is frequently seen as an outlier among European countries, not only in geographic terms (which is undeniable) but in economic and demographic terms as well. During the first half of this century, Ireland had some claim to being the demographic freak of the Western world. It usually topped international league tables in relation to late age at marriage and permanent celibacy (or non-marriage). Despite the retreat from marriage, fertility remained stubbornly high down to the 1960s. Conversely, fertility outside marriage was low by international standards. Alone among European countries, Ireland had suffered persistent population decline between the mid-19th and the mid-20th centuries. In many decades it had the highest rate of emigration of any country in Europe. Some of the more melodramatic commentators warned of impending race suicide (O'Brien, 1953).

In the century before 1850 a very different, if no less distinctive, demographic regime was in operation. Marriage was apparently early and frequent, and Ireland enjoyed the highest rate of population growth of any European society between the 1740s and the 1840s, with the possible exception of Finland. As this whole period was marked by a net outflow of people from Ireland, this means natural increase actually exceeded the expansion of population. At the end of the 20th century Ireland, North and South, seems to have lost much of its distinctive demographic identity, appearing to merge unobtrusively with the experience of other societies within northern and western Europe.

Clearly there is a complex story to be told here, and it becomes more elusive the farther back in time one ventures. The purpose of this chapter is to provide an overview of the current state of knowledge of Irish demographic behaviour, with particular emphasis on marriage, during the last four centuries. The first part of the paper discusses population estimates and population growth rates. The second part addresses, wherever possible, the typical age at marriage and the frequency of marriage through time. The final interpretative section meditates on some possible explanations for the dramatic shifts in behaviour over time.

II. Population through time

Most historians believe Ireland was thinly populated in the early 16th century, in view of the strong pastoral orientation of the economy, the existence of much unreclaimed bog and wasteland, and the low level of urbanization. The century witnessed much debilitating warfare, due to what some see as the unloosing of anarchic forces within Irish society and the viciousness of the Elizabethan conquest (Canny, 1977). There is dispute as to the course of Irish population change in the period, though there seems little doubt that the growth rate over the century as a whole was low if not actually close to zero. Some writers conjecture that in 1500 or thereabouts the population of the island may have been little over three-quarters of a million. In 1600 it may have been one million (see Figure 3.1a) (Canny, 1977: 64; Lenihan, 1997; for a higher estimate, see Cullen, 1975). In the years of peace between 1603 and the rising and massacres of 1641, the population seems to have surged forward at a remarkably rapid pace, suggesting the potential for growth within Irish society, even after discounting the role of immigrants in swelling the population numbers.

Figure 3.1a Population of Ireland, 1600-1991

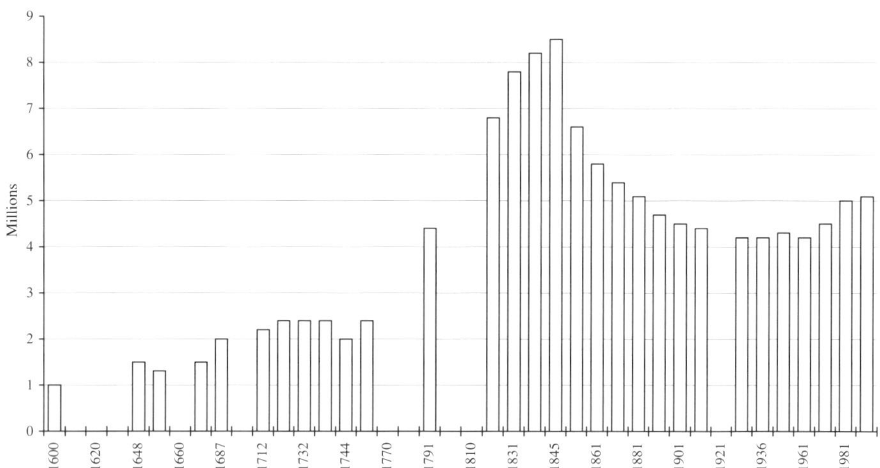

Recent evidence on the impact of war, subsistence crisis and plague on Irish population accompanying the Cromwellian conquest indicates a more severe check to population than had previously been suspected. According to Lenihan, this was of catastrophic proportions, with 15–20 per cent of the population being carried off by one or other of the riders of the Apocalypse during the crisis years of 1648–52 (Lenihan, 1997: 21). Population bounced back during the later 17th century, though it should be noted that the accelerated expansion during the 1670s and 1680s was due in part to settlers and newcomers from England and Scotland. Indeed, contrary to its reputation over the next three centuries as the land of emigrants and exiles, 17th-century Ireland experienced net immigration.

If the figures are to be believed, and it must the emphasized that all population estimates for Ireland before the first official census of population in 1821 are based on flimsy evidence, then high mortality during the second quarter of the 18th century, including the devastating famine of 1740–41, depressed population growth. There followed a sustained growth of population between the 1740s and the end of the Napoleonic Wars, mirroring a long wave of expansion in the Irish economy over the same period. Population levels continued to cascade upwards between 1815 and 1845, though the more significant fact is the deceleration of population growth as families and communities sought to adjust to narrowing economic opportunities.

Few historians today would see the Great Famine of the 1840s as a Malthusian crisis in the pure sense of a mortal confrontation between population and resources. There is even debate as to whether Ireland was overpopulated, in any meaningful sense, in the decades preceding the catastrophe. The question is sometimes posed in terms of, 'Was Malthus right?' (Mokyr, 1985: 38–60; O Grada, 1989, 1994; McGregor, 1989) My own view, based on statistical testing of the relationship between income per head and the population-resource base for a selection of parishes in four different regions of Ireland, is a diplomatic 'yes' and 'no'. In east Ulster and south Leinster there was little evidence of a connection between incomes and population density *circa* 1840, whereas in the poorer south and west of the island a negative relationship was apparent (Kennedy, 1994a). There is thus comfort both for advocates and critics of the Malthusian emphasis on an inverse relationship between population growth and living standards in rural economies.

Unlike the two previous catastrophes of 1648–52 and 1740–41, and famine experiences elsewhere, the population of Ireland did not bounce back after the Great Famine. Rather it went into long-run decline, due primarily to mass emigration, although changing marriage patterns also had a role to play, as we shall see shortly. The course of population is traced in Figure 3.1a, and changes in population growth rates are presented in Figure 3.1b and, using the same data, in a slightly different way in Figure 3.1c.

Figure 3.1b Population growth rates, 1600-1991

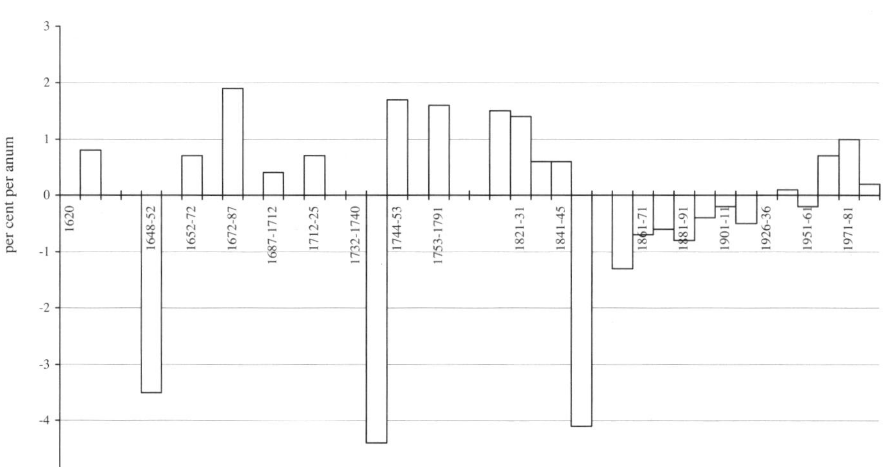

Figure 3.1c Population growth rates, 1600-1991

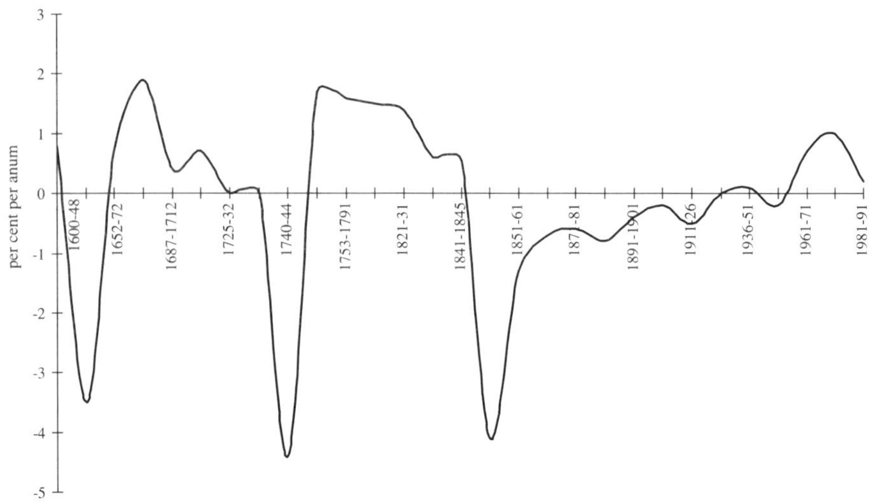

Much could be said about these patterns, including the tentative nature of the population estimates before 1821, but perhaps the overriding impression is the great diversity of growth rate experiences during the last four centuries. Particularly striking is the trinity of mortality crises, made up of cataclysms in the mid-17th, the mid-18th and the mid-19th centuries. It is curious, and mere chance, that these were evenly spaced in time. Viewed in comparative perspective, the remarkable thing is how rapid Irish population growth was in the century before the Famine, averaging 1.3 per cent per annum. In some decades the rate of increase of population exceeded 1.5 per cent per annum (Mokyr and O Grada, 1984). The long-run growth rate of 1.3 per cent may be compared with England's growth rate of 1 per cent and Scotland's of 0.8 per cent. The implication of course is that the size of Ireland's population increased relative to that of England and Scotland, with the gains concentrated in the second half of the 18th century. Still, if the figures underpinning Figure 3.2 can be believed, then an even more dramatic narrowing of population shares as between England and Ireland seems to have taken place in the preceding century, between 1650 and 1700. Then, in the century after the crisis of the 1840s, Ireland's position relative to England suffered a precipitous decline, as Ireland dropped from the top to the bottom of the population growth league for European countries. This relative decline continued into the present century.

Figure 3.2 Relative population size, Ireland and England, 1601-1911

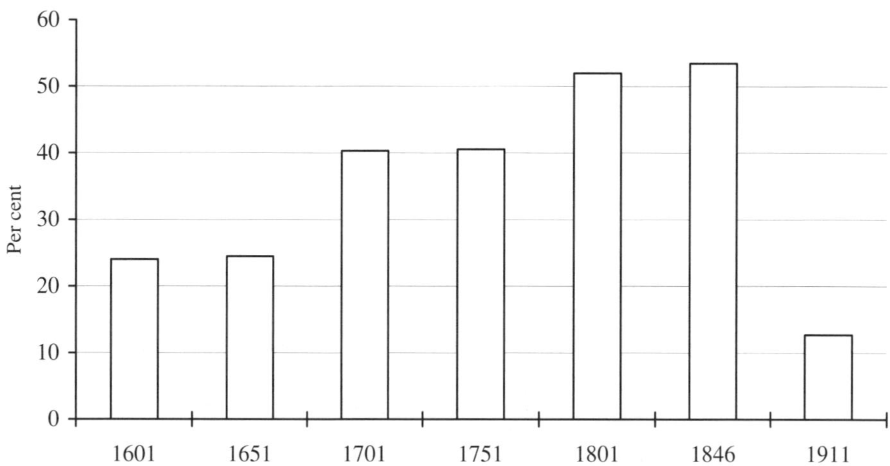

III. Marriage

We are accustomed to thinking of Ireland as conforming, broadly speaking, to a West European pattern of family formation, in which economic independence was a prerequisite to taking a mate and setting up home. The usual concomitants were a late (or later) age at marriage, as compared to societies outside Western Europe, and a variable proportion of the adult population never marrying. Some 17th-century commentators wondered, however, if the peoples of Ireland really came within the European orbit, in demographic as well as other matters. William Petty, an able colonial administrator with a passion for numbers, considered that Irish women married 'upon their first capacity' (Hull, 1889, vol. II: 608). Outsiders also affected to be shocked by the supposedly loose morals of the native Irish women, a perception which is at variance with the low incidence of illegitimate births recorded in later centuries (Connolly, 1975; on the dangers of English prejudice colouring observations of the demographic practices of other nations, see Houston, 1992).

The admittedly scanty evidence we have does not support this picture of early and near-universal marriage in 17th-century Irish society. David Dickson, using Cromwellian transportation certificates which described the family and household characteristics of a sample of households in the early 1650s, was struck by the numbers of servants and maids in their twenties who were unmarried (Dickson, 1991). The source allows a rough calculation of mean age at marriage for women and men. For Dublin county, this turns out to be 24 years of age for women (median age of 34 years), and for the socially more heterogeneous Munster sample the figures were a little lower. Mean age at marriage for Munster women was 23 years (median age of

22 years). These compare with an age at marriage for English women of 25.6 years, on average, in the 1650s (Wrigley et al., 1997: 134). There is little point in making much of the regional difference within Ireland, in view of the limited sample sizes. The significant point surely is that both samples point in the direction of women in Ireland delaying marriage until well after the onset of menarche. Men married some five years later, at 28 or 29 years of age, which is actually later than in the case of Englishmen, where mean age at marriage was 27 years and six months (Wrigley et al., 1997: 134). Demographic evidence on the better-documented Irish Quakers reinforces the impression that early marriage was not common (Eversley, 1981). Quaker women married, on average, in their twenty-fourth year, and Quaker men in their twenty-ninth. The age gap between spouses for Quakers and non-Quakers alike, it may be noted, was wide, being significantly greater than in the case of England at mid-17th century. What is suggested by these pieces of evidence is that Ireland was within the western European demographic system by the mid-17th century. Irish women may have been located towards the early-marrying end of the spectrum, but their menfolk were considerably more conservative in their approach to marriage.

Moving rapidly forward in time, we have solid data on age at marriage and the frequency of marriage from the Census of Ireland for 1841. The remarkable point perhaps is how unremarkable Ireland was in terms of age at marriage and proportions never marrying. What we find is a mean age at marriage of 26.3 years for women and 28.1 for men, with only a small degree of regional variation (Mokyr, 1985: 34). There is no support here for some of the more fantastic stories of Irish men and women marrying recklessly and at the first opportunity, even in the far west of the country. Malthus should have been proud of the restraint shown by the denizens of his neighbouring island. The proportion aged 45–54 years who were still single was 12.5 per cent for women and 10 per cent in the case of men, which indicates a degree of permanent celibacy similar to that for England at mid-century. Thus it seems that Ireland was undistinguished in relation to other West European societies in terms of its propensity to marry in the 1840s.

The big problem, however, is filling in the spaces for the 18th century. Parish-register demography is still in its infancy, and there are intrinsic difficulties in terms of the coverage and quality of the surviving registers. McAfee's study of a linen-producing and agricultural district in rural Ulster, the parish of Killyman, suggests a bridal age at marriage of 23 years for the 1770s, of 21 for the 1790s, rising to 24 years in the early 1840s (McAfee, 1987: 154). This pattern of falling age at marriage in the later 18th century but rising during the economically troubled decades after Waterloo would certainly fit with what we know of economy and population growth, but it is of course just one study and one may wonder about its representative character. A similar question mark hangs over the findings of Vann and Eversley who found that Irish Quakers married earlier than English Quakers, the average age at marriage for Irish Quaker women in the late 18th and early 19th centuries being 24–25 years (Vann and Eversley, 1992). O' Neill's study of Killashandra in County Cavan, in south Ulster, indicates a fall in marriage age in the late 18th century and a rise in the decades before the mid-century crisis (O'Neill, 1984: 177–86). The marriage data in the 1841 Census of Ireland, as re-worked by O Grada, are consistent with a gentle rise in marriage ages in the 1820s and 1830s, as is his evidence on Dublin working-class women attending the Rotunda Hospital in Dublin during the period 1810–45 (O Grada, 1994: 72–3).

So, what do we make of all this? We really do not know the course of change in marriage age or proportions single during the 18th century. It is possible that age at marriage was fairly high before the 1770s and that it fell subsequently, as K.H. Connell supposed in his pioneering *Population History of Ireland*. The tiny number of studies cited above points in this direction. Why and when age at marriage might have risen is not at all clear, however. Alternatively, and perhaps a little less plausibly, it may be that Dickson's estimates for the mid-17th century can be exported forward in time, with small change of detail, into the first half of the 18th century. In other words, women in Ireland enjoyed (if that is the right verb) a relatively early age at marriage, of 22–23 years on average, over a very long period of time, extending from the 1650s to the 1760s or 1770s. If this scenario approximates the truth, then the demographic regime of the first half of the 18th century must have been a high-pressure one, characterized by high fertility and high mortality. A lower plane of mortality after the 1740s would then have cleared the way for sustained population increase, in view of the comparatively early age at marriage and the absence of birth control. Whichever scenario is preferred, it seems clear that as the living standards of the rural poor came under pressure from 1815 onwards,[1] marriage was increasingly delayed, thus bringing Ireland more fully into the western European mainstream.

What happened to permanent celibacy is anyone's guess. Non-marriage or permanent celibacy was certainly low on the eve of the Great Famine in 1841, and may have been lower still a decade or two earlier (Kennedy, 1996). Arthur Young, writing in the 1770s, implies that the rate of marriage was high, the age of marriage low and family size large; in other words, the quintessential picture of early 19th-century Irish family life (Young, 1892). Independently of Young's remarks, there are some indirect reasons for suspecting that marriage was widespread in Irish society during the 18th century. Cullen believes that servants and labourers were less likely to live in with their employers during the 18th as compared to the 17th century.[2] The spread of potato cultivation would have facilitated the formation of labouring and cotter households. The rise of handicraft industry, in particular the linen and woollen industries, is also consistent with enhanced opportunities for marriage, even on the part of the rural poor from the 1740s or 1750s. We cannot offer any quantitative estimates of celibacy levels between the 1770s and the Great Famine, but in view of the diffusion of the potato crop, the spread of proto-industry, and the strengthening of a more labour-intensive agricultural sector, evidenced by a switch from pasture to tillage, it

[1] Real wage data for skilled and unskilled urban workers do not show a deterioration in living standards between 1815 and 1845, which is puzzling. There is little doubt, however, that the mass of cottiers and labourers in rural Ireland lived a precarious existence, close to the margin of subsistence, and that this class was expanding in absolute and relative terms during the period 1800-45. See Kennedy (1997).

[2] L.M. Cullen, Trinity College, Dublin, private communication.

seems unlikely that celibacy levels exceeded those which existed at the end of this period in 1841. If this indirect reasoning is correct, then celibacy levels were typically less than 12 per cent between the 1770s and the 1840s. It seems unwise to hazard even a guess for the first half of the century. The economic circumstances for marriage would seem to have been less propitious, though whether this might have reflected itself in a higher age at marriage or a lower rate of marriage, or a combination of the two, is simply unknowable at this remove in time.[3]

It is with a sense of relief, perhaps, that one turns from the uncertainties of the 18th century to the firmer statistical evidence of the second half of the 19th. Surprisingly perhaps, the Great Famine does not appear to have had a noticeable impact on either age at marriage or the extent of non-marriage. The regional diversity in celibacy in 1841, with the southeastern counties foreshadowing the retreat from marriage which was so pronounced a feature of Irish society in the late 19th century, suggests that a trend towards permanent celibacy had set in well before the catastrophe. While the poor western counties of Ireland held out longest against the national trend towards permanent celibacy, it is striking how widespread the rejection of marriage had become by the eve of the First World War. By 1911, some 25 per cent of older women would never marry and the proportion of permanently celibate men was higher still at 28 per cent. Or to take an extreme case, some 30 per cent of Monaghan women – Monaghan is a county of small farms and poor soil in south Ulster – were unlikely to ever marry. The situation of depressed nuptiality was in fact very similar to that found in some of the rural counties of Scotland. Anderson observes celibacy levels in the region of 25 per cent for both men and women in the 'Crofting Counties' and the Highlands of Scotland in 1911 (see Chapter 2).

Figure 3.3 Non-marriage of women, Ireland, 1841-1911

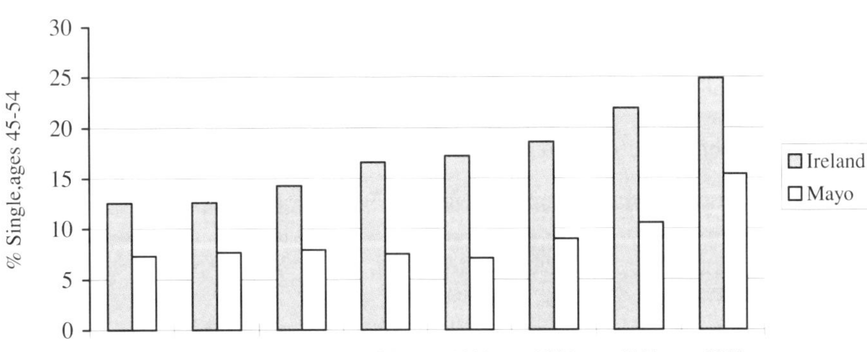

[3] For what it is worth (in terms of reflecting the wider society), when one compares Quaker women marrying in the two periods 1650-99 and 1700-1749, it transpires that the mean age at marriage changed only a little, from 22.7 to 23.2 years, a difference of half a year (Eversley, 1981: 64–65).

For rural Ireland, the position changed little before the 1950s. This was the decade in which the Commission on Emigration and Other Population Problems reported, reflecting the worries of the Irish government and official circles on what was deemed to be the anomalous state of Irish population, at least in the twenty-six counties of the Irish Republic. Certainly there were grounds for concern. Irish population had been in decline for a century or more and, second only to emigration, Irish marriage patterns were considered to be a subject of grave concern. Viewed comparatively, the Irish Republic (though less so Northern Ireland), by virtue of its late age at marriage and its high incidence of permanent celibacy, was at the upper-extreme of the western European marriage system.

Figure 3.4 Non-marriage of women, Ireland and England/Wales, 1851-1966

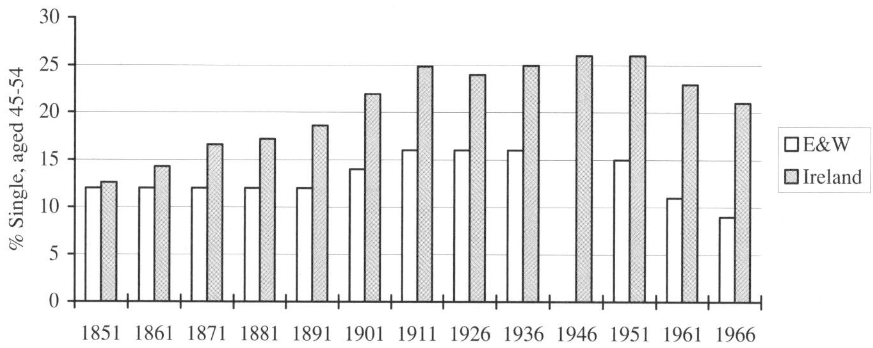

The comparison with England and Wales highlights the surge in celibacy in Ireland in the late 19th century and the remarkably high levels which were maintained into the second half of this century.[4] England is not necessarily the best reference point, but a comparison with other countries in Europe in the 1930s or the 1950s would see Ireland perched firmly at the top of the international celibacy tables. Thus, the proportions single among women aged 45 years or over in a number of countries in the 1960s included: France (10 per cent), Belgium (10 per cent), Netherlands (11 per cent), and Spain (14 per cent) (Kennedy, 173: 42). One has to move into colder climates to find an avoidance of marriage that approaches the Irish case. In Scotland, the proportion single was an impressive 18 per cent; the story was the same in Norway; while Iceland demonstrated the perils of love in a cold climate, being dangerously close to Ireland with permanent celibacy at the 20 per cent level (Kennedy, 173: 42).

Ireland was less extreme in terms of age at marriage, though it topped the late marrying league for European women in the mid-20th century, edging in just ahead of Switzerland (*Commission on Emigration*, 1954: 69). Thus while age at first marriage in the Irish Republic in 1946 was 28 years, it was 26 in Scotland and France,

[4] The figure for Mayo in 1871 is based on interpolation, being the mean of the values for 1861 and 1881.

27 in the Netherlands and England and Wales, and under 25 in Hungary. The contrast was stronger for men. As the Commission on Emigration remarked (1954: 69): 'while women in this country [Republic of Ireland] marry later than elsewhere, men marry markedly later. This relatively late age at which Irish people marry is a further unsatisfactory feature of our marriage pattern'. The most 'unsatisfactory' element in the eyes of the Commissioners, and indeed in the eyes of many writers this century, was of course the extent to which Irish people did not marry at all.

A picture of the evolution of the female age at marriage in the long run is portrayed in the panel below. It should be emphasized again that any estimates before 1841 are sited on a pinhead of evidence. Contrary to what is sometimes thought, marriage age in Ireland was quite stable in the decades immediately after the Great Famine. It was only towards the end of the century that marriage ages reached close to 29 years, on average, and they remained at this level into the 1930s. From the 1940s onwards, marriage age declined until the late 1980s when women in the Irish Republic typically married in their twenty-fifth year, exactly the same as the average for women in the European Union (twelve countries). Irish women, and the men also, had come in from the cold. Not only on this indicator, but on most other demographic indicators, Ireland was converging rapidly on western European norms (Kennedy, 1994; Drew, 1998). Ireland, North or South, was no longer an outlier, and with this loss of a distinctive demographic identity goes some of the interest in the Irish population story. Cultural change induced and accelerated by the mass media, music and entertainment industries, increased urbanization, and new forms of family and social life – less authoritarian and restrictive – were among the forces responsible for this transformation of marriage patterns in modern times. More fundamental, one suspects, were the economic changes: the shift of the Irish economy onto a higher growth path after 1960, culminating during the 1990s in the phenomenon of the Celtic Tiger; the associated harvest of jobs and incomes, for women as well as for men; sectoral changes in the distribution of labour, in particular the decline of the traditional rural economy; and the ease of exit and re-entry to the Irish economy through the medium of migration.

Figure 3.5 Mean age at marriage, Irish women

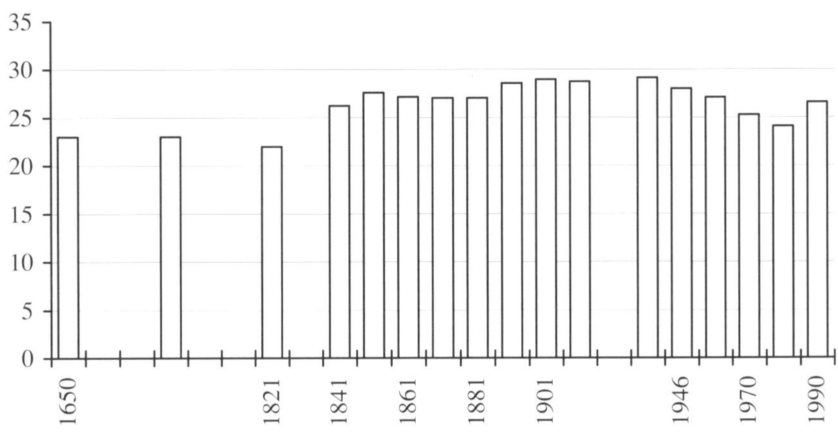

IV. Understanding change

One of the key questions is how the Irish shifted from being a people with a high propensity to marry in the century before 1845 to a people with a very low propensity to marry in the century after the Famine. In the earlier discussion, I identified some of the conditions which were favourable to marriage – a wave of economic expansion during the long eighteenth century, stretching from the 1740s to 1815, and affecting agriculture, particularly the tillage economy, and also proto-industry – serving to increase the demand for labour. The miracle tuber, the potato, played its own mysterious role, perhaps by improving nutrition, lowering mortality and reducing the duration of breastfeeding. The remarkable growth of population in Finland, comparable to that for Ireland, was in part attributable to the diffusion of the potato crop, according to Moring (1998: 183, 194–96). The likelihood, she believes, is that the addition of potatoes to an existing cereal-based diet had the effect of raising the general level of nutrition, and hence resistance to disease in southwest Finland. Also of potential relevance in the Irish case, she argues potato food was especially suited to small children, and would have helped reduce infant mortality. 'As potatoes became soft when cooked there was no necessity for anybody to chew them for the baby, and there was therefore less risk of the baby being infected through consuming contaminated food' (Moring, 1998: 194). More generally, one might argue that the land-economizing potato lowered the cost of household formation and child rearing (Connell, 1950: 159–62). Under Irish conditions, a family could grow enough potatoes to sustain itself for eight or nine months of the year on three-quarters of an acre of land. In addition, the possibilities of reclaiming wasteland, with the aid of the potato, meant frontier-like conditions in some of the remoter parts of the island where population growth was, paradoxically, most vigorous in the decades before the Famine. Real wages, if anything, declined in the second half of the 18th century. The conventional Malthusian argument would, however, regard this as unfavourable to marriage and population increase.

It is of course a simplification to speak of marriage, nationally or regionally, without reference to social class. Though the evidence is patchy, it seems likely that different marriage regimes operated among different agrarian classes before the Famine. It is clear that payment of dowries, and other forms of calculating behaviour, were practised by the tenant farmers, and indeed the gentry. O'Neill provides evidence on marriage ages for a single parish, that of Killashandra in County Cavan in 1841 O'Neill, 1984: 178). Large farmers married more than two years later in life than farmers generally, and four years later than male labourers, the mean age at marriage for labouring males being 24 years and six months.[5] More indirect evidence by David Miller, but relating to all of the country, suggests a similar finding: a later age at marriage for the farming community (Miller, 1994). What we seem to have, therefore, is two marriage regimes, stratified by social class, in Ireland before the Famine.

[5] Curiously though, the age at marriage for farmers' wives was little different from that of female labourers, each marrying, on average, in their twenty first or twenty second year (O'Neill, 1984: 178–9).

The low propensity to marry in the century after the Great Famine has perplexed not only contemporaries but historians as well. Tim Guinnane's authoritative work, *The Vanishing Irish*, offers a fundamental re-appraisal of the historiography. He reviews three sets of explanations for the low propensity to marry: the Malthusian interpretation, and variations on it; institutional barriers to marriage such as the necessity of acquiring a dowry in the case of women, or land in the case of men; and finally religious and cultural explanations (Guinnane, 1997). Each in turn is found wanting, though to varying degrees. This clears the way for Guinnane's own perspective on marriage, which emphasizes the changing costs and benefits of marriage and the increasing availability of substitutes for marriage in post-Famine Irish society.

Guinnane is particularly concerned to understand the rise of permanent celibacy or non-marriage in post-Famine society. This followed distinctive spatial and temporal patterns during the period 1850–1914, with celibacy spreading gradually from east to west and increasing in all counties during the period. Guinnane invokes three historical forces to explain the retreat from marriage: the introduction of a poor law in 1838, the land reforms of the later 19th century, and the agricultural depression of the 1870s and 1880s. The problem is that the poor law was pretty well a constant in time and space and the social impact of the Land Acts is not really known. This leaves the agricultural depression of the 1870s and 1880s, which may be unambiguously connected with a decline in marriage. However, marriage had been declining in some regions of Ireland, most notably the southeast, from as early as the 1830s. The fit between the explanatory model and the empirical evidence on the geography and sequencing of change seems less than comfortable.

Of older vintage, and for long the standard interpretation, is that due to Robert Kennedy (Kennedy, 1973). This is a modified Malthusian argument, which accepts that standards of living were rising in post-Famine society. But, Kennedy argues, material expectations may have been rising still faster. A rise in the *desired* minimum standard of living meant that marriage was postponed or deferred indefinitely. Increasing contact with North America, in particular through the medium of emigration, meant that a greater consciousness of the gap in living standards between Ireland and abroad was fostered during the age of mass emigration between 1850 and 1900.

Still, many questions remain. As Guinnane emphasizes, a large minority of well-off farmers in the east of Ireland, and elsewhere, never married (Guinnane, 1997: 204–08). Consideration of living standards can hardly have been the binding constraint. There is also the problem, as the work of Jeffrey Williamson and Kevin O'Rourke has shown, that the wage gap between Ireland and Britain, and Ireland and the United States, had narrowed appreciably by the end of the 19th century (Williamson, 1994). Yet celibacy continued to increase.

My own view, tempered by the knowledge that the propositions have not been sufficiently tested, is a Malthusian-style perspective on the course of change. There is little doubt that expectations of material comfort were rising during the 19th century, initially (one assumes) in the emigration-prone regions of the east and the north-east where celibacy was most noticeable before 1845, and eventually extending to all parts of the island. Moreover, employment niches in the Irish rural economy were disappearing from the Famine onwards, with the decline of opportunities for farm labour, the disintegration of handicraft industries, and the contraction of certain forms of service occupations. Such change would have reduced the aggregate of marriages over time, without necessarily increasing the proportions unmarried in the population. In practice, however, declining occupations were likely to have been associated with a rising incidence of non-marriage.[6] As the occupational structure varied by region – rural labourers being more heavily represented in Leinster and parts of Munster, for example – the effect on celibacy tends to show up unevenly also. In addition, the poverty of many households, particularly in the west of Ireland, did not favour the retention of surplus unmarried sons and daughters within the ancestral homestead. Emigration drained the economically marginal, leaving fewer unmarried adults in the west as compared to the east. What of those left behind? Despite low standards of living, men and women were still prepared to occupy the niches afforded by their smallholdings and embark on marriage on a widespread scale. Notions of rising material expectations of life, it would seem, were slower to penetrate the distinctive cultural zones of the western seaboard, where Gaelic-speaking, clachan settlements, seasonal migration and a relatively egalitarian landholding system prevailed. Indeed the different marriage patterns of the West between the Great Famine and the Great War are a useful antidote to an overly mechanical reliance on notions of rising economic expectations as a barrier to marriage.

The position in the midlands and the east of the country was very different. On the larger farms of the east, the labour contribution of an unmarried son or daughter had some value, and the resources to maintain an assisting relative were more plentiful. Permanent celibacy, consequently, was more pronounced. Another way of putting this is to say the pressure on non-inheriting children to migrate was somewhat less. The larger puzzle is with those who did inherit property, and who still did not marry. In some cases, delayed inheritance must have mattered. However, why a large minority of household heads – some of them quite comfortably off – never married, is not easy to understand, and Guinnane's notion of the possibility of more attractive alternatives to marriage ('marriage substitutes') has much to commend it (Guinnane, 1997: 230–33).

By the mid-20th century, in a reversal of earlier regional patterns, the incidence of permanent celibacy was more firmly rooted in the west of Ireland as compared to the eastern seaboard counties. This is consistent with conventional standard of living concerns, as the west failed to diversify its primarily agricultural base or bridge the gap in farm incomes between east and west (Brody, 1973). Small farms were inherited and manned, but were less than sufficient to maintain, at conventional standards of comfort, a prospective wife and children. Gender is important here. Women may

[6] In 1946, admittedly a later moment in time, 50 per cent of rural labourers aged 45-54 years were unmarried, whereas middling sized farmers (30 to 50 acres) had a much lower celibacy level, the corresponding figure being 25 per cent, or exactly half that for farmers. *Commission on Emigration* (1954: 84).

have been more reluctant than inheriting males to embrace marriage and a lifetime of drudgery on the western smallholdings.

Marriage rates in the Republic of Ireland and Northern Ireland remained low by international standards in the 1950s, an economically depressed decade which witnessed a huge exodus of people from rural Ireland. However, under conditions of more buoyant economic growth and expanding employment in the 1960s and the early 1970s, the Irish Republic enjoyed a marriage boom. The proportions marrying increased dramatically, and marriage ages fell. Mean age at marriage for women had been 29 years in 1926, 28 in 1946, and was still as high as 27 years in 1960. But, by 1970 it had fallen to 25 and then 24 a decade later (Kennedy, 1994b: 27–32). These radically new marriage patterns were not, however, to be sustained. In the final quarter of the century the Irish Republic joined, with a time lag, the wider West European trend towards falling marriage rates and rising age at marriage. By then, of course, the meaning of marriage was undergoing profound change, and comparisons with the propensity to marry in earlier time periods make only limited sense. Throughout the twentieth century marriage rates had been higher in Northern Ireland than in the Irish Republic, reflecting the more urban, industrial character of the North. Marriage ages also tended to be lower.[7] After 1970 the rate of marriage fell, and, again in line with European trends, the mean age at marriage moved upwards. As Ireland, North and South, moved close to the modal European demographic experience, the assumption must be that the forces determining marriage patterns in western Europe were also shaping marriage behaviour on the island of Ireland.

Set against the backdrop of a changing society, marriage patterns in rural Ireland were also, and inevitably, undergoing change. By the final quarter of the 20th century these were no longer determined by conditions on the land, inheritance practices among farm households, or even the prosperity of the agricultural community. Farming occupations accounted for a minority of livelihoods among those living in rural areas. Other social groups – professionals, industrial workers, service workers – now predominated. In the 1950s and the 1960s social commentators were lamenting the exodus of young people from the countryside, some predicting the imminent death of rural Ireland (examples include Healy, 1968; Scheper-Hughes, 1979). Such prophecies of doom were, to say the least, premature, failing as they did to notice the quickening pace of economic development, even in rural areas. Processes of industrialization and service sector growth, economic decentralization, suburbanization, and commuting were gradually changing the material conditions of life in the Irish countryside. By the close of the 20th century, rural Irish society was more vibrant demographically than at any time since the Great Famine.

---

[7] The mean age at marriage for women in Northern Ireland in 1950 was 26.5 years, 25.3 in 1960, 23.6 in 1970, the remarkably low figure of 22.4 in 1980, and then a rise to 24.3 years in 1990. The corresponding figures for men were 30, 28, 23.6, 24.4 and 26.2 years. Kennedy (1994b: 32).

Bibliography

Brody, H. (1973) *Inishkillane: Change and Decline in the West of Ireland*, London.

Canny, N. (1977) 'Early modern Ireland: an appraisal appraised', *Irish Economic and Social History*, 4, pp. 56–65.

Commission on Emigration and Other Population Problems, 1948-1954 (1954), Dublin.

Connell, K.H. (1950) *The population of Ireland, 1750–1845*, Oxford.

Connolly, S. (1979) 'Illegitimacy and pre-nuptial pregnancy in Ireland before 1864: the evidence of some Catholic parish registers', *Irish Economic and Social History*, 6, pp. 5–23.

Cullen, L.M. (1975) 'Population trends in seventeenth-century Ireland', *Irish Economic and Social History*, II, pp. 149–65.

Dickson, D. (1991) 'No Scythians here: women and marriage in seventeenth-century Ireland', in M. McCurtain and M. O' Dowd (eds), *Women in early modern Ireland*, Edinburgh.

Drew, E. (1998) 'Reconceptualising families in Ireland: changes in demography and family forms', Centre for Women's Studies, Trinity College, Dublin.

Eversley, D.E.C. (1981) 'The demography of the Irish Quakers, 1650–1850', in J.M. Goldstrom and L.A. Clarkson (eds), *Irish population, economy and society: essays in honour of the late K.H. Connell*, Oxford.

Guinnane, T. (1997) *The vanishing Irish: households, magration, and the rural economy in Ireland, 1850–1914*, Princeton.

Healy, J. (1968) *The Death of an Irish Town*, Cork.

Houston, R.A. (1992) *The population history of Britain and Ireland, 1500–1750*, London.

Hull, C.H. (ed.) (1899) *The economic writings of Sir William Petty*, Cambridge.

Kennedy, L. (1994) 'Malthusian models and Irish history: an assessment', unpublished paper, Queen's University of Belfast.

Kennedy, L. (1994) *People and population change: a comparative study of population change in Northern Ireland and the Irish Republic*, Dublin.

Kennedy, L. (1996) 'The other great hunger: non-marriage in nineteenth-century Ireland', paper read to the American Conference for Irish Historians, Belfast.

Kennedy, L. (1997) 'Prices, wages and living standards in Ireland, 1700–1850', paper to the National Historical Accounts Group at the Economic and Social Research Institute, Dublin.

Kennedy, R.E. (1973) *The Irish: emigration, marriage and fertility*, London.

Lenihan, P. (1997) 'War and population', *Irish Economic and Social History*, 24, pp. 1–21.

Macafee, W. (1987) 'Pre-famine population in Ulster: evidence from the parish register of Killyman' in P. O'Flanagan, P. Ferguson and K. Whelan (eds), *Rural Ireland: Modernisation and Change, 1600–1900*, Cork, pp. 142-61.

McGregor, P. (1989) 'Demographic pressure and the Irish Famine: Malthus after Mokyr', *Land Economics*, 45, 228–38.

Miller, D.W. (1994) 'Fertility and social change in Ireland, 1841–61', paper to the annual meeting of the Social Science History Association, Atlanta.

Mokyr, J. (1985) *Why Ireland starved: a quantitative and analytical history of Ireland, 1800–1845*, London.

Mokyr, J. and O Grada, C. (1984) 'New developments in Irish population history, 1700–1850', *Economic History Review*, 37, pp. 473-88.

Moring, B. (1998) 'Motherhood, milk, and money: infant mortality in pre-industrial Finland', *Social History of Medicine*, 2, pp.177-96.

O Grada, C. (1989) *The Great Irish Famine*, London.

O Grada, C. (1994) *Ireland: a new economic history, 1780–1939*, Oxford.

O'Brien. J.A. (ed.) (1953) *The vanishing Irish: the enigma of the modern world*, New York.

O'Neill, K. (1984) *Family and farm in pre-famine Ireland: the parish of Killashandra*, Madison.

Scheper-Hughes, N. (1979) *Saints, sinners and schizophrenics: mental illness in rural Ireland*, Berkeley.

Vann, R. and Eversley, D. (1992) *Friends in life and death: The British and Irish Quakers in the demographic transition, 1650–1900*, Cambridge.

Williamson, J. (1994) 'Economic convergence: placing post-Famine Ireland in comparative perspective', *Irish Economic and Social History*, 21, pp. 5–27.

Wrigley, E.A., Davies, R.S., Oeppen, J.E. and Schofield, R.S. (1997) *English population history from family reconstitution, 1580–1837*, Cambridge.

Young, A. (1892) *Arthur Young's Tour in Ireland (1776–1779)*, ed. A.W. Hutton, London.

4 Marriage and economic conditions since 1700: the Belgian case.

Isabelle DEVOS, University of Ghent

I. Introduction

The purpose of this chapter is to give a succinct picture of the social and economic background underlying the Malthusian pattern of late marriage and the reasons for its disappearance during the course of the 19th and 20th centuries in Belgium. We start with a description of nuptiality trends prior to 1850 and the explanatory hypotheses put forward by Franklin Mendels and Chris Vandenbroeke. We then continue with a discussion on the modernization of nuptiality between 1850 and 1980 and its implications for population change, mostly depending on the research of Ron Lesthaeghe. Data on Belgian nuptiality are presented in an appendix.

Most of the theories formulated to explain marriage patterns are 'economic at bottom' (Stone, 1977: 51). They consider age at marriage to be a function of the age at which men can achieve an independent living adequate to support a family. Hajnal found a unique pattern of late and non-universal marriage in 17th and 18th-century western Europe. According to this pattern, 10–15 per cent of the population remained single throughout life, and the mean age for first marriage of women was in general above 24 years (Hajnal, 1965). The Western European Marriage Pattern was associated with a peasant economy and an inheritance system which demanded a certain amount of property as a prerequisite to marriage. More simply, in order to get married, men had to save or, in most cases, wait until their father died and a piece of land, a workshop or a cottage became available. According to Dupâquier, delays in the deaths of the holders of the land, the result of declining death rates tended to rise the age at marriage (Dupâquier, 1972: 202). People who did not inherit or could not find another source of income would defer marriage. In homeostatic terms, this means that definite celibacy and the age at marriage were influenced by the rate of adult mortality. Habakkuk ascribes the uniqueness of the Western European Marriage Pattern to the European stem-family: when property descends to a single heir (primogeniture), late marriage fulfils an important economic role (cited in Lesthaeghe, 1977: 65). Sons who did not share their father's property had to postpone marriage and work as day labourers or seasonal workers, or seek a source of income in ways other than agriculture. A system with partible inheritance and equal sharing increases nuptiality intensity and leads to a drop in marital fertility, because parents want to limit further division of property through limitation of family size. The Malthusian framework might have been valid for describing long-term trends in Belgian nuptiality. In the short term, however, Franklin Mendels argues that during the 18th century, large sections of the population tried to escape from it.

II. Proto-industrialization

The literature on proto-industrialization states that employment in cottage industry (cash income) allowed earlier marriages than had been possible under the traditional marriage system. A clear presentation of this argument appears in Mendels's Ph.D. dissertation on 18th-century Flanders (Mendels, 1969, also 1972). His work examines the statistical relationship between wages, prices, family formation and the growth of rural industry. Mendels attributes periodic fluctuations in marriage frequencies to the development of the linen sector, the main proto-industrial activity in Flanders.[1] In his opinion, the decline in the age of marriage was not the result of increased prosperity but of what was called 'the proletarization of the rural population'. At the end of the Ancien Régime, nearly half of the Flemish population was engaged in the rural linen industry, at least on a part-time basis. The supplementary income was not used by peasants for investment, but was used to support entry into a marriage which otherwise would have been delayed. The symbiosis of agriculture and cottage industry (with the agricultural sector producing flax and the industrial sector spinning and weaving it into linen) brought on a steady decline in age at marriage and growth of rural population. Agricultural viability was no longer a prerequisite to marriage, but the presence of textile employment was (Seccombe, 1995: 189). The necessity to wait for an available farm had disappeared; only a handloom needed to be procured. As Lesthaeghe (1977: 69) states, 'the basis of the subsistence of these classes was labor, not property'. Hence, if we are to believe Mendels, the self-regulating mechanisms of Dupâquier did not exist in 18th-century Flanders. The new group of wage-earning people tried to break away from the old Malthusian pattern and married earlier. The restrictive function of marriage lost its capacity to maintain the balance between population and economy. Mortality remained the only important check. According to Mendels model: 'whereas population growth had been the principal cause of impoverishment and peasants thought of industry as a means of alleviating their poverty, the poverty did not disappear because proto-industrialisation in turn had the unfortunate feedback effect of promoting poverty by breaking down the old self-regulating demographic system. This happened primarily through marriages which were facilitated by the expectation of a cash income from industry'(Mendels, 1982: 85).

Low marriage ages were associated with poor economic conditions. The fact that the proto-industrial phase in Flanders was a period of poverty is, however, very much contested. Chris Vandenbroeke – the most important challenger of Mendels theory on proto-industry – nuances this picture and points out only the start and the end of proto-

[1] Within Belgium, the Flemish and Walloon patterns of economic development should be distinguished. Mendels described 18th-century inland Flanders as an examplar of proto-industrialization. Especially in the area between Ghent, Oudenaarde, Aalst, Roeselare and Thielt, relations between the small-scale, intensive agriculture and the cottage industry were very tight. Flanders had to cope with strong population pressures (250–300 inhabitants per km^2) which resulted in extreme parcelling of the land. The northern part of Flanders, on the other hand, was characterized by large land holdings and market farming. In Wallonia, the first phase of industrialization occurred only at the beginning of the 19th century.

industrialization were characterized by a pauperization of rural population, while the intermediary phase had relative affluence. Evidence can be found in the real wages of agricultural workers and linen weavers (see Figure 4.1). The second and third quarter of the 18th century was a period of high purchasing power for the people in the countryside, and was described as a golden age by contemporaries. Dérival, a French nobleman on a journey through the Austrian Netherlands in 1782–83, noted : 'All the inhabitants of the towns of the Low Countries live if not in opulence at least in great abundance: but this is even more to be remarked in the countryside than in the towns; in towns and in the countryside one cannot be struck by the good fortune enjoyed by the inhabitants' (quoted in Vandenbroeke, 1987: 156). Flanders was one of the most prosperous regions in the world.[2]

However, the situation deteriorated rapidly during the first half of the 19th century when proto-industrialization had to compete with mechanization in the textile sector. The strong competition between domestic linen and foreign cotton, together with the potato blight and the harvest failures of the 1840s, represented a major catastrophe. Between one-quarter and one-half of the Flemish population became indigent and needed assistance. Flanders was referred to as 'the Ireland of the continent'. Yet, this impoverishment was not a consequence of a linear trend in the development of rural industry, as stated by Mendels. In Vandenbroeke's description, the prosperity of the Flemish regional economy around the middle of the 18th century cannot be denied.

[2] A comparative analysis of the physical product -in real terms- confirms the relative prosperity of the Flemish people around 1800 (Vandenbroeke, 1987: 156) :

	Flanders	France	England
Wheat (L.)	1.282	1.140	857
Meat (Kg.)	255	230	254

Figure 4.1 Real wages of agricultural workers (A) and linen weavers (B) expressed in litres of wheat

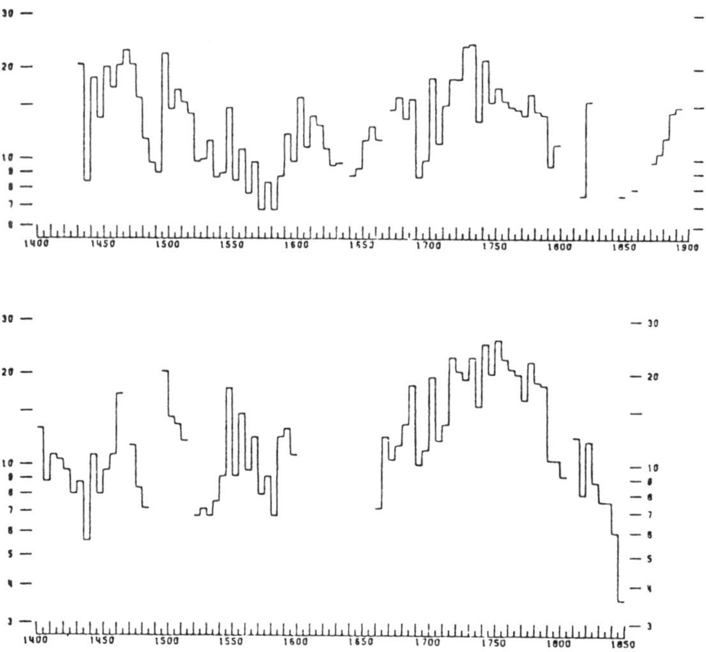

Source: Vandenbroeke (1984: 922)

At the Economic History Congress in Budapest in 1982 the two visions were confronted (Vandenbroeke, 1984; Mendels in 1984). Vandenbroeke offered Flemish data that contradicted Mendels's model by showing that the age of marriage did not decline during proto-industry. Using a large collection of local monographs, he showed the existence of a restrictive attitude. On a long term basis, the 18th century was characterized by a strong decrease of crude marriage rates from 13 to 8 per cent, which continued into the 19th century when it reached an absolute minimum of 5.5 per cent. Only at the end of the 19th century was an improvement was noted (see appendice, Table 1). Especially striking was the high age at which marriage was concluded during the period 1620–1899, as shown in Figure 4.2

Figure 4.2 Age at first marriage of men (1) and women (2), Flanders

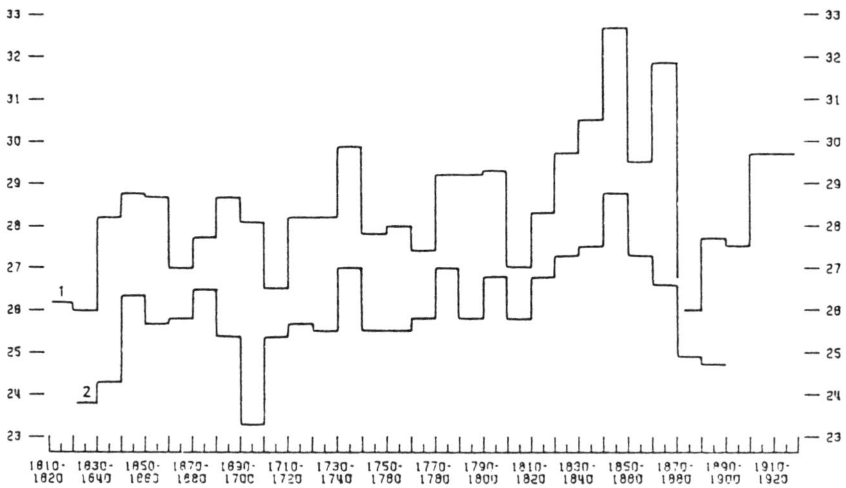

Source: Vandenbroeke (1984: 929)

While women's average age of marriage was between 25 and 26 years around 1700, it reached 27.5 years in the period 1790–99 and a peaked at 29.7 years in 1850–59 as a result of the economic crisis (appendice, Tables 3, 5 and 6). Twenty-eight per cent of women between 30 and 35 at the end of the 18th century were single, the figure rose to 46 per cent in 1846 and 54 per cent in 1856. Additional evidence can be seen in the increasing number of never-married people: the percentage of definitive celibacy at age 50 rose from 15 per cent at the beginning of the 18th century to 21 per cent at the end (appendice, Tables 13 and 14). These values all indicate a very restrictive nuptiality pattern, as described by Hajnal for most West European populations. The gradual increase in marriage age since the 1750s means that the so-called favourable influence for nuptiality patterns during the proto-industrial phase (1750–1840) was untenable. The transition from an agrarian-artisanal to a more industrial proletarian pattern was anything but positive for marriage frequencies. In most areas of Flanders the I_m index, the proportion married among women of childbearing age between 15 and 50 years, was even lower than .450 (appendice, Table 10). In East Flanders, for instance, the 1700 level of .470 was only matched at the beginning of the 20th century (appendice, Table 9). The acceleration of I_m values during the early 18th and the first half of the 19th centuries confirms the increasing restrictive marriage pattern, and is taken by Vandenbroeke as a clear refutation of arguments put forward by Mendels, Levine and others who centre on the relationship between proletarization and nuptiality. At the end of the Ancien Régime the areas where proto-industry played an important role such as Roeselaere, Thielt, Oudenaarde, Ghent and Aalst did not manifest exceptionally high I_m values (see Figure 4.3). Neither does there appear to be an epicentre of extremely high or low values of I_m or even a different pattern for linen and non-linen areas. In 1796, the I_m index for the East Flemish and West Flemish rural areas were respectively .462 and .487, for the urban areas .430 and .464, and the city of Ghent .414, which does however illustrate the negative influence of the urban environment on nuptiality (Jaspers and Stevens, 1985: 72; Gyssels et al., 1986: 72).

Figure 4.3 I_m, Antwerp, East Flanders and West Flanders, 1796

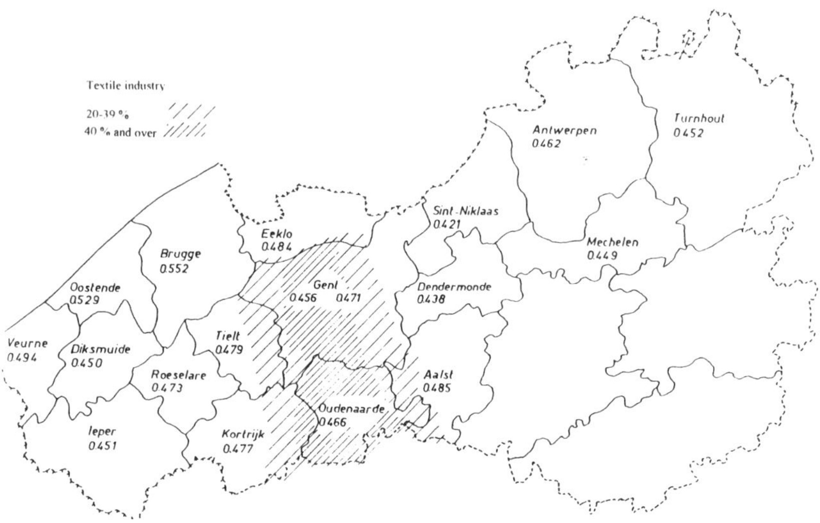

Source: Schelstraete (1986: 73)

The research of Myron Gutmann on Walloon localities confirms Vandenbroeke's findings about the relationship between industrial development and nuptiality. Gutmann's study of Wandre brought to light no marked decline in the age at marriage as industry evolved during the 17th and 18th centuries (Gutmann, 1980). Gutmann also compared the industrialized town of Verviers with four more rural parishes in its hinterland for 140-year period (1650–1790) (Gutmann, 1987). Marriage ages were high in all localities, and the trend of marriages was similar in both urban and rural settings. From a minimum of 24.9 years around 1650, the age of marriage rose to a maximum of 27.8 years in the early 18th century, fell to a minimum again in the 1730s, and then rose to a peak just around 1770 (appendice, Table 4). Increasing industrialization did not bring marriage ages down. The reported ages at first marriage were high and remained high both before and after the onset of proto-industrialization. Leboutte and Gutmann suggested marriage ages stayed high in the Verviers region because 'a peasant mentality continued to operate, even after industrialization'. This mentality was evoked by Faipoult, prefect of the department of the Scheldt (1801): 'La certitude d'un gain journalier rendit ici tout homme laborieux : le villageois prit l'habitude d'une activité constante ; et, comme son premier goût est la terre, il s'y appliqua avec ardeur, mais en donnant à celui du tissage ou de la filature de lin et de la laine, tous les moments qu'il en pouvait employer à la culture. Beaucoup de villageois acquérant quelque aisance par cet avantageux régime, voulurent être fermiers, et non simples journaliers'(Faipoult, 1801). The research of Paul Servais, which shows that the workers in the Hervé district remained fairly prosperous and continued to try to purchase land, confirms this hypothesis (Servais, 1982).

Gutmann also compared a series of mean marriage ages and annual changes in the number of marriages to various measures for economic conditions (real wages, food prices, rural income). Nuptiality did not display the characteristics asserted by the proto-industrialization hypothesis. The economic variables were not significant. Furthermore, he demonstrated that the ability to measure the relationship between nuptiality and economic conditions depended on the measure of nuptiality employed. Mendels, for instance, had to rely on the periodic fluctuations in overall frequencies since better measures of nuptiality were lacking. His demographic data were based on the number of marriages per year which measure short-term phenomena and are closely related to short-term economic conditions. Mean or median marriage ages, according to Gutmann, measure changes taking place over a longer period of time. He states that 'the persistent high ages at first marriage for women in Belgium represent a consistent social stability which in fact changed only slowly : they masked changes taking place beneath them. Individual level data would enable to determine the susceptibility to changing economic conditions'(Gutmann, 1980: 171). Such material is, however, rarely available, but we do have a few indications about marriage behaviour by professional class (see Table 4.1).

Table 4.1 Age at first marriage by professional category, Evergem

	1806–08	1814–16	1824–26	1845–47	Increase
Farmers	31.6	29.8	32	36.4	15.2%
Agricultural workers	31.2	30.8	27.7	33.5	7.4%
Textile workers	28.3	29.4	29.4	35.7	26.1%
Servants	26.4	34.0	29.6	36.8	39.4%
Artisans	28.3	27.8	32.3	34.9	23.3%
All categories	30.1	29.6	30.1	35.0	16.3%

Source: Parijs (1982: 94–5)

The table shows that there was an overall movement toward a more restrictive nuptiality pattern. The tendency to marry late increased to a greater extent amongst textile workers – and servants – than in other occupations and illustrates the depression of rural industry during the 1840s.

To summarize, it is possible that during proto-industrialization certain areas were characterized by a fall in age of marriage. In England, women's age at first marriage fell very substantially (by an estimated 2.5 years during the 18th century). Belgium, on the other hand, offers no proof of this evolution. The proto-industrial phase had no positive influence on nuptiality patterns. The overall pattern appears to be one in which marriage ages were rising, not falling. Even Hans Medick, one of the most prominent proponents of the proletarization hypothesis, reconsidered the theory and wrote in 1997: 'Es fällt besonders auf, dass auch in der Hochphase der gewerblich proto-industriellen Entwicklung...keineswegs eine Tendenz zur Senkung der Heiratsalters festzustellen ist' (Medick, 1997: 319). For Belgium, both Vandenbroeke and Gutmann noted a decrease of nuptiality at the end of the 19th century, although not before. Nevertheless, a contradictory pattern could be found in urban areas.

III. Industrialization

Compared to the 1850s, when the age at marriage reached its peak, the 1961 figures show a decline of almost six years (appendice, Table 7). The I_m-index moved towards a more intense pattern, reaching a value of .700 by 1961 (appendice, Table 11). Turning to definitive celibacy, we see the same picture: in the middle of the 19th century 15 per cent of the men and nearly 18 per cent of the women were still single at age 50, while in 1947 this had fallen to about 10 per cent for both sexes (appendice, Table 16). More people were getting married, and life expectancy of marriages had also increased (appendice, Tables 18 and 19). Mortality improvements were the major factor, and the proportion of marriages ending in widowhood had declined. By 1930, however, the mortality effect was overshadowed by increase in divorce and the average duration of marriage decreased once more. Divorce more than tripled between 1888 and 1945 (from 4 per cent to 14 per cent), though it remained at a fairly low level by comparison with other Western countries (Schoen et al., 1984).

These results indicate a substantial break from the Malthusian marriage pattern that existed during the Ancien Régime. From the middle of the 19th century, a gradual decline in definitive celibacy and age at marriage was evident and continued for more than a century.[3] This transition from a pattern of late marriage to one of much earlier and more universal marriage, described as 'the modernization of nuptiality', was observed in many western countries. Ron Lesthaeghe found, however, several gradations of marriage patterns within the overall Western European picture (see Table 4.2). In France, where already before 1850 I_m had reached a value of .500, a much more modern nuptiality behaviour prevailed than elsewhere. A second pattern was observed in Belgium, the Netherlands and Germany. This was characterized by a gradual upward trend, starting around the middle of the 19th century and continuing until the 1960s. A third pattern existed in most of the other western European countries, where the change in I_m was insignificant during the 19th century and the beginning of the 20th century. These countries exhibited a nuptiality revolution after 1930, especially after the Second World War, and reached I_m-levels of .700 in only a few decades.

[3] The marriage boom came to an end in the 1960s. The last decades nuptiality has been declining considerably (Appendix, table 7). In 1995 the average age at marriage nearly matched its 1850s level.

Table 4.2 I_m, Belgium, Germany, France and the Netherlands, 1840–1910

approx. date	Belgium	Germany	France	Netherlands
1840			0.516	
1845	0.375		0.520	
1850			0.526	0.389
1855	0.366		0.530	
1860			0.531	0.406
1865		0.454	0.530	
1870		0.472	0.529	0.438
1875		0.495	0.533	
1880	0.435	0.501	0.538	0.469
1885		0.494	0.541	
1890	0.436	0.497	0.540	0.450
1895			0.541	
1900	0.479	0.513	0.543	0.450
1905				
1910	0.517	0.524		0.469

Source: Lesthaeghe (1977: 55)

Within Belgium, regional variation was substantial. A clear distinction was observed between the northern and the southern parts of the country. For instance, in the arrondissement of Tielt in 1880, the average age at marriage was 28.4 years and 30.5 per cent of women at the age of 50 were still single, while in the arrondissement of Charleroi the average age was 25 and only 9.2 per cent of the women were single. The highest marriage frequencies in the middle of the 19th century were found in the province of Hainault, and the lowest in the provinces of East Flanders and West Flanders and Limburg (appendice, Table 2). These three provinces also had a proportion of single people consistently above the national average (appendix, Table 15). These provincial differences in nuptiality at the middle of the 19th century persisted until the 1960s, when the marriage boom reached its end. The rise in nuptiality was more or less equally pronounced in all provinces. Only between 1961 and 1970 did an important change in the ranking of the provinces occur: all the Walloon areas underwent a decrease, while the Flemish areas continued to rise (appendice, Table 12).

What determined the modernization of Belgian nuptiality? Most theories associate a change in marriage behaviour with economic change. The Dutch historian E. Hofstee points to the proletarization movement linked to increasing industrialization as an explanation for the increase in nuptiality during the 19th century. A map of I_m values for Belgian arrondissements (Charleroi, Thuin, Mons, Soignies, Philippeville) in 1900 shows that high marriage intensities coincide with early industrialization.[4] Testing the proletarization hypothesis with Belgian data, Ron Lesthaeghe found that

[4] Wallonia, emerging in the 1840s as the most industrialized area on the continent, lost its primacy by 1914. The two pivotal sectors of Walloon industrialization were the heavy industry (coal, steel and iron) in the central part of the province of Hainaut and the suburbs of Liège and the mechanized wool center in the Verviers area.

modernization of marriage patterns occurred indeed earlier in the new group of wage earning classes, which seems to support Hofstee's theory. He discovered, however, major differences between marriage behaviour of rural and strictly urban wage-earners. The typical industrial working class developed an earlier pattern of marriage, whereas the landless rural proletariat (day labourers, cottagers, servants) continued to marry late. The analysis in Wallonia showed that wherever a large group of industrial labourers was found, there were high I_m-values. In Flanders, the lower nuptiality intensity was caused by the high percentage of rural labourers.[5]

Figure 4.4 Im, Belgian arrondissements and four urban areas, 1900

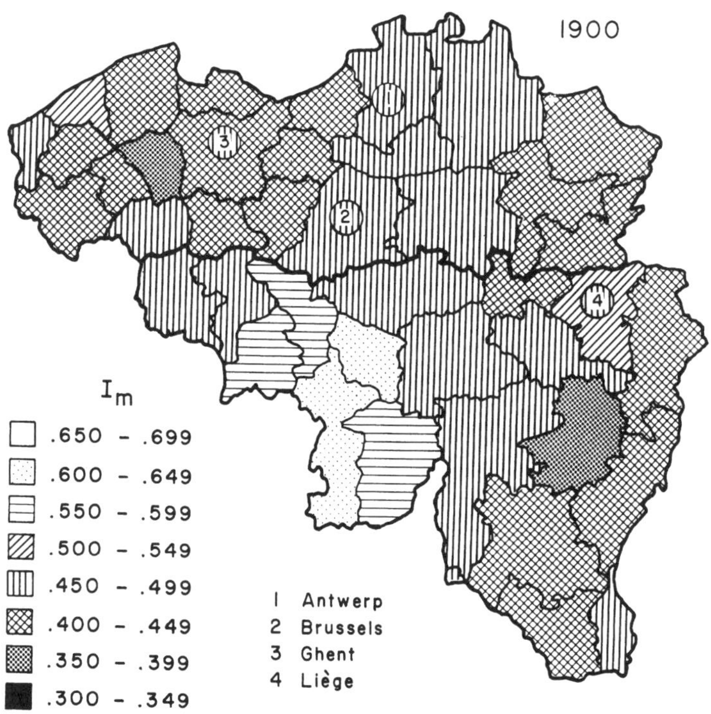

Source: Lesthaeghe (1979: 61)

[45] The nuptiality differences between rural and urban areas at the end of the 19th century are most probably the continuation of earlier regional marriage patterns, as described by Jaspers and Gyssels for the end of the Ancien Régime, and seem to provide some evidence for Vandenbroeke's theory.

Thus, Lesthaeghe deemed the proletarization theory too general and emphasized the impact of occupational structure on nuptiality. In his opinion, Hofstee also overlooked the effect of the type of industrialization on nuptiality in urban areas. For instance, in industrial towns such as Charleroi and Seraing, which specialized in heavy industry, a much more modern nuptiality pattern prevailed. However, provincial towns with light industries (Kortrijk, Ostend, St Niklaas, Aalst) and metropolitan areas (Ghent, Antwerp, Brussels) had substantially lower values of I_m and a higher concentration of single women (Lesthaeghe, 1977: 76–87). The research of George Alter, which demonstrates the migration of a large number of unmarried women from surrounding rural areas into the city of Verviers to work in the wool industry and the domestic service, supports these results (Alter, 1988: 63–90).

These regional differences in nuptiality, however, were not simply the result of economic differences. Lesthaeghe found that between 1890 and 1910, the two areas of greatest industrial development, the province of Hainault and the province of Liège, had different nuptiality patterns. In Hainault, adjacent to early marrying France, nuptiality was higher whereas the area of Liège, on the border with Germany and the Netherlands, was behind in the nuptiality transition. Furthermore, the fact that regional variations in nuptiality persisted throughout the 19th and 20th centuries, even when economic differences between regions muted, suggests that other factors were at work. The nuptiality differences seem to correspond to internal cultural variations. Susan Watkins has examined the change in variation in nuptiality between the provinces of most western European countries for the period 1870–1960 (Watkins, 1986). Her evidence shows that, after controlling for differences in industrialization and occupational structure, those provinces that were contiguous, and especially those which shared a language, a religion or more generally a common culture, had similar nuptiality levels. I_m was homogeneous for provinces within the regions, while the regions differed substantially from one another. However, regional variation decreased in countries such as France when regional economies were replaced by a national economy or because of the growth of a national culture. In Watkins's opinion, the persistence of nuptiality differences between the north and the south of Belgium reflects long-standing historical divisions. The country is characterized by a high degree of cultural heterogeneity, as witnessed by the presence of two major linguistic communities (Flemish in Flanders, French in Wallonia) and different past histories. Watkins's analysis reminds us here of Hajnal's typology of marriage, and takes us back to the start of the chapter. The basis of his typology was clearly geographical. Hajnal detected a late and non-universal marriage pattern west of a line running from Trieste on the Adriatic Sea to St Petersburg on the Baltic. I_m values varied in these regions between .300 and .600. In the eastern half of Europe nuptiality was considerably higher.

Evidently, marriage patterns vary with geographical regions. On the other hand, we cannot deny Watkins's critique when she states that 'geography as an explanation for age at marriage ranks with 'biology as a destiny' for women's roles' (Watkins, 1986: 327).

IV. Implications for population change

What were the effects of the modernization of nuptiality for household structures? Hofstee suggested that the increase in nuptiality was more than the transition from a pattern of tardy marriage to one of earlier and universal marriage, but also implied the change from an extended to a nuclear family system. Considering the high percentage of definitive celibacy during the Ancien Régime, he argued that single people joined other households, mostly those of relatives. In his description, when the father of a family died, only the eldest son would get married; other siblings would continue to live on the property as dependants. From the evidence gathered in Belgium, however, it seems that extended households have rarely been the practice. In fact, given the pattern of late nuptiality and high fertility, the average family size was quite small, about 4–5 people (see Table 4.3).

Table 4.3 Household density, Flanders

1670-1699	4,59	-1600	4,07
1700-1729	4,88	1600-1650	5,03
1730-1759	4,87	1650-1700	4,57
1760-1789	5,26	1700-1750	4,32
1790-1820	5,25	1750-1800	4,5
1840-1870	4,88	1800-1820	4,47
1875-1884	4,78	1840-1870	4,7
1895-1904	4,5	1880-1900	4,4

Source: Vandenbroeke (1976b: 8)

According to Vandenbroeke, the smaller households before 1700 can be explained by repeated mortality crises, while declining death rates and an increasing restrictive nuptiality pattern were responsible for the maximum values of the second half of the 18th century. The higher household density in this period can be definitely related to the development of the cottage industry. Compared to the north, inland Flanders had much larger households (Vandenbroeke, 1976b: 9–11). There was again a striking difference between urban and rural areas. The average household in the countryside had between 4.5 and 5.5 people, while in the cities the average was between 4 and 5 people. The lower values in the cities were the result of in-migration of single women from the countryside, often short-term labor migrants. According to Alter, these women had an important impact on the marriage market for local women. His work on the marriage prospects of women born in 19th-century Verviers demonstrates that a high proportion of them remained unmarried and continued to live with their families of origin. He points to moral obligations and parental authority, more than economic contributions, as binding them to their families. This is in sharp contrast with the picture painted by Anderson and Shorter, who attributed independence and individualism to young people in 19th-century cities. Rather than the urban experience, it was marriage which represented 'a distinct break from the family of origin' (Alter,

1988: 89). Married women rarely lived with their parents, although they continued to live in their proximity.

Nuclear families represented 80–90 per cent of family structures. This percentage would only increase in the 20th century, when marital fertility was brought under control. During the Ancien Régime, fertility was regulated by means of marriage. The delay of marriage was, in Chaunu's terms, 'la véritable arme contraceptive de l'Europe classique'. Areas with low nuptiality values had higher marital fertility; areas with a more intensive nuptiality pattern had lower fertility. A correlation test between I_m and I_g for Flemish regions in 1796 gives a high inverse correlation (-0.733). Again, there was no outright association with rural industry. Marital fertility, with values well above .700, was very near the expected maximum and we may assume that contraception was not widespread (Jaspers and Stevens (1985: 77).

Figure 4.5 I_g, Belgian arrondissements and four urban areas, 1900

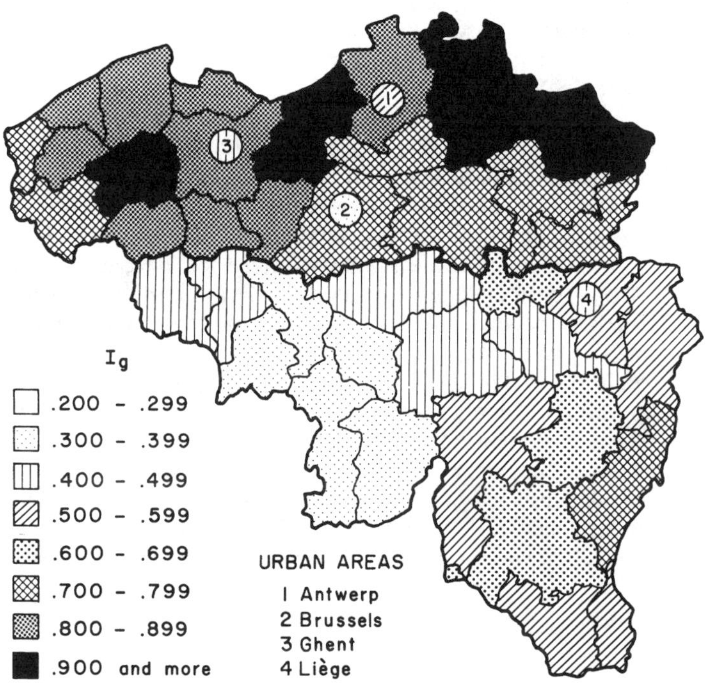

Source: Lesthaeghe (1977: 109)

For Belgium as a whole, the I_g index only began to decline after 1870 and followed an uninterrupted downward movement until the 1970s.[6] The change began first in Wallonia. The areas with lower fertility were all on the Walloon side (see Figure 4.5). Flanders, apart from the urban areas, remained behind; it was not until after the turn of the century that a strong decrease appeared in most Flemish areas. The more urbanized and industrialized areas in Belgium were definitely those where fertility declined earlier and faster. The map also confirms the consistent difference between the two language regions, the sharpness of which can be observed along the entire length of the language border. For instance, Lesthaeghe found that within pairs of Walloon and Flemish villages, with an average distance of four miles from each other, Flemish villages had a much higher fertility. Furthermore, indications of earlier fertility control were found among the Francophone populations of the Flemish cities. From this perspective, he states that the impact of language and secularization (the break from organized religion) cannot be overlooked. For a given level of industrialization, the Walloon arrondissements had a considerably higher level of secularization than their Flemish counterparts. The Walloon population had a more flexible mentality toward fertility control, while in Flanders, constraints toward contraceptive practices reflected a deeply rooted traditionalism and a strong attachment to Catholicism (Lesthaeghe, 1977: 111–14, 154–58, 183–89).

In most Flemish areas, the nuptiality change occurred before the marital fertility change; but in Wallonia, there was only a weak indication of time lag. Thus, marital fertility started to drop after the incidence of marriage had decreased. Consequently, at the beginning of the 20th century Flanders was confronted with an accelerated population growth which led to the loss of the Walloons' numerical hegemony in the country. Under conditions of restrained fertility, a decline in age at marriage would have translated into excessive population growth. Thus, a long-term continuation of the decline in age at marriage necessitated a change in the mentality toward fertility control. As Van de Walle states, 'the decline in age at marriage was not provoked by a decline in marital fertility; the latter was a permissive agent without which the nuptiality trends would not have persisted in the long run' (Van de Walle, 1972: 151). Lesthaeghe discovered that in Belgium the effect of nuptiality on marital fertility was fairly small: in fact, 'the relationship was virtually spurious as they were both responding to the same exogenous conditions' (Lesthaeghe, 1977: 151). The gradual breakdown of the Malthusian pattern was the result of increasing industrialization, urbanization and secularization.

[6] The decline of marital fertility occured almost simultaneously with the decline in illegitimate fertility. Illegitimate fertility was, however, never very high : it rarely exceeded 10 per cent of marital fertility.

Figure 4.6 Boundaries of Belgium, provinces and arrondissements, 1840–1919

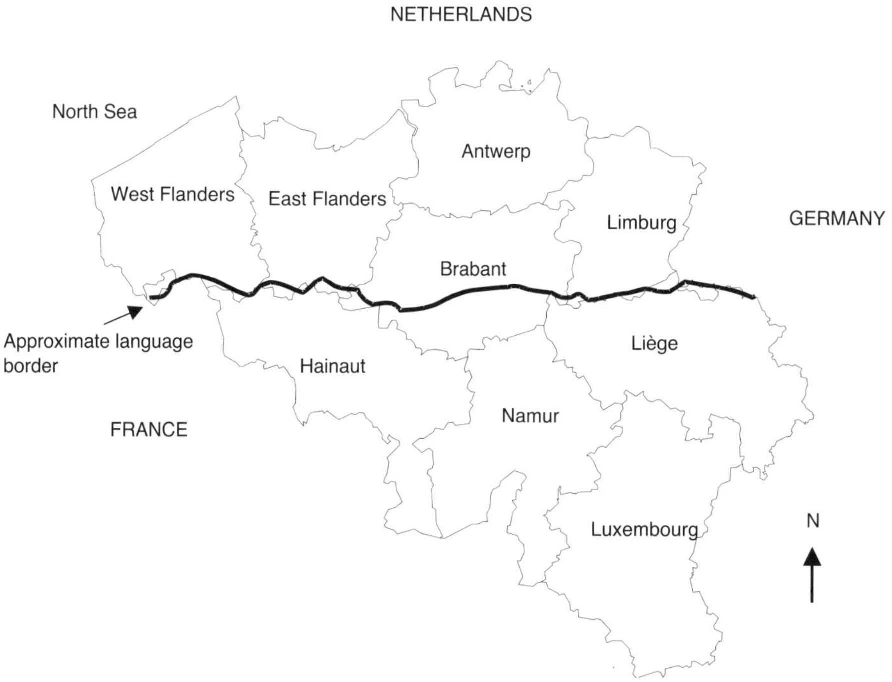

Appendice

Table 1 Crude marriage rates, Flemish countryside

1670-89	15
1680-89	13.1
1690-09	12.9
1700-19	12.8
1710-29	13.4
1720-39	12.4
1730-49	10.3
1740-59	8.9
1750-69	8.5
1760-79	8
1770-89	8.7
1780-99	8.6
1800-09	8.3
1815-30	7.9
1831-40	6.8
1846-50	5.5
1851-56	5.9
1856-60	7.5
1861-65	6.7
1871-75	6.7
1881-85	6.6
1891-95	7
1901-05	7.4
1911-15	9

Source: Vandenbroeke (1976b: 52-53)

Table 2 Crude marriage rates, Belgian provinces, 1803-1850

	Antwerp	Brabant	East Fl.	West Fl.	Hainaut	Liège	Limburg	Luxemburg	Namur
1803	8.4	8.3							
1804	7.5	7.6	7.3	7.5	7.8	6			7.3
1805	7.4	6.9	7.1	7.3	7.6	5.7			5.3
1806	7.6	7.4	7.3	7.4	8.4	6.4			6.9
1807	6.9	7.1	6.9	7	7.8	6.7			7.7
1808	6.6	6.8	6.7	5.9	7.7	6.5			8.3
1809	6.7	7.1	6.5	7.1	7.9	6.8			8.5
1810	7.7	7.5	7.6	7.7	8.3	7.3			8.3
1811	7.6	7.1	7.3	7.6	8.1	6.2			7.5
1812	7.7	6.8	6.9	6.7	7.1	6			7.6
1813	10.9	9.6	8.4	10.8	10.1	8.4			10.6
1814	6.4	6.3	6.7	6.4	6.3	5.7			4.6
1815	13.3	8.2	6.6	7.6	8	8.5			7.7
1816	7.4	7.3	7.0	6.6	7.2	6.1			6.7
1817	6	6.7	5.5	5.4	5.6	6			5.5
1818	7	7.9	6.4	6.4	6.9	6.6			6.6
1819	6.6	8.4	6.6	7.1	8.2	6.8			8.2
1820	6.8	8.5	6.4	7.0	8.6	7.6			7.8
1821	7.2	8.4	7.3	7.7	8.5	7.6			7.7
1822	7.6	8.4	7.9	8.1	8.7	7.7			7.6
1823	7	7.9	7	7.5	8.5	8.2			7.2
1824	7	6	6	7.2	7.3	6.5			6.6
1825	7.5	7.8	6.6	7.6	8.4	7.4			7.7
1826	7.2	8.6	6.7	7.8	8.5	7.8			8.2
1827	6.5	8.1	6.3	7.1	7.1	7.7			7
1828	7.6	8.4	6.7	7.1	7.7	7.8			7.7
1834	8.1	7.1	6.9	7.2	7.9	7.7			7.4
1835	8.3	8.3	7.3	7	8.1	8.8			8.0
1836	7.7	7.9	7.0	7.5	6.8	8.6			7.5
1837	7.7	7.9	7.3	7.4	7.9	7.9			7.3
1838	7.6	8	7.2	7	7.9	7.6			7
1839	7.6	8.1	7.0	7.1	7.7	7.4			6.9
1840	7.8	8.2	7.1	7	7.9	7.7	7.3	7.1	7
1841	7.6	7.9	6.7	6.5	7.5	7.3	8.1	7.4	7
1842	7.5	7.9	6.3	6.2	7	7.3	7.7	6.7	7.1
1843	7.2	7.5	5.9	6	6.8	7.6	6.5	6.7	6.7
1844	7.3	7.4	6.4	6.3	6.9	7.8	7.1	6.4	6.8
1845	7.1	7.6	6.2	6.3	7.1	7.4	6.3	6.1	6.5
1846	6.4	6.6	5.1	5.2	6.1	6.5	5.7	5.6	6.5
1847	6.1	6	4.5	4.7	6.2	6.3	5.1	5.7	6
1848	6.5	6.8	6	7.7	7	7.1	6.4	6.7	6.6
1849	7.5	7.5	7.1	7.3	7.2	7.4	7.1	6.7	7
1850	7.8	7.8	7.6	7.7	7.9	7.8	6.6	6.7	7.2

Source: Hofstee (1978: 201)

Table 3 Women's age at first marriage, Flanders/Brabant

	average	median
1620-39	24.3	23.8
1640-49	25.6	24.3
1650-59	27.9	26.4
1660-69	26.7	25.7
1670-79	28	25.8
1680-89	26.8	26.5
1690-99	25.5	25.4
1700-09	25.3	23.3
1710-19	26.7	25.4
1720-29	26.3	25.7
1730-39	26.7	25.5
1740-49	28.5	27
1750-59	26.3	25.5
1760-69	26.6	25.5
1770-79	26.6	25.8
1780-89	27.3	27
1790-99	27.5	25.8
1800-09	27.9	26.8
1810-19	26.8	25.8
1820-29	27.7	26.8
1830-39	28	27.3
1840-49	28.9	27.5
1850-59	29.7	28.8
1860-69	28.2	27.3
1870-79	27.5	26.6
1880-89	26.8	24.9
1890-99	26.2	24.7

Source: Vandenbroeke (1976a: 111)

Table 4 Women's age at first marriage, Walloon localities

	Verviers	Ensival, Limbourg, Soiron, Thimister
1650-59	25.54	24.89
1660-69	25.79	26.26
1670-79	25.87	25.67
1680-89	26.61	26.75
1690-99	27.06	26.63
1700-09	27.22	27.83
1710-19	26.73	27.57
1720-29	26.47	26.21
1730-39	25.79	25.93
1740-49	26.74	26.73
1750-59	26	26.65
1760-69	27.03	27.03
1770-79	27.92	26.84
1780-89	27.16	27.11
1650-1790	26.71	26.74

Source: Gutmann (1987: 153)

Table 5 Average age at first marriage, Flemish localities, 1765, 1796 and 1840

	1765		1796		1840	
Parish (Arrondissement.)	Males	Females	Males	Females	Males	Females
Astene (Ghent)	30.30	27.50	30.10	27.20		
Evergem (Ghent)	26.97	26.21	27.52	26.35	35	31.40
Munte (Ghent)	33.14	27.53	31.03	27.48	29.94	28.04
Poeke (Ghent)	27.60	26.50	31.80	28	34.70	29.90
Ronsele (Ghent)	32.80	26.45	31.20	29	35.70	33.40
Wachtebeke (Ghent)	29.30	26.44				
Zeveneken (Ghent)	30.22	27.21	29.45	26.78		
Moerzeke (Dendermonde)	29.20	27.59				
Wetteren (Dendermonde)	30.70	30				
Adegem (Eekloo)	28.72	30.50			36.40	30.30
Kluizen (Eekloo)	32.05	26.59	31.70	27.16	31.24	28.49
Watervliet (Eekloo)	31.59	27.14	29.65	25.46	31.42	27.99
Daknam (St.Niklaas)	34.63	29.61	31.30	29.57	31.67	28.60
Elversele (St.Niklaas)	34.20	29	34.20	29		
Mullem (Oudenaarde)	30.36	29.33	32.19	29.95	30.58	28.44
Zingem (Oudenaarde)			30.40	27.30	31.30	29.20
Zulzeke (Oudenaarde)	30.85	28.85	30.12	27.04	29.80	27.32
Denderhoutem (Aalst)	28.98	27.16	28.98	27.16		
Herzele (Aalst)	29.76	27.08	29.76	27.08		
Velzeke (Aalst)	29.07	28.18	29.13	26.90		
Dentergem (Thielt)	29.52	25.44				
Kaster (Kortrijk)	28.82	27.26				
Kalmthout (Antwerpen)	28.54	25.10	28.75	25.68		
Geetbets (Leuven)	28.45	26.96	28.41	27.58		
Gaasbeek-Itterbeek-St.Martens-Lennik (Brussel)	29	27.10	29.10	29.10		

Source: Schelstraete (1986: 206-07)

Table 6 Age at first marriage, Flemish localities

	Males		Females			Males		Females	
Parish (Arro.)	average	median	average	median	Parish (Arro.)	average	median	average	median
Astene (Ghent)					Kluizen (Eekloo)	27.9	26	24.7	23.7
1670-1709	28.6	27.6	26.2	26.2	1660-1689	29	27	25	23.7
1710-1749	28.9	28.1	27	25.6	1675-1704	27.3	25.3	25.6	24
1750-1789	30.3	28.2	27.5	27.1	1690-1719	28.2	26	28.4	26.5
1790-1829	30.1	29.5	27.2	26.2	1705-1734	32.8	30	26.6	25
Oudburg (Ghent)					1720-1749	33.3	30.7	25	23.5
1680-1699	26		24.5		1735-1764	32.3	30.8	26.6	25.2
1700-1719	27.3		25.2		1750-1779	31.8	30.7	26.6	25
1720-1739	27.9		26.3		1765-1794	31.3	29.8	27.1	25.1
1740-1759	26.3		24.2		1780-1799	32.1	30.3	27.3	25.6
1760-1778	24.2		22		1790-1809				
Evergem (Ghent)					Watervliet (Eekloo)	33.5	33	26.5	29
1759-1794	27	26.8	26.1	26.3	1635-1659	33.6	33	33.2	33
1806-1808	30.1	28.5	27.1	24.8	1655-1669	38.9	40.5	35.6	37
1814-1816	29.6	27.8	26.9	25.1	1665-1679	34.9	36.5	28.1	24
1824-1826	30.1	27	28.6	26.7	1675-1689	26.9	25	24.5	24.2
1845-1847	35	34.2	31.4	28.5	1685-1699	29.4	29.3	26	25
Wachtebeke (Ghent)					1695-1709	29.7	29.5	26.3	25
1650-1674	28.8	27.2	24	24.1	1705-1719	31.4	28.6	26.7	25.8
1675-1699	26.6	24.8	24.8	24.2	1715-1729	33.5	32.5	27.1	25.7
1700-1724	28.8	26.6	23.1	23.1	1725-1739	35.1	35	27.8	26
1725-1760	29.3	27.1	26.4	25.3	1735-1749	32.3	30.5	27.1	26
Zeveneken (Ghent)					1745-1759	30.8	28.3	27	25.2
1678-1700	28.4	28.4	25.5	25.5	1755-1769	32.4	30.8	29	26.2
1701-1725	28.3	27.9	26.2	26.8	1765-1779	31.1	29.8	26	25
1726-1750	29.4	29.2	27.2	27.5	1775-1789	28.9	29	24.9	24.3
1751-1775	30.2	30.8	27.2	27.4	1785-1799	30.4	29.8	26	24.9
1776-1796	29.5	29.5	26.8	26	1795-1809	30	28.6	25.3	24.7
Munte (Ghent)					1805-1819	29.8	28.5	27.5	26.4
1685-1729	35.7	35	27.3	26	1815-1829	31.4	30.8	28	27.2
1705-1749	36.5	36.5	27.1	26	1825-1840				
1725-1769	33.2	31	27.5	27	Daknam (St.Niklaas)	33	32	29	29
1745-1789	30.3	29.7	27.5	26.9	1625-1664	33.7	33.5	29.9	29
1765-1809	31	30.2	27.5	26.5	1645-1684	30.5	30	30.1	30
1801-1830	29.6	28.1	27.4	26.5	1665-1704	30.6	30.3	28.2	27.5
1816-1840	30	29.4	28	27	1685-1724	32.2	30.6	28.1	28
Poeke (Ghent)					1705-1744	32.9	31	29.6	29.5
1760-1769	27.6		26.5		1725-1764	34.6	34.5	29.6	29
1770-1779	28.1		28.7		1745-1784	31.4	30	29.6	29
1780-1789	27.9		25.4		1765-1804	31.2	28.8	28.5	27
1790-1799	31.8		28		1785-1824	31.7	30.3	28.6	27.2
1800-1804	31.1		26.2		1805-1840				
1800-1809	30.1		26.2		Elversele (St.Niklaas)	27.2	27.2	24.5	25
1810-1819	29.2		28.2		1608-1649	29.6	28.3	26	26.1
1820-1829	29.9		29.5		1650-1699	29.5	28.1	27.5	27
1830-1839	31.5		30.9		1700-1749	34.2	29.4	29	28.3
1840-1849	34.7		29.9		1750-1796				

Ronsele (Ghent)				
1700-1729	26.1		27.9	
1715-1744	26.1		27.9	
1730-1759	26.7		27	
1745-1774	31.4		26.1	
1760-1789	34.2		27.6	
1775-1796	31.2		29	
1802-1809	30.7		27.3	
1810-1819	29		27.2	
1820-1829	31.2		29.3	
1830-1839	33.8		28.9	
1840-1849	35.7		33.4	
Wetteren (Dendermonde)				
1745-1768	30.7	29.4	30	29
1755-1779	30.7	29.9	28.9	27.9
Hamme (Dendermonde)				
1851-1855	31.4	30.1	29.2	28
1861-1865	30.9	28.1	28	26.1
1875-1879	30.1	28.1	26.4	24
1885-1889	28.9	26	26	24
1895-1899	27.9	26	24.9	23
1905-1909	26.8	25	24.7	23
1915-1919	28.9	27	25.6	23
1920-1924	25.9	24	24.1	22
Moerzeke (Dendermonde)				
1750-1759	29.2	27	25.6	25
1760-1769	29.2	28	27.6	27
1770-1779	30.5	29	28	27
1780-1789	28.1	28	27.4	27
Adegem (Eekloo)				
1700-1709	30.6		25.5	
1710-1719	28.9		24.5	
1720-1729	30.1		25.3	
1730-1739	29.9		28.2	
1740-1749	27.9		27.8	
1750-1759	30		26.1	
1760-1769	28.72		30.5	
1770-1779	31.7		28.6	
1780-1789	29.9		28.3	
1830-1842	31.8		29	
1843-1845	33.8		29.7	
1846-1847	36.4		30.3	
1849-1851	33		31.6	
1852-1955	33		31.3	
Rumbeke (Roeselare)				
1815-1824	31.3	26.8	27.9	26.2
1825-1834	36.1	28.5	27.8	27.2
1835-1844	32.1	30.7	30	28.7
1845-1854	33.3	31.6	30.1	29.3
1855-1864	32.9	31.8	29.7	28.8
1865-1874	32.2	30.6	25.5	27.7
1875-1884	31.8	30.5	27.3	25.1
1885-1889	27.2	26.6	23.8	24.8
Mullem (Oudenaarde)	32.4	27.7	27.7	26
1650-1694	34.2	35	30.1	28
1680-1709	32.8	31	29.8	26.5
1695-1724	32	33	26.8	26
1710-1739	30	30	26.6	25
Zingem (Oudenaarde)				
1797-1806	30.4		27.3	
1830-1839	31		28.5	
1840-1849	31.3		29.2	
1850-1859	32.6		30.1	
1860-1869	32.6		29.9	
Zulzeke (Oudenaarde)				
1670-1699	28.1	28	28.8	28.7
1685-1714	28	28	29.6	28.6
1700-1729	29.5	29.2	29.5	27.6
1715-1744	31.9	31	29.7	27.5
1730-1759	30	29	28.2	27.7
1745-1774	30.3	29	28.1	27.7
1760-1789	30.8	28.6	28.1	26.6
1775-1804	29.9	28.2	27.3	26.2
1790-1819	30.3	28.5	26.8	25.6
1805-1834	30.1	28.4	26.9	26
1820-1840	29.8	28.56	27.3	26.1
Herzele (Aalst)				
1643-1719	28.3		25.8	
1720-1796	29.8		27.1	
Zottegem (Aalst)				
1871-1880	30.3		27.4	
1881-1890	27.1		24.7	
1891-1900	29.6		25.5	
Velzeke (Aalst)				
1648-1699	27.5	26	26.1	24.4
1700-1724	28.3	25.4	25.7	24.4
1725-1749	28.5	25.7	26.3	25.1
1750-1774	29.1	27.8	28.2	26.8
1775-1796	29.1	28.1	26.9	25.1
Denderhoutem (Aalst)				
1701-1750	29.7	27.9	28.6	25
1751-1795	29	29	27.2	25.6
Dentergem (Thielt)				
1760-1769	29.5	27	25.4	25
1770-1779	29.2	28	26.7	26
1780-1789	29.7	30	27.2	26

Kaster (Kortrijk)				
1730-1754	28.2	26.5	27.2	26.5
1755-1779	29.3	28.1	27.3	26.5
Anzegem (Kortrijk)				
1775-1779	30.1	29	27.6	27
1780-1784	33.1	30	26.3	25
1785-1789	28.7	27	27	25
Avelgem (Kortrijk)				
1775-1779	27	26	26.6	24
1780-1784	27	24	25.9	24
1785-1789	26.5	25	25.9	24
Oelegem (Antwerpen)				
1650-1690	27.5	27.2	24.6	24.9
1691-1725	28.6	27.9	26.4	25.8
1726-1755	28.1	27.3	26.6	25.9
Kalmthout (Antwerpen)				
1725-1749	28.1		23.9	
1750-1774	28.5		25.1	
1775-1797	28.8		25.7	
1805-1828	29.2		26.3	
Gierle (Turnhout)				
1594-1700	27.5	26.6	25	24.3
Geetbeets (Leuven)				
1720-1739	29.3	27	25.6	
1740-1759	27.9	26.5	26.9	27
1760-1779	28.5	27.5	27	25.8
1780-1799	28.4	27	27.6	27
1800-1819	29.4	28.4	27.4	25.3
1820-1832	27.3	25.9	27	25.7
Walem (Mechelen)				
1674-1755	29.8	28	28.4	26.5
Gaasbeek-Itterbeek-St.Martens-Lennik (Brussel)				
1600-1699	27.2	24.8	27.2	24.9
1700-1724	27.7	26.8	27.2	25.1
1725-1749	28.5	27.1	26.4	25.4
1750-1774	29	27.8	27.1	26.2
1775-1796	29.1	28.8	28.1	26.6

Source: Mendels (1984: 951-952); Vandenbroeke (1984: 930); Schelstraete (1986: 190-205)

Table 7 Age at first marriage, Belgium, 1852-1995

	Males	Females	Both sexes	
1852-1856	30.5	28.6	1985	25
1862-1866	30.0	28.0	1990	26.1
1886-1890	28.6	26.7	1995	28.9
1896-1900	27.6	25.7		
1906-1910	27.3	25.2		
1916-1920	27.5	25.6		
1926-1930	26.6	24.2		
1947	26.3	23.4		
1961	24.9	22.4		

Source: 1852-1930: Van de Walle (1965: 46); 1947: Wattelaer (1966: 419); 1986-95: Bevolkingsstatistieken (1996: 19)

Table 8 Women's age first marriage, Belgian provinces, 1862-1930

	1862-66	1896-1900	1926-30
Antwerp	28.8	25.3	24.1
Brabant	28.7	25.8	24.2
East Flanders	28.5	26.4	24.8
West Flanders	29.1	26.2	24.8
Hainaut	26.6	24.3	22.6
Liège	27.6	26.1	24.3
Limburg	28.7	27.0	25.2
Luxemburg	28.2	26.9	25.5
Namur	27.9	25.6	23.9

Source: Van de Walle (1965: 47)

Table 9 **I_m, West and East Flanders**

	West Fl.	East Fl.
1699-1703		.473
1742-1757		.406
1796	.470	.420
1802-1812	.407	.417
1846	.347	.345
1856	.326	.303
1866	.375	.361
1880	.400	.384
1890	.401	.395
1900	.437	.439
1910	.463	.473
1920	.432	.446
1930	.551	.561

Source: Vandenbroeke (1976b: 37)

Table 10 **I_m, Flemish localities**

Parish		
St.Denijs-Westrem	1699	.574
	1703	.418
Etikhove	1742	.336
Balegem	1755	.397
Lovendegem	1757	.439
	1796	.485
Oudegem	1796	.501
Zeveneken	1796	.438
St.Pauwels	1796	.366
Vurste-Wassene	1796	.413
Moortsele	1796	.428
Landskouter	1796	.333
Wortegem	1796	.471
Denderwindeke	1796	.254
Ename	1796	.427
Etikhove	1796	.364
Maarke	1796	.466
Melden	1796	.413
Ossenisse	1796	.386
Kanton Lede	1796	.434
Evergem-Zomergem-Knesselare-Ronsele	1796	.431
Schelderode	1804	.501
Munte	1808	.379
Scheldedepartement	1802	.445
	1812	.389
Elene	1842	.285

Source: Vandenbroeke (1976a: 135)

Table 11 I_m, Belgium, 1846-1970

1846	.375	1910	.517
1856	.366	1920	.501
1866	.403	1930	.602
1880	.435	1947	.617
1890	.436	1961	.705
1900	.479	1970	.703

Source: Lesthaeghe (1977: 52)

Table 12 I_m, Belgian provinces, 1806-1970

	Antwerp	Brabant	East Fl.	West Fl.	Hainaut	Liège	Limburg	Lux.	Namur
1806 low est.	.400	.419	.389	.400	.385	.403			.407
1806 high est.	.446	.420	.445	.414	.410	.416		.453	.419
1846	.365	.384	.345	.347	.411	.404	.359	.421	.415
1856	.365	.374	.303	.326	.424	.390	.347	.400	.405
1866	.395	.408	.361	.375	.464	.401	.370	.398	.432
1880	.457	.440	.384	.400	.489	.434	.406	.424	.457
1890	.457	.431	.395	.401	.502	.433	.380	.412	.444
1900	.482	.470	.439	.437	.572	.468	.411	.432	.497
1910	.518	.509	.473	.463	.617	.509	.448	.476	.546
1920	.512	.507	.446	.432	.597	.503	.427	.449	.520
1930	.604	.602	.561	.551	.699	.605	.529	.524	.621
1947	.623	.622	.596	.579	.694	.612	.558	.547	.625
1961	.709	.703	.676	.672	.766	.720	.671	.682	.717
1970	.721	.691	.696	.710	.715	.689	.700	.653	.679

Source: 1806: Duchêne and Lesthaeghe (1975: 44); 1846-1970: Lesthaeghe (1977: 57)

Table 13 Percentage of single women at age 50, East Flanders

1699-1703	15.2	1856	27
1742-1757	18.8	1866	27
1796	20.9	1880	27.1
1846	25.4	1890	24.6

Source: Vandenbroeke (1976a: 117)

Table 14 Percentage of people never married at age 50, Flemish localities

	Males			Females		
	Average	min.	max.	average	min.	max.
Walem, 1674-1755				3.9		
Elversele, 1750-1796					8	27
Astene, 1730-1779		1	9.8		1.2	6.9
Astene,1780-1829		5.1	12.3		4.1	10.8
Kalmthout, 1805-1825	16.8			7.3		
Rumbeke, 1815-1854	16.2			19.1		
Rumbeke, 1855-1889	25.9			30.7		

Source: Vandenbroeke (1976a: 116)

Table 15 Percentage married and unmarried, Flanders, 1796-98

	Males			Females		
	Unmarried	married	widowed	unmarried	married	widowed
15-19	99.9	0.1		99.1	0.9	
20-24	94.4	5.5	0.1	85.2	14.6	0.2
25-29	71.5	28	0.5	53	46.5	0.5
30-34	46.9	52.5	0.6	31.1	66.8	2.1
35-39	31.4	67.5	1.1	19.2	76.6	4.2
40-44	21.9	75.1	3.0	17.3	76.6	6.1
45-49	18.5	76.9	4.6	14.4	78.6	7.0
50-54	17.3	75.4	7.3	14.5	71.1	13.8
55-59	15.9	73.6	10.5	18.9	64.3	16.8
60-64	15.4	69.4	15.2	17	53.1	29.9
65-69	14.8	68.2	17	15.9	49	35.1
70-74	17	55.2	27.8	23.4	37.2	39.4
75-79	15.5	54.6	29.9	26.4	26.4	47.2
80+	20.1	39.6	40.3	26.5	19	54.5

Source: Vandenbroeke (1976b: 34)

Table 16 Percentage of persons never married at age 50, Belgium, 1829-1947

	Males	Females
1829	15.0	23.5
1846	15.3	17.7
1856	19.5	19.2
1866	19.4	18.2
1880	18.1	18.9
1890	17.3	17.5
1900	15.9	16.8
1910	14.5	16.4
1920	13.0	15.4
1930	10.5	13.3
1947	9.1	10.4

Source: 1829-1930: Van de Walle (1965: 51); 1947: Wunsch and Wattelaer (1967: 5)

Table 17 Percentage of single women aged 50, Belgian provinces, 1866-1930

	1886	1900	1930
Antwerp	17.7	16.0	12.3
Brabant	16.6	16.5	14
East Flanders	22.6	21.1	17.2
West Flanders.	25	22.5	16.4
Hainaut	15	11.2	8.4
Liège	14.8	16	12.8
Limburg	18.8	18.2	15.2
Luxemburg	13.4	15.8	15.8
Namur	12.6	15.2	12.6

Source: Van de Walle (1965: 52)

Table 18 Marital status life tables for Belgian male cohorts born 1888-1945 and 1975

	1888-92	1893-97	1898-1902	1903-07	1908-12	1913-17	1918-22	1923-27	1928-32	1933-37	1938-42	1943-45	1975
Expectation of life at birth	46.4	48	49.2	51.7	52.8	54.6	56.7	58.7	59.9	62.1	62.2	63.5	68.5
Proportion ever marrying	.594	.609	.621	.651	.666	.697	.724	.749	.769	.790	.784	.797	.836
Proportion ever marrying of those surv. to age 15	.836	.831	.832	.841	.853	.875	.884	.889	.902	.897	.888	.884	.858
Average age at first marriage	27.4	27.1	26.4	26.3	26.4	26.5	26.1	25.7	25.2	24.8	24.5	24.2	24.1
Proportion of marriages ending in divorce	.041	.045	.051	.057	.068	.079	.083	.088	.101	.117	.133	.146	.157
Proportion of marriages ending in widowhood	.358	.350	.336	.332	.326	.323	.326	.318	.313	.307	.301	.297	.293
Proportion of marriages ending in death	.600	.605	.613	.611	.607	.598	.591	.594	.586	.576	.566	.557	.550
Average age at divorce	39.7	40.6	41.6	40.8	41.2	40.6	40.9	42	41.7	40.8	39.8	38.8	37.8
Average age at widowhood	61.2	62.3	63.5	64.7	66.1	67	67.4	68.6	69	69.3	69.3	69.3	69.4
Marriages per person marrying	1.14	1.13	1.13	1.12	1.11	1.11	1.11	1.10	1.10	1.11	1.13	1.15	1.16
Proportion of widowed persons remarrying	.256	.246	.231	.195	.162	.136	.118	.092	.079	.073	.071	.073	.071
Proportion of divorced remarrying	.726	.697	.699	.732	.716	.727	.714	.689	.682	.686	.704	.732	.752
Average age at remarriage for widowed persons	46.4	46.9	44.8	43.5	43.5	44.5	46	49.5	52	53.6	54.1	53.3	54
Average age at remarriage for divorced persons	40.9	41.5	42.5	41.9	42	41.6	42.3	44	44.3	44.3	43.5	42	40.5
Average duration of a marriage	32.2	33.3	34.5	35.4	36.1	36.4	37.1	37.9	38.2	38	37.5	37.1	36.8
Average duration of a widowhood	8.8	8.6	8.0	8.1	8.1	8.3	8.6	8.8	8.9	8.9	8.9	8.9	8.9
Average duration of a divorce	7.7	8.5	8.2	7.6	7.8	7.8	8.4	9	9.5	10	10	9.2	8.6
Proportion of life spent never married	.480	.473	.464	.457	.449	.437	.425	.418	.407	.407	.409	.408	.422
Proportion of life spent married	.469	.478	.492	.499	.506	.516	.525	.532	.540	.538	.533	.535	.522
Proportion of life spent widowed	.046	.043	.038	.038	.037	.038	.040	.039	.039	.039	.038	.038	.037
Proportion of life spent divorced	.005	.005	.006	.006	.007	.009	.010	.011	.014	.017	.019	0.19	0.19

Source: Schoen et al. (1984:90)

Table 19 **Marital status life tables for Belgian female cohorts born 1888-1945 and 1975**

	1888-92	1893-97	1898-1902	1903-07	1908-12	1913-17	1918-22	1923-27	1928-32	1933-37	1938-42	1943-45	1975
Expectation of life at birth	51.9	53.9	55.9	58.4	59.4	61.1	63.7	65.8	67	69.3	69.3	70.7	75.2
Proportion ever marrying	.605	.632	.659	.692	.710	.730	.769	.804	.825	.855	.851	.868	.912
Proportion ever marrying of those surv. to age 15	.815	.825	.845	.861	.880	.890	.906	.926	.941	.944	.942	.941	.929
Average age at first marriage	25.4	25.6	24.6	24.1	23.9	24.4	24.2	23.6	23	22.6	22.4	22.3	22.2
Proportion of marriages ending in divorce	.040	.042	.046	.054	.063	.076	.082	.085	.094	.111	.127	.140	.156
Proportion of marriages ending in widowhood	.598	.601	.611	.608	.607	.606	.601	.595	.593	.582	.572	.564	.553
Proportion of marriages ending in death	.362	.357	.343	.338	.329	.318	.317	.320	.313	.307	.301	.297	.291
Average age at divorce	37.8	37.6	38.5	38.8	38.5	38.1	38.2	39.2	39.5	38.7	37.7	37	35.6
Average age at widowhood	61.3	61.9	62.3	62.2	62.5	62.9	63.9	64.8	64.7	64.9	64.9	65	65
Marriages per person marrying	1.12	1.11	1.11	1.11	1.11	1.11	1.10	1.09	1.09	1.09	1.11	1.12	1.14
Proportion of widowed persons remarrying	.125	.118	.113	.104	.089	.074	.053	.040	.034	.028	.026	.024	.023
Proportion of divorced remarrying	.715	.715	.695	.696	.709	.711	.693	.662	.637	.632	.634	.658	.694
Average age at remarriage for widowed persons	44.3	45	44.3	43.6	42.9	42.6	43.7	44.7	47.1	49.4	49.8	51.3	52.6
Average age at remarriage for divorced persons	40.3	39.7	40.4	40.6	40.5	40.2	40.3	41.6	42.4	42.3	42.3	41.3	39.3
Average duration of a marriage	32.3	32.8	34.3	34.9	35.4	35.4	36.5	37.9	38.3	37.2	37.7	37.2	36.6
Average duration of a widowhood	14.4	14.4	14.8	15.7	16.3	16.5	16.5	16.3	16.7	16.8	16.9	16.9	16.9
Average duration of a divorce	11.9	11.5	12.1	12	11.6	11.8	12.5	13.3	14.2	14.9	15.6	14.9	13.8
Proportion of life spent never married	.461	.452	.424	.406	.389	.386	.372	.352	.336	.330	.330	.331	.336
Proportion of life spent married	.420	.428	.450	.460	.470	.470	.483	.504	.513	.516	.512	.510	.505
Proportion of life spent widowed	.112	.113	.119	.126	.131	.133	.131	.129	.133	.132	.131	.131	.129
Proportion of life spent divorced	.006	.006	.007	.009	.010	.012	.014	.015	.018	.022	.027	.029	.030

Source: Schoen et al. (1984:91)

Bibliography

Alter G. (1988) *Family and the female life course: the women of Verviers, 1849–1880*, Milwaukee.

Duchêne, J. and Lesthaeghe, R. (1975) 'Essai de reconstitution de la population belge sous le régime français: quelques caractéristiques démographiques de la population féminine', *Population et Famille*, 36, pp. 1–47.

Dupâquier, J. (1972) 'De l'animal à l'homme: le mécanisme auto-régulateur des populaitons traditionnelles', *Revue de l'Institut de Sociologie*, 11, pp. 177–211.

Faipoult, F. (1801) *Mémoire statistique du Département de l'Escaut.*

Hajnal J. (1965) 'European marriage patterns in perspective', in D.V. Glass and D.E.C. Eversley (eds), *Population and History*, London, pp. 101–43.

Gutmann, M. (1980) *War and rural life in the early modern Low Countries*, Princeton.

Gutmann, M. (1987) 'Proto-industrialization and marriage ages in Eastern Belgium', *Annales de Démographie Historique*, pp. 143–73.

Gyssels, C. and Straeten, L. Van der (1986) *Arbeid en tewerkstelling in West-Vlaanderen (1796–1815)*, Ghent.

Jaspers, L. and Stevens, C. (1985) *Arbeid en tewerkstelling in Oost-Vlaanderen op het eind van het Ancien Regime*, Ghent.

Lesthaeghe, R. (1977) *The decline of Belgian fertility, 1800–1970*, Princeton.

Medick, H. (1997) *Weben und Uberleben in Laichingen 1650–1900*, Göttingen.

Mendels, F. (1969) 'Industrialization and population pressure in 18th century Flanders', Ph.D. dissertation, University of Wisconsin.

Mendels, F. (1972) 'Proto-industrialization: the first phase of the industrialization process', *Journal of Economic History*, 32, pp. 241–61.

Mendels, F. (1982) 'Proto-industrialization: theory and reality', paper presented to the International Economic History congress, Budapest.

Mendels, F. (1984) 'Faut-il modifier le modèle flamand?' *Annales, Economies, Sociétés, Civilisations*, 39, pp. 939–56.

Parijs, L. (1982) 'Demografische en sociaal-economische studie van de gemeente Evergem (1798-1846)', MA dissertation, University of Ghent.

Schelstraete, G. (1987) 'De relatie tussen de proto-industrie en de huwelijksleeftijd in Oost-Vlaanderen', MA dissertation, University of Ghent.

Schoen, R., Baj, J. and Woodrow, K. (1984) 'Marriage and divorce in twentieth-century Belgian cohorts', *Journal of Family History*, 9, 1, pp. 88–97.

Seccombe, W. (1995) *A millennium of family change*, New York.

Servais, P. (1982) 'Les structures agraires du duché de Limbourg et des Pays d'Outre-Meuse du XVIIe et XIXe siècle', *Annales, Economies, Sociétés, Civilisations*, pp. 303–19.

Stone, L. (1977) *The family, sex and marriage in England 1500–1800*, New York.

Vandenbroeke, C. (1976) 'Karakteristieken van het huwelijk- en voortplantings-patroon. Vlaanderen en Brabant 17e-19e eeuw', *Tijdschrift voor Sociale Geschiedenis*, 5, pp.108–45.

Vandenbroeke, C. (1976) 'Prospektus van het historisch demografisch onderzoek in Vlaanderen', *Handelingen van het Genootschap voor Geschiedenis 'Société d'Emulation' te Brugge*, 113, pp. 1–85.

Vandenbroeke, C. (1984) 'Le cas flamand : évolution sociale et comportements démographiques au XVIIe-XVIIIe siècles', *Annales, Economies, Sociétés, Civilisations*, 39, pp. 915–39.

Vandenbroeke, C. (1987) 'The regional economy of Flanders and industrial modernization', *Journal of European Economic History*, 16, pp. 149-70.

Walle, E. Van de (1965) 'La nuptialité en Belgique de 1846 à 1930 et sa relation avec le déclin de la fécondité', *Population et Famille*, 6–7, pp. 37–56.

Walle, E. Van de (1972) 'Marriage and marital fertility', in D.V. Glass and R. Revelle (eds), *Population and social change*, London, pp. 137–51.

Watkins, S. (1986) 'Regional patterns of nuptiality', in A.J. Coale and S. Watkins (eds), *The decline of fertility in Europe*, Princeton, pp. 314–36.

Wattelaer, C. (1966) 'Evolution et comparaison de la nuptialité en Belgique', *Recherches Economiques de Louvain*, pp. 407–41.

Wunsch, G. and Wattelaer, C. (1967) 'La situation démographique de la Belgique', *Dossiers de l'action sociale catholique*, pp. 65-78.

5 Access to marriage in the East Ardennes during the 19th century

George ALTER, Indiana University
Michel ORIS, University of Liège

I. Background

This chapter derives from an international research project, The EurAsia Project for the History of Population and Family, initiated in 1994 by Akira Hayami. This project includes Japanese, Chinese, Swedish, Italian, Belgian and Dutch teams. The factor unifying this obviously heterogeneous group is the availability of population registers that permit a complete study of population and family dynamics, including migrations. Such a source naturally leads to a strong interest in longitudinal analyses. Among the participants, some were especially interested in the relationships between demography and economy, while others were more concerned with family history, the household life cycle and domestic privilege as sources of differential demographic behaviour. The project is the result of a scientific accord between these two interests. Its goal is to see: firstly, how different civilizations, which for us are essentially defined by their family systems, have chosen different demographic responses (mortality, fertility, nuptiality, migrations, household dynamics); and secondly, to see how they have managed various kinds of stress (Malthusian or long run stress, short-term stress, or familial stress like the loss of a parent). In other, perhaps more lively words, we want to describe the ways in which the family systems distributed the burdens of hard times within families. Research on mortality has been most developed, especially in terms of reactions to short-term economic stress and to the death of the father. Fertility analyses are now progressing rapidly and research on marriage has just begun.

The EurAsia Project shares some common goals with the CORN network: the desire to promote a more accurate form of comparative history through the development of standard measures, the importance given to the influence of economic conditions, the focus on the countryside, the attempt to reconstruct the 'longue durée', and of course the interest in marriage. Nuptiality is a component of the demographic regime that is central to the EurAsia Project. Indeed, the classic comparison between Asia and Europe stresses this element. In pre-transitional Europe, historians following in Malthus's footsteps have emphasized the role of late marriage and definitive celibacy in adjusting the rate of population growth to economic conditions (Flinn, 1981). By denying marriage to those without the means to support an independent household, the 'European Marriage System' restrained household formation in times of scarcity. However, when the population was low, as in the aftermath of an epidemic, marriage became younger and more universal and the population recovered rapidly (see the influential work of Wrigley and Schofield (1981), and many others since). In contrast, it has been assumed that demographic adjustment in Asian societies operated primarily through the 'positive check' of mortality. In Japan, the debate has been centred largely on infanticide, while in China, overpopulation, famines and their connections with social disorders have been stressed (Saito, 1992; Lavely et al., 1990). However, recent work suggests that Euro-centric perceptions must be substantially revised, and that Asian populations had their own solutions for coping with economic stress and avoiding the positive check of mortality (see Hayami, 1987; Lee and Campbell, 1997; Tsuya and Kurosu, 1998b).

In the present study, we do not propose a major departure from the prevailing model of the European Marriage System. Indeed, the case we investigate, the municipality of Sart-lez-Spa, is a good illustration of how this model worked. Sart is located in the extreme east of Belgium in a region called the 'Hautes Fagnes', which is considered the poorest rural area of the kingdom. Although this commune is geographically quite large (56.9 km2), it has always been sparsely populated (42 inhabitants per km^2 in 1846). During the 19th century, the late ages at marriage that we observe in Sart were clearly a response to poverty and lack of economic opportunity within the commune.

However, this paper does represent a different point of view concerning the factors affecting the timing of marriage. First, in contrast to most previous work, we emphasize individual and household characteristics, particularly the relationships between parents and children and among siblings. Although discussions of the European marriage pattern have often implied that the intergenerational transmission of wealth, particularly the inheritance of farms, had an important effect on the timing of marriage, this process has rarely been studied at the individual level (Alter, 1988, 1996). Marriage was usually earlier in times of high mortality, but we have little direct evidence that young people were waiting for their own parents to die. The results presented here are broadly consistent with assumptions about the role of inheritance in marriage, but they suggest a more complicated process in which female inheritance was also important. Second, we consider the influences of general economic conditions on the probability of marriage at the individual level. The rural family was an economic unit that had the function of smoothing consumption during periods of economic stresses (Bengtsson, 1998). We will look for the effects of structural (long-term) changes in the local economy of Sart, as well as short-term stress due to annual movements in prices. Third, we compare marriage to out-migration from the commune of Sart. Migration was the most likely alternative of those who wished to marry but could not find either the means or a suitable partner. While Sart is as isolated as a village can be in densely populated Belgium, it was in a region undergoing rapid industrialization. A major textile centre was located only 20 km away, and heavy industry was not much further. Migration out of Sart was not simply an individual choice. Higher female than male out-migration created an unbalanced marriage market.

The kind of analysis presented here is only possible because we can base it on population registers. Although these are rich sources of data, they have received considerably less attention than other sources of historical demographic data. This is partly due to the limited number of locations in which population registers are found. However, the complexity of these sources has also impeded analysis. Etienne Van de Walle (1976) was the first to recognize the advantages of historical population registers and to apply some of the lessons of the family reconstitution to their study. Recent work by participants of the EurAsia Project expand on Van de Walle's approach and apply techniques from the rapidly developing field of event history analysis (Alter and Oris, 1997; Lee and Campbell, 1997; Breschi et al., 1998; Tsuya and Kurosu, 1998b; and especially for the study of marriage Alter, 1988). Bengtsson (1993) incorporated series of prices and wages into this analytical framework. His work brings together events within households with the study of short-run fluctuations in economic conditions. This synthesis of two previously separate methodologies is a foundation for the research proposed here. The wealth of information in the population registers allows us to construct models combining variables from three perspectives: the individual life course, the family life cycle and external economic conditions.

Although the Belgian team has been developing databases from several urban and/or industrial populations since the mid-1980s, we have constructed new samples of rural municipalities for comparison with the other groups engaged in the EurAsia Project. Sart is our first rural database. Indeed, the system of population registers was organized in the whole kingdom in 1846, and access to nominative documents after 1900 is normally restricted. This allows coverage of a relatively limited period of 56 years. In some towns like Verviers, annual lists of inhabitants exist for the period 1806–46, but this is extremely rare in the countryside. Sart is a very special case because the local administration organized a true population register in 1811–12, which was kept up to date until 1843. A small register covers the short period 1843–46. We have linked these documents, as well as the registers opened in 1846, 1866, 1880 and 1890, in order to reconstitute the life course of 11,402 persons who lived in Sart between 1812 and 1899, accumulating a bit more than 200,000 person-years. Some missing dates of birth or death have been found in the civil registration which also permitted us to create a data base with the 1,268 marriages celebrated in Sart between 1812 and 1890.

II. Nuptiality trends and patterns

II.1. Marriage and population: simple words, ambiguous realities

Detailed documents like the population registers offer the opportunity to highlight some ambiguities in the concepts currently used in the demographic analysis of marriage. Table 5.1 presents four different estimates of mean age at marriage and two different estimates of proportions never marrying at age 50. Although they are all similar, especially for males, they each refer to fairly different populations. The singulate mean age at marriage (SMAM) is based on information on marital status in the population registers weighted by time at risk. The marriage registers give us all persons who married in Sart. People who married in Sart but lived somewhere else are included, while those who married elsewhere but lived in Sart are not included in the marriage registers. The estimates from 'observed marriages' are based upon marriage dates reported in both the marriage registers and the population registers for people who were reported in the marriage registers. The survival analysis estimates are computed by life table analysis using observed marriages and time at risk by age for never married persons in the population registers.

Table 5.1 Various measures of mean age at first marriage and proportion never married, Sart, 1812–99

	Females	Males
Mean age at marriage		
Singulate mean age at marriage	28.3	31.5
From marriage registers	25.8	28.8
From observed marriages	26.9	30.0
Survival analysis	28.2	30.7
Per cent not married at age 50		
Population registers	11.8	14.0
Survival analysis	19.6	22.8
Quartiles of age at first marriage by survival analysis		
25 per cent	23	26
50 per cent	26	29
75 per cent	30	34

The greatest differences are between the two methods based on marital status (SMAM and survival analysis) and those that average ages observed in the marriages themselves (marriage registers and observed marriages). For females, the two former methods result in estimates of 28.3 and 28.2, compared to 25.8 and 26.9 for the latter methods. This difference may be due to the different ways that the methods are affected by out-migration. Indeed, it has been shown that migrants from Sart tended to marry earlier: between 1812 and 1890, there was at least a one-year difference in the average age at first marriage between the stayers and the movers. Among males, the average was respectively 29.7 and 28.6; among females it was 26.7 and 25.6 (Oris, 1997: 16). Thus, out-migration leads to an upward bias in SMAM and survival analysis. This can also explain why the survival analysis results in higher estimates of celibacy at age 50 than we get from the marital statuses of persons aged 50–54.

These comparisons stress the difficulties of comparative studies but, more positively, highlight two points that must be remembered: firstly, the population living in a municipality and the population marrying in this municipality are not exactly the same; and secondly, the mobility of young people causes this discrepancy, so we can not assume similar behaviours for stayers and movers.

II.2. Demography, migrations and the sex differential in the access to marriage

Whichever estimates are chosen, it is obvious that 19th century Sart followed the 'European Marriage Pattern' of late marriage and high proportions never marrying. The average ages at marriage were about 28 for women and 30 for men. Even the median ages at marriage were 26 and 29 respectively (see Table 5.1). The percentage not married at age 50 reaches a maximum of 22.8 for males and 19.6 for females. For comparison, the level of female definitive celibacy was under 10 per cent in coal and iron towns such as Tilleur and Ougrée, between 17 and 19 per cent in the textile centres of Verviers and Dison, and around 20 per cent in historic cities such as Huy and Liège (Oris, 1995: 37).

Such high levels can be seen as the results of population pressure. After the Napoleonic wars and the mortality crisis of 1816–17, the population of Sart increased in the first half of the 19th century, from 1,815 inhabitants in 1812 to 2,549 in 1851. It gradually decreased due to out-migration in the second half, to 2,091 inhabitants in 1900. This loss of 450 persons hides a much more intense out-migration flow. Indeed, the balance of births and deaths remained largely positive (around one per cent of the population each year), maintaining a constant pressure. The effect of the mid-century change in the demographic dynamic is shown very clearly in Figure 5.1, where we consider five-year moving averages of average ages at first marriages. The 'population' is the 'observed marriages' of Sart citizens contracted between the ages of 20 and 40. In 1856, exactly when the population decline starts, the male age at first marriage increases to an average of 32.2. It decreases in the 1870s to around 28, but rises again after 1881 and stays above 30 until 1900. What is remarkable is not the responsiveness of males but the contrast with female indifference. While the coefficient of variation (standard deviation divided by the average) is 0.039 for the male curve, it is only 0.025 for the female one, which shows more stable behaviour with a slow tendency towards a lower average age at first marriage. Consequently, the age gap between spouses, which was small during the first half of the 19th century, reaches approximately four years during the period 1852–60 and 1881–1900.

Figure 5.1 Average age at first marriage (mariages rages 20-39) by sex, five-year moving averages, Sart, 1812-99

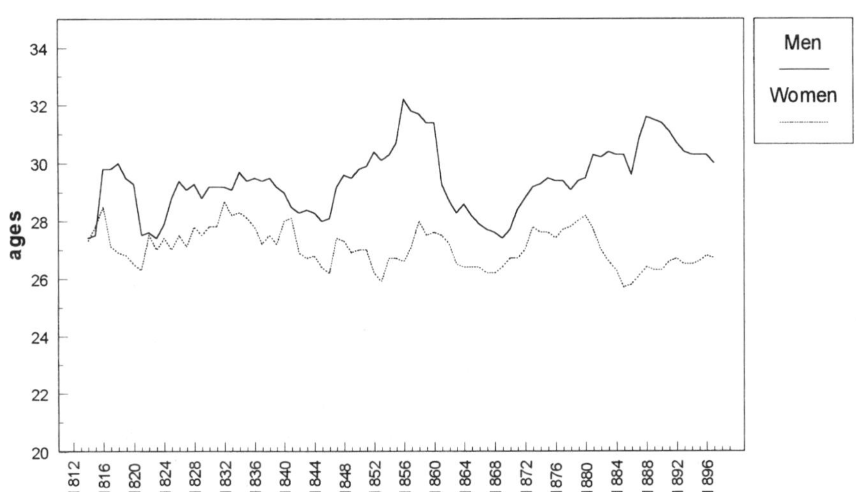

The appearance and nature of this sex differential in access to marriage appear even more clearly in Figure 5.2, which presents movements in the proportion of married persons in the age group 25–34 by sex. Among these young adults, male and female curves are surprisingly close to each other between 1812 and 1835. It is in the early 1830s that we observe the final destruction of rural proto-industrial spinning, killed by competition from the modern factories of Verviers (see Patriarca, 1986). However, after 1845 the distance between men and women became huge: 30 to 35 per cent of males attained the status of being married in the age group 25–34, against 50 to 55 per cent among females. The depression of the male curve between 1845 and 1854 creates the gender gap and contrasts with the relative stability of women.

Figure 5.2 Proportion married in the age group 25-34 by sex, Sart, 1812-99

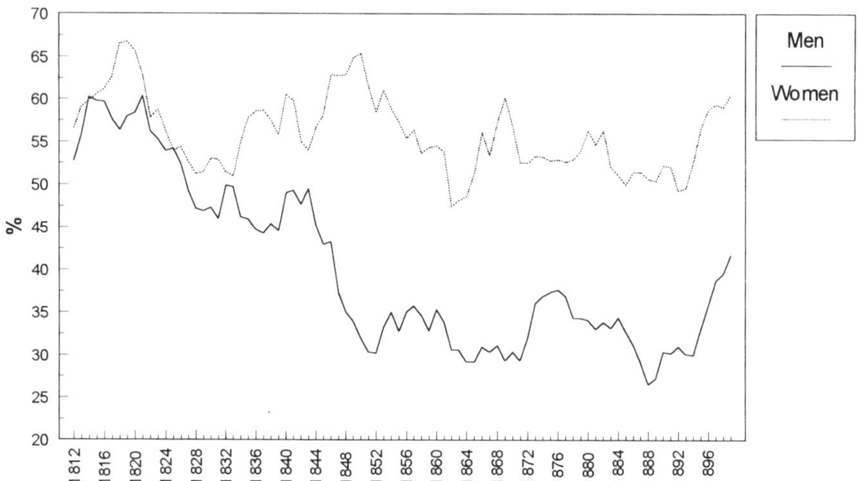

Of course, the evolution of nuptiality must be related to important changes in the economic conditions in Sart, but we reserve this discussion for Part 3 of this chapter. Here, we want to consider the 'most proximate determinant' of population dynamics, through which the economy most obviously influences population size: migration, which was sex-selective and consequently modified the structure of the marriage market. The woollen textile centre of Verviers attracted more women than men, which explains the sex ratio of 108 males per 100 females in Sart in 1846, 104 in 1890. However, these aggregate numbers have little explanatory value. We prefer following the annual evolution of the sex ratio among the never-married aged 20–39 in Figure 5.3, which we consider to be a better approximation of the marriage market for first marriages. Again, exploitation of the population register yields a dramatic picture. In 1812–1815, the marriage market was extremely bad for women: there were only 85 men for 100 women. But this statistic probably does not reflect the true situation. In the context of the Napoleonic wars, under-enumeration of unmarried males in the ages of military service was common, and many young men were tempted to avoid military obligations by assuming a precocious marriage and family responsibility.[1]

[1] These points have been observed by various historians from Adolphe Quetelet in 1847 to Jean-François Potelle (1998: 95).

Figure 5.3 Sex ratio among never-married aged 20-39, Sart, 1812-99

However, even if the starting point is artificially low, the tendency can not be contested: there was a strong and almost continuous deterioration of the male position from 1812 to 1851. In the middle of the 19th century, a value of 175 never-married men for 100 women describes a completely unbalanced marriage market. An amelioration is observed from 1855 to 1872, but the sex ratio remains around 155. After 1872, a second phase of improvement continues until the end of the century.

It is interesting to make a comparison between Sart and Tilleur. The latter was an industrial boom-town depending on coal, iron, and steel in the suburbs of Liège. Its explosive growth was due to massive flows of immigration that created a very unbalanced marriage market, similar to the one observed in Sart: 150–160 men per 100 women. However, women in Tilleur married at 25 or 26, two or three years earlier than female first marriages in Sart, and even men in Tilleur were one or two years younger than Sart men at their first marriages (Oris, 1997:4). These contrasts reflect the different opportunities that young people found for establishing a household in a rapidly expanding economy like Tilleur compared to a rural backwater such as Sart.

From all the evidence presented above, we can conclude that the nature of the marriage market changed fundamentally during the first part of the 19th century, from a surplus to a deficit of women, because of female out-migration and that a consequence was a strong gender differential in the access to marriage during the second part of the century. It seems that the marriage market had a variable influence on the timing of marriage for males who did marry: it is the probable cause of the increase in the average age at first marriages in the years 1852–60, and perhaps also the origin of the improvement between 1860 and 1880, but surely not the explanation of the increase observed in the two last decades of the 19th century. It is also astonishing not to see a deterioration of the male age at first marriage before 1851, in view of the strong rise in the sex ratio.

In other words, our results confirm the conclusions of an important debate between David Weir (1984) and Roger Schofield (1985): namely, the ability to marry and age at marriage are more or less independent.

II.3. Marriage, demographic regime and family system

As in a classical Malthusian regime, nuptiality played a decisive role in the adjustment of population to local resources. While the total marital fertility rate (from age 20) was 9.2, the total fertility rate was only 4.9. Thus, family size was reduced by four births per woman, 46 per cent, by the high proportion of fertile unmarried women (disregarding the effect of mortality). From this point of view, Sart was surely at one extremity of the scale. At the opposite end was Tilleur, an industrial boomtown in eastern Belgium, where the Malthusian brake was broken. In 1857–66, legitimate fertility was 9.2 children per married woman in Tilleur, and the general fertility rate was 6.8.

Figure 5.4, which presents the Coale index of proportions married, I_m, shows that the age and marital composition of women living in Sart becomes less and less favourable to high fertility. I_m initially declines from a level of 0.491 to 0.391 between 1816 and 1831. There are then twenty years in which the nuptiality brake is relaxed until population decline begins in the 1850s. The next period is characterized by stability, and I_m stays around 0.400. Finally, there is a brief accentuation of control during the late 1880s and early 1890s before nuptiality begins to recover at the end of the 19th century. This downward movement of I_m contrasts with the continuity of age and access to marriage among females (Figures 5.1 and 5.2). The explanation is again the higher propensity of couples married at young ages to leave Sart, and this propensity increased during the 19th century.

Figure 5.4 I_m, Sart, 1812-99

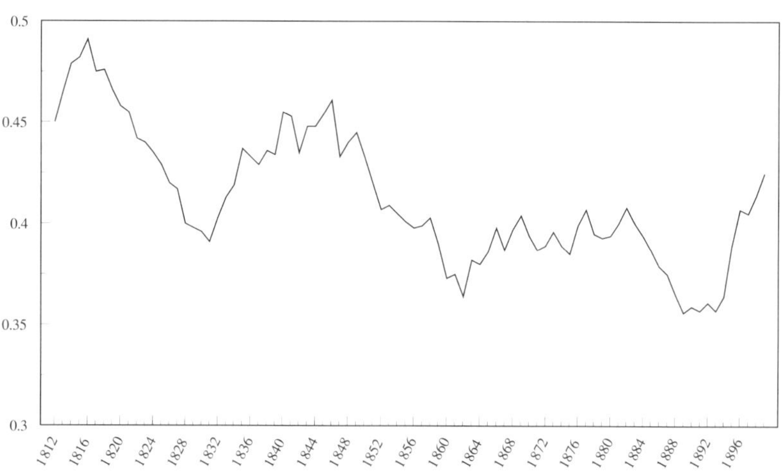

Nuptiality and out-migration acted together to control the population size at an aggregate level, but they also acted together at the household level, and their respective roles cannot be clearly distinguished. In Sart as well as in the whole Walloon area, the rule of neo-localism was followed and marriage implied departure from the parental family, if not immediately, then at least after a short time. As we have seen above, emigration was sometimes linked to a marriage outside Sart. We often have no trace of union in our data, but we do have a record of the departure. We have used this information to compute life tables of 'leaving home' which are summarized in Figure 5.5 in the form of survivors curves (for data and methods, see Capron and Oris, 1997). The higher curve on these graphs can be read as follows: under the conditions observed in Sart between 1812 and 1846, among 100 male babies, 99.3 per cent of those alive at their fifth birthday still lived with at least one of their parents. At age 25, 76 per cent of this cohort were still at home, and 31 per cent were so at the age of 35. However, these data only consider the effects of the mobility of children.

On the upper curve, we have added the effects of parents' deaths to the effects of child mobility. Parental mortality permitted children who stayed at home to succeed the previous generation. With child mobility and parental death acting together, there are now 62 per cent of the males living with parental presence/control at the age of 25, and 19 per cent at the age of 35. This means that in the process of 'emancipation' from the preceding generation the 'push' effect of mortality affected 14 per cent of children at age 25 and 12 per cent at age 35. If we now compare males with females, it appears that daughters' departures were more precocious and intense (64 per cent of survivors at 25 and 22 per cent at 35, if we only consider the 'child mobility effect'), but the impact of the parents' deaths is of a similar magnitude for those who stayed at home.

If we look at the evolution of leaving home over time, we find a sex differential again. Among women, the decrease of adult and old age mortality during the 19th century is more than compensated by increased child mobility, but this is not the case among men. From the life tables for the males of Sart, the 'average age at living independently' was 27.2 in 1812–46, 28.2 in 1847–70 and 28.7 in 1871–1900. Among females, it was respectively 25.5, 25.9 and 24.9. Simple cross-sectional data confirms the deterioration of the male situation. In 1846, in the age group 25–59, 68.2 per cent of the men were head of their household. In 1890, this proportion had fallen to 62.8 per cent.

Most historical studies of the 'leaving home' process confuse the effects of children's departures and those of parents' deaths, and their methodologies vary (see the excellent critical synthesis in Dribe, 1997). Nevertheless, when we view our results in comparison to other studies, the family system in Sart appears to have been extremely tense. If living apart from parents was the ideal, the situation of Sart children, though not the worst observed, was surely one of the worst (Dribe, 1997: 5–6; Capron-Oris, 1997: 24–25; Steckel, 1996: 515; Janssens, 1993: 134). The difficulties they faced are illustrated by the results discussed above: couples who married at a younger age had a higher propensity to out-migrate than those who married later. Michel Oris has analysed the duration of time between marriage and departure from

Figure 5.5 Children surviving in cohabitation with their parents, by sex and period, Sart, 1812-1900

Sart in another publication (Oris, 1997: 16–17). Among the 'movers', only one third of the women and one man in four left the village less than one year after the marriage. Consequently, we cannot say that the union was usually part of a plan to migrate or a preparation for the dangerous world of big industrial cities. The alternative interpretation is that those who did not respect the traditional brake of delayed marriage were less able to constitute a viable autonomous household and were finally obliged to leave Sart to find resources elsewhere, especially in the growing towns.

III. Event history analysis

III.1. Methods

Table 5.3 presents the results of an event history analysis of marriage and migration for 19th-century Sart (averages for the explanatory variables are in Table 5.2). We include only persons who had never been married at ages 18–39. The data and methods have been described more extensively elsewhere (Alter, 1988; Alter and Oris, 1997), so we include only a brief explanation here.

Table 5.2 Means of covariates used in the event history analysis

	Females	Males
Time period		
1812–1846	0.39	0.32
1847–1875	0.32	0.37
1876–1900	0.29	0.32
Occupation of head of household		
Agriculture	0.63	0.61
Unstable	0.08	0.08
Industry and crafts	0.07	0.06
Service	0.05	0.07
No profession	0.07	0.08
No occupation listed	0.11	0.10
Relationship to head of household		
Head of household	0.02	0.02
Non-kin of head	0.03	0.06
Siblings present in household		
Older brother	0.33	0.32
Younger brother	0.56	0.53
Older sister	0.30	0.29
Younger sister	0.52	0.52
Parental mortality and co-residence		
Both alive	0.33	0.32
Mother only	0.16	0.17
Father only	0.15	0.13
No parents	0.17	0.18
Father died < 3 years, mother alive	0.07	0.07
Father died < 3 years, mother dead	0.02	0.03
Mother died < 3 years, father alive	0.05	0.05
Mother died < 3 years, father dead	0.03	0.03
Both died < 3 years	0.02	0.01
Prices		
Price level	2.30	2.30
Difference from trend	0.00	0.00

The entries in Table 5.3 are estimates of the relative risk of marriage associated with a one unit change in an explanatory variable. A relative risk of 2.0 implies that a one unit increase in that variable doubled the likelihood of marriage. A relative risk of 0.5 implies that the risk of marriage decreased by 50 per cent. For example, the estimate of 1.53 in the model of female marriage during the period 1847–75 means that women were 53 per cent more likely to marry during that period than in the reference period, 1812–46. All of the explanatory variables used in the model are binary ('dummy') variables, except for the two price variables.

Table 5.3 Estimated relative risks of marriage and migration by sex for never-married persons, ages 18-39, Sart, 1812–1900

	Marriage		Migration	
Covariates	Females	Males	Females	Males
Time period				
1812–1846	1.00	1.00	1.00	1.00
1847–1875	1.53	1.04	17.07	5.15
1876–1900	1.18	0.80	13.75	4.98
Prices				
Price level	0.74	0.66	0.35	1.30
Difference from trend	0.72	0.83	1.51	1.63
Occupation of head of household				
Agriculture	1.00	1.00	1.00	1.00
Unstable	0.74	0.82	2.99	2.10
Industry and crafts	0.87	1.05	1.53	1.92
Service	0.89	0.60	2.01	2.90
No profession	0.72	0.59	1.40	1.43
No occupation listed	1.13	1.07	1.93	1.81
Relationship to head of household				
Head of household	0.80	0.82	0.70	1.07
Non-kin of head	0.42	0.23	1.46	1.92
Siblings present in household				
Older brother	0.87	0.72	0.79	0.67
Younger brother	0.78	0.87	0.91	0.92
Older sister	0.77	0.70	0.69	0.73
Younger sister	0.96	0.71	1.27	1.07
Parental mortality and co-residence				
Both alive	1.00	1.00	1.00	1.00
Mother only	1.22	1.15	1.14	1.17
Father only	0.96	0.99	1.06	1.35
No parents	1.06	0.97	2.57	2.46
Father died <3yrs, mother alive	1.60	0.99	0.55	0.97
Father died <3yrs, mother dead	0.97	1.10	0.63	1.71
Mother died <3yrs, father alive	1.27	1.39	0.84	1.07
Mother died <3yrs, father dead	1.49	0.79	2.33	2.83
Both died <3yrs	1.88	3.04	2.10	3.33
Partial max. log likelihood	-6150.43	-5388.28	-2955.29	-4765.92
Overall model Chi-squared	76.22	87.55	515.91	128.64
Overall p-value	0.00	0.00	0.00	0.00
Total time at risk	13125.8	18290.7	13125.8	18290.7
Total events	957	817	494	764

Estimates in this table were obtained using the Cox partial likelihood procedure. The Cox procedure estimates the effects of covariates without explicitly describing the shape of the 'baseline hazard'. In this case, the baseline hazard describes the way in which risks of marriage/migration change with age. While we know that marriage and migration vary systematically by age, the shapes of these age profiles are not our focus here. Thus, the estimates presented in Table 5.3 are adjusted for the effects of age, even though changes in risk with age are not explicitly described.

III.2. Time period

The first panel of Table 5.3 compares marriage and migration patterns across three broad time periods. We see here the effects of important changes in Sart and the economy of eastern Belgium.

During the first half of the 19th century Sart experienced a certain amount of de-industrialization, as pre-industrial forms of iron and textile production moved from rural areas to industrial agglomerations. There was little change in agricultural techniques during this period, and inhabitants of Sart depended upon forest products and swidden agriculture from extensive communally owned lands. This was a period of slow population increase. The years from 1847 to 1875 were the peak of the industrial revolution in Eastern Belgium. Production was expanding rapidly in Verviers, a nearby woollen textile centre, and in the coal and iron industries around Liège. Under pressure from the national government, some communal lands were sold to private owners during this period. Inhabitants of Sart continued to have rights to use communal forests and peat bogs on the plateau known as the *hautes fagnes*, but the population of Sart began to decline. After 1875 industrial expansion in Verviers slowed, and new agricultural techniques such as artificial fertilizers were applied in the Ardennes, without clear success. Exploitation of the forests to furnish timber for the coal mines also increased. Overall, the local economy required less and less labor.

These economic adaptations are quite evident in the estimates shown in Table 5.3. Out-migration from Sart accelerated dramatically after 1846. The risk of migration for men was five times greater after 1846, but even this increase is dwarfed by the changes that affected women. Compared to 1812-46, women were seventeen times more likely to migrate from 1847-75 and more than 13 times more likely from 1875–1900. Part of this difference may be due to defects in the reporting of migration in the population registers before 1846, but it corresponds to other evidence that the balance of migration shifted after 1846. Furthermore, it is noteworthy that the change is greatest for women. The textile factories of Verviers were heavily dependent upon female labour. While men could find work in Verviers too, the demand for male labour was greater in the coal mines and iron mills in the Meuse valley.

Changes in marriage behaviour were less dramatic than those in migration, but no less important. Women were 53 per cent more likely to marry in the second period (1847–75), and the estimate for the third period is also positive. The risk of marriage for men hardly changed after 1846, but men were 20 per cent less likely to marry after 1875. Both of these patterns are explained by the heavy out-migration of women.

On the one hand, women whose marriage prospects in Sart were poor could leave the village and find work in the textile mills. On the other hand, female out-migration made it more difficult for the men who remained to find wives.

III.3. Prices

An unusual feature of this model is the inclusion of two variables derived from national price series, which are measured annually. The price variables are specific in time but apply to all individuals in the community during that time. We use statistical software developed by Goran Brostrom that associates prices with the corresponding time periods in individual lives.

Figure 5.6 Price series, Sart, 1812-99

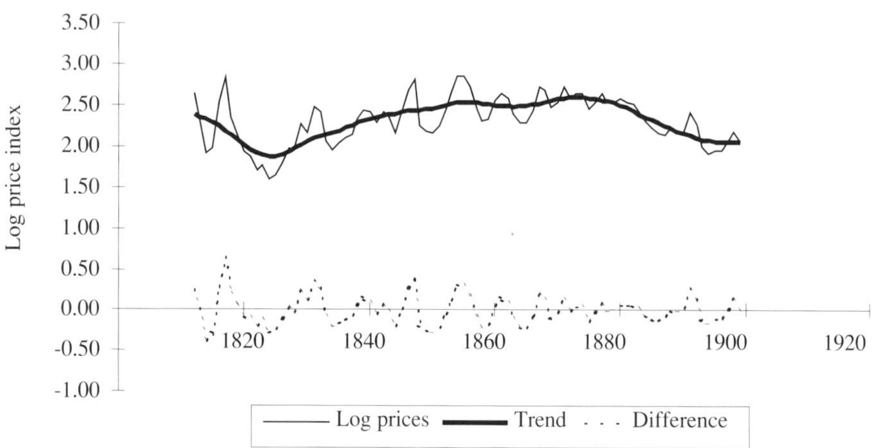

Our price variables are based on an index of the prices of several agricultural commodities, particularly grains, measured in Verviers, the largest nearby market.[2] Although detailed information on wages is not available, we believe that this index provides a good measurement of short-term changes in real incomes. High prices are usually caused by poor harvests that reduce agricultural incomes, but an agricultural population can also benefit from high prices because the value of any marketable surplus will be increased. However, Sart was always a marginal agricultural area that depended on the sale of forest products to supplement grain and livestock production.

[2] The construction of this index is detailed in Oris (1998).

The two price variables included in the model are intended to distinguish between long-run and short-run influences. Prices were high after the Napoleonic wars, fell during the first half of the century, rose to a peak in the 1870s, and then fell again after that. We have used the Hodrick-Prescott algorithm to smooth the price series and remove the effects of short-run changes while leaving the long-run pattern. The variable labelled 'price level' in Table 5.3 is the series of annual prices after application of the Hodrick-Prescott filter (for a detailed discussion, see Alter and Oris, 1997). The variable labelled 'difference from trend' is the difference between the original series and the price level. Our focus is on these short-run changes in prices, and the price level is included only as a control for other unmeasured variations in the economy (Bengtsson, 1997).

Although only one of the four estimated relative risks achieves statistical significance, short-run changes in prices affected both marriage and migration. Young people of both sexes were less likely to marry and more likely to migrate in years of high prices. Since our price variables are calculated on a logarithmic scale, a one unit increase in the difference from the trend means that prices would double. When prices doubled, the likelihood of marriage decreased by about 20 per cent and the likelihood of out-migration increased by more than 50 per cent.

III.4. Occupation

Since occupations were often not reported for children, we classify individuals according to the occupation of the head of household. The most common occupation was agriculture, which included about two-thirds of the population. The main occupation in the 'unstable' group was *journalier* (day labourer). Those with 'no profession' reported an occupation like *ménagère* (housewife) or *rentier*. Occupations were often missing in the earlier registers, and many of those who did not list an occupation were actually engaged in agriculture. There was a clear difference between farmers and others in Sart. Young adults living in non-agricultural households were less likely to marry in Sart and more likely to migrate.

III.5. Relationship to head of household

Most unmarried persons in Sart were living in a household headed by a parent, but small percentages were living with non-kin or headed their own households. Both of these groups were less likely to marry, and those living with non-kin were much more likely to migrate.

III.6. Siblings in the household

While the Belgian Civil Code followed the Napoleonic Code in requiring an equal division of the inheritance, siblings were still differentiated by sex and birth order. Elder siblings would be expected to help their parents to support siblings too young to work, while the labour of younger siblings might make it easier for their elders to leave the nest. Custom also prescribed that siblings, especially sisters, should marry in birth order. The marriage of the *cadette* was generally regarded as a bad omen for her older sister. In addition, the labour of sons and daughters was qualitatively different. While males could command higher wages in the labour market, female labour was no less essential on the farm. For these reasons, variables have been included in the model to indicate the presence in the household of siblings of each sex and relative ages.

The main finding is that an unmarried person who lived with any type of sibling was less likely to marry or to migrate. On the one hand, this may have been due to some kind of increasing returns to scale in large households. Families that had more adult children at home may have been more adept at finding ways to employ them and less willing to let them go. On the other hand, this result may be due to unmeasured differences among households in terms of preferences about celibacy or the timing of marriage. If siblings in some families shared some kind of propensity toward permanent bachelorhood and spinsterhood, the best indicator of their lower likelihood of marriage would be the fact that their siblings were still unmarried and living at home.

There is one noteworthy exception to this overall pattern, however. Women with younger sisters were more likely to migrate, and the presence of younger sisters had no effect on their marriage chances. This may have been an adaptation to the interests of the younger sister in a system that preferred marriage in birth order. Even if the elder sister were not successful in a different marriage market, her absence would have served the interests of the *cadette*.

III.7. Parental mortality and co-residence

Finally, we examine the effects of intergenerational transfers on marriage by looking at the effects of mortality and co-residence with parents. We divide the sample into nine categories that identify which parent or parents they lived with and also whether their mother or father died in the preceding three years. The reference category is persons living with both parents. Next, we identify persons whose parent died more than three years earlier, and lastly we consider those with a parental death in the previous three years according to whether this was the first or second parental death. The results of this analysis are both dramatic and surprising.

The most striking finding is that both marriage and migration were much more likely if both parents had died in the preceding three years. When this occurred, men were more than three times more likely to marry or migrate, and the risks for women almost doubled. Of course, this occurred in only a handful of cases, but these effects are strong enough to be statistically significant for males.

The surprising findings are that parental deaths had larger effects on the marriages of women than men, and that the mother's death was just as important as the death of the father. These results are surprising because we expect farmland to pass from father to son. Even though the Civil Code required equal inheritances, it was not necessary to actually divide the property among the heirs. One child could take over the farm and compensate his siblings in cash or other goods (possibly by mortgaging the land), or the siblings could all continue to own shares of land that was farmed by one son who regularly compensated his siblings. If inheritance of the farm was the obstacle delaying the marriages of young men (and we have no doubt that many men in 19th-century Sart were waiting to take control of their father's land), then the risk of marriage for young men should have increased after a father's death. Instead, we find almost no effect when only the father died, even though there is an enormous effect when the father and mother died both. Moreover, the father's death has a large and statistically significant effect on female marriage, and males were more likely to respond to the deaths of their mothers by migrating.

Of course, inheritances could stimulate marriages by passing through daughters as well as through sons. A young woman with a dowry was much more eligible in the marriage market, and her contribution was just as important to the success of the new household as was her bridegroom's. One of the peculiarities of demographic analysis is that we always measure the fertility and nuptiality of women, even when we theorize about the behaviour of men. We need to know more about female inheritance and the behaviour of widows. Clearly, we also need to know more about how property was transmitted from generation to generation in Sart.

IV. Conclusions

This chapter has taken some first steps in the study of marriage in 19th-century rural Belgium. Our basic point is the close connection, in our data but also in past family strategies and individual behaviours, between nuptiality and mobility. We have shown that aggregate statistics, such as the average age at first marriage, are affected by migration in different ways, and we have emphasized the need to place individual behaviour in a family and household context. Our most original and surprising result is the better capacity of women, compared to men, to cope with economic stress.

All of these findings suggest that marriage in 19th-century Sart was a source of tension in a very strained family system. This tension is an aspect of a regional family culture that certainly requires further study. But it is also understandable as a consequence of a spatial and chronological distortion: while the industrial revolution broke down the traditional limitations described by Thomas Malthus at the national and even international level, Malthusian population pressure was rising in Sart and the East Ardennes throughout the 19th century.

Bibliography

Alter, G. (1988) *Family and the female life course: the women of Verviers, Belgium, 1849–1880*, Madison.

Alter G. (1996) 'The European Marriage Pattern as solution and problem: households of the elderly in Verviers, Belgium, 1831', in A. Bideau et al. (ed.), *Les systèmes démographiques du passé*, Lyon, pp. 3–19.

Alter G. and Oris, M. (1997) 'Mortality and economic stress: individual and household responses in a 19th century Belgian village', *EurAsia Population Project Working Paper* 13.

Bengtsson, T. (1993) 'Combined time-series and life-event analysis: the impact of economic fluctuations and air temperature on adult mortality by sex and occupation in a Swedish mining parish, 1757–1850', in D. Reher and R. Schofield (ed.), *Old and new methods in historical demography*, Oxford, pp. 239–59.

Bengtsson, T. (1997) 'Combined life event and time series analysis: the impact of economic fluctuations and household cycles on mortality in rural Sweden, 1750–1850', *EurAsia Population Project Working Paper* 5.

Bengtsson, T. (1998) 'Why dad dies: the mortality of men in their working ages in the 18th and 19th centuries', paper presented to the European Science Foundation Conference 'When dad died: family stress and household dynamics in historical societies', Venice, 23–24 May.

Breschi, M., Derosas, R. and Manfredini, M. (1998) 'Fatal seasons in children's survival: Italy, 19th century', *EurAsia Population Project Working Paper* 15.

Capron, C, and Oris, M. (1997) 'Ruptures de cohabitation entre parents et enfants dans les villes et les campagnes du Pays de Liège au 19e siècle', paper presented at the Entretiens Jacques Cartier 1997, Lyon, 8–10 December.

Dribe, M. (1997) *Rural youth migration from a household perspective: a study of the age at leaving home in Scania, Sweden 1829-1870*, Lund.

Flinn, M.W. (1981) *The European demographic system, 1850–1820*, Baltimore.

Janssens, A. (1993) *Family and social change: the household as a process in an industrializing community*, Cambridge.

Hayami, A. (1987) 'Another Fossa Magna: proportion marrying and age at marriage in late 19th century Japan', *Journal of Family History*, 12, pp. 57–72.

Lavely, W., Lee, J. and Wang Feng (1990) 'Chinese demography: the state of the field', *Journal of Asian Studies*, 49, pp. 807–34.

Lee, J. and Campbell, C. (1997) *Fate and Fortune in rural China: social organization and population behavior in Liaoning 1774–1873*, Cambridge.

Oris, M. (1995) 'Le cours de la vie féminine dans les villes industrielles du Pays de Liège au 19e siècle. Premiers résultats', paper presented for the International Congress of Historical Sciences, Montréal, 27 August–3 September.

Oris, M. (1997) 'The age at marriage of migrants during the industrial revolution', EurAsia Population Project Working Paper 3.

Oris, M. (1998) 'A brief discussion on the economic series in 19th century Belgium', *EurAsia Population Project Working Paper* 19.

Patriarca, S. (1986) *Farmers, spinners, weavers and their families: proto-industry and the factory system in Charneux, Belgium, 1770–1870*, MA thesis, University of Texas at Austin.

Potelle, J.-F. (1998) 'Dison au milieu du 19e siècle. Prosopographie d'une population industrielle', in C. Desama and M. Oris (ed.), *Dix essais sur la démographie urbaine de la Wallonie au XIXe siècle*, Brussels, pp. 91–124.

Saito, O. (1992) 'Infanticide and Japan's pre-transition demographic regime', in *Historiens et Populations. Liber Amicorum Etienne Hélin*, Louvain-la-Neuve, pp. 249–57.

Schofield, R. (1985) 'English marriage patterns revisited', *Journal of Family History*, 9, pp. 2–20.

Steckell, R.H. (1996) 'The age at leaving home in the United States, 1850–1860', *Social Science History*, 20, 4, pp. 507–32.

Tsuya, N. and Satomi, K. (1998a) 'Patterns and covariates of fertility in 18th and 19th century rural Japan: evidence from two Northeastern villages', *EurAsia Population Project Working Paper* 16.

Tsuya, N. and Kurosu, S. (1998b) 'The mortality effects of adult male death on women and children in household in 18th and 19th century rural Japan: evidence from two northeastern villages', paper presented to the European Science Foundation Conference 'When dad died: family stress and household dynamics in historical societies', Venice, 23–24 May.

Walle, E. van de (1976) 'Household dynamics in a Belgian village, 1847–1866', *Journal of Family History*, 1, pp. 80–94.

Weir, D. (1984) 'Rather late than never: celibacy and age at marriage in English cohort fertility, 1541–1871', *Journal of Family History*, 8, pp. 340–54.

Wrigley E.A. and Schofield, R.S. (1981) *The population history of England, 1541–1871: a reconstruction*, London.

6 Economic opportunities and age at marriage: an analysis of 19th-century micro data for the Netherlands

Frans van Poppel, Netherlands Interdisciplinary Demographic Institute
Jan Nelissen, Brabant University

I. Introduction

Short-term economic fluctuations such as harvest failures and economic recessions were a continuous characteristic of pre-industrial society. These forms of economic distress had provoked considerable demographic responses. Studies of England, France, Sweden, the Netherlands and other countries have shown that nuptiality, mortality and fertility were affected by variations in the supply of agricultural products and yearly changes in prices and real wages. In particular, the close connection between grain prices and other indicators of short-term economic change and marriage frequency has attracted the attention of contemporary observers and of historians as well.

The idea that short-term economic fluctuations influenced nuptiality was based on the norm in northwestern Europe whereby a minimum amount of resources – often in the form of savings – had to be accumulated prior to marriage. During periods when real wages were low, the time needed to accumulate savings may have been relatively long, and hence age at marriage relatively high. In an agrarian economy, the price of food was a very important factor in determining the level of the standard of living, and fluctuations in the price of grain were the primary determinants of variations in the real wage from one year to another. Annual variations in the price of grain affected nearly every sector of the European economy before the industrial era: for the majority of farmers lower prices meant loss of income, labourers lost employment and income, townspeople were forced to spend more on provisions, and therefore demand for services and products of industry fell off. In an economy where expenditures on food accounted for a high proportion of all consumption, fluctuations in grain prices caused large variations in the purchasing power available for other goods and services (Galloway, 1988).

In the course of time, the impact of poor harvests on nuptiality has diminished. This was the consequence of increased market integration, expansion of transport networks and more efficient distribution. As industrialization progressed and large classes of the population were no longer dependent upon agricultural production, grain prices became less relevant as an indicator of real income. As a consequence, the relation between grain prices and nuptiality as it existed until the first half of the 19th century has totally disappeared. This is not to say that from that time on a relation between marriage frequency and the economic situation no longer existed: many nineteenth-century and early twentieth-century statisticians have shown that non-agricultural short-term economic indicators such as exports and unemployment rates were strongly related to the annual variations in marriage frequency (for an overview, see Thomas, 1925 and Southall and Gilbert, 1996). Economic and demographic historians have shown less interest in the relationship between nuptiality and economic conditions in the industrial period, and have been much more concerned with an understanding of behaviour in an agricultural pre-industrial society (Southall and Gilbert, 1996; Schellekens, 1997).

This is not the only aspect of the relation between economy and marriage which has been relatively neglected. Most modern studies which examine the relationship between short-term economic variations and nuptiality follow the same procedure: they remove the general movement upward or downward – the secular trend – from the economic and demographic time series so that they are able to isolate the fluctuations. For prices, this removes most of the influence of secular real income change, but leaves behind variance closely related to short-run changes in real income.

The link between marriage and the secular trend in the economy itself has not received much attention, apart from studies dealing with the effect of proto-industrialization on age at marriage.[1] An adequate treatment in which the relationships have been expressed in quantitative terms was lacking until recently. Wrigley and Schofield (1993: 422), however, have pointed out the important role which long-term economic trends might have played in marriage decisions. They argue that precisely because marriages lasted for a long time, not only did short-term prospects affect marriage decisions, but the evaluation of the probable course of events over half a lifetime also played a part.

Timing and incidence of marriage were influenced by, for example, the trend in real wages because the savings for marriage were accumulated over a period of years – ten or twenty years on the part of parents, five to ten for the children – and a sudden upturn in wages would not have such a large impact on the amount saved (Macfarlane, 1986: 262–90). Before the prospective spouses decided that the time was good for marrying, the prospects over the likely term of the marriage had to match some standard in the actors' minds. This in turn partly depended on their reaction to trends over a preceding period of some length. Financing a viable marriage required not only some prior accumulation but also a viable economic future, and the perception of these future prospects might have been influenced by long-term economic trends. This does not imply a knowledge of trends in real wages and a conscious attempt to adjust behaviour accordingly. Other mechanisms might have been at work

---

[1] Thomas (1925: 36) referred to the work of Aftalion (*Les crises périodiques de surproduction*, Paris, 1913) and Hector Denis (*Les index des phénomènes moraux*, Brussels, 1911) both of whom in tracing the economic influences upon the marriage rates, distinguished between secular and cyclical movements.

which could have produced an impact of changing real wages on marriage patterns over a longer period of time. Wrigley and Schofield suggest that changes in the trend of real wages must initially have been difficult to distinguish from the random annual fluctuations in real wages produced by the varying fortunes of the harvest: 'Only the slow accumulation of new readings over a period of years after the retrospectively identified turning point can have provided the "information" needed to convince the "system" that a change of trend had occurred' (Wrigley and Schofield, 1993: 434). Wrigley and Schofield describe two mechanisms through which long-term economic trends might influence the couple's perceptions. In a situation in which marriage decisions were partly made by the parental generation, or in which the bride and groom perceived their prospects largely through the eyes of their parents, a parental generation brought up in a downward phase in the real wage cycle without ever reaching the standard of living they had known in childhood and early youth might communicate their pessimistic experience to the next generation. An 'appropriate' change in marriage behaviour would then be very slow to appear. Wrigley and Schofield also argued that the social mechanisms that translated the pressure of economic circumstances into changing marriage practices could have been insensitive to slight changes in the trend of real wages as a consequence of which marriage patterns responded only after the new trend in real wages was well established.[2]

In this chapter, we study the relationship between long-term economic changes and marriage using data for the Netherlands for the 19th and early 20th centuries. It is not only the period to which we direct our attention, and the fact that we concentrate on the effects of long-term economic developments which differentiates this study from earlier papers.[3] What is also important is that we make use of demographic data which allow us a clearer insight into the mechanisms through which the economy affected the marriage decisions of the population. To illustrate this point, we must first give a short review of some of the characteristics of the studies dealing with the short-term effects of the economy on marriage.

II. Literature review

The existing literature provides little assistance in determining the mechanisms by which the state of the economy affected marriage patterns. This is in part due to the fact that in most of the relevant studies, only very crude data have been used. This

[2] Weir (1984: 341; see also Schellekens 1997) has suggested that the relationship between the long-term trend and age at marriage might be more complicated than is suggested above. When people could choose between saving for late marriage and downward mobility, prospective couples may have decided to opt for downward mobility and a fall in the wage could then reduce the waiting time for marriage. Why would one waste one's life savings when so little could be saved?

[3] For an analysis of short-term changes in marriage in the Netherlands as a consequence of economic fluctuations, see van Zanten and Van den Brink (1939), De Jonge (1968: 263–64) and, for a more sophisticated analysis, Galloway (1988).

applies to economic as well as demographic indicators. Although the demographic literature has stressed that the timing of marriage did not always run parallel to the intensity with which marriages were contracted, both aspects of marriage usually are not separately analysed. Additionally, a distinction between first marriages and remarriages and a sex-specific analysis of the effects of the economy are lacking. One might expect that people marrying for the first time were more strongly affected by the economic situation than remarrying couples, and that economic constraints played a greater role for marrying men than for marrying women. From a theoretical point of view, one could expect that some socio-economic groups and couples living in specific regions might be much more vulnerable to the up and downs of the economy; yet the usual type of analysis does not consider socio-economic differences in the response to the changes of the economy, nor does it discuss differences in regional susceptibility. Each of these aspects will be elaborated on below.

The fundamental problem affecting many of the studies dealing with the impact of changing economic situations on marriage behaviour is that they are based on aggregated demographic and economic data. Yet, the way the household responded to economic change was conditioned by the norms, traditions and values of the region and social class in which the family members were embedded. Using data for a whole country or region makes it difficult to examine the impact of regional and social differences in these reactions, and thus to detect the direct causal determinants of marriage change. The most extensive account of the way in which decisions regarding marriage were rooted in cultural norms and customs specific to each social class is given by Macfarlane (1986: 262–90). According to Macfarlane, each marriage was the outcome of a calculation of costs and benefits by the couple, their friends and close relatives. In marriage, individuals could satisfy their psychological, sexual and social needs, but they knew that if marriage occurred at the wrong time or to the wrong person, there would be serious consequences in terms of socio-economic position and personal happiness.

To establish a new household, a couple had to have saved enough and had to have the skills necessary to run a household. Marriage involved substantial initial expenses – the acquisition of such items as pots, pans and furniture as well as the ability to meet rent payments or their equivalent – and a relatively high level of continuing costs and skills were required to be able to run the household independently. There might be capital costs because the household was often a workshop (farm equipment and stock to be bought and as well as continuing commitments in the form of rents, rates, payments in kind and so on). Acquiring the resources and skills necessary for marriage was a protracted process for both potential partners, but the length of time involved varied over time and between different groups (Wrigley et al. 1997: 123–25).

For those who commanded greater resources, the timing of marriage might be a matter of choice. For this group, it was important to marry only at an age at which they could be sure that they were able to maintain the standard of living to which they had been accustomed when single. Fear of poverty, of loss of social status, of loss of leisure and pleasure held them back from marriage, while illicit intercourse made it possible to compensate for the lack of sexual satisfaction. The pressure on farmers and tradesmen was different: they were only expected to marry when they were settled in a business or on a farm which enabled them to support a family. People were thus restrained from marriage by the shortage of remunerative employment, the shortage of farms or businesses, or in merchant and professional employment, the lack of a salary sufficient to keep a wife and family. For other groups, the speed with which they acquired the skills and assembled the resources needed for marriage could vary considerably.

In judging the consequences of the decision as to whether or not to marry and in balancing the costs and advantages of marriage, the economic situation played an important role. In periods of lowered real wages and with uncertain prospects for employment, marriage might be postponed or cancelled. Men would save their earnings for some years, and only when their savings had reached a certain level could they consider marriage. A continued period of increased wages and greater opportunities for labour would result in a weakening of the pressures against marriage, and might lower the age at marriage. Increased wages might lead to a shortening of the period normally necessary to accumulate the savings for marriage. Children could also benefit from the fact that their parents had saved enough over a period of rising real incomes to release their marriage portions while they were still relatively young. When the demand for labour increased, people would find themselves moving faster up career structures and hence attaining earlier the level at which it would be considered reasonable and safe to marry.

Yet periods of economic growth might also raise levels of expectation. What was considered a 'reasonable level of maintenance' for one generation might not be so for the next. As wealth increased, general expectations could rise, and the desire for upward social mobility might cause individuals to defer marriage for a few years longer. By that time they might have reached a higher level of wealth, which could then be cemented by a better marriage. In the absence of a fixed standard, people found that increases in the wealth of the society, instead of making marriage easier to enter into, might have the effect of raising the threshold (Macfarlane, 1986).

The question is, how did members of the different social classes, given their ideas about the standards of savings, expected income, comfort or vocational training, react to changes in their economic situation? Many studies dealing with the relationship between economic changes and changes in marriage either assume implicitly or mention explicitly that different segments of the population were affected differently. The 19th-century Dutch statistician Sandberg argued in the 1860s that to examine whether marrying men and women were indeed reacting to the prices of the basic necessities of life, 'special statistics, regarding in particular the diversity of social classes and states in society, have to be consulted'. When marriage rates did not correspond to the prices of wheat, the reason probably had to be found in 'circumstances which only come to light by descending to the statistics of the separate regions and social classes' (Sandberg, 1866). The Dutch professor of medicine Evers (1882: 21–22) argued that the changing economic circumstances 'did not effect the lower classes; neither did those people, who were rich enough to comply with all the requirements demanded to establish a household. These people also marry whenever they feel inclined to do so. This is not the case with the other members of society.'[4]

Present-day researchers, studying the reactions to fluctuations in harvest and grain prices, also mention differences in reactions according to the sector of the economy. Galloway (1993) suggested that poor harvests generating high cereal prices may have benefited the large grain producers and distributors, but may also have caused suffering for landless labourers, small farmers and most urban dwellers. The profits of businessmen in control of distribution probably increased. The urban poor suffered along with their rural counterparts as the prices of provisions rose, at the same time as the demand for their services and products fell away. The rich had ample provisions or funds to insulate themselves effectively against the vagaries of the harvest (Galloway, 1993; Richards, 1984; Faber, 1976: 15).

Social differences are not the only reactions to economic changes that can be observed. Economic opportunities might also differ greatly between regions and between urban and rural areas, making it much more difficult to establish a viable family economy in some regions than in others. Thomas (1925), for example, believed that the agricultural population would be less affected by business cycles than the more industrialized population. Glass (1938: 278) argued that this depended on the type of agricultural economy; an agricultural system based largely upon hired labour and catering mainly for export would be strongly affected, and even an economy which produced only for the home market would be severely hurt by a depression which saw the home market flooded with foreign agricultural produce.

It is clear that using aggregated data for a country as a whole to study the reactions of marriage to economic changes has serious shortcomings. This approach only allows us to detect the average response of the average person, and it is insensitive to regional and social differences in the reaction to the economy. A strong reaction to prices by part of the population might be hidden within a broader weak or moderate reaction by the whole population (Lee, 1993). Essentially, the demographic reaction of the most numerous sector of the population to economic variations will dominate any analysis conducted at the national level. Only by comparing the direction, magnitude and timing of the marriage response from region to region, and from social group to social group, might one begin to understand the implications of economic change for the behaviour of households and individuals embedded within them (Bengtsson 1993).

There have been some earlier attempts to approach this question. Galloway (1993) studied how demographic responses to price increases varied between rich and poor European countries, rich and poor districts in a rural portion of Denmark and rich and poor parishes in the French city of Rouen. Southall and Gilbert (1996) studied differences in vulnerability to economic fluctuations by comparing absolute numbers of marriages per social group in periods of economic distress and in periods of eco-

[4] For contrary ideas regarding the reactions of the lower class, see Glass (1938).

nomic upswing for one parish in Bolton, Lancashire. Of course it is difficult to analyse these fluctuations in nuptiality using the more common econometric or time series methods, as random variations tend to become too large if the number of events is small. It is also difficult to find homogeneous regions of appropriate size consisting, for example, of rich peasants or poor farmers.

The micro-analysis of individual nominative data and the macro-analysis of aggregate data have recently been combined by Bengtsson (1993), who also included macro-level indicators of economic conditions such as price series as covariates in a micro-level life event analysis of the determinants of demographic behaviour. Through such an approach, and by interacting measures of macro-level conditions with covariates measuring other characteristics of individuals, it is possible to differentiate the demographic impact of changes in economic conditions by occupation and other personal attributes. It is this approach that will be followed here, albeit by using other methods.

The studies published so far on the relation between the economy and marriage have other shortcomings as well. The model normally used in interpreting the effects of the economy on marriage is based on the assertion that a minimum amount of resources must be accumulated prior to marriage, and that this accumulation is taken mainly from labour earnings. The time required to accumulate any fixed sum therefore increases as the wage falls, implying that the age at marriage rises. The model does not however specify which sex is responsible for what share of accumulation, nor is there any predictable effect of changing relative wages of men and women. In general, female wages will have been too low to constitute the majority contribution to the savings (Weir, 1984). It is thus usually incumbent on the male or his parents to provide a living for his wife and children, as well as for himself. Marriage for women seemed relatively unaffected by economic conditions; for most women, the economic incentives and disincentives to marriage were minimal (Dixon, 1970: 317). Sandberg (1867: 461) therefore argued that 'Where it is about finding a criterion with which to judge the prosperity of the population, male marriages outweigh those of women. For, a women does not ask a man's hand in marriage, at least not yet in our time, and as soon as it becomes more difficult to earn a livelihood and to find the necessary means to establish a household, men *will* marry at higher ages but women will not, for, as soon as a man possesses the means to support a family, he might as well marry a young girl as a woman of a more advanced age'.

Economic constraints thus should affect the timing and prevalence of male nuptiality directly, and of female nuptiality indirectly. Given the fact that marriage rates and ages at marriage for male and female populations might be different, it is essential, particularly when studying local populations, to make a distinction between the effects of economic development on male and female marriage indicators.

A substantial proportion of marriages in the past included people who had been married before. In the 19th century, in 20–25 per cent of all marriages, one or both spouses had been married before. This percentage clearly decreased from the 1860s on, reaching 10 per cent by around 1910. When using data for all marriages, a large proportion of marriages will consist of remarriages which, by definition, might be assumed to be less susceptible to changes in the economic situation. In the past, the presence of children provided a strong stimulus for remarriage for widows and widowers alike. Widowers needed a new spouse to take care of the children, whereas widows needed a spouse to provide an income for the family. Consequently, both sexes generally had relatively low standards for the 'minimal acceptable match' (Oppenheimer, 1988). The pressure to remarry may have been so strong, in particular among widowed people with young children, that little attention could be paid to matters of 'secondary' interest such as economic prospects and cultural similarity. Besides, in the case of those who married for the first time a new family was established, whereas in the case of a remarriage only a continuation of an existing marriage was at stake. Sandberg (1867: 453) argued that first marriages 'are regulated to a much higher degree by the symptoms of social prosperity and distress than the second and following marriages. They depend directly on the means available to set up and provide for a family'. Earlier research on the effect of short-term economic disturbances on marriage rates in the Netherlands and in Amsterdam during the 19th century has confirmed the idea that the correlation between economic indicators and first marriages rates was somewhat higher than for those including first and second marriages (van Zanten and van den Brink, 1939). Glass (1938), on the other hand, argued that remarriages were more affected by changes in prosperity than marriages by younger men. Widowers might have been at the peak of their earnings, and economic depression would make them ripe for dismissal as employers attempted to reduce costs. This would reduce their ability to remarry. Given this uncertainty about the relative influence of first and succeeding marriages, it would be interesting to make a distinction between the effects of economic circumstances on first and on second marriages.

As mentioned above, it is assumed that economic fluctuations have an effect on age at marriage because the time required to accumulate the necessary resources increases as wages fall. Yet in almost all studies dealing with the influence of economic factors on marriage, it is implicitly argued that high or low ages at marriage find a direct expression in the marriage rate. In fact, (crude) marriage rates capture the effects both of changes in the timing of marriage (age at marriage) and of changes in its incidence (the proportion of each generation who marry). According to Eversley (1965: 43–46), it is a fair assumption that during the years when there were few marriages, the average age at marriage was also high, and vice versa. It is thus assumed that celibacy is just one step beyond delayed marriage, that it is a quantitative rather than a qualitative step. Although in the abstract it makes sense that the timing and prevalence of marriage should be highly correlated, and that the social, economic and demographic factors causing large numbers of men and women to delay their marriage should also cause high proportions to remain unmarried, the relation between late or early marriage and high or low proportions marrying might in reality be more complicated (see Dixon, 1970, 1978). One might argue that the impact of a recession would have been greater on the young, who had less chance to accumulate savings, and hence the mean age at marriage would increase and the marriage rate would decrease. One might also envisage a situation in which all age groups were affected to more or less the same degree; in which case the marriage rate would be affected but age at marriage would not, or at least would be affected only slightly. Finally, one could imagine a situation in which age at marriage was affected but the marriage rate did not show any variation. This could for example be the case when rising incomes stimulated marriages among the young, whereas at the same time older bachelors who had put off marriage could not compete for brides with these younger males, or become reluctant to give up their freedom because they had become adjusted to single life. The question is whether it is correct to interpret celibacy as an unintended consequence of individuals waiting too long, or whether celibacy might vary independently of age at marriage. Weir (1984) has argued that it is necessary to distinguish between figures for age at marriage and for celibacy. Gutmann (1987) also showed that indices based on numbers of marriages and on the mean age at marriage cannot be used interchangeable. He argued that to measure social changes taking place over a longer period of time, mean or median ages are better suited than indices such as marriage rates. Marriage ages smooth out the changes which might be seen in a time measure, and partly reflect the individual conditions of a family's life. Therefore, it might be useful to use a more direct measure for the possible delay in marriage instead of a measure which combines marriage delay and marriage abstention.

III. Data sources

Data on year of marriage, age at marriage, marital status and occupation of the spouses were available from marriage certificates for the period 1811–1912, for a total of twenty-two Dutch municipalities. The total number of marriages included was 66,198. Table 1 gives an overview of the number of marriages for each of the regions included in the analysis.

The selected regions had a highly diverse socioeconomic structure, ranging from large farms producing for the market economy with sharp differences between workers and farmers (Midwolda and Zeeland) to subsistence farming (the area in Rural North Brabant, known as the 'Kempen') or fishing communities (Katwijk), and from communities dominated by domestic industry (Oldenzaal) to cities (Delft, The Hague, Naarden and Arnhem) where many industrial activities and relatively large numbers of civil servants, artisans, shopkeepers, servants and military personnel were found. Although our data do not give a balanced overview for the Netherlands as a whole (the provinces of Friesland, Drenthe and Utrecht are not included, and there are only limited data for North Holland, Overijssel and Limburg), their national representativeness as far as age at marriage and the proportion of first marriages is concerned is quite good (van Poppel, 1992).

In order to classify individuals by social class, only the occupations of the bridegroom, as stated on the marriage certificates, were used. These provide partial information on the exact status of occupations. It is not clear in many cases whether the individuals concerned were self-employed or employed by others. A more detailed and precise classification of occupations would require a further study of local labour relations. By putting the emphasis on the comparison of broadly-defined social classes, however, we can avoid this problem.

Table 6.1 Number of marriages per municipality

Municipality/region	Number	Period
Arnhem	10,350	1812–1900
Delft	16,701	1812–1911
Dodewaard	289	1812–1868
Elsloo	811	1812–1912
Bommelerwaard	3,724	1812–1912
Goes	4,142	1811–1900
Katwijk	3,781	1812–1912
Kempen	4,891	1812–1912
Midwolda	2,742	1812–1912
Naarden	2,068	1812–1912
Oldenzaal	2,757	1812–1912
Rotterdam	1,656	1812–1899
(Rural) North Holland	1,207	1815–1909
(Rural) South Holland	3,772	1812–1912
The Hague	4,135	1850–1882
Wageningen	852	1812–1868
(Rural) Zeeland	2,320	1811–1912
Total	66,198	

The socioeconomic classification used in our study is a slightly modified version of the one designed by Giele and Van Oenen (1974) and distinguishes five broad groups: upper class (professionals and high ranking military personnel), learned professionals and lower civil servants (including supervisors of various kinds), farmers, petty bourgeoisie (shopkeepers, small entrepreneurs and merchants, self-employed artisans), and manual workers (craftsmen in small businesses, industrial and building craftsmen, servants, casual and unskilled labourers, lower grade military, agricultural labourers and fishermen). We grouped agricultural labourers and other labourers together, as in rural communities in particular the expression 'labourer' could refer to both labourers working in agriculture and all other kinds of labourers. We also classified together all those persons without any occupation.

Next, the rank number of marriage for males and females was used to create the following categories: first marriage for males and females, first marriage for females, first marriage for males, non-first marriage for males, non-first marriage for females and non-first marriage for both spouses.

As we also wanted to study whether the effects of the secular changes in the economy differed according to region and whether those involved came from a rural or urban background, we further divided our data set into four groups: rural regions in the north and west, rural regions in the south and east, urban regions in the north and west, and urban regions in the south and east. The cities of Rotterdam, The Hague and Delft, which had both a large population in terms of size and a high population density, were classified as urban regions in the north and west, and Arnhem was similarly classed as an urban region in the south and east.[5] Goes, Katwijk, Midwolda, Naarden, rural Zeeland, rural North Holland and rural South Holland were classified as rural north and west, whereas the Bommelerwaard region, Dodewaard, Elsloo, the Kempen area, Oldenzaal and Wageningen were included as rural south and east. This division is more or less in line with results of previous demographic research on differences in family structure and family relations between the western and northern part of the Netherlands on the one hand, and the south and the east on the other (see for example van Poppel, 1985; Lesthaeghe and Wilson, 1986). It is also very similar to the division used by van Zanden (1985) in his study of the development of agriculture in The Netherlands and by Wichers (1965) in his study into the emergence and continuation of regional cultural differences. In general, the west and north had much more intensive contacts with the outside world through a well-developed transportation network, the seaports and the highly market-oriented agricultural activities. As a consequence, they showed more of an individualistic orientation.

To measure the secular changes in the economy, we used two variables: the per capita national income in constant prices of 1913 (Smits et al. 1997: 45, 78) and annual data on the price of wheat at the markets in the cities of Arnhem and Middelburg. Unfortunately, reliable economic indicators are difficult to find at the local level, and we thus had to rely on the national data. The national income data are the result of a recently completed effort to reconstruct the economic development of the Netherlands since the beginning of the 19th century, and in particular the resulting long-term growth pattern of national income may be considered as reliable. Wheat prices have been published for the period until 1900 (see Overzicht, 1903; Overzicht 1904). The prices farmers received for their agricultural products corresponded very closely with the prices of the products sold in the various marketplaces. We also know from several studies that the prices of wheat in the various Dutch market cities during the 17th and 18th centuries followed each other very closely. The same might be assumed for other products in which trade was intensive, such as dairy products and other commercial crops (van Zanden, 1985: 109). As the price of wheat in Middelburg generally proved to have insignificant effects, we show here only the results for the price of wheat in the city of Arnhem.

Per capita national income increased only slightly between 1820 and 1860, whereas the price of wheat at the market in Arnhem increased strongly. During the next period, the opposite trend could be observed: whereas per capita income increased rather quickly, prices decreased between 1865 and 1890. After 1890, per capita national income increased only slightly and the price of wheat decreased to some extent.

[5] At the beginning of the period studied, in 1809, Arnhem had 9,400 inhabitants; Delft counted 14,000, Rotterdam 59,100, and The Hague 41,900. A century later, in 1910, these numbers had increased to 64,700, 34,200, 417,800 and 270,100, respectively.

This leaves us with the following explanatory variables: the annual gross national per capita income, region in combination with rural or urban residence (dummy variables), socio-economic class, price of wheat and marital status of bride and groom.

IV. Methods of analysis

By restricting the analysis to first marriages for men and women, and assuming that the age at marriage is linearly dependent on the above-mentioned factors,[6] we can formulate the following relationships between age at marriage for men and for women respectively, and the explanatory variables (we delete further indices for the various years and the individuals for reasons of readability):

$$AM_m = \alpha_{0,m} + \sum_{i=1}^{3} \alpha_{1i,m}.Region_i + \sum_{j=1}^{5} \alpha_{2j,m}.SE_j + \alpha_{3,m}.NIpcc + \alpha_{4,m}.Pwheat + \alpha_{5,m}.AM_f + \epsilon_m$$

and

$$AM_f = \alpha_{0,f} + \sum_{i=1}^{3} \alpha_{1i,f}.Region_i + \sum_{j=1}^{5} \alpha_{2j,f}.SE_j + \alpha_{3,f}.NIpcc + \alpha_{4,f}.Pwheat + \alpha_{5,f}.AM_m + \epsilon_f$$

In this equation, AM_g is the age at marriage for a person of sex g (g=m (male) or f (female)), $Region_i$ refers to the three regions distinguished here, SE_j to socio-economic class, NIpcc to the per capita national income in constant prices and Pwheat to the price of wheat in Arnhem. ϵ is the error term (the deviation of the dependent variable Y from its expected value) with mean zero and variance σ^2.

It is clear from this equation that we do not assume that there exists a one-way relationship between the dependent variables AM_f and AM_m and the explanatory variables, the economic time series. We assume on theoretical and empirical grounds that there is a strong relationship between the age at marriage of both spouses, thus between male and female ages at marriage. Therefore each of the variables AM_f and AM_g appear as variables on the right side of the equation of the other, the result of the theory that suggests this specification. As a consequence, one dependent variable, male age at marriage, might explain the development of another dependent variable (female age at marriage) and can itself be explained by this other variable. If we have such a two-way causation in a function, this implies that the function cannot be treated in isolation as a single equation model: the application of least squares to a single equation assumes among other things that the explanatory variables are truly exogenous. If this is not true, that is if the independent variables are at the same time determined by the dependent variable, one central assumption of ordinary least squares estimation techniques (OLS), the assumption that the error terms ϵ_m and ϵ_f are uncorrelated is violated. The application of this method yields biased and inconsistent results. We must use a multi-equation model which includes separate equations in which AM_f and AM_m appear as endogenous variables, although they might appear as indepen-

[6] The use of a loglinear specification resulted in about the same elasticities and thus did not lead to other conclusions. The same happened when the analysis was based on three-years or five-year lagged per capita income, or the use of a moving average or on the use of lagged prices.

dent variables in other equations of the model. A system describing the joint dependence of variables is called a simultaneous equations model.

A technique that is appropriate for estimating this system of equations is two-stage least squares (2SLS), which is used extensively in econometrics (see for example Judge et al., 1985; for a more basic introduction, see Godwin, 1985). In the first stage, each of the two dependent variables in the model is regressed on all the independent variables in the model. The second stage involves using the estimated values of the dependent variables derived in the first stage as independent variables to obtain two-stage least squares (2SLS) estimates. In this way, the endogenous variables that appear in the equation which is to be estimated are purified and become uncorrelated with the disturbance term in that equation. The predicted values for the dependent variable from the first stage remove the source of simultaneity bias from the 2SLS estimates, and thus can be used to produce unbiased coefficients of the relationships in the model.

The complete system of equations which describes the structure of the relationships of all the variables, and in which the endogenous (dependent) variable is expressed as a function of the other endogenous variable, of the independent variables and of disturbances (random effects) is called the structural model. The parameters in this model are the direct effects of each explanatory variable on the dependent variable. Indirect effects can only be computed by the solution of the structural system. The model in which the endogenous variables are expressed as a function of the independent variables only is called the reduced form of the structural model. The reduced form parameters measure the total effect, the direct plus the indirect effect, of a change in the independent variables on the dependent variables, after taking into account the interdependence among the jointly dependent endogenous variables.

V. Results

Table 6.2 gives the 2SLS results for the period 1811–1912. The table gives the regression coefficients and the β-coefficients. Levels of significance are indicated by asterisks. The R^2 values give the proportion of the variance in the dependent variable explained by the explanatory variables.[7]

[7] Empty cells relate to the fact that the reference categories of the dummy variables (labourers, rural southeast) are not given. Due to multicollinearity, Table 6.2 does not include a value for women in the urban southeast area.

Table 6.2 Two-stage least squares estimation result for first marriage, 1811-1912

Variable	Women Regression coefficient	β-coefficient	Men Regression coefficient	β-coefficient
Per capita national income	-0.0041 ***	(-0.067)	0.0037 ***	(0.054)
Rural/northwest	-0.6466 ***	(-0.058)		
Rural/southeast				
Urban/northwest	0.4392 ***	(0.031)	-0.7536 ***	(-0.064
Urban/southeast			-1.1909 ***	(-0.076)
Upper class	-1.6667 ***	(-0.060)	2.9665 ***	(0.096)
Learned professionals	-0.4374 ***	(-0.023)	1.0594 ***	(0.050)
Farmers	-0.3656 ***	(-0.022)	0.9659 ***	(0.053)
Petty bourgeoisie	-0.1264 **	(-0.009)	0.3811 ***	(0.025)
Labourers				
Without occupation	-0.0670	(-0.012)	0.7616 ***	(0.013)
Price of wheat in Arnhem	-0.0202 **	(-0.011)	0.0332 ***	(0.015)
Female age at marriage			1.2574 ***	(0.253)
Male age at marriage	0.5863 ***	(0.186)		
Constant	11.1824 ***		-6.0159 ***	
R^2_{adj}	0.049	0.083		
N	52,657		52,665	

Note: Significance levels: * = 10%; ** = 5%; *** = 1%.

The first impression is that economic factors do affect the age at marriage for both men and women. At least, per capita national income and the price of wheat are significant for both sexes. However, we expected a negative sign for per capita national income (rising income leading to decreasing ages at marriage) and a positive one for the price of wheat (rising prices leading to increasing ages at marriage). For men, we found the reverse sign for per capita national income, and for women the reverse sign for the price of wheat. In addition to these direct effects, we also have indirect effect of the economic changes. Changes in per capita national income and the price of wheat also affect the age at marriage for the other sex via AM_m and AM_f, and so on. Only by including this indirect effect (or in other words by looking at the reduced form coefficients) do we get an impression of the total impact.[8]

If we limit ourselves to the direct effects, we might conclude that an increase of per capita national income by one guilder (in prices of 1913, which implied a per capita gross national product of 484.7 guilders in that year) decreased the age at marriage for women by 0.0041 years and increased the average male's age at marriage by 0.0037 years. Its direct elasticity amounted to -0.042 and +0.038, respectively. This implies that a 1 per cent increase of GNP lowered the age at marriage for women by 0.042 per cent and increased that age for men by 0.038 per cent.[9] The total impact (calculated by including the indirect effect via AM_m and AM_f respectively) showed an elasticity of -0.072 and -0.057. The sign is now as expected. At first sight, these elasticities seem rather small. However, a doubling of the per capita GNP (which occurred between about 1820 and 1910) lowered the average age at marriage by about 25 months for women and 19 months for men. In fact, the age at first marriage decreased slightly more than eight months for women, whereas it decreased by four months for men during that period.

What might be concluded about the impact of the price of wheat? An increase in prices of 1 per cent directly increased the age at marriage of men by 0.010 per cent whereas that of women was lowered by 0.006 per cent. The total effect (including the

---

[8] These reduced form coefficients might be calculated in the following way. Starting from the equations

(1) $Y_1 = \alpha_1.X + \beta_1.Y_2 + ...$ and (2) $Y_2 = \alpha_2.X + \beta_2.Y_1 + ...$

we get after substitution:

(3) $Y_1 = [(\alpha_1 + \alpha_2.\beta_1)/(1 - \beta_1.\beta_2)].X + ...$ and

(4) $Y_2 = [(\alpha_2 + \alpha_1.\beta_2)/(1 - \beta_1.\beta_2)].X + ...$

The reduced form coefficients for X are now $(\alpha_1 + \alpha_2.\beta_1)/(1 - \beta_1.\beta_2)$ with respect to Y_1 and $(\alpha_2 + \alpha_1.\beta_2)/(1 - \beta_1.\beta_2)$ with respect to Y_2.

[9] The elasticity of the variabele Y with respect to the variabele X has been defined as $(\Delta Y/\Delta X).(Xav/Yav)$. Here, for men $\Delta Y/\Delta X$ is the derivative of AM_m to NIpcc. In our application this is the coefficient for AM_m(0.0041). Xav and Yav are the average values of NIpcc and AM_m for the period of estimation. These amount to 278.46 guilders and 27.56 years. So we get for this elasticity: 0.0041.(278.46/27.56)= 0.041. The elasticity for the total impact is found in the same way. We use the reduced form coefficient instead of the coefficient given in the equation of AM_m(see the foregoing footnote).

indirect effect via AM_f and AM_m) resulted in a coefficient for men of +0.0297 and for women of -0.0028. The coefficient for women still has the unexpected sign, but is no longer significant. The elasticity for men now amounts to 0.0091, implying that a doubling of the price of wheat increased the average male's age at marriage by less than three months. As in the period 1860–1910 the price of wheat decreased by about one-fifth, this implied a decrease in the average age at marriage of men by less than one month.

Although we found an impact of the economic variables, the β-coefficients were very small, implying that economic factors contributed only to a very limited extent to the explanation of the equations. This was proven most clearly by a comparison between the expected effect of the change in per capita national income and the actual development of the age at marriage. The development of the wheat prices explained only 0.01 per cent of the variance in the equation for men and 0.02 per cent of that for women. Per capita national income explained 0.45 per cent for men and 0.29 per cent for women, respectively. Thus, on the basis of this first analysis, we have to conclude that in spite of the significant signs, the direct contribution of these economic variables to the explanation is very limited. The regional and socio-economic factors appeared to have much more importance. Region explained 0.43 per cent of the variance for women and 0.99 per cent for men. For the socio-economic status of the groom, these percentages were 0.48 per cent and 1.53 per cent, respectively.

Thus far the entire period has been treated as if it were homogeneous. However, during the 19th century there were important structural changes in the Dutch economy. Processes such as the industrial revolution, urbanization, major shifts in occupational distribution and improvements in transportation with consequent reductions in regional price differences may well have altered the relationship we have been studying, and it is therefore important to examine each sub-period separately. We repeated our analysis for sub-periods of varying length, again restricting ourselves to first marriages. This both reinforces the earlier analysis by confirming or rejecting its assumptions, and gives a more detailed picture of the relationships among the series.

It was found that the impact of the macroeconomic changes on age at marriage was limited to only part of the period 1811–1912. For example, if we limit the analysis to the years 1821–60, we get insignificant results for both per capita national income and the price of wheat for women. National income is also insignificant in the equation for men, and the price of wheat is significant only at the 10 per cent-level, contributing only 0.16 per cent to the explanation of the equation. Using periods of five years (e.g., 1821–25) did not result in significant coefficients for the per capita national income either. The coefficient for this variable is always larger than -0.0013 and the picture is very solid. Comparable results were found for the years after 1890, where the absolute value of the coefficients was even smaller. Thus, the impact of the economic variables appears to be limited to the period 1861–90 and in this case the results, which are shown in Table 6.3, also conform to the theoretical expectations.

Table 6.3 Two-stage least squares estimation result for first marriage, 1861-90

Variable	Women Regression coefficient	β-coefficient	Men Regression coefficient	β-coefficient
Per capita national income	-0.0068 ***	(-0.078)	0.0066 ***	(-0.067)
Rural/northwest	-0.7315 ***	(-0.062)		
Rural/southeast				
Urban/northwest			-0.9333 ***	(-0.082)
Urban/southeast	0.6014 ***	(0.045)	-1.6577 ***	(-0.113)
Upper class	-1.5439 ***	(-0.058)	3.2109 ***	(0.110)
Learned professionals	-0.4500 ***	(-0.026)	1.2225 ***	(0.064)
Farmers	-0.1523	(-0.009)	0.8932 ***	(0.045)
Petty bourgeoisie	0.0311	(-0.002)	0.2146 ***	(0.015)
Labourers				
Without occupation	0.4830	(-0.010)	0.3035 ***	(0.058)
Price of wheat in Arnhem	-0.0409	(-0.014)	0.0461 ***	(0.014)
Female age at marriage			1.3624 ***	(0.278)
Male age at marriage	0.5199 ***	(0.178)		
Constant	13.9024 ***		-9.4587 ***	
R^2_{adj}	0.050		0.095	
N	20,342		20,344	

Note: Significance levels: * = 10%; ** = 5%; *** = 1%

Table 6.3 shows a direct negative impact of per capita national income on age at marriage for women, which is significant at the 1 per cent-level, whereas the effect is significantly positive for men (p-value = 0.081). Looking at the total effect, which also takes into account the indirect effect via AM_m and AM_f, respectively, we find a coefficient of -0.0108 for women and -0.0077 for men. With respect to the price of wheat, we find reduced form coefficients (total effects) which equal -0.0544 for women and -0.0026 for men. Both effects thus have the wrong sign.

These coefficients result in a reduced-form elasticity with respect to per capita national income of -0.123 for women and -0.082 for men. As NIpcc increased by 75 per cent between the first and the last five-year period, this causes a decrease of the age at marriage by 31 months among women and almost 23 months among men. Actually, the average age at marriage decreased by 21 months and by more than 18 months, respectively. We might conclude that in the period 1860–91, national income indeed appears to have had a large impact on the development of age at marriage. The observed effect is in accordance with the findings for the whole period (Table 6.2) and thus confirms our earlier conclusion that the impact of changes in national income on the age at marriage only holds for the period 1861–90.

In the next step, we studied whether changes in the national income had a varying effect on the different socio-economic classes, regions and rank orders of marriage. Table 6.4 shows the direct coefficient, the β-coefficient and the total impact of per capita national income for various subgroups. The first two panels refer to first marriages.

Table 6.4 Two-stage least squares estimation result per national income by subgroups, 1861–90

Subgroup	N (Average)	Women Regression coefficient	β-coef	Total effect	Men Regression coefficient	β-coef.	Total effect
Region							
Rural/northwest	5,067	-0.0108 ***	-0.148	-0.0135	0.0120 ***	0.150	-0.0096
Rural/southeast	3,214	-0.0086 ***	-0.100	-0.0111	-0.0255 ***	-0.252	0.0051
Urban/northwest	8,383	-0.0100 ***	-0.104	-0.0111	0.0051 *	0.048	-0.0112
Urban/southeast	3,679	-0.0105 ***	-0.121	-0.0112	-0.0296 ***	-0.329	-0.0105
Socio-economic status							
Upper class	780	0.0014	0.016	0.0003	-0.0048	0.041	-0.0036
Learned professionals	1,932	-0.0083 ***	-0.092	-0.0085	0.0063	0.063	-0.0084
Farmers	1,823	-0.0025	-0.025	-0.0018	0.0040 **	0.033	0.0035
Petty bourgeoisie	3,706	-0.0068 ***	-0.074	-0.0106	-0.0035 -	0.037	-0.0077
Labourers	11,864	-0.0075 ***	-0.090	-0.0134	0.0061 ***	0.070	-0.0111
Without occupation	238	-0.0103	-0.072	-0.0041	0.0227	0.139	0.0168
Rank number marriage							
First marriage for males and females	20,343	-0.0068 ***	-0.078	-0.0108	0.0066 *	0.067	-0.0077
First marriage females non-first marriage males	2,504	0.0064	0.043	-0.0230	-0.0153 ***	-0.085	-0.0000
Non-first marriage females, first marriage males	958	-0.0119 *	-0.080	-0.0116	-0.0022	-0.014	-0.0073
Non-first marriage for both spouses	1,070	0.0035	0.022	0.0209	0.0118	0.062	0.0298

Note: Significance levels: * = 10%; ** = 5%; *** = 1%.

Disaggregation by region shows significant direct results in all regions for women. Strikingly enough, national income changes have a positive impact on male age at marriage in the north and west and a rather strong negative one in the south and east. This holds for both rural and urban areas in these regions. The total impact, however, is about equal for men and women in all regions, being about 0.011. There is only one exception: for men in the rural southern and eastern areas, the effect of national income is about half that found in the other regions.

The effect of national income also differs according to the socio-economic class of the husband. As far as the total impact is concerned, the effect is only visible in three out of the six categories. The effect is strongest for labourers, both for men and for women married to a labourer. The petty bourgeoisie shows about average impact, whereas women married to learned professionals are slightly less affected. Strikingly, no effect of national income is visible for farmers. Further, we did not find a significant impact of national income for men and women from the upper classes, or for persons without occupation. For this last group the limited number of observations might have a bearing on the result.

Finally, Table 6.4 also shows the effects for non-first marriages. National income has about the same overall effect on age at marriage in those cases in which a man was marrying for the first time and the bride had been married before, as in cases in which neither had been married before. As expected, cases where the woman was marrying for the first time and the man had been married at least once before show a rather high effect of national income on the marriage age of women, but no effect on the man's age. If both partners had been married before, however, we find a positive effect of national income, an result which clearly runs counter to the theoretical expectations. In these cases other elements (such as the presence of children), which could not be considered here, may have played an important role.

The impact of the price of wheat is shown in Table 6.5; as noted above, we use only prices at the market in Arnhem.

Table 6.5 Two-stage least squares estimation result for the price of wheat in Arnhem by subgroups, 1861–90

Subgroup	N	Women			Men		
	(Average)	Regression coefficient	β-coef	Total effect	Regression coefficient	β-coef.	Total effect
Region							
Rural/northwest	5,067	-0.1433 **	-0.060	-0.1620	0.1927 ***	0.073	-0.0678
Rural/southeast	3,214	-0.0594	-0.021	-0.0463	-0.0583	-0.017	0.0264
Urban/northwest	8,383	-0.0228	-0.007	-0.0244	-0.0151	-0.004	-0.0565
Urban/southeast	3,679	-0.0001	-0.000	-0.0016	-0.0261	-0.010	-0.0234
Socio-economic status							
Upper class	780	0.0001	0.000	0.0001	-0.0001	-0.000	-0.0000
Learned professionals	1,932	-0.0239	-0.006	-1.0117	0.0254	0.006	-1.0518
Farmers	1,823	0.0654	0.016	0.0841	0.0281	0.006	0.0858
Petty bourgeoisie	3,706	-0.0741	-0.026	-0.0482	0.0704	0.023	0.0516
Labourers	11,864	-0.0415	-0.015	-0.0788	0.0308	0.011	-0.0704
Without occupation	238	0.0129	0.002	0.0270	0.3153	0.030	0.3110
Rank number marriage							
First marriage for males and females	20,343	-0.0409	-0.014	-0.0028	0.0461	0.014	0.0297
First marriage females non-first marriage males	2,504	0.1448	0.029	-0.4669	-0.3441 **	-0.058	-1.4534
Non-first marriage females, first marriage males	958	-0.2872	-0.061	-0.3265	-0.1146	-0.023	-0.2357
Non-first marriage for both spouses	1,070	-0.1928	-0.036	-0.1673	0.1873	0.030	0.0435

Note: Significance levels: * = 10%; ** = 5%; *** = 1%.

The picture that arises from Table 6.5 is that the price of wheat generally does not have a significant effect on age at marriage. Moreover, we seldom find the expected (positive) sign. The price of wheat only had a statistically significant effect on age at marriage in the rural areas of the north and west, but for both men and women the sign of this effect was contrary to expectations. When we look at the total effect, we find a positive impact of wheat prices on age at marriage for farmers and for persons without occupation. That the impact of wheat prices on age at marriage for other socio-economic groups was less might be related to the fact that we included national income in constant prices. The development of this variable has also been affected by the price development of wheat. We also found a positive total impact of wheat prices on male age at marriage among the petty bourgeoisie, and in cases where both parties were remarrying. Among farmers, the total elasticity amounted to 0.025 for both men and women. This implies that a decrease in the price of wheat by 30 per cent (which occurred between 1860 and 1890) lowered the age at first marriage by about nine months. Actually, the age at marriage decreased by twenty-three months for women and fourteen months for men. For those without occupation, we find an elasticity of about 0.01 for women and 0.09 for men. This implies a lowering of the age at marriage (based on a reduction of the price of wheat by 30 per cent) of about 3.5 months for women and thirty-two months for men. The actual decrease amounted to 5.5 months for women, whereas age at marriage increased by twenty-two months among men. Again, we should realise that the number of persons in this group was very small (N=238) and that the group was rather heterogeneous.

VI. Conclusions

In western Europe, the decision to marry reflected a vast range of pressures and incentives, of which only a limited number were of an economic nature. Social customs, established conventions, personal preferences and sexual drives all played a part (Wrigley et al. 1997: 123–25). In this chapter, we have concentrated on only one of these factors, namely, secular economic development. Although we have tried to study this factor in a wider context than is usually the case, we realise that our data still contain many shortcomings. Parallel to the growth of national income, there were processes of industrialization, proletarianization and urbanization which can hardly, if at all, be distinguished from the process of income growth. Several authors have argued that it was precisely these changes in the structure of the economy which led to changes in the age at marriage: the spread of rural industry and industrialization (Kriedte et al., 1977: 122–24; De Jonge, 1968: 264–65; Lynch, 1986), urbanization (Shorter, 1977: 140–46) and proletarianization (Tilly, 1984: 13–43; Tilly and Scott, 1978: 91–96; Hofstee, 1954). Only a part of this set of factors is captured in our study through the inclusion of variables such as socio-economic position and urban–rural background. A second problem is that we only used data on national income. Per capita real income is simply an abstract arithmetical expression of national income, showing no relation to a specific class of people. Although in the period under study an integrated national economy did emerge, regions and social classes continued to differ in terms of income. We were not able to take these differences into account.

It appears that changes in the national income were indeed a factor that played a role in the marriage decisions of Dutch men and women. During the period 1811–1912 as a whole, the total effect of the change in GNP on age at marriage was considerable, leading to a decrease in the average age at marriage for both men and women. Structural changes in the price of wheat during this period caused a small increase in the age at marriage of men, while the effect on female age at marriage was not statistically significant. Although we found that the economic variables did have an impact, the direct contribution of these variables to explaining changes in age at marriage over time was very limited.

Next, we took into account the changing character of the Dutch economy and studied the effect of the economic changes per sub-period. It turned out that the impact of the chosen economic variables was limited to the period 1861–90. Changes in national income during this period caused a considerable decrease in age at marriage among women and men. Wheat prices during this period had an unexpected decreasing effect on age at marriage for the population as a whole.

By using individual units of analysis (limiting ourselves again to first marriages), we could distinguish the responses of the different socio-economic classes and regions to changes in national income. Increases in national income reduced male and female ages at marriage in all regions, and in both rural and urban areas in these regions. The total impact was about equal for men and women, but for men in the rural southeastern areas the effect was considerably smaller. Differences within the overall change in income might have played a role in the differences in reaction between the southeastern region and the other parts of the Netherlands. Available evidence suggests indeed that this part of the country lagged behind in the increase in national income during the period under study.

The effect of national income also differed according to the socio-economic class of the husband. Increases in national income caused decreases in age at marriage only among labourers, and among women marrying labourers. The petty bourgeoisie show a similar effect, though less strongly, and women married to professionals were also clearly affected. Farmers were not affected by the growth of national income, nor were men and women from the upper classes or persons without occupation. National income had about the same total effect on age at marriage in all cases where the man was marrying for the first time, but in cases where the woman was marrying for the first time but the man was remarrying, national income had a rather strong effect on female marriage age and no effect on the male's age at marriage. If both partners had been married before, national income had a positive effect.

The impact of the price of wheat was generally not significant except in the rural areas of the northwest; but here, for both men and women, the sign of this effect was contrary to expectations. We observed a positive impact of wheat prices on age at marriage for farmers and for persons without occupation.

These results are only partly in line with current concepts of differences in susceptibility to economic growth between social classes. Thomas (1925: 85), and in her footsteps Southall and Gilbert (1996), have argued that 'people living near the poverty level would probably not be greatly affected by cycles of prosperity and depression. Their condition tends to be but little improved in times of prosperity, and one degree worse does not hold many extra burdens. Prudence is an unaccustomed attitude, for their general condition seems to be beyond the possibility of improvement. Hence, persons at the lower extremes of society probably marry without much relation to present or prospective business conditions. Similarly, the very rich would probably not be affected to a degree to prevent marriage during a business depression'.

During the first part of the 19th century, the age at marriage among labourers indeed did not show any effect of changes in national income, and this lack of reaction is what one would expect. After 1860, however, there certainly is a response to the increase in national income among members of this group. For the upper class, however, as was expected on the basis of Thomas's assumptions, no reaction is visible.

As far as farmers are concerned, the fact that they did not show a reaction to the secular development of national income might be related to the fact that couples from this social class could only marry until they were economically independent, that is, had acquired land. For a large part of the population, land became available through intergenerational transfers. Here mortality might have affected the feasibility of marriage through the timing of inheritances and the amount of competition between siblings for shares in inheritances (Schellekens, 1997).

The differences which were found between sub-periods in the relationship between economic development and the age at marriage more or less correspond to those observed in the UK in the period 1854–1913 (Thomas, 1925). The arguments given by Thomas to explain the difference between the period 1875–94 and earlier and later periods also apply to the Dutch situation. That the correspondence was much closer in the years 1860–90 than before is probably due to the later industrialization of the Netherlands in comparison with the United Kingdom. An agricultural population is influenced to a lesser extent by the development of national income, and is more dependent on the harvest, the price of grain and the availability of land. Marriage was usually followed quickly by the birth of a first child, and when entering into marriage this possible future burden had to be taken into account. When knowledge of contraceptives became available and accepted, the increase of the family could be postponed until better times. This removal of one of the economic obstacles to marriage might explain the weaker link between marriage and the economy in the post-1890 period, when effective methods of birth control were gradually diffused.

Finally, it is interesting to compare the results of our analysis with the 19th-century ideas on the proper age at marriage. In the continuing debate between the supporters of Thomas Malthus and his opponents on the causes of working-class poverty, implicit and explicit reference was often made to the economic requirements for marriage. Those who took part in this discussion contrasted middle-class attitudes towards marriage with their views of the marriage patterns of the lower class. The poverty of the working classes was assumed to be the result of 'the improvident way in which marriages are contracted'. Beucker Andreae (1851: 185, 188) for example, discussing the situation in the province of Friesland, argued that instead of remaining in service for a few more years as farm hand or farm maid, thus saving more money, 'most younger people marry at ages below 30 (sometimes 25, 26) without having other means of subsistence than the husband's arms and the wife's knowledge of managing the household'. The labouring class lacked deliberate thought, order and thrift. According to Bogaard (1852: 166–67), referring to the situation in the province of Gelderland, the rural population 'marries in a very improvident way without worrying about the future, whereas the bare necessities for establishing their household are lacking...'. Among the lower classes the rule was that 'as soon as someone from this class earns more than he needs to support himself, and sometimes even before he is able to do so, he will seize the first possible opportunity to enter into a marriage and usually it is not hard to find a girl who, without thinking, is prepared to join her destiny with his...' The middle classes, on the other hand, wished to postpone marriage until a decent level of living had been secured; in particular, from the 1860s onward, middle-class men were accused of being afraid of giving up an established standard of living.

During the period in which the complaints about the irresponsibility of working-class men were most vehement (that is, in the period until around 1860–65), the age at marriage in this class was on the rise. It was only after the 1860s that a strong drop in age at marriage occurred among labourers, learned professionals and the petty bourgeoisie, and that differences in the age at marriage between these groups and the upper class increased considerably. We have observed that during the first part of the 19th century, secular changes in the economic situation did not have an effect on the age at marriage, while after 1860, members of the lower class did react to the changing economic situation. Increases in income stimulated them to establish a new family at an earlier age than before.

The members of the upper and middle classes, on the other hand, did not react to the changing economic situation. Among upper-class women, the age at marriage increased continuously from the beginning of the 19th century onwards, and it remained stable at a rather high level after 1870 at a time when a clear decrease in the age at marriage took place in other layers of society. We showed that rising incomes after 1860 did not stimulate earlier marriages among the well-to-do. Why did the social classes differ in their reaction to the secular rise in income? One might suggest that this was due to a more than proportional rise in incomes among members of the lower class compared to other groups. It might also be that in the upper class, the standards for setting up a new household rose faster than the means for realizing this goal, whereas this was not the case in other classes (Dixon, 1978). There are indications that rising material aspirations and increased consciousness of the costs of rearing a family might have played a role in the Netherlands, as was the case in England (Banks, 1954). Schuurman (1989: 211–16) argued that in the 19th century a rise in domesticity took place, leading to an increase in the number of durable goods which a household had to possess before entering into marriage. Although this process was not limited to one social class, the upper and middle classes were the first to make changes in this 'culturally determined moral economy'. This discussion illustrates the point that strong discrepancies existed between the real world and the views that contemporaries had of their society.

Bibliography

Banks, J.A. (1954) *Prosperity and parenthood: a study of family planning among the Victorian middle classes*, London.

Bengtsson, T. (1993) 'Combined time series and life event analysis: the impact of economic fluctuations and air temperature on adult mortality by sex and occupation in a Swedish mining parish, 1757–1850', in D.R. Reher and R. Schofield (eds), *Old and new methods in historical demography*, Oxford, pp. 239–58.

Beucker Andreae, J.H. (1851) 'Rapport ingediend voor het vijfde landhuishoudkundig congres te Leijden, 11, 12, 13 Juni 1850 Betreffende een onderzoek naar den zedelijken en materiëlen toestand der arbeidende bevolking ten platten lande en van de middelen om dien zooveel mogelijk te verbeteren', *Tijdschrift voor Staathuishoudkunde en Statistiek*, 6, pp. 156–96.

Bogaard, P.T. (1852) 'Verslag van den stoffelijken en zedelijken toestand der Arbeidende Volksklasse ten Plattelande, in het zuidelijk deel der Provincie Gelderland', *Verslag van het verhandelde op het zesde Nederlandsche Landhuishoudkundig Congres, gehouden te Goes, van den 10den tot den 14den juni 1851*, Goes, pp. 163–70.

Dixon, R.B. (1970) 'The social and demographic determinants of marital postponement and celibacy: a comparative study', unpublished Ph.D. dissertation, University of California: Berkeley.

Dixon, R.B. (1978) 'Late marriage and non-marriage as demographic responses: are they similar?', *Population studies*, 32, pp. 449–66.

Evers, J.C.G. (1882) *Bijdrage tot de bevolkingsleer van Nederland*, 's-Gravenhage.

Eversley, D.E.C. (1965) 'Population, economy and society', in D.V. Glass and D.E.C. Eversley (ed.), *Population in history: essays in historical demography*, London, pp. 23–69.

Faber, J.A. (1976), *Dure tijden en hongersnoden in pre-industrieel Nederland*, Amsterdam: Rodopi.

Galloway, P.R. (1988) 'Basic patterns in annual variations in fertility, nuptaility, mortality, and prices in pre-industrial Europe', *Population Studies*, 42, pp. 275–303.

Galloway, P.R. (1993) 'Short-run population dynamics among the rich and poor in European countries, rural Jutland, and urban Rouen', in D.R. Reher and R. Scho-field (eds.) *Old and new methods in historical demography*, Oxford, pp. 84–108 .

Giele, J.J. and Oenen, G.J. van (1974) 'De sociale struktuur van de Nederlandse samenleving rond 1850', *Mededelingen van de Nederlandse Vereniging voor Sociale Geschiedenis*, 45, pp. 2–32.

Glass, D.V. (1938) 'Marriage frequency and economic fluctuations in England and Wales, 1851 to 1934', in L. Hogben (ed.), *Political arithmetic: a symposium of population studies*, London, pp. 251–82.

Godwin, D.H. (1985) 'Simultaneous equations methods in family research', *Journal of Marriage and the Family*, 49, pp. 9–22.

Gutmann, M.P. (1987) 'Protoindustrialization and marriage ages in eastern Belgium', *Annales de Démographie Historique*, Paris, pp. 143–73.

Hofstee, E.W. (1954) 'Regionale verscheidenheid in de ontwikkeling van het aantal geboorten in Nederland in de 2e helft van de 19e eeuw', *Academiedagen*, VII KNAW, Amsterdam, pp. 59–106.

Jonge, J.A. de (1968) *De industrialisatie in Nederland tussen 1850–1914*, Amsterdam.

Judge, G.G., Griffith, W.E., Hill, R.C., Lütkepohl, H. and Lee, T.C. (1985) *The theory and practice of econometrics*, New York.

Kertzer, D.I. and Hogan, D.P. (1991) 'Reflections on the European Marriage Pattern: sharecropping and proletarianization in Casalecchio, Italy, 1861–1921', *Journal of Family History*, 16, pp. 31–46.

Kriedte, P., Medick, H. and Schlumbohm, J. (1977) *Industrialisierung vor der Industrialisierung. Gewerbliche Warenproduktion auf dem Land in der Formationsperiode des Kapitalismus*, Göttingen.

Lee, R. (1993) 'Short-term variation: vital rates, prices, and weather', in E.A. Wrigley and R.S. Schofield (eds) *The population history of England, 1541-1871: a reconstruction*, Cambridge, pp. 356–401.

Lesthaeghe R. and Wilson, C. (1986) 'Modes of production, secularization and the pace of the fertility decline in Western Europe, 1870–1930', in A.J. Coale and S.C. Watkins (eds), *The decline of fertility in Europe*, Princeton, pp. 261–92.

Lynch, K.A. (1986), 'Marriage age among French factory workers: an Alsatian example', *Journal of Interdisciplinary History*, 16, pp. 405–29.

Macfarlane, A. (1986) *Marriage and love in England: modes of reproduction 1300–1840*, Oxford.

Oppenheimer, V.K. (1988) 'A theory of marriage timing', *American Journal of Sociology*, 94, pp. 563–91.

Overzicht (1903) 'Overzicht van marktprijzen van granen te Arnhem in de jaren 1544–1901', *Bijdragen tot de Statistiek van Nederland*, Nieuwe volgreeks 26, 's-Gravenhage.

Overzicht (1904) 'Overzicht van marktprijzen van granen te Middelburg', *Bijdragen tot de Statistiek van Nederland*, Nieuwe volgreeks 26, 's-Gravenhage.

Poppel, F. van (1992) *Trouwen in Nederland*, Wageningen.

Poppel, F. van (1985) 'Late fertility decline in The Netherlands; the influence of religious denomination, socio-economic group and region', *European Journal of Population*, 1, pp. 343–73.

Richards, T. (1984) 'Weather, nutrition and the economy: the analysis of short run fluctuations in births, deaths and marriages, France 1740–1909', in T. Bengtsson, G. Fridlizius and R. Ohlsson (eds), *Pre-Industrial population change; the mortality decline and short-term population movements*, Stockholm, pp. 357–89.

Sandberg, W.T. (1866) 'Statistische studiën. Eene statistiek van den echtelijken staat in Nederland', *De Economist (Bijblad)*, 15, pp. 579–605.

Sandberg, W.T. (1867) 'Statistische Studien. Eene statistiek van den echtelijken staat in Nederland. III De huwelijken naar den burgerlijken staat', *De Economist (Bijblad)*, 16, pp. 445–78.

Schellekens, J. (1997) 'Nuptiality during the first industrial revolution in England: explanations', *Journal of Interdisciplinary History*, 27, pp. 637–54.

Schuurman, A.J. (1989) *Materiële cultuur en levensstijl. Een onderzoek naar de taal der dingen op het Nederlandse platteland in de 19e eeuw: de Zaanstreek, Oost-Groningen, Oost-Brabant*, Wageningen.

Shorter, E. (1977) *The making of the modern family*, Glasgow.

Smits, J.P., Horlings, E. and Zanden van, J.L. (1997) *The measurement of gross national product and its components, The Netherlands 1800–1913*, Research Memorandum N.W. Posthumus Institute no. 1, Rotterdam.

Southall, H. and Gilbert, D. (1996) 'A good time to wed?: marriage and economic distress in England and Wales, 1839–1914', *Economic History Review*, 49, pp. 35–57.

Thomas, D.S. (1925) *Social aspects of the business cycle*, London.

Tilly, L.A. and Scott, J.W. (1978) *Women, work and family*, New York.

Tilly, C. (1984), 'Demographic origins of the European proletariat', in D. Levine (ed.), *Proletarianization and family history*, Orlando, pp. 1–85.

Weir, D.R. (1984) 'Rather never than late: celibacy and age at marriage in English cohort fertility, 1541–1871', *Journal of Family History*, 9, pp. 340–54.

Wichers, A.J. (1965) *De oude plattelandsbeschaving: Een sociologische bewustwording van de 'overherigheid'*, Assen/Wageningen.

Wrigley, E.A. and Schofield, R.S. (1993) *The population history of England, 1541–1871: a reconstruction*, Cambridge.

Wrigley, E.A., Davies, R.S., Oeppen, J.E. and Schofield, R.S. (1997) *English population history from family reconstitution 1580–1837*, Cambridge.

Zanden, J.L. van (1985) *De economische ontwikkeling van de Nederlandse landbouw in de negentiende eeuw, 1800–1914*, Wageningen.

Zanten, J.H. van and Brink, T. van den (1939) *Population phenomena in Amsterdam in comparison with other big towns*, statistical communications of the Municipal Bureau of Statistics of Amsterdam, No. 103a, Amsterdam.

7 Marriage in Twente: nuptiality, proto-industrialization and religion in two Dutch villages, 1800-1900

François M.M. HENDRICKX, University of Nijmegen

I. Introduction

This chapter is based on research into the demographic aspects of largescale preindustrial and industrial textiles manufacture in the region of Twente, the Netherlands, in the 19th century (Hendrickx, 1997) (see Figure 7.1).

Figure 7.1 The three regions of the province of Overijssel, 1850

In 1972, Franklin Mendels published his famous article on the origins and development of what came to be known as proto-industrialization (Mendels, 1972; see also Mendels, 1981). In a study of the development of the linen industry in 16th- and 17th-century Flanders, he observed that the numbers of marriages increased when the industry was booming, but did not necessarily decrease again when linen weaving experienced a downturn. In Mendels's view, this mechanism was a break-up of the selfregulating demographic mechanisms of the European Marriage Pattern (1972: 149–52). He argued that this fundamental change in marriage behaviour, and the rise in the numbers of births it generated, were responsible for the population increase that was observed in Flanders during the rise of the linen industry in the 16th and 17th centuries.[1]

Some years later, this argument was taken one step further by Medick (1976), who argued that increases in nuptiality and fertility and hence in population size were all necessary consequences of the rise of proto-industrialization throughout Europe in this period. By offering additional income opportunities to land poor and landless families, proto-industrialization provided a larger proportion of these groups with an opportunity to marry and have children. This in turn led to an increasing dependence of these very groups on proto-industry. Since at the same time the tie with agriculture was growing weaker and would eventually disappear, this implied that a growing proportion of the population working in proto-industry was becoming increasingly dependent on their own labour alone. In Medick's view, in order to maximize their chances of survival, these families therefore had to be large and their members had to marry comparatively young so as to gain maximum benefit from their early years of strength.

It would thus seem that if the observations of Mendels and Medick are correct, in a system of developing or developed proto-industrialization, one would find a substantial group of families who are heavily involved in domestic industry, and who would be characterized demographically by earlier and more frequent marriage than other socioeconomic groups.

To test these hypotheses, research was carried out in two communities, Borne and Wierden, in the Dutch region of Twente (see Figure 7.2).

[1] For a summary of the criticism of Mendels's views with respect to Flanders, see Chapter 4 in this volume.

Figure 7.2 Borne, Wierden and the three main cities of Twente, 1850

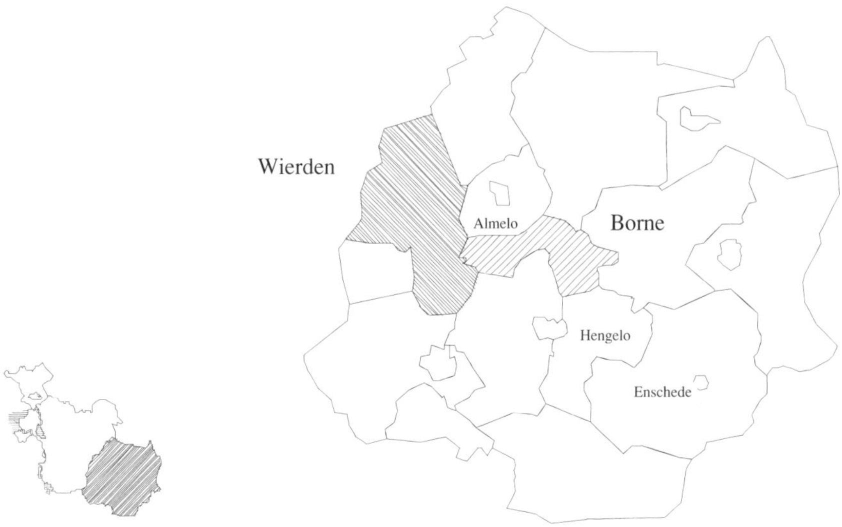

In this region, which produced linen and cotton cloth, we can distinguish three phases in the process of industrialization, each concentrating on different textiles products. The first phase was the flowering of linen production between roughly 1675 and 1750, organized as a cottage industry in the form of a puttingout system. This phase was Twente's first phase of protoindustrialization, and during this period linen weaving became the most important industry in the region, although it was still to a very large extent supported by agriculture (for an introduction to the history of early linen weaving in Twente, see Trompetter (1997)). From 1750 on there followed a period of stagnation in textiles production and a partial reorientation to halflinen fabrics, which lasted until 1833. After this date, a second phase of proto-industrialization occurred in Twente. The existing cottage industry, still producing mainly linen and halflinen cloth using the traditional hand shuttle, was reoriented to cotton production, technically modernized, intensified and enlarged to accommodate the increasing demand from the colonies and European markets. However, in spite of its technical advances, the traditional organization of production in the form of cottage industry and putting-out work by entrepreneurs was maintained, and cotton production in Twente therefore remained in its organization protoindustrial (Boot, 1935; Boot and Blonk, 1957; Fischer, 1983; Griffiths, 1979). It should be added here that with regard to labour, this second phase of protoindustrialization focused mainly on weaving; spinning was proportionally underrepresented in Twente well into the subsequent period of factory industrialization. Yarn was mainly bought from abroad, and therefore spinning offered comparatively little employment for women and children.

The 1860s saw the beginning of the final stage in textile production, that of factory industrialization. This phase, in which textile production began to be concentrated in the central area of the region, lasted until the 1970s. Then, in the general turmoil of the European textile crisis, the Twente producers, who had failed to adapt to changing market conditions, failed or shut down their businesses almost without exception, and the region returned to its agricultural roots (Vylder, 1995; Hendrickx, 1995, 1997).

During Twente's second phase of proto-industrialization after 1833, there were also important changes in agriculture which eventually altered structurally the way the population used the soil, and in so doing, changed the economic structure of the communities in the region (van Zanden, 1985: 152–66). Up until the 1830s, agriculture had mainly been a smallscale operation, based on a type of commonfield tillage in which landpoor or landless families were allowed to use parts of the commons to graze their cattle and to harvest turf to fertilize their plots (Slicher van Bath, 1977: 410–18). Beginning in 1837, under the influence of changing conditions on the world market for grains, a division of the commons and their transformation into private property was started. This development gradually excluded the small and smallest peasants from commercial agriculture. At the same time, agricultural production was gradually reoriented from labour intensive arable farming to a more capital intensive cattle breeding. Thanks to this double adjustment, the smallest farmers eventually lost their minuscule holdings as well as their rights to the commons (van Zanden, 1985: 331). The entire process took some thirty five years to complete, but led to a fundamental restructuring of agriculture in the direction of commercialization and rationalization.

To sum up, during the 19th century, important structural changes took place in Twente in both agriculture and industry, which thoroughly restructured both sectors. From an economy based for the most part on a combination of subsistence agriculture and the weaving of linen or halflinen cloth, it was transformed into a society in which agriculture and industry became more intensively involved in international markets, eventually leading to increasing commercialization, rationalization and factory-based industrialization.

II. Nuptiality in Borne and Wierden

Against this background of structural changes both in industry and in agriculture, demographic aspects of the theories of protoindustrialization were tested. A second dimension was introduced by extending the demographic analyses into the period of early industrialization (after 1860), in order to study the demographic behaviour of a population that had lived with the presence of protoindustrialization for two centuries and then moved into an age of factory industrialization. To this end, two family reconstitutions were carried out in two adjoining communities, Borne and Wierden (Figure 7.2). In both communities, two separate ten year marriage cohorts were analysed, the first cohort consisting of people married between 1831–40, the second including people married between 1871–80. The cohorts were chosen in such a way that they covered the period of the second proto-industrialization as well as that of early factory industrialization.

In Borne and Wierden, the second phase of protoindustrialization evolved, one might say, by the book, although in Borne, protoindustrialization was more dominant than it was in Wierden. In a later stage, beginning in the 1860s, Borne developed into an industrialized community, while in Wierden, factory industry developed to a noticeably lesser extent and instead a specialization in agriculture was observed. We have therefore a comparable evolution in Borne and Wierden during the protoindustrial period, but with the beginning of industrialization the two communities began to diverge.

Figure 7.3 Population growth, Borne and Wierden, 1811–1911

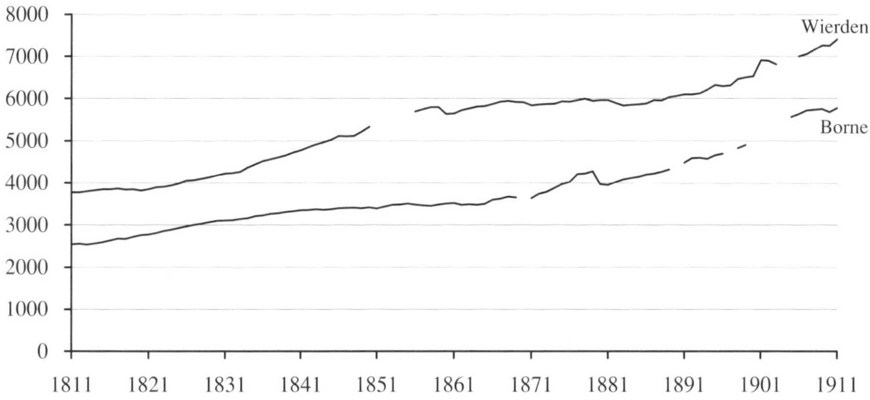

Although the two communities differed considerably in size, the rate of population growth over the 19th century was comparable (see Figure 7.3). The population of both Borne and Wierden doubled in size during the 19th century. In 1811, Borne had 2,442 inhabitants and Wierden had 3,770. By 1911, Borne had 5,784 inhabitants while Wierden had 7,413. However, compared to the population growth in some other communities within the region, especially in the last quarter of the 19th century, this growth was quite moderate (see Figure 7.4). To get an idea of the vital statistics of both communities, gross marriage, birth and death rates are presented in Figures 7.5 and 7.6.

Figure 7.4 Population growth, Borne, Wierden and the three main cities of the Twente, 1818–1909

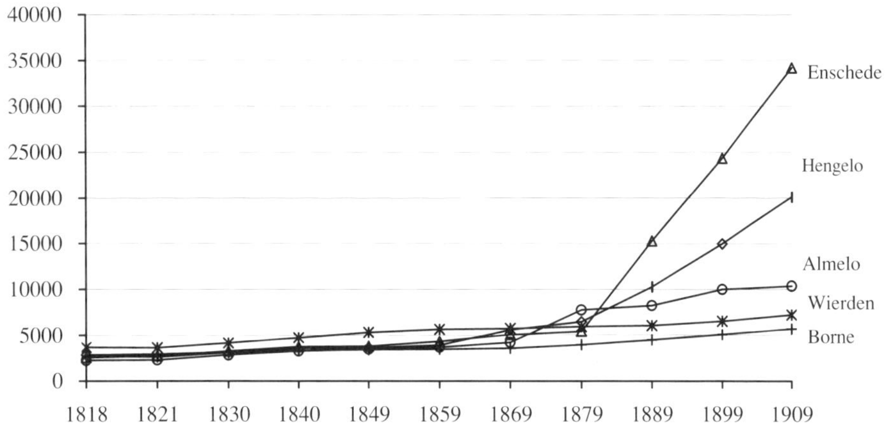

Figure 7.5 Gross marriage, birth and death rates, Borne, 1811–1911 (five-year moving averages)

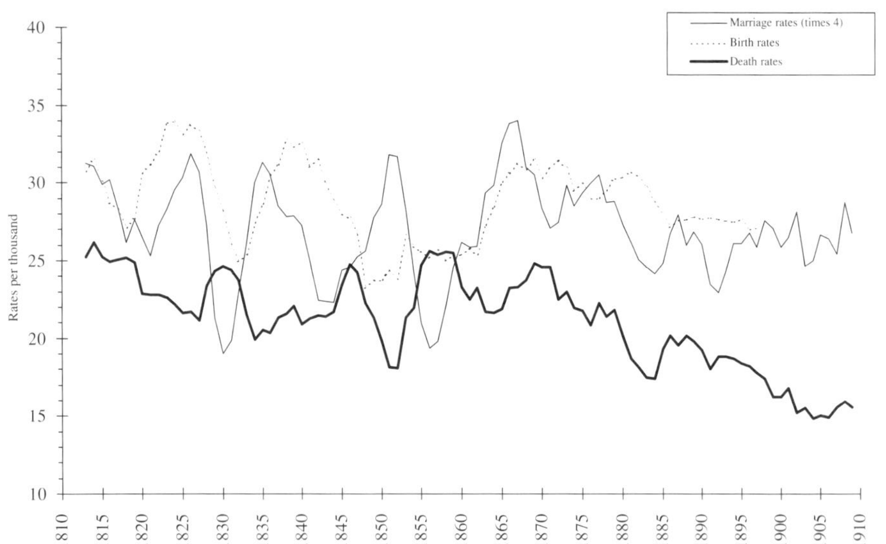

Figure 7.6 Gross marriage, birth and death rates, Wierden, 1811–1911 (five year-moving averages)

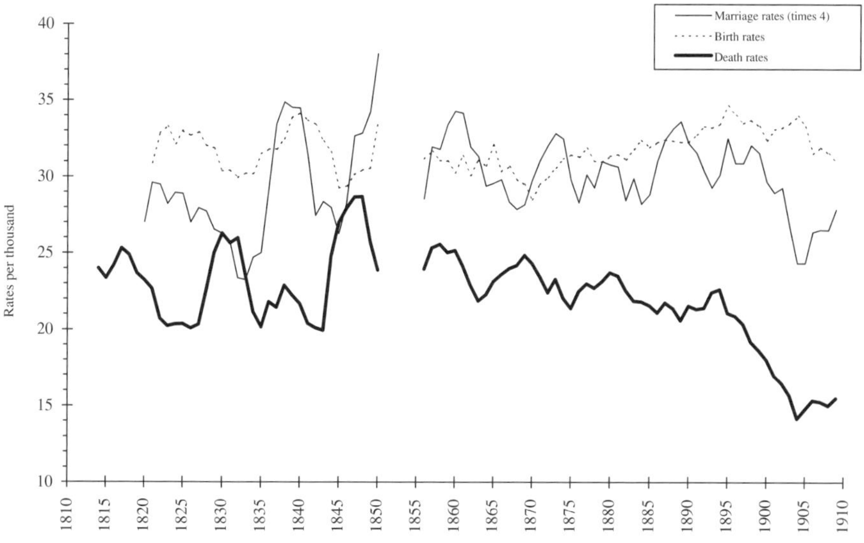

Two phenomena, the presence of the European marriage pattern and the beginning of the subsequent demographic transition, are clearly distinguishable. The European marriage pattern was characterized by high mortality, low marital frequency, a high age at marriage, and high marital fertility (Hajnal, 1965: 101–42). In Figures 7.5 and 7.6, the high levels of fertility and mortality are clearly visible during the first part of the 19th century. During this period also, birth and death rates still at times equalled each other. In some instances, mortality even rose above fertility (although this is concealed by the five year moving averages in Figures 7.5 and 7.6). The marriage rates were at a level that was normal by national (and European) standards, that is, between five and ten per thousand over the entire period (Hofstee, 1981: 146).

The transition to a new demographic pattern is also clearly visible.[2] In both communities, it was not until the beginning of the 1870s before birth and death rates began definitively to diverge. After 1865–70, death rates started to fall while the birth rates maintained their previous high levels; in Wierden, they initially even showed a tendency to rise.

Considering the gross marriage rates in Figures 7.5 and 7.6, it is immediately obvious how closely the trends in birth rates and marriage rates were connected for both communities. However, in contrast to the expectations aroused by theories of proto-

[2] For an extensive introduction to the theories and models concerning the demographic transition, see Andorka (1978). For an overview of results of European research on the demographic transition, see Coale and Watkins (1986).

industrialization, there was no noticeable increase in marriage rates in Borne and Wierden during the 19th century. Neither during the proto-industrial period (1830–60), nor during the subsequent period of industrialization (as of 1870), was there a significant rise in the number of marriages per 1,000 inhabitants. We do observe short periods of rising marriage rates (in Borne, for example, between 1830 and 1835 and between 1855 and 1865, in Wierden between 1835 and 1840 and between 1847 and 1850), but these rises were followed immediately again by falling rates, which suggests that in those periods marriages that had previously been postponed were now realized, rather than that there was an increase in the general level of nuptiality. On the contrary, during the period of industrialization (between 1870 and 1900) Borne in particular shows a slightly downward trend, while in Wierden over this period the trend of the gross marriage rate was in general stable.

To determine whether marriage rates were influenced by changes in the age distribution of the underlying population, population pyramids were constructed for the census years between 1879 and 1909. These are shown in Figure 7.7 and 7.8. For those years, at least, age structure in the two communities was very stable. In general, substantial changes in age structure rarely happen very rapidly, except for the occurrence of sudden mortality crises or other calamities. Since we have no evidence of such profound tragedies, we may assume that the stable age distribution of the last quarter of the 19th century is an adequate reflection of the situation in previous decades. We may therefore assume that the variations in gross marriage patterns reflect changes in actual marriage behaviour rather than changes in the underlying population.

Figure 7.7 Population pyramids, Borne, 1879–1909

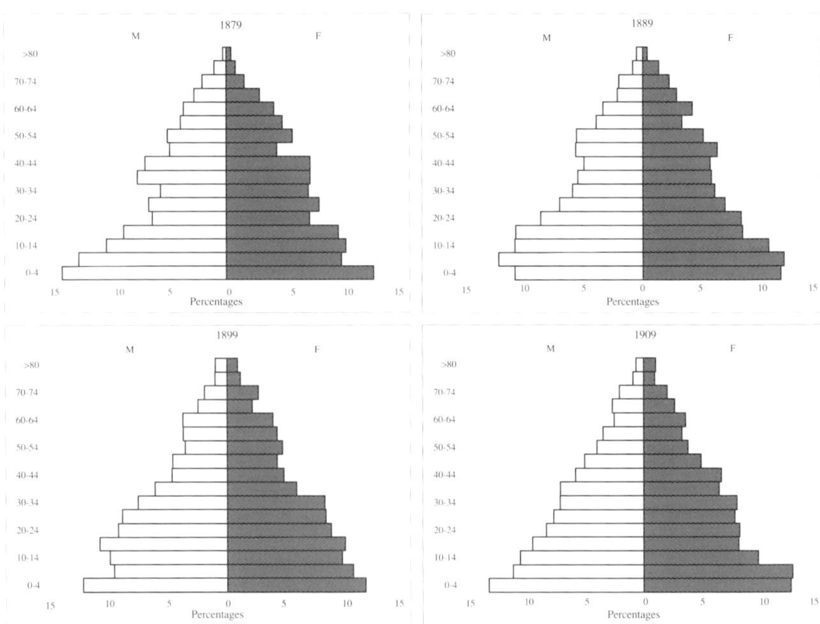

Figure 7.8 Population pyramids, Wierden, 1879–1909

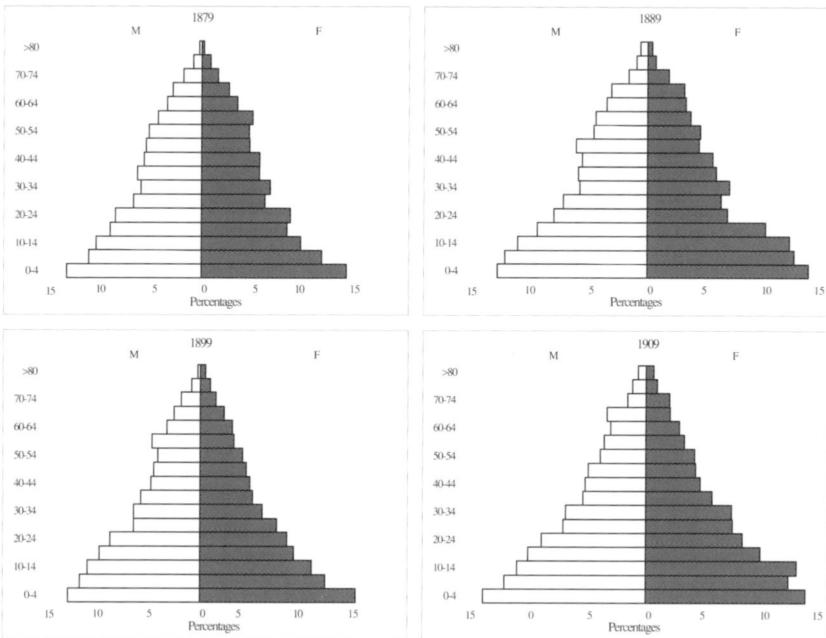

The sex ratios for Borne and Wierden between 1818 and 1909 are presented in Table 7.1. In Wierden, the proportion of men to women was consistently higher than in Borne. The age pyramids show that, at least during the last quarter of the 19th century, this structural difference between Borne and Wierden is age-independent. However, the variation in the sex ratio over the 19th century followed a similar trend in both communities.

Table 7.1 Sex ratio, Borne and Wierden, 1818-1909

	Borne	Wierden
1818	98.9	112.3
1821	105.4	115.7
1830	99.0	113.7
1840	101.4	112.0
1859	98.3	105.8
1869	100.3	105.7
1879	103.4	108.3
1889	104.3	110.6
1899	103.4	110.5
1909	103.3	110.9

For the last three decades of the 19th century, the censuses allow for a calculation of percentages never married 50–59 years (Table 7.2).

Table 7.2 Proportions never married, Borne and Wierden, 1818-1909

	Borne		Wierden	
	Men	Women	Men	Women
1879	19.32	17.68	9.25	5.11
1889	19.53	19.89	12.89	13.36
1899	19.35	21.46	12.50	6.55

These results show that in Borne, the proportions of both men and women never married were consistently (and considerably) higher than in Wierden. It seems that with regard to marriage, Borne maintained a pattern which was closer to the high proportions of final celibacy observed in the European Marriage Pattern than was the case in Wierden. This is confirmed by the I_m rates for the same years (Engelen et al., 1987: 37) (Table 7.3).

Table 7.3 I_m, Borne, Wierden, Overijssel and the Netherlands, 1879-99

	Borne	Wierden	Overijssel	Nederland
1879	0,452	0,583	0,476	0,469
1889	0,461	0,603	0,476	0,451
1899	0,444	0,604	0,483	0,451

The case is not, however, that Borne has exceptionally low rates of nuptiality; rather, Wierden has exceptionally high rates. One reason for this may have been the relatively high proportion of enforced marriages taking place in Wierden in comparison to Borne. We will come back to this later. With regard to our initial hypotheses regarding the increase of nuptiality upon the (re-)introduction of proto-industrialization in Twente, our conclusion must be that the gross rates offer no indications in this direction. On the contrary, it seems that during the 1830s the proportions married have decreased rather than increased. A rise in the proportions of people never married only begins to take place after 1840, and decreases again after 1880.

III. The results of the reconstitutions

The family reconstitutions which were carried out in Borne and Wierden allow us a more precise view of nuptiality, especially with regard to age at marriage. The first results are summarized in Table 7.4.

Table 7.4 Age at first marriage for men and women by community, first and second cohort

	Borne		Wierden	
	Men	Women	Men	Women
Cohort 1 (1831-40)	30.47	27.01	29.60	26.06
Cohort 2 (1871-80)	31.46	28.07	29.78	26.09

A first conclusion must be that in both cohorts, age at first marriage is relatively high for both men and women. This is especially true in view of the hypotheses which were raised at the beginning of this chapter. A comparison with some results from other family reconstitution studies confirms this (see Table 7.5).

Table 7.5 Mean ages at first marriage in comparison

	Borne, Wierden	German villages	Shepshed	Auffay	Tilburg	Marlhes	Spenge
Cohort 1	1831-40	1825-49	1825-51	1831-40	1830-9	1841-70	1818-43
Men	30.0	29.4	24.1	28.3	27	30.6	26.1
Women	26.4	26.9	22.6	26.6	25	25.6	24.7
Cohort 2	1871-80	1875-99			1870-9	1871-98	1844-68
Men	30.4	28.3			26	29.8	26.7
Women	26.8	25.5			25	25.1	24.4

An inquiry carried out by David Levine into the demography of Shepshed in view of its protoindustrial development became a showcase in favour of these hypotheses in the early 1980s (Levine, 1976). For Shepshed, in the 1825–51 cohort Levine found an average age at first marriage of 24.1 for men and of 22.6 for women. When compared to these results, ages at first marriage of both men and women in Borne and Wierden were still rather high. Moreover, compared to analogous periods in other studies, the mean ages at first marriage in Borne and Wierden were high, both for women and men and in both cohorts. It is becoming clear that Shepshed may well have been an exception from the western European perspective, for none of the other figures (all derived from communities that had intensive cottage industry, except for most of Knodel's fourteen German villages (Knodel, 1988)), even came close to the values for Shepshed. The ages at first marriage in Borne and Wierden are also fully comparable to values for other Dutch and Belgian cases.

For six communities in the region of Kempen, Meurkens (1985: 189) found an average age at first marriage for women of 27 years for the period 1880–84. For men, he found a result of 31 years. For the community of Hooge and Lage Mierden around the middle of the 19th century, Van der Heijden found an average age at first marriage of 28.7 years for women (31.1 years for men), while in the community of Nuenen between 1850–1900, he found 29.5 years for wives of smallholders and farmers (32.6 for men), and 28.2 years for wives of weavers (29.8 for the men) (Heijden, 1981: 109). Vandenbroeke, summarizing results of a number of family reconstitution studies carried out for Flanders and Brabant, reaches results which are slightly lower: for the period 1830–39, women's average age at first marriage was 28.0 years, while for the period 1870–79 it was 27.5 years (Vandenbroeke, 1976: 111). Compared to the results for North Brabant, Flanders and Belgian Brabant, in Borne and Wierden age at first marriage was on average somewhat lower (Table 7.5). However, for Krommenie, a village in the region of Zaanstreek north of Amsterdam, where during the 19th century proto-industrialization was present in the form of canvas-weaving, average ages at first marriage were 25.7 years for men and 25.6 years for women, which the authors refer to as being comparatively high for the region, but which is around one year lower than the grand mean for Borne and Wierden together (Damsma et al., 1985) (see Table 7.5)

Returning to Borne and Wierden, we see that the average age at first marriage for both men and women was consistently higher in Borne than in Wierden, although Borne was the community with the more pronounced protoindustrial and industrial character. Therefore, as was the case with the proportions never married, these results do not seem to confirm the hypotheses formulated by Mendels and Medick.

However, it could still be the case that ages at marriage by weavers, for example, do correspond with Mendels's and Medick's idea but are concealed in the larger averages. To examine whether this was indeed the case, the two cohorts were each divided into three occupational categories – agriculture, textiles and other occupations – based on the occupation of the groom at marriage. The occupational structure of the cohorts reflects the already mentioned separate economic developments in Borne and Wierden (see Table 7.6).

Table 7.6 Distribution of men's occupation at marriage, first and second cohorts

	Borne	%	Wierden	%
		Cohort 1 (1831-40)		
Agriculture	91	41.94	146	44.79
Textiles	79	36.41	86	26.38
Others	47	21.66	94	28.83
Total	217		326	
		Cohort 2 (1871-80)		
Agriculture	125	43.25	232	50.66
Textiles	88	30.45	61	13.32
Others	76	26.30	165	36.03
Total	289		458	

Note: First and non-first marriages included

The shares of agriculture in both communities are comparable: in the first cohort, around 40% of the men in each town were employed in agriculture. In Borne, however, the textiles sector was represented more strongly, while in Wierden the 'other' category was more developed.

For the second cohort, the situation had changed: in both communities, the share of agriculture had risen, but a more dramatic change had taken place with respect to textiles. In Borne, the share of men working in this sector had decreased, but in Wierden the share had been halved. The general decrease of textiles in the second cohort might be due to the phase in which this cohort was positioned: at the time, in the 1870s, cottage weaving was already retreating while industrial production was not yet fully established. However, the specific decrease of this sector in Wierden was of a more structural nature: here, mechanized industry would never gain the importance that domestic industry had had in previous decades.

The results of the calculation of average age at first marriage for these occupational groups is shown in Table 7.7. It is clear that male textile workers have the lowest mean ages at marriage, and this is true for both cohorts. Their dispersion, expressed by the standard deviation, is also smaller than that of farmers (a difference of 2.0 years for the first cohort, and of 0.9 years for the second cohort), indicating a relatively small age range in which the majority of men in the textiles category got married. Male farmers, on the other hand, were much more conservative regarding age at first marriage in that, on average, in accordance with the structure of the European Marriage Pattern, they married very late: both their average age at first marriage and the dispersion around the average are the highest of all occupational categories. This indicates that among farmers there was less uniformity as far as age at first marriage was concerned than among the other groups. The men in the 'other' category take a middle position in both cohorts, but are closer to textile workers than they are to agricultural workers.

Table 7.7 Age at first marriage for men and women by occupational category

	Agriculture		Textiles		Other	
	Men	Women	Men	Women	Men	Women
			Cohort 1 (1831-40)			
Mean	31.55	26.80	28.25	26.77	29.54	25.48
Median	30.21	25.85	27.52	26.12	28.73	24.99
St.dev.	7.05	5.25	4.99	4.85	4.86	4.76
N	190		146		120	
			Cohort 2 (1871-80)			
Mean	31.39	26.97	27.94	26.06	30.64	27.16
Median	30.16	25.77	26.78	25.50	29.11	26.47
St.dev.	6.54	5.71	5.68	4.81	5.76	5.09
N	291		132		206	

Contrary to what one might have expected, the change in age at first marriage between the first and the second cohort is generally marginal. For the men with occupations in agriculture and textiles, mean ages at first marriage fell slightly, whereas for the men in the 'other' category they rose by over one year.[3] Thus, although the 'other' group takes a middle position in both cohorts, the trend in the age at first marriage of men in this category between the first and second cohort is precisely the opposite of the trend of the other two categories. On the other hand, in the second cohort, textile workers do have mean ages at marriage that are lower than those of men in the other two categories, and the ages at marriage of farmers are significantly higher than those of men in the other two categories. Whether in Borne and Wierden the differences between weavers and other occupational groups are as large as could be expected might be a matter of debate, but the fact remains that even the comparatively low ages at first marriage for weavers in Borne and Wierden are still a long way from the values Levine found for Shepshed.

If we break down the data in Table 7.7 by community, the image presented above does not alter dramatically (see Table 7.8). The men working in textiles were still the youngest to marry, in both the first and in the second cohort and in both communities. More remarkable, however, is the fact that within occupational categories, there are consistent differences between the two communities. In all occupational groups and in both cohorts, men in Borne married later than their colleagues in Wierden. The

[3] In the 'other' category, the rise in the age at marriage appears to have been a structural phenomenon: between the first and the second cohort, for all significant occupations within this category the average age at first marriage for men rose, in one case (the clog-makers of Wierden) by as much as 4.9 years. The number of clog-makers rose from 18 in the first cohort to 69 in the second, so that their influence on the mean age at marriage rose correspondingly. The only exception to this rule were the merchants, whose mean age at first marriage fell by 7.7 years. Their number rose from 6 in the first cohort to 17 in the second.

reasons for this behaviour are not entirely clear, but may have to do with the different dominant religions in Borne and Wierden, or with differences in economic opportunities in the two communities. We will elaborate on this when dealing with women's age at first marriage below.

Table 7.8 Age at first marriage for men by occupational category and community, first and second cohort

	Agriculture		Textiles		Other	
	Borne	Wierden	Borne	Wierden	Borne	Wierden
			Cohort 1 (1831-40)			
Average	31.73	31.44	28.91	27.66	30.99	28.78
Median	29.20	30.55	28.61	26.43	30.23	27.39
St.dev.	7.38	6.91	4.92	5.05	4.75	4.91
N	71	119	69	77	37	83
			Cohort 2 (1871-80)			
Average	33.74	30.13	28.81	26.68	31.02	30.48
Median	32.25	29.07	27.83	25.54	29.52	28.96
St.dev.	7.29	5.74	6.09	4.85	6.22	5.59
N	102	189	78	54	61	145

It is also remarkable that in agriculture, the changes between the first and the second cohort are very different in Borne from those of Wierden. In Wierden, the age at first marriage for men dropped by more than one year, while for the farmers, small landholders and labourers in Borne, it rose by more than two years. That the development in neither Borne nor Wierden was caused merely by a few exceptions is illustrated by the values for the median and the standard deviation. In both communities these values follow the mean, indicating that the groups as a whole changed their marriage behaviour between the first and second cohort. In Wierden, the standard deviation decreased markedly, indicating that the differences within the group of farmers and small landholders became smaller.

In Borne, the 'textiles' group showed little change between the first and second cohort, while in Wierden the age at first marriage decreased by one year. Upon closer inspection of this group for the second cohort, it turns out that in Wierden, the decrease in the age at first marriage was caused especially by the factory weavers. Their average age at first marriage was 24.83 years (in Borne, it was more than three years higher, at 28.04 years). In contrast, hand weavers in Wierden had an average age at first marriage of 27.76 years (in Borne, as was to be expected, hand weavers married much later, on average at 31.60 years, a difference of nearly four years). Moreover, it has to be noted that in Wierden the group of factory weavers was comparatively small (20 persons), while the hand weavers were more numerous (34 persons). In Borne, this was exactly the reverse: there were 61 factory weavers and only 17 hand weavers.

In the 'other' category, age at first marriage in Borne remained stable between the first and second cohort, while in Wierden it increased by nearly two years. No single occupation within this group can be made responsible for this increase. The most numerous occupations (merchants (12 persons), carpenters (13), bargees (17) and clogmakers (61)) all married between 30.2 and 31.2 years on average. The rise in the age at marriage therefore seems to have been a general phenomenon within this group.

The image one is left with after surveying the ages at marriage for men seems a little paradoxical. On the one hand, there were undeniably differences in ages at first marriage among the three occupational categories. In the first cohort, the 'agriculture' category did distinguish itself from the other two categories, while in the second cohort the textile workers stood out. On the other hand, the differences were not so large as one might have expected them to be in the light of the hypotheses raised at the beginning of this chapter. Compared to the values Levine found for Shepshed, in Borne and Wierden men generally had very high ages at first marriage, while men working in textiles in particular (28.25 in the first cohort, 27.94 in the second cohort) were still a long way from the values Levine found. Moreover, these values did not develop downward significantly between the first and second cohorts.

These results therefore contradict vital positions in the canon of proto-industrialization theory. They do not support the theoretical assumption of a generally low age at marriage in proto-industrial communities: if this had been the case, it would have shown in the results for the first cohort. Moreover, they do not support the thesis that proto-industrial workers will have a significantly lower age at first marriage than will other occupational groups: in Borne and Wierden, the differences in ages at first marriage among men of different occupational status were not very large and, in the proto-industrial first cohort, as far as 'other' and 'textiles' were concerned, the differences were not even statistically significant. On the contrary, in the first cohort it was the farmers who stood out with an above-average age at marriage, while the age of the weavers was below average. The expected lower age at marriage for occupations in textiles only occurred in the second cohort, in a phase and under economic conditions in which the lower age at marriage cannot be connected to proto-industrialization.

These conclusions seem to apply even more so with regard to women's age at first marriage (Table 7.4). As was the case throughout Europe, age at first marriage for women in Borne and Wierden was lower than it was for men. On the whole, this difference amounted to about 3.5 years. There was also some occupation-specific variation for women, (Table 7.7), although the differences among women were less clear-cut than among men. In the first cohort, for example, which includes women married in the period of the booming cottage industry, contrary to expectations there was no difference in the mean age at first marriage of women marrying farmers and those marrying weavers. Even the median ages and the standard deviations differed only marginally. Paradoxically, in the first cohort it was the women in the 'other' category who were the first to marry, on average more than one year younger than the other two groups. In the second cohort, on the other hand, the structure is rather different. Between 1871 and 1880, weavers' wives *had* become the first to marry. On average, though, they committed themselves less than one year earlier than women marrying farmers. The average age of the latter group had barely changed. And oddly enough, the wives of small shopkeepers and craftsmen, who had been the first to marry in the first cohort, now had become the last.

It would be interesting to see whether further breaking down the data in Table 7.7 by community reveals any underlying structures. After all, there were some differences in economic structure between Borne and Wierden, with the former community having a more pronounced industrial structure than the latter, which remained more agriculturally oriented. These differences might appear when looking at ages at first marriage for women by occupational categories in each of the two communities separately (see Table 7.9).

Table 7.9 Age at first marriage for women by occupational category and community, first and second cohort

	Agriculture		Textiles		Other	
	Borne	Wierden	Borne	Wierden	Borne	Wierden
			Cohort 1 (1831-40)			
Mean	27.49	26.39	27.44	26.17	25.30	25.55
Median	28.31	25.07	26.31	25.42	25.40	24.78
St.dev.	5.02	5.34	4.50	5.06	4.43	4.90
N	71	119	69	77	37	83
			Cohort 2 (1871-80)			
Mean	29.20	25.77	26.93	24.81	27.61	26.97
Median	27.57	24.73	26.50	24.38	26.66	26.32
St.dev	6.08	5.11	4.98	4.25	4.82	5.18
N	102	189	78	54	61	145

This new perspective on the data reveals some interesting additional characteristics of the marriage behaviour of women in both communities. In the first cohort, for example, the largest differences in age at marriage were those between the two communities, and not those between occupational groups: in Borne, weavers' and farmers' wives married at almost exactly the same mean age. The same was the case in Wierden. Between Borne and Wierden, however, there was a difference of over one year for these two groups. And contrary to what one might expect in view of the theoretical predictions concerning demographic behaviour in proto-industrial communities, it was the women of Borne, the more pronouncedly proto-industrial community, who married later. For women in the 'other' category, there is no noticeable difference in the average age at marriage between the two communities.

For the second cohort, the situation had changed. In half of the groups, the average age at first marriage had risen ('agriculture' in Borne, and the 'other' category in both communities), while in the other half it had fallen (by around half a year for the wives of farmers in Wierden and for the wives of weavers in Borne, and by nearly 1.4 years for the wives of weavers in Wierden). In the period 1871–80, it was the spouses of weavers who married at the youngest age, although their ages at marriage had fallen only marginally in Borne. One might regard their fall in age at first marriage as a coincidence, to be attributed to the relatively small number of cases in this category in Borne: the mean value for weavers' wives in Borne has only declined marginally while the median has risen marginally and, statistically speaking, the differences between the ages at first marriage for the first and second cohort in Borne are not significant.[4]

The same conclusion can be drawn for weavers' wives in Wierden: from a statistical point of view, the fall in their age at first marriage between the first and second cohort was not significant. Although in Wierden the average age at first marriage had fallen by nearly 1.4 years, in the second cohort in particular the number of cases involved is so small that random fluctuations cannot be ruled out. This was confirmed by an analysis of variance, comparing the ages at first marriage for weavers' wives in Wierden for the first and second cohorts, which revealed no significant differences between the values.

What is more interesting than the drop in the age at marriage *per se* is again the differences between the two communities. It is striking that in Borne both the mean and median ages at first marriage are higher than they are in Wierden, for all occupational groups and for both cohorts, with the single exception of the mean value for the 'others' category in the first cohort, which is marginally below the corresponding value of Wierden. The differences are not always large, but they are consistent.

IV. The role of religion

A possible explanation for these differences might be religion. One of the notable disparities in social structure between the two communities is the difference in the proportions of Catholics and Protestants in Borne and Wierden. In Wierden, around 65 per cent of the population were Protestants, while in Borne, we find 60 per cent were Catholics. This does not mean that the two communities were extreme representatives of either religion, but it is a structural difference none the less. From the literature, it is known furthermore that in general, among 18th- and 19th-century Catholics, age at first marriage was higher and the proportion of premarital pregnancies and illegitimacy were lower than among Protestants (van Poppel, 1992; Engelen and Meyer, 1979). In the case of Borne and Wierden, with respect to mean ages at first marriage, we concluded that these were nearly always higher in the community of Borne, in which the dominant religion was Catholicism (Engelen and Meyer, 1979). Therefore, it seems plausible to link the higher ages at marriage to religion (Table 7.10).[6]

---

[4] An analysis of variance (age at first marriage against cohort) yielded an F ratio of 0.402 (degrees of freedom between groups: 1; within groups: 145), resulting in a p value of 0.53.

[5] Analysis of variance (age at first marriage against cohort) yielded an F value of 2.57 (degrees of freedom between groups: 1; within groups: 129), resulting in a p value of 0.11.

[6] In Table 7.10, only marriages within a single religious category were included. Mixed marriages between Catholic and Protestant spouses were not included. This does not affect the results since it involves only 5 out of 377 first marriages in the first cohort for which we know the religion of bride and groom.

Table 7.10 Mean age at first marriage by religion and community, first cohort

	Borne			Wierden		
	Men	Women	N	Men	Women	N
Protestant	30.02	27.58	35	30.81	26.58	174
Catholic	31.77	27.43	114	29.08	26.87	54

Before the data are interpreted, one important comment needs to be made. It may have been noticed that the total numbers of persons in this table does not correspond to the total numbers of first marriages observed in other tables, and that their average ages at first marriage are noticeably higher. This is due to the fact that the data in Table 7.10 were derived from baptismal records and not from civil birth records (which as a matter of principle did not record religion). Copies of the baptismal records were attached to the marital records for persons born before the introduction of civil registration in 1811, for whom of course no civil birth record existed, or for those persons who were born after 1811 but who were still not registered by the civil authorities. This leads to the situation whereby the people included in Table 7.10 were all born before or shortly after 1811, while those births which occurred after 1811 and which were registered with the civil authorities are not included, since for those people no religion was known. Consequently, the average age at marriage of the groups represented in Table 7.10 is higher than that of the marriage cohort as a whole. One should therefore take care in interpreting the ages at marriage as such, since they are not representative of the entire cohort. However, the people whose religion was unknown were fairly evenly distributed across the two communities: in Borne, there were 14 per cent with an unknown religion, while in Wierden this was the case with 18 per cent of all those engaging in first marriages. Since the groups with an unknown religion are therefore firstly comparatively small, and secondly proportionally similar in size in both communities, there is no objection to using the data in Table 7.10 as a basis for analysis, because the groups involved are comparable.

The analysis shows that once again, the major differences are those between communities. The observation that women in particular married earlier in Wierden than did those in Borne remains intact when controlled for religion. Irrespective of their religion or the occupation of their husbands (as demonstrated in the previous section), the women in Wierden married on average between 7–12 months earlier than the women of Borne. On the other hand, it is also clear that religion as such did not play a determining role: the differences in age at first marriage between Protestant and Catholic women within each community are far smaller than the differences between the two denominations as between the communities. We may therefore conclude that in the first cohort, the religion of an individual does not play a major role in the explanation of the differences in age at first marriage between the two communities.

An alternative way of explaining the discrepancy between the two communities might be to look at the numbers of pre-nuptial pregnancies in each community. If, as was demonstrated by Engelen and Meyer, it is correct that Protestants had proportionally more pre-nuptial pregnancies than Catholics, this might influence their age at marriage (Engelen and Meyer, 1979). Since pre-nuptial pregnancies ordinarily led to enforced marriages, one can assume that these marriages took place on average at an earlier age than did ordinary marriages (see Table 7.11).

Table 7.11 Age at first marriage for women by community and interval between marriage and first birth, first and second cohort

	Interval < 7 months		Interval>7 months	
	Borne	Wierden	Borne	Wierden
		Cohort 1 (1831-40)		
Mean	27.12	24.79	26.76	26.33
Median	26.23	24.56	26.29	25.07
St.dev.	3.39	4.04	4.85	4.96
N	16	85	122	147
		Cohort 2 (1871-80)		
Mean	26.55	24.35	26.99	25.95
Median	25.93	24.13	26.63	25.26
St.dev.	4.78	3.63	4.28	4.26
N	27	103	142	198

If one considers those women who were pregnant at marriage, there is a difference of over two years in mean age at first marriage between Borne and Wierden in both cohorts. However, in Borne there was no significant difference in the age at first marriage between brides who were pregnant at marriage and those who were not, while in both cohorts, this difference was around 1.5 years in Wierden. This suggests that at least in Borne the desired age at marriage moved within certain bounds, based on a set of rules and morals with regard to what was an acceptable age at marriage. The relatively small difference in Borne between the age at marriage for women who were pregnant at marriage and those who were not also suggests that in Borne, sexual activity between partners was either postponed until the date of the marriage was fixed, or that in Borne a more effective set of preventive techniques was applied than in Wierden. Although at first sight there seems to be little reason why in one community such techniques should be used while in the next community they were not, it is a possibility that deserves further research (see also Schellekens, 1991).

It must however be kept in mind that in Wierden there were proportionally far more pre-nuptial conceptions in both cohorts than was the case in Borne. Moreover, in Wierden the difference in age at first marriage between women who were pregnant at marriage and those who were not is much larger than in Borne. This suggests that in Wierden, sexual activity between unmarried partners was more common and started at an earlier age than was the case in Borne. In combination with a generally accepted earlier age at marriage among Dutch Protestants than among Dutch Catholics, as is suggested by other research, this would lead to a situation in which firstly the general age at first marriage would be lower, and secondly the proportion of pre-nuptial pregnancies would be higher. All this suggests that there is indeed a connection between religion and the average age at first marriage. However, the relation is not a direct one, as was shown in Table 7.10: irrespective of whether a woman was a Catholic or a Protestant, in Borne she would marry on average at around 27.5 years, while in Wierden, she would marry on average at around 26.7 years. What seems to matter, therefore, is not an individual's specific religion but rather the dominant religion in the community. The dominant religion might have set out rules and beliefs regarding an acceptable frequency and age at marriage. We know this to have been the case in the Netherlands in the 19th century, where the Catholic clergy propagated celibacy as a first choice and a late marriage as the second best option.[7] It is therefore possible that this mechanism was responsible to a considerable extent for the observed phenomenon that there was less difference in age at first marriage between religions within a community than there was between the two communities as such.

For the first cohort, it is possible to test this by controlling the values in Table 7.10 for pregnancy at marriage (Table 7.12).

Table 7.12 Age at first marriage for woman pregnant at marriage by religion and community, first cohort

	Borne		Wierden	
	Protestant	Catholic	Protestant	Catholic
Mean	28.0	26.6	25.5	24.8
Median	28.3	25.4	24.9	25.2
St.dev.	3.7	4.2	4.3	1.6
N	7	5	56	5

To be sure, the values in Table 7.12 are generally too small to allow for firm conclusions based on these values alone, but they do support the conclusion from Tables 7.10 and 7.11. Irrespective of the religion of the individual women, the structural difference in age at first marriage between Borne and Wierden remains intact: Catholic women in Borne on average married later than did Catholic women in Wierden, and the same applies to Protestants and those whose religion is unknown. This suggests that the dominant religion in a community was apparently able to define rules with regard to what was considered to be an acceptable age at first marriage, and was even in a position to influence to some extent those inhabitants who did not belong to the dominant religion. In Borne, where the dominant religion was Catholicism, this led to a situation in which firstly, the number of pre-nuptial pregnancies was significantly smaller than in Protestant-dominated Wierden, and secondly, the average age at mar-

[7] See van Poppel (1992: 230–3) and his discussion of Irish and Dutch literature which confirms this pattern (van Poppel refers to Connell (1968) 113-61).

riage was structurally higher even in case of pre-marital pregnancies. The fact that this was so for all occupational categories, combined with the observation that the differences in age at first marriage appeared to exist primarily between communities rather than between occupational categories, suggests that the dominant religious culture in a community may have been a stronger determinant of age at marriage than occupation. With regard to the theoretical issues that are at the core of this study, this implies that whether one had an occupation in cottage weaving or in one of the other two occupational groups was not the factor of prime importance in the decision to marry at a certain age. Rather, it seems as if the majority of the couples responded to a certain extent to existing norms within the community, norms which, it is suggested, are first of all linked to the views generally held within the dominant religious culture in the community, not to the economic feasibility of early marriage or the personal desire to marry at a certain age.

V. Conclusions

The key results of these analyses, dealing with the age at first marriage, seriously challenge the positions taken by Mendels and Medick. The ages at first marriage of both men and women are generally too high and too undiversified with respect to occupational status to be interpreted with reference to proto-industrialization theories. Moreover, the differences between weavers and farmers/peasants are too small to allow the conclusion that in Borne and Wierden a group of truly proto-industrial labourers existed, a group whose marriage behaviour was structurally different from that of the other groups that surrounded them.

Among men, these differences are appreciable and indeed seem to point to a specific proto-industrial marriage pattern (in both cohorts, weavers were indeed the youngest ones to marry), but with women this was not the case. In the first cohort, women marrying weavers had the same age at first marriage as women marrying farmers and smallholders. In the second cohort, the former had indeed the lowest ages at first marriage, but by that time industrialization had started to develop in Borne and Wierden. All the same, statistical tests show that the distributions of the ages at marriage for women were all very close together. We then looked at the question of whether religion might play a role in the age at marriage, since it was discovered that the main differences in ages at marriage arose between communities, not between occupational groups. It was concluded that religion does apparently play a role, although not at the level of the individual but rather as a background variable. All this leads us to believe that the traditional proto-industrialization model does not hold under these circumstances, and that essential parts of it are contradicted by the material presented above.

Bibliography

Andorka, R. (1978) *Determinants of fertility in advanced societies*, London.

Bieleman, J. (1992) *Geschiedenis van de landbouw in Nederland 1500–1950. Verandering en verscheidenheid*, Amsterdam.

Boot, J.A.P.G. (1935) *De Twentsche Katoennijverheid 1830–1870*, Amsterdam.

Boot, J.A.P.G. and Blonk, A. (1957) *Van smiet- tot snelspoel. De opkomst van de Twents-Gelderse textielindustrie in het begin van de 19de eeuw*, Hengelo.

Coale, A.J. and Watkins, S. (eds) (1986) *The decline of fertility in Europe: the revised proceedings of a conference on the Princeton European Fertility Project*, Princeton.

Connell, K.H. (1968) 'Catholicism and marriage in the century after the famine', in *Irish peasant society: four historical essays*, Oxford, pp. 113-61.

Damsma, D., Siffels, N. and Weijers, I. (1985) 'Geen geld, geen goed. Het gezin van de zeildoekwever in Krommenie in de negentiende eeuw', *Tijdschrift voor Sociale Geschiedenis*, 11, pp. 101–29.

Engelen, T.L.M. (1987) *Fertiliteit, Arbeid, Mentaliteit. De vruchtbaarheidsdaling in Nederlands-Limburg 1850–1960*, Maastricht.

Engelen, T.L.M. and Meyer, M.M. (1979) 'Gedwongen huwelijken op het Nederlandse platteland', *A.A.G. Bijdragen*, 22, pp. 190–220.

Fischer, E.J. (1983) *Fabriqueurs en Fabrikanten; de Twentse katoennijverheid en de onderneming S.J. Spanjaard te Borne tussen circa 1800 en 1930*, Utrecht.

Griffiths, R.T. (1979) *Industrial retardation in the Netherlands, 1830–1850*, Den Haag.

Gullickson, G.L. (1986) *Spinners and weavers of Auffay: rural industry and the sexual division of labor in a French village, 1750–1850*, Cambridge.

Hajnal, J. (1965) 'European marriage patterns in perspective', in D.V. Glass and D.E.C. Eversley (eds), *Population in history: essays in historical demography*, London, pp. 101–43.

Heijden, C.G.W.P. van der, (1981) 'Een belichting van enige historisch-demografische aspecten van een Kempische plattelandsgemeente in de negentiende eeuw', *Varia Historica Brabantica*, 10, pp. 83–120

Hendrickx, F.M.M. (1995) 'The rise and fall of an industrial region: Twente, 1650–1960', in R. Leboutte and J-P. Lehners (eds), *Passé et avenir des bassins industriels en Europe*, Luxembourg, pp. 235–46.

Hendrickx, F.M.M., (1997) *'In order not to fall into poverty': production and reproduction in the transition from proto-industry to factory-industry in Borne and Wierden (the Netherlands), 1800–1900*, Amsterdam.

Hofstee, E.W. (1981) *Korte demografische geschiedenis van Nederland van 1800 tot heden*, Haarlem.

Janssens, A.A.P.O. (1993) *Family and social change: the household as a process in an industrializing community*, Cambridge.

Klein, P. (1991) 'Familie und agrarisch-heimgewerbliche Verflechtung. Eine demographische Studie zu Spenge (Ravensberg) 1768–1868', unpublished Ph.D. thesis, University of Bielefeld.

Knodel, J.E. (1988) *Demographic behaviour in the past: a study of fourteen German village populations in the eighteenth and nineteenth centuries*, Cambridge.

Lehning, J.R. (1980) *The peasants of Marlhes: economic development and family organization in nineteenth-century France*, London.

Levine, D. (1976) 'The demographic implications of rural industrialization: a family reconstitution study of Shepshed, Leicestershire, 1600–1851', *Social History*, 2, pp. 177–96.

Medick, H. (1976) 'The proto-industrial family economy: the structural function of household and family during the transition from peasant society to industrial capitalism', *Social History*, 2, pp. 291–315.

Mendels, F.F. (1972) 'Proto-industrialization: the first phase of the industrialization process', *Journal of Economic History*, 32, pp. 241–61.

Mendels, F.F. (1981) *Industrialization and population pressure in eighteenth century Flanders*, New York.

Meurkens, P. (1985) *Bevolking, economie en cultuur van het oude Kempenland*, Bergeijk.

Poppel, F. van (1979) *Trouwen in Nederland. Een historisch-demografische studie van de 19e en vroeg-20e eeuw*, Den Haag.

Schellekens, J. (1991) 'Determinants of marriage patterns among farmers and labourers in two eighteenth-century Dutch villages', *Journal of Family History*, 16, pp. 139–55.

Slicher van Bath, B.H. (1977) *Een samenleving onder spanning. Geschiedenis van het platteland in Overijssel*, Utrecht.

Trompetter, C. (1997) *Agriculture, proto-industry and Mennonite entrepreneurship: a history of the textiles industries in Twente 1600–1815*, Amsterdam.

Vandenbroeke, C. (1976) 'Karakteristieken van het huwelijks- en voortplantingspatroon. Vlaanderen en Brabant, 17de-19de eeuw', *Tijdschrift voor Sociale Geschiedenis*, 5, pp. 105–45.

Vylder, G. de (1995) 'Nederland gevangen in een textielweb', *Textielhistorische Bijdragen*, 35, pp. 120–32.

Zanden, J.L. van (1985) *De economische ontwikkeling van de Nederlandse landbouw in de negentiende eeuw, 1800–1914*, Utrecht.

8 Marriage and the early modern state: the Norwegian case[1]

Sølvi SOGNER, University of Oslo

I. Introduction

Marriage is the key to population growth, as Wrigley and Schofield have argued so well for England (Wrigley and Schofield, 1981). Marriage, however, is a very complex institution. Unlike births and deaths, marriage cannot be regarded as a purely demographic event (even though the medieval church came quite close to doing so in accepting copulation combined with promise of marriage as a *de facto* marriage). Marriage does not just happen as a result of the natural attraction between the sexes. Marriages are not created in heaven, or privately by two contracting parties. Historically, marriages are entered into according to rules that to a large degree are the consensus outcome of conflicting interests between the families of the parties, rules that are upheld by tradition, modified over time and heavily influenced by the dispositions of the state. Marriages are as a rule founded on an economic basis, whether solid or only makeshift. In so far as the state's policy had economic implications, the relevance for the marriage institution is immediately obvious.

In the first part of this chapter, we give an outline of the main traits in the development of the institution of marriage in the Nordic countries in general in the early modern period, from a demographic point of view. The focus will be on the 18th century, when for the first time there are adequate sources to study demographics in Scandinavia. We shall argue that the differential population growth of the five Nordic countries in the 18th century can best be understood in terms of differences in economic development.

In the second part of the chapter, we proceed to discuss the implications for marriage in Norway of certain aspects of the state's policy which have not been sufficiently drawn into the debate, probably because they are of a cultural or gendered nature. We will discuss marriage in a cultural context, supplementing insights from the demographic sources with findings from recent research on 17th- and 18th-century judicial sources. We shall focus on the Norwegian experience, but we believe this to be representative of Nordic development in general.

---

[1] A slightly different version of this paper has been presented at a seminar on 'Women's employment, marriage age and population change' in Delhi, 3-5 March 1997. The perspective has been elaborated in 'Illegitimitet i et kjønnshistorisk perspektiv på maktstaten i tidlig nytid', in *Folk og erhverv tilegnet Hans Chr. Johansen,* Odense 1995, pp. 33-45. For the present version, I am indebted to professor Kari Pitkänen, Helsinki, for his comments on the Finnish situation.

II. Population trends in the Nordic countries

II.1. Population growth c.1735–1900

Scandinavia had a population of about 3.5 million in 1750. By 1850, the population had more than doubled to 8 million. By 1900 the population had almost quadrupled from the earlier figure to 12.5 million.

Some of this growth must be attributed to falling mortality, which declined in Denmark, Norway and Sweden from the end of the 18th century. By 1870 mortality was declining in Finland and Iceland as well, and populations were growing quickly and quite evenly in all five countries.

High mortality in ordinary years and repeated demographic crises during the 18th century caused serious setbacks to population growth. However, growth patterns are strikingly different between the countries. In Denmark, Norway and Sweden there was a small but steady growth of 0.5 per cent per annum for the three countries taken together. In Iceland population hardly increased at all – 0.1 per cent per annum – whereas in Finland population was growing very fast, at a rate of 1.3 per cent per annum. We shall argue here that these spectacular differences in population growth are largely due to differential opportunities for marriage.

Table 8.1 Average annual population increase, 1735–1800 and 1801–1900, percentages

	Sweden	Finland	Denmark	Norway	Iceland
1735—1800	0.5	1.3	0.3	0.7	0.1
1801—1900	0.7	0.9	0.9	0.9	0.7

Source: Bengtsson (1992: 11); *Suomen taloushistoria, 3* (1983).

II.2. Marriage and celibacy in the 18th century

Age at marriage was high for both women and men in almost all of the Nordic countries. Only half of women in the age group 25–29 in Denmark, Norway and Sweden were married. In Iceland, age at marriage was even higher; there, half of all women were not married before entering the age group 30–34. In Finland, on the other hand, it is indicated that half of all women may have been married before age 25, i.e. in the age group 20–24.

Substantial proportions of women never married; some 10–15 per cent of women were still single around the age of 50 in Denmark, Norway and Sweden, while in Iceland in 1801, as many as 25 per cent of women were still single at around age 50. Even so this was a remarkable change since the census of 1703, when 40 per cent of women were still celibate at this age (Gunnarsson, 1980; Gunnlaugsson, 1988). The

Finnish situation is more complicated. In western Finland the situation is similar to central Scandinavia, whereas eastern Finland represents a development of its own, completely contrary to the Icelandic situation. Unfortunately there are no national statistics before 1880, but provincial figures from eastern Finland indicate that marriage here was almost universal in the 18th century – only 2–4 per cent were still single at age 50 – the European Marriage Pattern did not have a breakthrough in this area until the 19th century (Lutz and Pitkänen, 1986; Moring, 1998).

Table 8.2 Proportions single women, by age, Nordic countries, 18th century

		20-24	**25-29**	**30-34**	**35-39**	**40-44**	**45-49**	**50-54**
Sweden	1750	73	43	26	16	12	10	
Sweden	1800	78	48	30	20	15	12	
Norway	1801	81	54	34	27	19	18	13
Iceland	1703	95	79	51	48	41	43	
		20-29		**30-39**		**40-49**		**50-59**
Iceland	1801	69		34		26		23
		15-24		**25-34**			**45-54**	
Finland	1751	47		11			4	
	1800	71		20			2	
	1880	86		32			14	
		20	**25**	**30**	**35**	**40**	**45**	**50**
Denmark	1801	98	78	36	17	17	6	9

Source: Gunnarsson (1980); Gunnlaugsson (1988: 62); Hofsten and Lundström (1976: 35; Johansen (1975: 90); *NOS B 134*.(1980: 96); Lutz and Pitkänen, (1986).
Note: The figures for Finland 1751 and 1800 are based on only one community, Kitee, but for 1880 they cover the entire county of Viborg.
Data on age at marriage at a national level in Norway go back to the middle of the 19th century. Men were on average 29 years old and women were 27 years old when they married for the first time. Not until the 1930s did the age at marriage for men not previously married fall below 27, and for women below 25. Local parish studies for the 18th century indicate that marriage age was high then as well.

In sum, we seem then to be confronted with three different 18th-century nuptiality patterns:
1. An Icelandic pattern where women typically marry in the age group 30–34, and 25 per cent of the women never marry.
2. A central Scandinavian pattern –coinciding with John Hajnal's European Marriage Pattern– where women marry in the age group 25–29, and 10–15 per cent of them never marry.
3. An East Finnish pattern where women typically marry at 20–24 years old, and only 2–4 per cent remain celibate throughout life.

This is indeed surprising, considering the generally accepted homogeneity of the Scandinavian countries. All five countries have small populations, scattered settlement, dominant agriculture, low levels of urbanization, Protestant Lutheran state churches and great similarity in their legal systems.

II.3. Illegitimate, legitimate and premarital fertility in Scandinavia

These differential nuptiality patterns of necessity influenced fertility. The great majority of children were born within wedlock in all five countries: 90 per cent in Iceland, 95–97 per cent in Sweden, Denmark and Norway, 96–98 per cent in Finland. The figures are as might be expected from the nuptiality patterns: values for the illegitimacy ratio will then be 10 per cent in late and seldom-marrying Iceland from 1771–1800, 5–7 per cent in Denmark, Norway and Sweden around 1800, and below 3 per cent in parts of Finland, where it is indicated that marriage at this time was still very early and almost universal.

Table 8.3 Illegitimacy rates in the Nordic countries, 1751–1820, percentages

	Sweden	Norway	Denmark	Finland	Iceland
1751–1760	2.4	-		1.4	
1761–1770	2.6	-			
1771–1780	2.9	4.2	3.6**		
1781–1790	3.9	4.8*	-	2.8***	9.6°
1791–1800	5.0	-	-	-	-
1801–1810	6.1	6.3	7.4	-	-
1811–1820	6.8	7.4	-	-	-

Source: Hofsten and Lundström (1976: 31); *NOS XII 245* (1969: 44–45); Gille (1949–50: 32); Johansen (1975: 103); Gunnarsson (1980: 23)
Note: * = 1781–83; ** = 1751-1800; *** = 1761-1880; ° = 1771-1800

Fertility within marriage was very similar to rates that have been found for other European farmer societies. Children were born every two or three years throughout the time of marriage; mothers were in their early 40s when they gave birth for the last time. Prolonged breastfeeding is likely to be the cause of the generous spacing between births (Lithell, 1988).

The fertility of married women greatly exceeds that of unmarried women. Marriage, therefore, is a clear stimulant to raising the general birth rate. Marriage is selective. The women who married tended to be fecund: bridal pregnancy is a widespread phenomenon in the Scandinavian countries, with the exception probably of Finland in the 18th century. In the 19th century, the Finnish pattern becomes more like the rest of the Northern countries. Norwegian family reconstitution studies show that 39–52 per cent of the brides had a first birth before the wedding or 0–7 months after it (Sogner, 1984). If people did not marry for whatever reason, they might run the risk of conceiving illegitimate children, but on the other hand the exposure to becoming fertile was greatly reduced. Unwed mothers tend to be about the same age as brides, according to a representative survey for Norway for 1802–03 (Haavet, 1982). Unwed fathers, on the other hand, tend to be somewhat younger than the bridegrooms, and were most probably not yet ready to support a family. The interpretation most widely favoured is as follows: illegitimate children are born to parents who act according to the norms of rural society. Pre-nuptial sexuality was accepted as part of the mate-seeking culture. What was exceptional was that a prenuptial conception proved to be not prenuptial after all, and resulted not in a wedding but in an illegitimate birth.

II.4. Marriage, household formation and livelihoods

The economic opportunities for young people to marry and set up a household of their own have always varied enormously. To marry or not to marry was the question everywhere. Iceland and parts of Finland represent the two extremes, and the answer to the question differed in the two countries.

In parts of Finland, the decision to marry varied according to whether people were farmers or were without property. In the former case, the parents would have been able to exert some influence. The multiple family household was favoured in connection with the slash and burn form of agriculture, but also in other areas. A father and his sons and their families might agree to form a joint household, or brothers and their wives might keep house together. The young couple did not necessarily need to economic basis to create an autonomous household; they could make do with their own labour as part of a larger unit (Moring, 1994).

Conditions in Iceland, on the other hand, seem to have been excessively restrictive: 'The Icelandic poor law was intended to deal with the problem of poverty in a rural society...to ensure social discipline, and prevent vagrancy, guarantee farmers a steady supply of relatively cheap labour, *prevent paupers from marrying*...in general to maintain the existing social order' (Gunnlaugsson, 1988; my emphasis). In 1824, ministers were actually forbidden to marry people who were in debt for poor relief received during the ten years preceding the proposed marriage, a regulation which was not abolished until 1917. This can be seen as indicative of very strict regulation of marriage, an interest shared by central and local authorities as well as by the propertied classes (Gunnlaugsson, 1985).

In central Scandinavia, household formation in the 18th century falls between these two extremes. It was becoming increasingly neo-local, and the trend is characterised by a multiplication of simple nuclear households. The old model – the *stem-family*, when families of two generations kept house together – was still to be found on farms and involved the parent family and the heir to be, usually the eldest son and his family. There may be several reasons for this development. First, the retiring farmer as well as the son who would inherit increasingly seemed to prefer separate lodgings. This can explicitly be read out of retirement contracts, where after the 1720s the retiring parents less frequently 'join at the table' – which was the traditional way – but instead took out in goods and services what was due to them and lived in a separate household (Sogner, 1998).

Also, and more importantly, improved economic conditions including new industries outside agriculture made it easier in the course of the 18th century for young couples to find the resources set up house in separate lodgings. The possibilities for doing so varied according to region, and Central Scandinavia was most favoured in this respect. Nuclear family households were rapidly increasing in numbers, outbalancing all other family household forms. Younger siblings were able to find economic openings which would allow them to set up a household of their own. It is thus true that the typical family household in 18th-century Scandinavia was the nuclear family household. In charge was the married couple, two adults sharing the work and the responsibility of running the household unit. In the household of the married couple could be found their biological children, resident relatives, lodgers and servants.

II.5. The centripetal and the centrifugal family

The distribution of household members in the various households indicates that we have two main types, the centripetal and the centrifugal type (Löfgren, 1977). The production activity of the former requires labour, and it tends to attract people from outside and to have a larger number of members. The latter is smaller in size, has less household production activity and hence less need for extra hands from outside the family. Indeed, the tendency for a household of this type is quite the opposite; supernumerary members are forced to go out to work for their living. Again, Eastern Finland represents a distinctive development. In Northern Karelia in the 18th century there were large families and few servants, whereas in the 19th century families grew smaller and the number of servants increased.

The situation in 1801 in Rendalen, a rural parish in East Norway, may illustrate this finding. Ninety-five per cent of households here were headed by married couples. The households can be sorted according to social groups, with farmers on the one hand and cottars on the other. Each group shows a definite structural pattern, which however becomes somewhat blurred if the mean is considered. Farmers' households were more than twice the size of the cottar household, 7.6 persons versus 3.7. Each component of the household was smaller in the cottar household: there were fewer resident children, fewer resident kin, fewer lodgers and above all, hardly any servants.

These same differences between farmer households and cottar households is found elsewhere. Examples are given from the parish of Dala in Sweden in 1780 – 5.4 versus 3.0 – and the parish of Krønge in Denmark in 1787 – 5.2 versus 3.6. Also, the distribution of persons within categories is very similar (Sogner, 1978; Winberg, 1977; Nygård Larsen, 1976).

Table 8.4 Household structure of farmers and cottars, parishes of Dala, Sweden, 1780, Krønge, Denmark, 1787 and Rendalen, Norway, 1801

	Farmers			Cottars		
	Dala	Krønge	Rendalen	Dala	Krønge	Rendalen
Nuclear family	4.5	3.9	4.8	2.9	3.1	3.3
Kin	0.2	0.4	0.9	0.1	0.2	0.2
Foster children	-	-	0.1	-	-	0.03
Servants	0.8	0.9	1.4	0.1	0.1	0.03
Coresidants	-	-	0.4	-	-	0.2
Total	5.4	5.2	7.6	3.0	3.6	3.7

Source: Winberg (1977: 300); Sogner (1978: 291), Nygård Larsen (1976: 139)

In Norway, the 18th century was characterised by a marked increase in the number of «centrifugal» households. This was due to new industries offering opportunities for young people to marry and set up a new household. For instance, in the parish of Rendalen referred to above, practically all households – 97 per cent – had been farmer households in the 1660s. By 1801, the number of households had tripled, but only 50 per cent of all households were now farmers' households: the other 50 per cent were cottars and lodgers' households. A social cleavage had taken place, in this particular case in the wake of commercial exploitation of the forests. The new development opened up for the simpler type of household, making it possible for more young couples to marry and set up house and start a family and thus contribute to the population growth.

The same development took place to some extent everywhere in the region. The nature of the economy might differ, as might the pace of development. But judging by the very revealing structure of the households, the trend is clear: young people were increasingly marrying into households of their own, households which might be simpler than those they had come from, but which still gave shelter to families of their own.

The important exchange of children, young and old, between households in the capacity of servants was underpinned by legal bindings (Imhof, 1974). In the 18th century, all the Scandinavian countries passed laws to the effect that young people were obliged to serve, and for low wages. The most restrictive period was between 1733 and 1754, but enforcement lasted until between 1788 and 1805. The efficiency of the enforcement, however, must have varied considerably, being affected by the push and pull of the market forces.

From a family household point of view, a major issue centred who was to draw the rewards from the new economic life: the old heads of centripetal household through their unmarried servants, young and old, male and female, or the newcomers who aspired to set up centrifugal households of their own. The latter won, but the battle was long and drawn-out and is difficult to describe clearly.

First, there was an exodus of male servants from the households (Dyrvik, 1986; Sogner, 1997). Already at the beginning of the 18th century, the sex ratio among servants in Norway was 45 (that is, there were 45 male servants for every 100 female servants). In 1801 the situation was the same. There was a constant demand for male labour, in agriculture and elsewhere. The cottar group, which comes into its own in agriculture during the 18th century, represents a married servant with a family household of his own. Outside agriculture, male wages in the new trades – shipping, mining, forestry and so on –readily attracted young men away from service and into new, possibly more independent positions. The military employed soldiers and sailors in the army and navy. The earnings were limited, but opened up the possibility of establishing modest family households, whose survival would depend upon the consolidated labour of husband, wife and children. Age at marriage for men and women of the new lower-order social groups was clearly higher than for farmers, indicating their greater difficulties in getting established.

Table 8.5 Mean age at first marriage of farmers and cottars, parish of Rendalen 1733–80 and 1781–1828

	Males		Females	
	1733–80	1781–1828	1733–80	1781–1828
Farmers	28.8	29.5	25.4	26.2
Cottars	34.0	32.9	31.3	31.0

Source: Sogner (1979: 336)

To conclude this discussion, the general economic situation in the 18th century opened up the prospect of new livelihoods outside traditional structures, and thus favoured marriage on the basis of limited incomes. In Norway, this development was discernible from at least the middle of the 17th century, but was overshadowed by the war in which the country was involved until about 1720.

So far, we have established some important demographic indicators regarding marriage that the Nordic countries seem to have in common: (1) late marriage, (2) bridal pregnancy and (3) considerable illegitimacy. How are we to interpret this pattern within a wider context? We have touched upon the general economic conditions as the backdrop against which marriage most naturally will and must be seen. We should, however, reflect on some other aspects that may be of influence in this regard, whether positive or negative.

III. Marriage: institutional impediments and stimulants

The early modern states in Scandinavia were intensely occupied in state-building projects. The policy of their governments involved creating an apparatus of civil servants, building up national armies, defending or expanding the nation's borders, stimulating new and old industries, and bolstering the state finances through taxes. All this activity could not help but have an effect on marriage, even if only indirectly.

III.1. Marriage and law

In Norway in the Middle Ages, marriage was a private contract, an agreement between the parent families of the young couple, with clear economic bindings. After the christianization of society around the year 1000 the church gradually set its imprint on marriage, but the blessing of the newly-weds in church was more an optional extra. It was not part of civil law and had no legally binding consequences. The new household was economically founded on contributions from either side, and land that women brought into marriage would return to her kin in the event that she bore no children in the marriage.

This situation changed with the Reformation. According to the Marriage Ordinance of 1589, two ecclesiastical ceremonies were now required for a marriage to become legitimate: a formal betrothal before witnesses, and a wedding. Being legitimate had important economic consequences for the child, as only legitimate children could inherit from their father. This was of great importance in a society based on access to land and with strict rules regarding the transfer of property, for example, the right of the eldest son to take over the farm. In fact, illegitimate children could not inherit from their fathers until 1915. By then, landed inheritance had to a certain degree lost its unique importance, and the right to take the father's family name had become more crucial.

Children born to parents who were publicly betrothed, however, were accepted as legitimate as if their parents were already married, until 1799 when betrothal was abolished. Then followed a period of uncertainty as to the legitimacy status of the child, but in 1851 unambiguous rules were introduced, to the effect that a child was illegitimate if its parents were not married at the time of the child's birth. The subsequent marriage of the parents would, however, legitimise it. In the 18th century we find examples where the local clergy could and did influence what kind of baptismal status was conferred upon the child, bringing pressure on the couple to marry in exchange for a legitimate baptism.

III.2. Marriage and religion

The early modern Nordic state was also religiously fundamentalistic. The kings adopted the Reformation principle of *cuius regio, eius religio*, and the evangelical Lutheran religion became the state religion for nearly all inhabitants (except in Eastern Finland, where a small part of the population was Orthodox). Church and State were the two sides of the same coin. Symptomatic is the use in court of the Bible as a legal reference. The concern of the state was protection against God's punishment, which would fall upon a country with a sinful and ungodly people. From about 1600 onwards one decree after the other was passed, penalising sexual offences: fornication, adultery, incest, cohabitation with persons too closely related, infanticide. Having children outside of marriage was made a criminal offence in all the Nordic countries, and was punishable by heavy fines. So was being pregnant at the wedding, but in this case the fine was considerably reduced. Not until the time of the Enlightenment around 1800 did these public reactions become less rigid. It is natural to assume that a lasting imprint had been made on people's way of thinking.

These crimes have been a major theme in recent Nordic research. A deep conflict has been uncovered, between the demands of the powerful state on the one hand and the practices of traditional society on the other, between the norms set by the state and upheld and persecuted vigorously in court, and the norms by which people traditionally lived (Telste, 1993). We are concerned here with these norms in so far as they regard marriage.

In 1617, very strict legal prosecution was introduced regarding fornication. Public norms and social norms were brought into conflict. From then on we are confronted with two types of crime, which are treated differently by the courts: fornication, the new crime, which consists of unmarried persons having illicit sex, and the traditional offence, breach of promise, called *møykrenking* in Nordic languages, which means 'offending a virgin'. The former crime was on the increase, as we can read so vividly in judicial sources and as we have already seen in the parish registers discussed above, whereas the latter was gradually being done away with. This was done by the state through legislation. Fornication became the crime most frequently committed by women. The clergy reported from the parish registers to the bailiff, and legal persecution was based on these lists.

'Offending a virgin' concerns sex between an unmarried couple, where the sexual act itself is regarded as synonymous with a promise of marriage. The offence can be traced back to the national codex of 1274. It was repeatedly renewed, in 1558, 1589, 1604 and even 1687. An offended virgin could take her case to court and sue a faithless lover for breach of promise. If she did, she would have her honour restored, as and would also receive financial compensation (which might come in useful when she went looking for a better husband). Cases of this kind before the courts were numerous until 1734, when according to an ordinance of that year they were no longer accepted.

The transition came gradually. The new important national codex of 1687 gave a forewarning of what was to come. The law, although still upholding the offence as such, introduced the concept of 'ill-famed woman'. For such a woman, the law did not apply. And, what was also new, if the man denied that the sexual act had taken place and the woman could not prove him wrong, he could swear himself free. She, on the other hand, would fined as a liar because she was 'displaying her shame and turning herself into a whore'. It is a far cry from the offended virgin. Traditionally, an unmarried pregnant woman could either expect marriage – the sexual act constituting a promise of marriage – or, if the man remonstrated, she could sue for breach of promise, with the probable outcome of having her honour restored as well as a remuneration, both of which would enhance her future marriage prospects. Now this line of action was no longer possible. The woman was punished and heavily fined, and had to undergo a ceremony in church for her public absolution. The man might go almost scot-free.

The formal as well as real responsibility for the crime of fornication was now laid entirely at the door of the woman. Her honour could no longer be restored, which was quite fatal since women's honour was intimately tied to sexuality, far more so than for men. The responsibility for the child became hers and hers alone (and there is always a child in these cases, otherwise they are usually not raised). The father's economic responsibility for the child had to await the future (1763) to be legally upheld; in practice, this responsibility has been poorly acknowledge until this day.

III.3. The military state

If the father of the illegitimate child was a soldier, which he very frequently was in the militarised state that was being built up from the 17th century onwards, the state supplied him with other legal loopholes to rid himself of the responsibility for the illegitimate child. In 1671, soldiers were being automatically pardoned from civil litigation for their first and second cases of fornication (from 1696 this was limited to first offences only).

The importance of this legal provision can be seen when considering that the state from the middle of the 17th century was building up a military system based on what may be termed general conscription. The most recent research on the military history of the period claims that conscription in Norway was without doubt the most comprehensive in Europe (Lind, 1994). During the period 1650–1725 a military state was established. Soldiers were being protected from commitments other than military. This led to control over the marriage of the soldiers, who could not marry without a written permit from their officer; which pleased Malthus immensely when informed of it during his visit to Norway in 1799. Untimely lawsuits, family providing duties and fines for soldiers were not popular in the army. There are more ways of hindering a marriage than outright forbidding the minister to perform the ceremony, as happened in Iceland.

As the outcome of the state's normative intervention into the private lives of men and women in cases that naturally involve a person of each sex, we find an asymmetric judicial persecution. Women more and more frequently appeared alone before the court or in church to take their punishment. The very serious economic and social consequences of this development for women led eventually to changes in the legal system. Where King Christian IV in the beginning of the 17th century had fought sorcery and vice in order that God should not punish his lands, the lawyers of the Enlightenment no longer saw the moral crime, only the economic consequences. In 1812, women were pardoned for their first and second offence, more than a century after men had got off this particular hook.

IV. Conclusion

The state-building project of the 17th and 18th centuries had dire consequences for the relationship between men and women. The policy pursued by the state had helped to disturb or worsen an earlier existing, albeit precarious, balance between the genders regarding sexuality and marriage – at least if the woman did not have a family to support her in her claims. In theory, the new laws made individual women legally responsible in fornication suits, on a par with men. Practice, however, proved much more inimical to women. The position of the individual woman in her negotiation with her partner was undoubtedly seriously impaired thanks to the legal provisions introduced by the early modern state. The long-term impact on popular attitudes is hard to assess.

Bibliography

Bengtsson, T. (1992) *Den demografiska transitionen*, Lund.

Dyrvik, S. (1986) 'Hushaldsutviklinga i Norge 1800–1920', in *Odense University Studies in History and Social Sciences. Vol. 96. Familien i forandring i 18- og 1900-tallet*, Odense, pp. 33–38.

Gille, H. (1949–50) 'The demographic history of the Northern European Countries in the eighteenth century', *Population Studies*, 3, pp. 3-65.

Gunnarsson, G. (1980) *Fertility and nuptiality in Iceland's demographic history*, Meddelande från Ekonomisk-historiska institutionen, Lunds universitet, no. 12, Lund.

Gunnlaugsson, G.Á. (1985) 'The poor laws and the family in 19th century Iceland', in J. Rogers and H. Norman (eds), *The Nordic family: perspectives on family research*, Uppsala, pp. 16–42.

Gunnlaugsson, G.Á. (1988) *Family and household in Iceland 1801–1930*, Uppsala.

Haavet, E. (1982) 'Avvik eller uhell? Ugifte foreldre omkring 1800 – en sosial analyse', unpublished MA thesis, Bergen.

Hofsten, E. and Lundström, H. (1976) *Swedish population history*, Stockholm.

Imhof, A.E. (1974) 'Der Arbeitszwang für das landwirtschafliche Dienstvolk in den nordischen Ländern im 18. Jahrhundert', *Zeitschrift für Agrargeschichte und Agrarsoziologie*, pp. 59–74.

Johansen, H.C. (1975) *Befolkningsudvikling og familiestruktur*, Odense.

Lind, G. (1994) *Hæren og magten i Danmark 1614-1662*, Odense.

Lithell, U.-B. (1988) *Kvinnoarbete och barntillsyn i 1700- och 1800-talets Österbotten*, Uppsala.

Löfgren, O. (1977) 'Potatisfolket', in *Forskning och framsteg*, nr. 56.

Lutz, W. and Pitkänen, K. (1986) 'Tracing back the eighteenth century "nuptiality transition" in Finland', paper for the International Institute for Applied Systems Analysis, Laxenburg.

Moring, B. (1994) *Skärgårdsbor*, Helsingfors.

Moring, B. (1998) 'The Finnish stem family in historical perspective: strategies for economic and social survival of the land-holding group', paper presented to the International Economic History Congress, Madrid, August.

NOS XII 245. Historisk statistikk 1968 (1969) Oslo.

NOS B 134. Folketeljinga 1801 (1980) Oslo.

Nygård Larsen, H. (1976) 'Familie- og husstandsstrukturen på landet i det 18. århundrede', in H.C. Johansen (ed.), *Studier i dansk befolkningshistorie 1750–1890*, Odense, pp. 121–88.

Sogner, S. (1978) 'Familie, husstand og befolkningsutvikling', *Heimen* 17, pp. 699–710.

Sogner, S. (1979) *Folkevekst og flytting*, Oslo.

Sogner, S. (1984) '''...a prudent wife is from the Lord'': the married peasant woman of the eighteenth century in a demographic perspective', *Scandinavian Journal of History*, 9, pp. 113–33.

Sogner, S. (1997) 'Domestic service in Norway: the long view", in A. Fauve-Chamoux and L. Fialová (eds) *Le phénomène de la domesticité en Europe, XVe - XXe siècles*, Prague, pp. 95–104.

Sogner, S. (1998) 'The Norwegian stem family: myth or reality?' paper presented to the International Economic History Congress, Madrid, August.

Suomen taloushistoria, 3: Historiallinen tilasto (1983) Helsinki.

Telste, K. (1993)*Mellom liv og lov. Kontroll av seksualitet i Ringerike og Hallingdal 1652-1710*, Oslo.

Winberg, C. (1977) *Folkökning och proletarisering*, Lund.

Wrigley, E.A. and Schofield, R.S. (1981) *The population history of England 1541–1871*, Cambridge.

9 Marriage and economic change in Sweden during the 18th and 19th century[1]

Christer LUNDH, Lund University

The focus of this chapter is the marriage pattern in Sweden in the 18th and 19th centuries. This period begins when the economy was characterised by traditional peasant family farms and noble estates, but it covers also the commercialization of agriculture in the early 19th century and the urbanization and industrial breakthrough in the last decades of that century.

From the 1860s onward, there are available national statistics on average marriage ages. For the period prior to that, the average marriage ages must be reconstructed, either from family reconstitutions or by means of indirect methods from the censuses. Both these ways of calculating the average marriage age will be utilised here.

The first question is whether Sweden was dominated by the Western European Marriage Pattern even before the end of the 19th century (that is, the period that Hajnal refers to in his classification of 1965). If so, how far back can one trace the Western European Marriage Pattern in Sweden? Second, we examine the temporal variations of the ages in marriage. Did economic change result in increasing or decreasing ages of marriage? Were there other long-term changes, such as long cycles, in the average marriage ages? Finally, the influence on average marriage ages of some economic and demographic variables will be discussed on the basis of a simple model.

I. The data

Sweden is reputed to have population statistics that not only go far back in time, but are also of high quality. We start with an overview of the availability of the data required to make possible calculations of Hajnal's measures of the Western European Marriage Pattern; namely the proportion of people never married, and the average age at first marriage.

Complete information on the Swedish population by sex, age and marital status is available in the census of 1870 and in all censuses after that. The main problem of the censuses prior to 1870 is that information on age, sex and marital status is never presented together. However, at the beginning of the twentieth century the Swedish

---

[1] This research has been conducted as part of the project 'From Uncertainty to Modern Economic Growth. Family and Household Behaviour in Sweden, 1650–1900', funded by the Swedish Council for Research in Social Science and Humanities, the Swedish Council for Social Research and the Bank of Sweden Tercentenary Foundation. I would like to thank Tommy Bengtsson, Martin Dribe and Mats Hagnell for comments on the draft version.

demographer Gustav Sundbärg reconstructed yearly population tables containing these variables for the entire period 1750–1900 by using censuses and other official statistics. These tables, in which the entire Swedish population is divided by sex, age (five-year groups) and marital status (never married, married, widowed/divorced) can be used for calculations of the proportions of never married (Sundbärg, 1907a).

Official statistics on marriages by sex, age and marital status are available from 1861 and onwards. The official figures for the period 1861–79 were revised by Sundbärg at the turn of the century. From these vital statistics, ages at first marriage can be calculated at the national level from 1861 and onwards (Sundbärg, 1907b). For periods prior to 1861, calculations of ages at marriage in Sweden usually have been based on family reconstitutions. One attempt has also been made to calculate average age at first marriage by indirect methods (singulate mean age at marriage)[2] from census data on marital status by age (Lundh, 1997).

II. The marriage pattern in a long-term perspective

In his renowned essay, 'European marriage patterns in perspective', Hajnal maintained that there were two different marriage patterns in Europe around 1900 (Hajnal, 1965: 101–04). In western Europe[3] the age at marriage was relatively high and the proportion of never married was large. In eastern Europe, that is to say east of an imaginary line drawn from St Petersburg to Trieste, the marriage pattern was characterized by lower age at marriage and a considerably smaller proportion of never married. Non-European countries showed approximately the same pattern as eastern Europe.[4]

Regarding the period before 1900, Hajnal claimed that the Western European Marriage Pattern dated from at least the 17th century. What then applied in the period before 1600? From the limited source material available, Hajnal suggested that the Western European Marriage Pattern had existed in the 16th century. He found support for this mainly from data on the aristocracy in England, Germany and Switzerland. For these groups, the pattern of marriage only became western European in the 16th century. That the Western European Marriage Pattern was preceded by a pattern of more traditional, East European type is confirmed by the sparse sources from medieval and ancient times, according to Hajnal (1965: 113–25, 134).

Sweden was one of the countries cited by Hajnal as an example of the Western European Marriage Pattern around 1900. Here, Hajnal relied on the Swedish official statistics. For the discussion of the marriage pattern during the centuries prior to 1900, however, Hajnal did not refer to Sweden at all. Most Swedish family reconstitutions

[2] This method was used by Hajnal (1953).

[3] Hajnal uses the term 'European Marriage Pattern' but refers to western Europe.

[4] The term 'Eastern European Marriage Pattern' is here synonymous with 'Non-European Marriage Pattern' and 'Traditional Marriage Pattern'.

were made after 1965 when Hajnal published his article, and Hajnal was probably not aware of the existence of Sundbärg's reconstruction of the Swedish population by age, sex and marital status for the period 1750–1900.

In 1900, the year representing Hajnal's point of reference, 13.5 per cent of men and 19.4 per cent of women in the age group 45–49 were never married in Sweden. The average age at marriage was over 28 for men and over 26 for women. Compared to eastern Europe, the proportion of never married was large and the age at marriage high, making Sweden well suited for inclusion in the Western European Marriage Pattern. How far back did this pattern go and were there any tendencies to change? Can one find support for the idea of a transition from an earlier traditional marriage pattern?

Figure 9.1 Proportion of never married by sex, ages 45-49, Sweden, 1750-1900

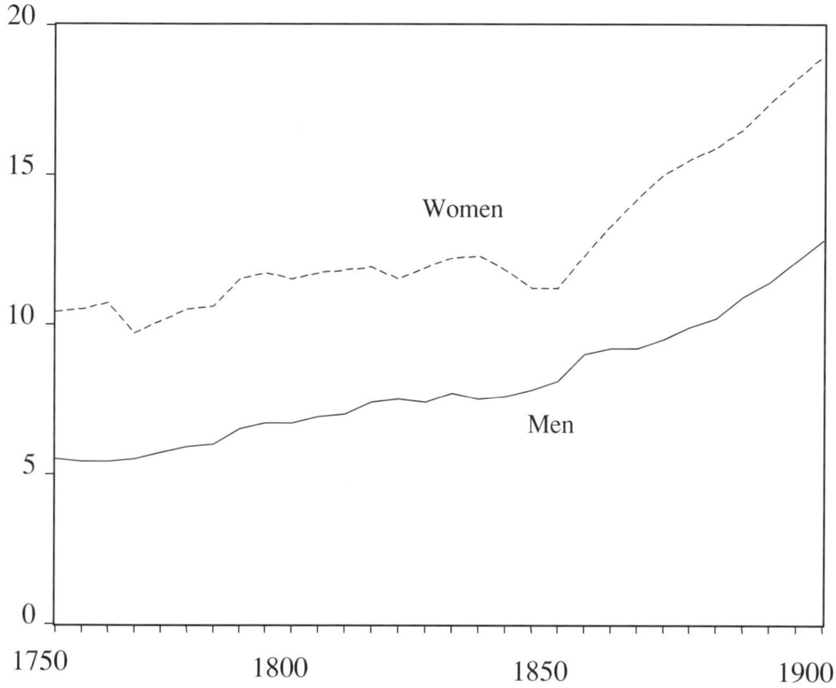

Source: Sundbärg (1907)

Figure 9.1 shows that the proportion of never married increased continuously between 1750 and 1900. This was also the case for all age groups (Lundh, 1997, appendix). The unit of measurement used by Hajnal (i.e., proportions of never married in the age group 45–49) was as little as 5.5 per cent for men in 1750. The proportion of women never married in the same age group was larger, nearly 10 per cent. For both men and women, this meant that the proportion of never married doubled between 1750 and 1900. The low proportion of never married men in 1750 is on the same level as the figures for several countries used by Hajnal to illustrate the East European pattern, for example, Greece (9 per cent), Hungary (5 per cent) and Rumania (5 per cent). In most East European and non-European countries, however, the proportion of never married men was lower in 1900 than it was in Sweden in 1750. Even though the proportion of never married women in Sweden was considerably smaller in 1750 than in 1900, the level was significantly higher than for those countries in eastern Europe and outside Europe referred to by Hajnal. The Swedish proportion of 10 per cent never married women in the age group 45–49 must then be set against a level varying between 0 and 4 per cent.

Figure 9.2 Crude marriage rates, 1650–1900

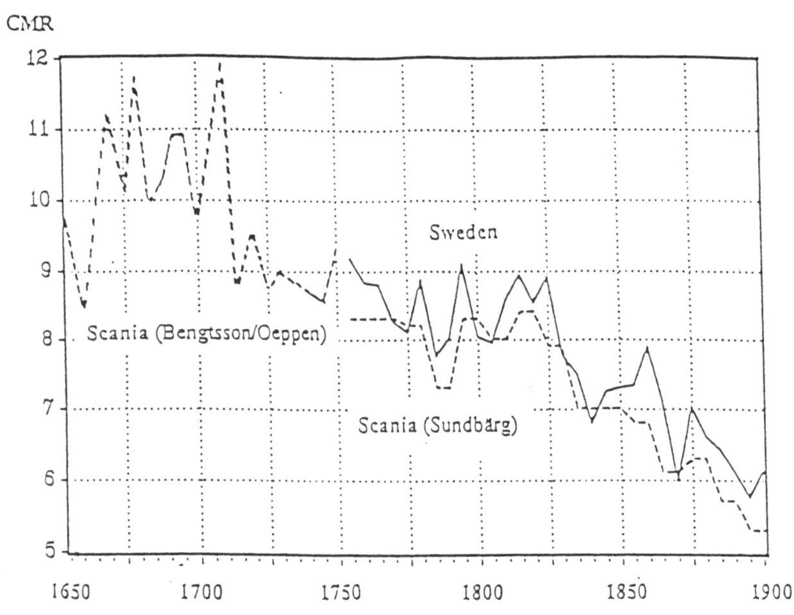

Source: *Historisk statistik för Sverige (*1969); Sundbärg (1910); Bengtsson and Oeppen (1993)

Unfortunately, it is not possible to follow the proportion of never married in the age group 45–49 further back than 1750. The question is whether the trend in 1750–1900 also characterised the centuries before 1750. There are some signs that point to this. Bengtsson and Oeppen, with the help of inverse projection, have reconstructed the population for a number of parishes in Scania from the middle of the 17th century, making it possible to calculate crude marriage rates for the period before 1750 (see Figure 9.2). Bengtsson and Oeppen's series of crude marriage rates show that marriage frequency declined since the late 17th century (1993).[5] Even though the crude marriage rate is a rough measurement which does not take into account shifts in the age structure, its decline between 1650 and 1900 points to the fact that the proportion of never married probably increased from as early as the middle of the 17th century.

Table 9.1 Mean age at first marriage, Sweden, 1861–90

	Men	Women
1861/1870	28.8	27.1
1871/1880	28.8	27.1
1881/1890	28.5	26.8
1891/1900	28.8	26.8

Source: *Historisk statistik för Sverige* (1969)
Note: that the ages of marriage for the period 1861–79 are calculated from Sundbärg's revision of the vital statistics.

We now turn to the age at first marriage, the second unit of measurement used by Hajnal to characterise marriage patterns. From 1861, when official statistics started to contain vital statistics on marriage by sex, age and marital status, until 1900, the average age at first marriage for men did not change at all while for women it decreased somewhat (see Table 9.1). For the period before 1861, we get two different pictures of how the long-term average marriage ages developed, depending on whether the average is calculated from family reconstitutions or indirectly from proportions never married.

Let us first deal with the picture obtained if one proceeds from the calculations of the marriage age carried out in investigations based on family reconstitutions.[6] When one arranges the results of Swedish investigations carried out chronologically, one gets a rough picture of the manner in which changes in age at marriage might have developed. In Figure 9.3, the results of different local studies are presented without paying attention to the size of the parishes under study. Results from different part-periods for one and the same parish have also been included in the figure.

[5] Bengtsson and Oeppen feel that the results are less certain for the period 1650–80.
[6] A few investigations are based on marriage age information from marriage registers, so that family reconstructions were not necessary. Apart from such exceptions it is necessary in Sweden, as in other countries, to carry out family reconstructions to calculate the age at marriage.

The trend seen in Figure 9.3 is that the marriage age of men declined between the beginning of the 17th century and the 1860s, but it is doubtful as to whether there was a corresponding decline for women. The mean age of men at first marriage declined from over 30 years to about 28 years, while the mean marriage age of women was quite stable, about 26 years. Apart from the problem of method, in which all studies were given equal weight, there is a further shortcoming in that the picture of the trend in average marriage age in Figure 9.3 is based on parish information for limited part-periods in different parts of the country. The majority of parishes in the 17th century were situated in central Sweden, whereas most of the parishes in the 19th century were in southern Sweden. Therefore, it is difficult to determine whether the tendency towards declining marriage ages was a real trend or was due to regional differences.

Figure 9.3 Mean age at first marriage, Sweden, 1620–1870

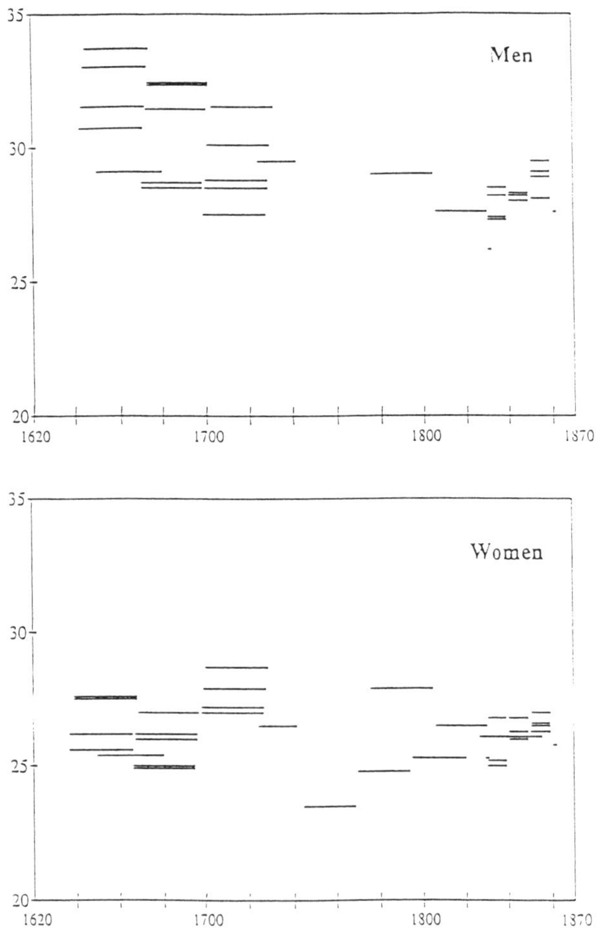

Source: Lundh (1993)

Table 9.2 Mean age at first marriage, Scanian parishes, 1646–1860

	Age	N
Men		
1646–1750	34.3	239
1751–1810	32.2	372
1811–1860	29.3	687
Women		
1646–1750	29.1	216
1751–1810	27.7	384
1811–1860	26.8	1,014

Source: Family reconstitutions from parish records for Ekeby, Frillestad, Halmstad, Hög, Kävlinge, Sireköpinge and Stenestad, Scanian Demographic Database.

Our own investigation of the age at first marriage in seven parishes in Scania[7] between 1646 and 1860, however, makes it possible to eliminate regional differences as the reason for the decline in the age at marriage. Table 9.2 shows that in the seven Scanian parishes, the marriage age declined sharply for both men and women. For both sexes, the age at first marriage during the period 1811–60 is at about the same level as the figures in the national statistics for Sweden as a whole during the period 1861–70 (see Table 9.1). The high marriage age during the first period is striking, particularly for men.

[7] Ekeby, Frillestad, Halmstad, Hög, Kävlinge, Sireköpinge, and Stenestad parishes, The Scanian Demographic database. This database is a collaborative project between the Provincial Archives in Lund and the Research Group in Population Economics at the Department in Economic History, Lund University.

Table 9.3 Age distribution of men and women, first marriages, Scanian parishes, 1646–1860

	1646–1750	1751–1810	1811–1860
Men			
14–19	3.3	2.7	0.6
20–24	15.9	14.8	17.0
25–29	27.6	31.2	44.0
30–34	18.8	23.9	19.9
35–39	10.9	12.4	9.9
40–45	7.1	6.5	4.1
45–w	16.3	8.7	4.5
Women			
14–19	9.3	7.3	7.2
20–24	27.8	30.7	36.8
25–29	26.4	33.1	33.6
30–34	19.0	15.9	15.3
35–39	6.0	9.1	3.8
40–44	6.0	1.6	1.6
45–w	5.6	2.4	1.7

Source: Family reconstitutions from parish records for Ekeby, Frillestad, Halmstad, Hög, Kävlinge, Sireköpinge and Stenestad, Scanian Demographic Database.

Thus, the trend of declining age at first marriage seems to be clear.[8] As can be seen in Table 9.3, this decline was the result of a lower proportion that married when older than (at least) 40. Apart from that, the proportion of marrying young people (15–19) also declined. Along with the decrease in marriage age, the deviation from the mean age at marriage diminished. During the period 1646–1750 about 60 per cent of the men and 70 per cent of the women who married in the seven Scanian parishes were aged 20–34. For the period 1811–60, the corresponding figures exceeded 80 per cent for men and 85 per cent for women.

If the picture of marriage age changes presented by family reconstitutions is correct, the Western European pattern, with high marriage ages, was even more pervasive in Sweden in the 17th, 18th and 19th centuries than around 1900, which was the point of reference for Hajnal. It is still possible that the tendency towards declining marriage ages was a regional feature of western Scania and not characteristic for Sweden as a whole. Therefore, a more cautious interpretation might be that the West European Marriage Pattern was already dominant in the 17th century, and that the high marriage age has prevailed since then.

[8] A possible drawback in the calculations of the age at marriage based on family reconstitutions is the difficulty of excluding with certainty all the previously married. Therefore, a decreasing proportion of undiscovered people remarrying may be falsely interpreted as a decrease in the average age at *first* marriage. In my investigation it is not probable that this alone can explain the decrease in marriage age. For a further discussion, see Lundh (1997).

A quite different picture is obtained if the average age at first marriage is calculated indirectly from the population distributed by sex, age and marital status. This approach, useful in cases where data on age at marriage is lacking but data on proportions of married by certain ages is available, was used by Hajnal in the early 1950s (Hajnal, 1953).

Figure 9.4 Male/female mean age at first marriage, Swedish counties, 1901-10 (Index 100 = mean age at first marriage by sex in Sweden as a whole)

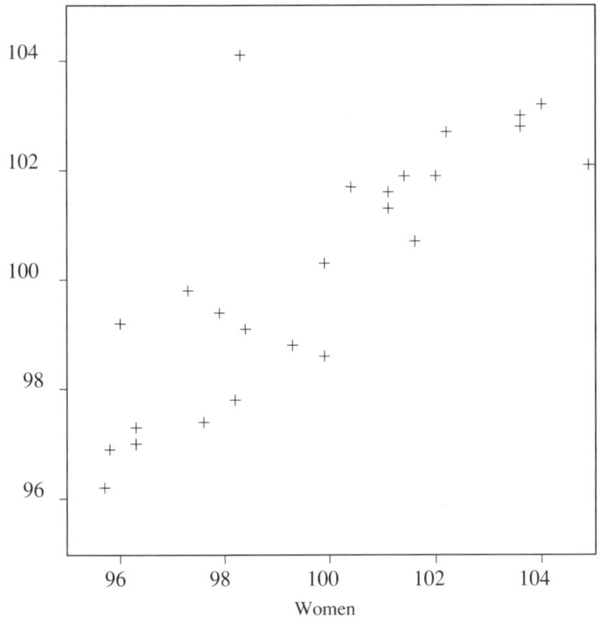

Source: Calculated from *SOS Befolkningsrörelsen. Översikt för åren 1901-1910,* table 17-18

Calculations of the 'Singulate Mean Age at First Marriage' (SMAFM) for the period 1751–1900, based on Sundbärg's reconstruction of the Swedish population by sex, age and marital status, give a quite different trend from the one in the calculations based on family reconstitutions. As can be seen in Table 9.4, for both men and women the trend was for age at first marriage to increase during the period 1751–1900. One possible explanation for the opposite long-term trends in marriage age in the Scanian parishes referred to above is that there are regional patterns and development that deviate from the national average.[9]

[9] Since we know from local studies (see Lundh, 1993) that there were differences in marriage ages between social groups, regional differences in the process of social diversification in the 19th century might result in regional differences in the ages at first marriage.

Table 9.4 Singulate mean age at first marriage, Sweden, 1751–1900

	Men	Women
1751–1800	27.9	26.9
1801–1850	28.4	27.1
1851–1900	29.6	27.9

Source: Sundbärg (1907a)

Calculation of regional ages at first marriage from the official statistics is possible only for the 20th century. As can be seen in Appendice Table 1 and Figure 9.4, in the period 1901–10 mean age at first marriage was quite high in all parts of Sweden, in both urban and rural areas. Thus, there is no reason to believe that there were parts of Sweden that were not characterised by the Western European Marriage Pattern. On the other hand, there were regional variations of about plus or minus 5 per cent from the national average, and as is shown in Figure 9.4 these regional deviations were the same for both men and women. With regional variations of this magnitude, one can not exclude the possibility that regional marriage ages sometimes developed in a different way from the trends in SMAFM at the national level.

Haines (1996) drew attention to the occurrence of long cycles of nuptiality in North America between 1800 and the present. We also found long cycles in the ages of first marriage in Sweden between 1750 and present times (Lundh, 1997). We shall deal here only with the period prior to the 20th century.

Figure 9.5 Singulate mean age at first marriage, Sweden, 1751-1900

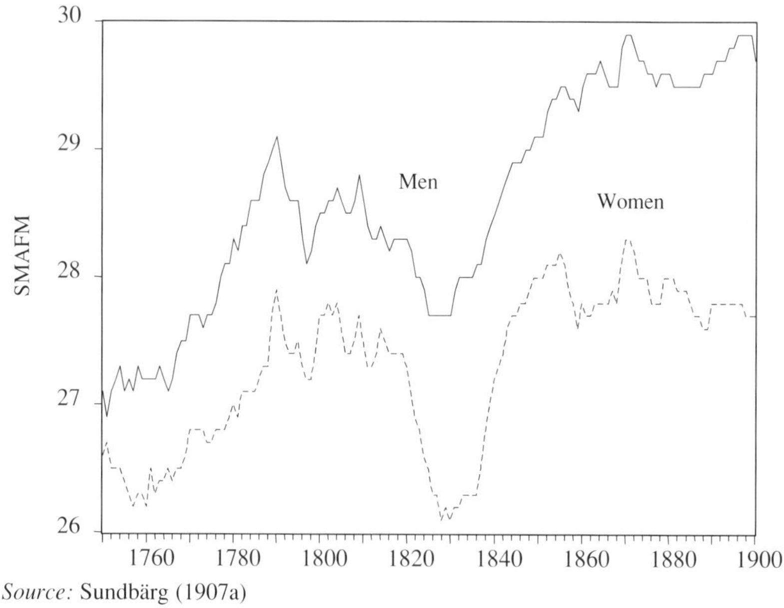

Source: Sundbärg (1907a)

From the calculations of the SMAFM for Sweden in the period 1751–1900, it is clear that the period can be divided into four sub-periods (see Figure 9.5). There seem to be two sub-periods of considerable increase in the marriage age (1750s–1790s and 1830s–1870s) and two sub-periods of decrease or stagnation (1790s–1830s, 1870s–1890s).

How reliable are these results? The pattern of the sub-period 1870s–1890s is approximately in accordance with what we know from the official statistics (see Table 9.1). The increasing trend for the entire period 1750–1900 and the existence of four sub-periods are further confirmed by using alternative indirect methods to calculate the average age at first marriage from data on population by sex, age and marital status.[10]

Figure 9.6 Mean age at first marriage, Scanian parishes, 1700/05-1890/94

Source: Family reconstructions in Ekeby, Frillestad, Halmstad, Hög, Kävlinge, Sireköpinge and Stenestad parishes, Scanian Demographic Database.

Also, when calculating the yearly mean age at first marriage in the seven Scanian parishes, a cyclical pattern appears (see Figure 9.6). However, the correspondence between the sexes is not quite complete. Men and women experienced much the same patterns in ages at marriage up until the 1840s. There were two sub-periods of decrease (1700s–1750s and 1800s–1840s) and one sub-period of increase/stagnation

[10] In a forthcoming study, a comparison between the SMAFM measure and alternative measures will be made with applications to the Swedish case.

(1750s–1800s). From the 1840s, men's age at first marriage decreased while that of women increased.

The main demographic methods to calculate the average age at first marriage (from family reconstitutions and indirectly from the censuses) are applicable only to periods with parish records or censuses. In Sweden, this means that they are useful from the 17th century onwards. Prior to that, there are only scattered data on age at marriage. The miracle collections of Stockholm, for instance, indicate a much lower age at marriage in the early 15th century, but the number of observations are too few to form a base for any generalizations (Myrdal and Bäärenhielm, 1994: 19–20).

In conclusion, it is clear that the Western European Marriage Pattern was predominant in Sweden from the 17th century and onwards. There might have been a transition from a traditional marriage pattern to the Western European Marriage Pattern during the 15th and 16th centuries, but much more data must be presented to support this hypothesis. From the end of the 17th century, the proportions of never marrying people increased in Sweden. The ages at first marriage at a national level seem to have experienced a corresponding increase from 1750–1900, although there were regional deviations from this general pattern. It is also clear that there were long cycles of nuptiality both at the national level and in Scania.

III. The marriage pattern and economic and demographic change

As market arrangements were often ineffective or gave rise to excessive transaction costs, the family fulfilled two important functions in the agrarian society. First, the family was an insurance institution that provided protection at sickness, old age or when one of the spouses died. Second, the family was the most important form of organisation of production for the household's consumption or for sales in the market. The family farm can be seen as an organizational solution to the problem of supervising labour that, for technological reasons, could not be gathered in one and the same work place.

Thus, there were strong motives for individuals to form a families. However, the scarcity of resources that characterised pre-industrial society limited the possibilities for young people to create separate households. They had to wait and save until they could take over a farm, or at least find some employment and housing which would make it possible to form a family. The Western European Marriage Pattern was to some extent a product of this scarcityof resources.

Even though the Western European Marriage Pattern was predominant in Sweden, there were variations in the average marriage ages. The expected marriage age was structurally determined by customs and institutions such as the Western European Marriage Pattern, the simple household formation system and the servant institution, but the actual timing of the marriage was influenced by economic and demographic conditions. Because of variations in such conditions, there was also room for variations in the average ages of marriage within the Western European Marriage Pattern. In this section, the influence of economic and demographic conditions on the average age at first marriage will be discussed.

Theoretically, it is easy to argue that economic growth should have a positive effect on the possibilities of marriage, and should thereby help to lower the average marriage ages. The rise in productivity that is the motor of economic growth provided higher earnings and a rise in the standard of living which increased the opportunities for young couples to invest in a dwelling and household goods and made it easier for them to take the step into marriage. This would be a quite traditional Malthusian interpretation of the determinants of changing marriage ages. Marriage was the regulator that brought about economical and demographic balance (Wrigley and Schofield, 1981).

On the other hand, economic growth and rising productivity were relying on an ongoing structural transformation of the economy. The general commercialization of the agrarian economy and an agrarian revolution in the early 19th century, and urbanization and the growing industrial sector in the later part of the 19th century created new job and housing opportunities and thereby new alternatives for forming families (Lundh, 1993, 1997; Guinnane, 1997.) The growth of new industries, new labour markets and jobs made it possible for occupational groups which had previously lacked opportunities for entering the marriage market, such as crofters and contract farm labourers (*statare*) to do so. The entrance of new occupational groups into the rural marriage markets alongside the peasants, who had previously been predominant, may have led to changes in the average age at marriage (Habakkuk, 1974; Knodel and Maines, 1976; Lesthaeghe, 1977; Levine, 1977). In this way, the economic development and modernization of society influenced the prerequisites for marriage and thereby influenced the average age at first marriage. The modernization process, including secularization and urbanization, may have also influenced preferences for marriage and concepts of the 'proper' age for getting married.

It is also clear that demographic changes may have influenced marriage ages. It is possible that we can find Easterlin effects, namely that the varying size of the birth cohorts with a lag of 20–30 years influences the possibilities of getting married (Easterlin, 1981). Large birth cohorts lead to increased competition for scarce resources such as land, jobs and housing, which in turn leads to postponed marriages and higher marriage ages. In this way, the sizes of cohorts expresses the extent of general crowding and competition for scarce resources.

In a similar way, structural imbalances or short-term changes in the sex ratio probably influenced marriage ages. A surplus of males and an increase in the proportion of males to females can be expected to have a positive effect on the age at marriage of men and a negative influence on the marriage age of women (Bergstrom and Lam, 1994). Even deaths among elderly can be supposed to have had some influence on the average marriage ages. In a situation characterised by scarce resources, the death of a head of a household made it possible for a young couple to take over the farm or to take up the craft (Ohlin, 1955, 1960; Schofield, 1976).

Figure 9.7 Logged real wages of agricultural workers, Sweden, 1750-1900

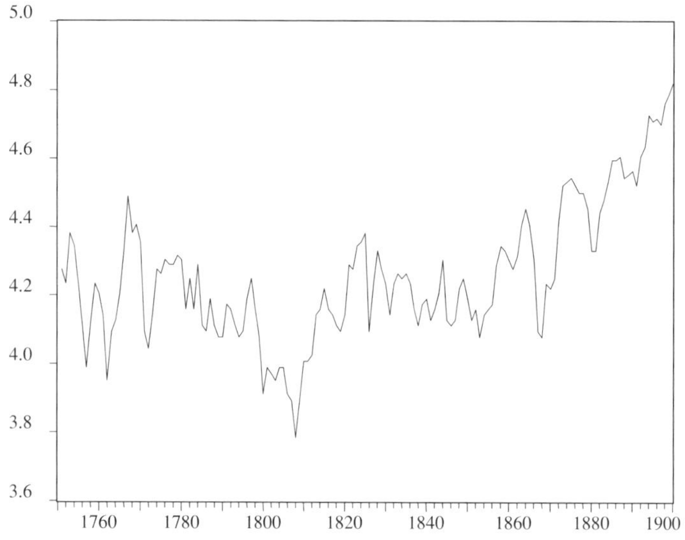

Source: Jörenberg (1972); Jörenberg and Bengtsson (1981)

Figure 9.8 Proportion of men and women, aged 20-29, Sweden, 1750-1900

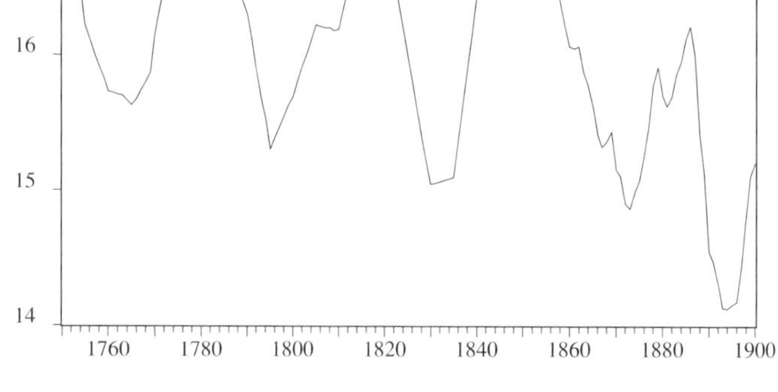

Source: Sundbärg (1907a)

Figure 9.9 Sex ratio, Sweden, 1750-1900

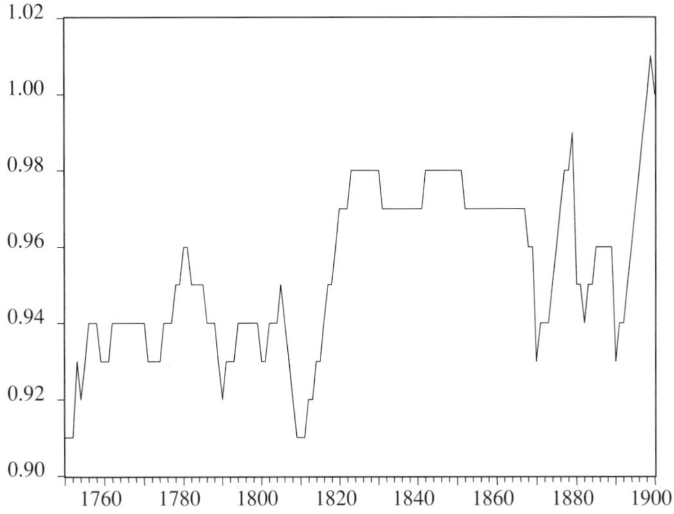

Source: Sundbärg (1907a)

Figure 9.10 Mortality of men over age 50, Sweden, 1750-1900

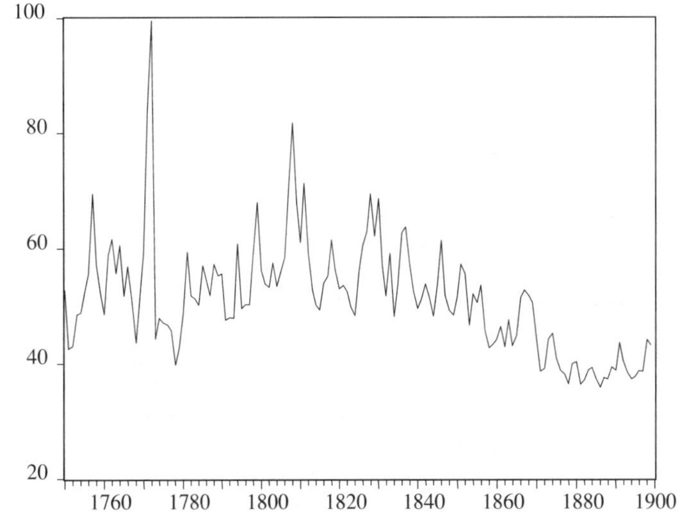

Source: Sundbärg (1907a); *Historisk statistik för Sverige* (1969)

In the following section, the influence on the marriage ages in pre-industrial Sweden of such economic and demographic factors will be discussed on the basis of a very simple model. The period of investigation is 1750–1900, and the dependent variables are male and female singulate mean ages at first marriage. The main independent variables are (logged) real wages of farm labourers (see Figure 9.7), the proportion of people aged 20–29 as a percentage of the total population (see Figure 9.8), the sex ratio (see Figure 9.9) and the age specific mortality of men over 50 years (see Figure 9.10).

A rise in productivity results in economic growth and increasing real wages. However, it may also be part of a process of economic transformation characterised by changes in technology and organization. In the model, real wages are assumed to reflect the development of the standard of living, but real wages are also an indication of economic development. This model does not distinguish between the Malthusian interpretation that real wages simply express the standard of living and the interpretation that changes in real wages also reflect the structural transformation of economy and the modernization of society. Since prices and wages in these times were set in the autumn, it is most likely that there was a lag in the influence of real wages on marriage ages. Therefore, real wages with a one-year lag are included in the model.

The proportion of people aged 20–29 is assumed to be a measure of the general crowding, and the sex ratio expresses the squeeze in the marriage market. The proportions of deaths of men over 50 are assumed to reflect the availability of free land, jobs and dwellings and thereby the possibilities to form new households.

From a theoretical point of view, one would expect there to be a positive influence on the marriage age of the proportion of people aged 20–29 and of the proportion of people of the same sex in the marriage market. On the other hand, one would expect a negative influence of real wages and the mortality of elderly men. To start with, OLS (ordinary least squares) was used, but because of serial correlation an AR(1) term (first-order autoregressive process) had to be included in the model.[11] The regressions are presented in Appendice Table 2.

According to regression 1, real wages in the year before the observation year had a strong significant negative influence on the marriage age of men. The influence of real wages in the same year was not significant. This is probably due to the institutional arrangements of price and wage formation and of marriage timing over the annual cycle. As has been mentioned, prices and wages were set in the autumn (early November). It is most likely that there was a lag in the influence of real wages on the marriage ages. Many people married before November and had no chance to react to changes in real wages, and some of those who married in November and December did probably not react immediately.

[11] The introduction of AR(1) into the model means that the values of the variables is being transformed. Since R^2 was estimated from these transformed values, it is much too high, which should be noted when the explanatory strength of the equation is being evaluated.

There was also a general crowding effect. The proportions of people aged 20–29 had a significant positive influence on the male marriage ages. This is a cohort effect. Young people belonging to a large cohort found it more difficult to form a family than the young people belonging to a small cohort. When the proportion of 20–29 year olds increased, the average male marriage age rose. This was as expected, and strengthens the picture of scarcity in the pre-industrial society.

Regression 1 does not indicate any statistically significant[12] influence of the sex ratio on the male SMAFM. This positive influence was not expected. One possible explanation is that the structural deficit of men (see Figure 9.9), especially in 1750–1820, created a situation in the marriage market in which the male marriage ages were not very sensitive to variations in the sex ratio.

When it comes to the last variable, the mortality of men over 50 years of age, we cannot find any statistically significant influence on the male SMAFM. This does not exclude the possibility of an 'inheritance' effect in the pre-industrial society. The scarcity of land and the lack of jobs for family providers and dwellings for families point towards the influence of the mortality of elderly on the possibilities for young people to marry. However, it is probably impossible to verify this at the aggregate level, since the distribution of elderly mortality is quite smooth with the exception of a few years of famine. Studies of individuals' marriage behaviour might very well show the influence of elderly mortality on the marriage decisions of young couples.[13]

Turning to regression 2 on the female SMAFM, the results are fairly similar to the results for men. As for males, there is a significant and distinct negative influence on female marriage age of real wages in the previous year. Increasing real wages means increasing possibilities for forming families, with falling marriage ages as a consequence.

Also, the general crowding effect seems to be the same for women as for men. According to the regression, there is a significant positive influence on the female SMAFM of the proportion of people aged 20–29. As for men, the mortality of elderly men was not found to have any statistically significant influence on female marriage ages.

Turning to the sex ratio, a difference between men and women was found. While the male SMAFM was not significantly sensitive to the sex ratio, there was a distinctive negative influence on the female SMAFM of the male-to-female ratio. An increase in the number of men per women helped to lower the female marriage age. One interpretation of this is that the structural male deficit, especially in 1750–1820, had a different meaning to men and women. An increase in the proportion of men led to a drop in the average female marriage age but had no importance to male marriage age, since there was a structural lack of men in any case.

---

[12] At the 5 per cent level.

[13] See for example Chapter 5 in this volume.

Figure 9.5 shows considerable similarity between the male and the female SMAFM. Even if the curves are not identical, they show the same long-term increase and similar cyclical trends. The correlation (Pearson's R^2) between the two curves is 0.9 for the period 1750–1900. The question is how the correspondence between the male and female marriage ages should be interpreted. On the one hand, they could be seen as independent of each other and determined by other explanatory variables (as in the model above). On the other hand, the possibility of mutual influence between male and female marriage ages cannot be excluded.

To determine whether there is a mutual influence, a Granger Causality Test with two lags was used (see Appendice Table 3). The test for the entire period 1750–1900 indicates that there is no mutual influence. However, if the period is divided into sub-periods, another pattern appears. In the 19th century one cannot rule out the possibility that the average male marriage age influenced the average female marriage age. On the other hand, in the sub-period 1750–99, the average male marriage age probably did not influence the female marriage age.

One interpretation of this is that the scarcity of resources in the 19th century contributed to a marriage pattern in which the male marriage ages were determined by real wages and demographic conditions, while the marriage ages of women were also influenced by the marriage ages of men. It was the man who became the head of household after the wedding, and therefore average male marriage ages were sensitive to the opportunities for young men to acquire land, jobs and housing. Real wage increases facilitated this, while increased crowding made it more difficult. As far as women were concerned, they too were influenced by economic change and by the general crowding, but this influence might have been indirect, as indicated by the possible influence of male SMAFM on female SMAFM. Squeezes in the marriage market and changes in the sex ratio might have had a more direct influence on women. One possible reason why one cannot find this pattern in the 18th century might be the structural male deficit (0.94–0.96).

IV. Concluding remarks

The Western European Marriage Pattern was already established in Sweden in the 17th century. There are scattered data that support Hajnal's thesis of a transition from the traditional to the Western European Marriage Pattern in the 16th century. However, more evidence must be presented before we dare to believe in this transition in the Swedish case. From the 17th century onwards, however, one can see the development of the marriage pattern with high age at marriage and a rather large proportion who never marry.

Between 1750 and 1900 there was a gradual rise in the proportion of never married. Regarding the possible trend-forming changes in the age at marriage before 1900, the results are somewhat contradictory. An estimation from censuses indicates that the average age at marriage in Sweden increased between 1750 and 1900, whereas investigations based on local family reconstitutions imply a declining marriage age after the 17th century. To some extent, this might be explained by regional differences. At the national level, the most likely trend was for ages at first marriage to rise. It is also clear, both from national calculations based on censuses and Scanian family reconstitutions, that there were long cycles in the marriage ages of both men and women.

Economic and demographic conditions influenced both male and female marriage ages. There was a clear negative influence of real wages (with a one-year lag) and a distinct positive influence of the relative cohort size of people aged 20–29. For women, there was also a clear negative influence of the male-to-female ratio. It is possible that men's marriage ages in a situation of scarce resources were directly influenced by changes in real wages and general crowding, while these influences on women's marriage ages were more indirect. Instead, female marriage might have been influenced more by men's marriage ages and by the sex ratio.

Alter has drawn attention to the fact that the Western European Pattern of Marriage persisted in spite of the increased standard of living in the 19th century. Even though the Malthusian trap was avoided, neither the age at marriage nor the proportion of never married decreased: 'Indeed, the persistence of late marriage throughout 19th-century Europe is a challenge to the Hajnal thesis' (Alter, 1991: 3).

The relative stability of the Western European Marriage Pattern can probably be explained by two phenomena. First, economic growth and society's modernization meant much more than simply an increase in the standard of living, and various aspects of this societal transition affected the marriage pattern in different ways. Certain trends indicate that the Western European Pattern of Marriage should have been reinforced, while others indicate that there should have been a weakening. Nor is it automatic that any change will affect the age at marriage and the proportion of never married in the same direction. Economic development led to an increased standard of living, which should have increased the marriage options at a younger age. On the other hand, economic development also created alternative income opportunities apart from family farming. Modern society's progress during the 19th century broadened the labour market and increased the likelihood of choosing celibacy as a strategy for raising the standard of living. Modernization also generated new possibilities for families to make a living without owning land, which had been the predominant combination of occupation and housing in the pre-industrial society.

Second, there was a temporal lag in the adjustment of the marriage pattern. The Western European Marriage Pattern can be functionally derived from the prerequisites that existed in European pre-industrial society. In a society characterised by inadequate resources, the expectation that the newly married couple would immediately start their own self-sufficient household made a high age at marriage necessary, which in turn was made possible by institutional arrangements such as the circulation of servants. Although institutions are affected by economic development, adaptation is usually preceded by a lag. Nor is it self- evident that institutions are always functional; they build on earlier institutional solutions, a phenomenon that North calls 'path dependency' (North, 1990). Social change certainly brought about an increase in the options open to an individual, but individual choices are not made entirely on economically rational grounds; they might also be influenced by prevailing norms, traditions, customs and formal rules. North expresses this as: 'in a world with institutions, only a limited number of responses to any change in relative prices are possible, with the response depending on the particular institutional environment' (North, 1985: 383).

Taking these two points into consideration, the influence of real wages on the average marriage ages in the regressions must be put into its temporal context. In the entire period, people responded to rising real wages by bringing forward their marriages, and to declining wages by delaying marriage. However, the interpretation of this influence is probably somewhat different for the former and later parts of the period.

In the 18th and early 19th centuries, society was characterized by a scarcity of resources that prevented young people who wanted to marry from actually doing so. These economic limitations on marriage could be interpreted as a long-term Malthusian preventive check. A rise in the standard of living (i.e., real wages) increased the opportunities for getting married, and some people took their chances as they appeared.

In the 19th century, the influence of the standard of living (expressed by real wages) on the marriage age remains. But in the 19th century, and especially in the second half, real wages should be interpreted as more than an indicator of the level of standard of living. Real wages also reflected the dynamic process of economic transformation, including changes in technology and organization. Therefore, the negative influence of real wages on marriage ages should also be interpreted in terms of the wider processes of economic and social change affecting Swedish society.

Appendice

Table 1 Mean age at first marriage by sex, Swedish counties, 1901–10

	Men	Women
Stockholms stad	29.2	27.7
Stockholms län	28.4	26.0
Uppsala län	27.9	25.8
Södermanlands län	27.5	25.3
Östergötlands län	28.3	26.2
Jönköpings län	29.4	27.0
Kronobergs län	29.4	27.4
Kalmar län	29.1	26.5
Gotlands län	29.1	26.7
Blekinge län	28.2	26.4
Kristianstad län	29.0	26.7
Malmöhus län	28.0	25.9
Hallands län	29.1	26.8
Göteborgs och Bohus län	28.8	26.8
Älvsborgs län	29.5	27.3
Skaraborgs län	29.5	27.4
Värmlands län	29.2	26.9
Örebro län	28.7	26.4
Västmanlands län	27.7	25.3
Kopparbergs län	27.8	25.4
Gävleborgs län	27.7	25.4
Västernorrlands län	28.5	25.7
Jämtlands län	29.8	25.9
Västerbottens län	28.4	25.8
Norrbottens län	28.4	25.4
Urban areas	28.6	26.2
Rural areas	28.6	26.9
Sweden	28.6	26.4

Source: Calculated from *SOS Befolkningsrörelsen. Översikt för åren 1901–1910*, Table 17–18.

Table 2 Regressions

1750–1900

Dependent variables	
Male SMAFM	Singualate mean age at first marriage for men
Female SMAFM	Singualate mean age at first marriage for women
Independent variables	
Real wages	Logged real wages of agricultural workers
Real wages (-1)	Logged real wages of agricultural workers the previous year
Proportion of 20–29	Number of men and women aged 20–29 as a percentage of the total population
Sex ratio	Number of men aged 20–29 divided by the number of women aged 20–29
Mortality of 50-w	Number of deaths of men aged 50 or more per 1,000 men aged 50 or more
AR(1)	First-order autoregressive process

Regression 1

Male SMAFM = Intercept + Real wages + Real wages (-1) + Proportion of 20-29 + Sex ratio + Mortality of 50-w + AR (1)

	Coefficient	Std. Error	t-Statistic	Prob.
Intercept	32.19763	4.136394	7.783985	0.0000
Real wages	0.041524	0.109451	0.379385	0.7050
Real wages (-1)	-0.209247	0.102078	-2.049887	0.0422
Proportion of 20–29	0.121215	0.052082	2.327383	0.0214
Sex ratio	-1.961263	1.174086	-1.670460	0.0971
Mortality of 50-w	-0.000681	0.001211	-0.561830	0.5751
AR(1)	0.992428	0.009736	101.9322	0.0000

Included observations	147
R^2	0.985179
Breusch-Godfrey Serial Correlation LM Test (Prob.)	0.303370
Prob. (F-statistic)	0.000000

Regression 2

Female SMAFM = Intercept + Real wages + Real wages (-1) + Proportion of 20-29 + Sex ratio + Mortality of 50-w + AR(1)

	Coefficient	Std. Error	t-Statistic	Prob.
Intercept	31.18882	1.776776	17.55360	0.0000
Real wages	-0.037176	0.122512	-0.303443	0.7620
Real wages (-1)	-0.311543	0.114246	-2.726948	0.0072
Proportion of 20–29	0.188231	0.058000	3.245382	0.0015
Sex ratio	-4.654400	1.314214	-3.541586	0.0005
Mortality of 50-w	-0.002113	0.001357	-1.556572	0.1218
AR(1)	0.983962	0.014504	67.83876	0.0000

Included observations	147
R^2	0.966126
Breusch-Godfrey Serial Correlation LM Test (Prob.)	0.582179
Prob. (F-statistic)	0.000000

Table 3 Pairwise Granger Causality Test (2 lags)

1750–1900			
Null Hypothesis:	**Obs**	**F-Statistic**	**Probability**
FEMALE SMAFM does not Granger Cause MALE SMAFM	149	2.76659	0.06622
MALE SMAFM does not Granger Cause FEMALE SMAFM		5.48405	0.00507
1750–99			
Null Hypothesis:	**Obs**	**F-Statistic**	**Probability**
FEMALE SMAFM does not Granger Cause MALE SMAFM	48	0.78438	0.46282
MALE SMAFM does not Granger Cause FEMALE SMAFM		8.79758	0.00063
1800–1900			
Null Hypothesis:	**Obs**	**F-Statistic**	**Probability**
FEMALE SMAFM does not Granger Cause MALE SMAFM	101	3.07681	0.05068
MALE SMAFM does not Granger Cause FEMALE SMAFM		2.12974	0.12445

Bibliography

Alter, G. (1991) 'New perspectives on European marriage in nineteenth century', *Journal of Family History*, 16, pp.1-5.

Bengtsson, T. and Oeppen, J. (1993) *A reconstruction of the population of Scania 1650–1760*, Lund Papers in Economic History 32.

Bergstrom, T. and Lam, D. (1994) 'The effects of cohort size on marriage-markets in twentieth-century Sweden', in J. Ermisch and N. Ogawa (eds), *The family, the market and the state in ageing societies*, Oxford, pp.46-63.

Easterlin, R. (1981) *Birth and Fortune*, London.

Guinnane, T.W. (1997) *The vanishing Irish: household, migration and the rural economy in Ireland, 1850–1914*, Princeton.

Habakkuk, H.J. (1974) *Population growth and economic development since 1750*, Leicester.

Haines, M.R. (1996) 'Long-term marriage patterns in the United States from colonial times to the present', *The History of the Family*, 1, pp. 15-39.

Hajnal, J. (1953) 'Age at marriage and proportion marrying', *Population Studies*, 7, pp. 111-36.

Hajnal, J. (1965) 'European marriage patterns in perspective', in D.V. Glass and D.E.C. Eversley (eds), *Population in history*, London, pp.101-43.

Historisk statistik för Sverige. (1969) Part 1, 'Befolkning. 1720–1967', Stockholm.

Knodel, J. and Maynes, M.J. (1976) 'Urban and rural marriage patterns in Imperial Germany', *Journal of Family History*, 1, pp. 129-69.

Lesthaeghe, R.J. (1977) *The decline of Belgian fertility, 1800–1970*, Princeton.

Levine, D. (1977) *Family formation in an age of nascent capitalism*, New York.

Lundh, C. (1993) *Giftermålsmönster i Sverige före det industriella genombrottet*, Lund Papers in Economic History 31.

Lundh, C. (1997) *The world of Hajnal revisited*, Lund Papers in Economic History 60.

Myrdal, J. and Bäärenhielm, G. (1994) *Kvinnor, barn & fester i medeltida mirakelberättelser*, Skara.

North, D. (1985) 'The growth of the government in the United States: an economic historian's perspective', *Journal of Public Economics*, 28, pp.383-99.

North, D. (1990) *Institutions, institutional change and economic performance*, Cambridge.

Ohlin, B.G. (1955) 'The positive and the preventive check: a study of the rate of growth of pre-industrial populations', unpublished Ph.D. thesis, Harvard University.

Ohlin, B.G. (1960) 'Mortality, marriage and growth in pre-industrial populations', *Population Studies*, 14, pp. 190-97.

Schofield, R. (1976) 'The relationship between demographic structure and environment in pre-industrial western Europe', in W. Conze (ed.), *Sozialgeschichte der familie in der Neuzeit Europas*, Stuttgart.

Sundbärg, G. (1907a) 'Fortsatta bidrag till en svensk befolkningsstatistik för åren 1750–1900', *Statistisk tidskrift*, häfte 139.

Sundbärg, G (1907b) 'Fortsatta bidrag till en svensk befolkningsstatistik för åren 1750–1900', *Statistisk tidskrift*, häfte 143.

Wrigley, E.A. and Schofield, R.S. (1981) *The population history of England 1541–1871: a reconstruction*, Cambridge.

10 Marriage and economy in rural Westphalia, 1750–1870: a time series and cross-sectional analysis[1]

Georg FERTIG, University of Münster

I. Introduction

In 1845, an anonymous Westphalian published a description of her province which caused some frowning among her countrymen (Anon. 1996: 75–79, 87–92). Annette von Droste-Hülshoff, whose authorship was revealed after her death, strongly emphasized cultural and socio-economic differences within Westphalia, and marriage patterns played a central role in the picture she put forward. The most striking contrast around which her text is built opposes the inhabitants of the Münsterland region in the northwest with those of Paderborn, in the southeast. If you travel from Paderborn to Münsterland, she claimed, you feel like an American who departs from the wigwams of the Iroquois and enters a pietist settlement. The Paderborner villagers, with their brownish skin, rebellious mind and wild temper, are to be esteemed for their 'pure nationality' or ethnic heritage. But it's the Münsterländer peasant – white-skinned, loyal and helpful – whom you actually can trust. Paderborn, according to Droste, was characterized by its smoky poor villages, full of little huts with broken roofs, and the cause of this deplorable state was that people used to rush into marriage without any capital but their labour power and a couple of wooden beams they somehow managed to collect. The poverty of Paderborn, as Droste argues, could not be overcome because of the widespread carelessness and passion which 'bring about' the poor – that is, induced parents to recklessly making children – and then, whatever property was left was taken away by advocates and innkeepers. In other words, marriage patterns are what we have to look at if we want to understand the poor economic conditions of Paderborn. Similarly, in Droste's view the wealth and the civilized state of the Münsterland was contingent upon the reluctant marriage behaviour of its inhabitants who rarely married without having secured their property in land. According to Droste, Münsterland peasants married 'like Moravians' (a pietist group); they followed the will and mind of their parents even in the choice of marriage partners. Of course childbirth out of wedlock was almost unknown, and population growth was – fortunately – lower than even the Prussian government would wish.

[1] Funding for the research underlying this paper has been obtained by Ulrich Pfister (Münster) from the Deutsche Forschungsgemeinschaft. Andreas Berger, Stefan Evers, Jens Fischer, Christine Große, Alexander Kessler, Georg Korte, Markus Küpker, Volker Lünnemann, Marcus Nümann, and Uwe Richter have spent many hours in Westphalian archives in order to mobilize source material. Patrick Galloway, Michael Haines, and several participants in the CORN conference have provided helpful comments on previous versions. I would also like to thank Franz Irsigler and Dietrich Ebeling of the Graduiertenkolleg Westeuropa (Trier) who have supported my first attempts at developing some ideas about marriage and the economy which are reflected in this empirical study.

This intriguing and somewhat controversial piece by the famous Westphalian poet was fairly typical of 19th-century thinking about marriage, culture and the economy. Some of the implicit assumptions prevalent in her text are first, that population growth is a dangerous thing; second, that the decision whether to marry or not should be made in accordance to the resources that are available; and third, there is quite a bit of variation in rural marriage patterns and attitudes. Some of these presuppositions still inform the views of historical demographers. To be sure, modern scholars tend to avoid ethnographic stereotyping so popular in the 19th century, and the notion of massive micro-regional variation in mentality and even skin colour can hardly be understood today. But the debate about reluctant and more growth-oriented marriage patterns, of peasant and other rural ways of marrying, is far from over.

It seems to be a generally accepted view that marriage in early modern and 19th-century rural western Europe was late, non-universal and elastic to economic circumstances. Some scholars have emphasized the role of neo-local household formation in bringing about this 'European Marriage Pattern' (Hajnal, 1965). A typical household was by no means self-sufficient: people were embedded in relations of communal economy, kinship, alms giving and factor markets. But whenever a new household was formed, this was a decisive movement in the context of all these relations. Marriage shifts the primary responsibility for generating income to a new unit in which labour and other factors such as capital and land are pooled, reproduced, co-ordinated and brought to the marketplace. Since in most cases marriage resulted in the formation of a new household, it implied costly decisions for the couples involved. It is therefore far from surprising that marriage behaviour reacted to the availability of resources beyond the couple's own labour power, including factors such as capital, land and labour, but also household consumer goods.

While Hajnal's 'European' pattern is largely agreed upon, the variations within this pattern are less well understood. Two major types of systems through which these resources were distributed are the family and the market. There is little consensus about the way marriage was regulated by these systems, and what variables determined how important each system was. One line of theorizing has emphasized the need for new couples – especially among peasants – to wait until a member of the old generation died and left his or her position to the new household (for a critique, see Ehmer, 1991). It has been argued that this 'chain between reproduction and inheritance' was broken in areas where proto-industrial production generated income from export markets (Tilly, 1971). However for peasants, the relative importance of subsistence and market production, and consequently, the positive or negative impact of high prices, has been debated (for two classical positions see Labrousse (1933) and Abel (1935)). A full understanding of the way marriage was embedded in the family economy and the market would require data analysis on a micro level, including information about both demographic and economic events in individual life courses (Schlumbohm, 1996). Such data are however very rare, and typically allow comparisons of very few parishes.

It is not the aim of this chapter to review the vast literature on marriage and the economy. In general, the question still does not seem to be settled. In the specific case of Westphalia, a couple of local and micro-regional studies have been carried out which touch upon some aspects of the problem (Hohorst, 1977; Göbel, 1989; see also the forthcoming study by Gehrmann), primarily in the context of non-dividing inheritance and proto-industry. Some important findings include the high proportion of remarriages, which did not decline during the 19th century (Klein, 1993); the failure of state policies aimed at linking marriage to inheritance (Krüger, 1977); and the observation that the rule of neo-local household formation was dropped by peasant households in times of hardship (Schlumbohm, 1996). There still seems to be room for a quantitative and explorative investigation of the way the economy influenced marriage in Westphalia.

II. Methods

In this paper, a research strategy on an aggregate level will be followed. This method, regression analysis of short-term fluctuations in demographic rates, has been introduced to modern social and economic history by Franklin Mendels in his famous dissertation which provided the starting point for the debate on proto-industrial versus peasant marriage patterns (Mendels, 1981). Moreover, a central chapter in Wrigley and Schofield's (1981) *Population history of England* exploits the Cambridge Group's English data with the help of a refined version of Mendels's technique, the calculation of cumulative elasticities from distributed lag regressions (Lee, 1981). Since then, distributed lag short-term analysis has been used in a large number of studies in historical demography (for an overview, see Galloway, 1988).

In the present study, the goal of the data analysis is to explain statistically the short-term variance of the local nuptiality series for a sample of thirty-four Westphalian parishes. Two determinants of these fluctuations are investigated: a rye price series from the Westphalian capital, Münster, which serves as an indicator for the fluctuating availability of resources on markets (rye prices can be expected to influence fluctuations in real wages and in the respective terms of trades of proto-industrial and peasant producers), and an estimate of the local non-infant deaths, which serves as an indicator for resource reallocations within the family system, most notably remarriages and inheritances. Since it is well-known that both variables may have an influence on marriage frequencies in rural societies, the main question to be explored is not whether such an influence can be detected in Westphalia as well. Rather, we are interested in exploring the conditions under which these influences were stronger or weaker. As such, two lines of investigation are followed. First, the level of aggregation is discussed with special attention to the non-infant death series. When we look at entire territories or sum up the local events of many parishes (Lee, 1981), our results may be quite different from what we find on the parish level. This is so because family systems are mainly local, while markets tend to be regional or even worldwide. Disaggregating the data even below the parish level is possible for one of our parishes only, where a local family reconstitution dataset is available (Schlien, 1993). Here, the local series will be broken down into sub-series such as first marriages, remarriages, deaths of previously married persons and the like. The second line of enquiry regards cross-sectional variables such as wealth, inequality, family forms or proto-industry which might determine how strong the influences of the two longitudinal series are. All series are pooled, and a distributed lag regression model is estimated for lags 0 to 3. Interaction terms with the cross-sectional variables are included in the model as are dummy variables for each parish.

Technically, the design follows the standard procedures developed by Lee, Galloway and Weir with small modifications in order to keep the results comparable. Non-infant deaths have been estimated following a method designed by David Weir (1984: 37)

$$nid_t = d_t - (imr \cdot (s \cdot b_t + (1 - s) \cdot b_{t-1})) \tag{1}$$

where nid_t = non-infant deaths in year t, d_t = all deaths in year t, imr = infant mortality rate, s = separation factor, i.e. the proportion of infant deaths occurring within the calendar year of birth, and b_t = births in year t. This method has been preferred over the one used by Lee because it minimizes the consequences of missing values in the birth series. The separation factor has been assumed to be 0.74, again following a suggestion by Weir. The infant mortality rate has been assumed to be 0.170, based on evidence from a family reconstitution study on one Westphalian parish.[2] All longitudinal variables z_t are transformed by dividing through a moving eleven-year average:

$$z_t^* = 11 \cdot z_t \div \sum_{i=-5}^{5} z_{t+i} \tag{2}$$

A consequence of this transformation, introduced by Lee, is that the regression coefficients can be interpreted as elasticities, that is, percentage reactions to percentage changes, and that they can be summed up to cumulative elasticities. The cross-sectional variables x_i are transformed by subtracting the minimum value and dividing by the span between minimum and maximum.

$$x_i^{**} = (x_i - min(x)) \div (max(x)-min(x)) \tag{3}$$

Thus, the cross-sectional variables take a value of 0 at the minimum and 1 at the maximum, which makes the interaction terms easier to interpret. This transformation is not used in other short term studies. The full regression model has the form:

$$n^*_{i,t} = \sum_{k=0}^{3} \beta_{1,k} p^*_{t-k} + \sum_{k=0}^{3} \beta_{2,k} x_i^{**} p^*_{t-k} + \sum_{k=0}^{3} \beta_{3,k}\, nid^*_{i,t-k} + \sum_{k=0}^{3} \beta_{4,k}\, x^{**}_i\, nid^*_{i,t-k} + \sum_{j=1}^{34} \beta_{5,i}\, d_{i,j} + \epsilon_{i,t} \tag{4}$$

for i = parish 1 to parish 34; t = year 1750 to year 1870; k = lag 0 to lag 3; where $n_{i,t}$ = nuptiality in place i at time t; p_t = price of rye at time t; $nid_{i,t}$ = non-infant deaths

[2] Infant mortality rates in the parish of Hartum varied between 0.158 and 0.210 in the period under study, as reported in Imhof (1990: 290). An even smaller infant mortality rate of only 0.138 has been found in Siegen (Göbel, 1988: 146, 311).

in place i at time t; x_i = the value of the cross-sectional variable in place i; $d_{i,j}$ = an array of parish dummy variables with the values 1 if $i = j$ and 0 otherwise; and $\epsilon_{i,t}$ = error term. Again, the model is closely designed after Galloway's work. One modification is that lag 4, usually insignificant, is not included in order to economise on missing values. Also, the regression coefficients $\beta_{1,k}$ through $\beta_{5,k}$ are estimated using maximum likelihood (ML) instead of ordinary least squares (OLS) regression. This was preferred because potential problems with the different sources of variation, cross-sectional and longitudinal, are thus avoided, and also because of more convenient software (Proc Mixed, by SAS). Experimenting with OLS and ML estimation has shown that while ML consumes much more computing time (several or even dozens of seconds as opposed to a fraction of a second on a Pentium PC), the estimates are identical up to the eighth decimal (as should be expected when the error term is normally distributed), and the ML results are slightly more significant. In ML estimation, R^2 is not reported. In some models without cross-sectional interaction terms, the parish dummies d are left out, and an intercept is included.

III. Sources and data

From each of the thirty-four *Kreise* or counties in Westphalia, one parish has been selected (see Figure 10.1). With one exception (Marl), the original parish registers (or microfilms of the originals) were evaluated.[3] As far as possible, random sampling was used as the selection method in order to arrive at results that are representative for rural Westphalia. However, several compromises were made. Löhne was selected because for this parish, a family reconstitution dataset was available (Schlien, 1993). Parishes the boundaries of which appeared to have changed during the 18th and 19th centuries were excluded, and parishes for which population enumerations from the 18th century have survived were preferred. We attempted to exclude those parish registers where there were many gaps before data collection even started. Also, very small (below 600 inhabitants in 1818) and very big (3,000 and more) parishes were excluded, and in the southwestern region of mixed religions, parishes with smaller minorities were preferred. The boundaries of political communities, parishes and taxation districts changed and overlapped during the period under study, as did the official definition of religious denominations (Calvinist, Lutheran and Catholic in the 18th century versus Evangelical and Catholic in the 19th century). On the one hand, it was impossible to select only parishes that were unaffected by all of these changes and inconsistencies: in several *Kreise*, there were no such parishes. But on the other hand, selecting a pure random sample would have forced us to refrain from linking any meaningful additional sources (including population numbers) to many of the local series.

[3] Parish registers are from Landeskirchliches Archiv Bielefeld, Personenstandsarchiv Detmold, Bistumsarchiv Münster, Bistumsarchiv Paderborn, Katholisches Gemeindearchiv Roxel, Katholisches Gemeindearchiv Selm. For Marl, data are from Krüger (1977). For Werther 1750–1767, data for the town only are not available; this gap has been filled using aggregated data for both town and parish of Werther. Both Catholic and Protestant parish registers were evaluated for Herringen in the period after 1816.

Figure 10.1 ***Kreise*** **and parishes**

Note: Boundaries represent Kreise as of 1861, ignoring enclaves and Kreis Münster-city. Dots represent geographical centres of parish areas. Cartography: Jens Fischer and Georg Fertig.

Members of minority denominations may be missing from most parish registers. Some of the birth and death series under study include a small number of stillbirths, mostly far below 4 per cent. The rye price series are edited post-harvest prices from the city of Münster; under normal circumstances, they should influence nuptiality only at lags 1 or higher. There were gaps in this series for the years 1846, 1848–49, 1855 and 1864–70. In order to fill these gaps, October prices of rye in the city of Münster as given in contemporary official publications and archival sources were used for the years up to 1867, and a published index of rye prices in the city of Berlin was

[4] Münster: Gerhard/Kaufhold, 1990, pp. 183-186; Amtsblätter der Regierung Münster; Staatsarchiv Münster (=STAM) Oberpräsidium Münster Nr. 352. Berlin, 1977, p. 404 / Tab. A 70.

used for the years 1868–1870.[4] In order to calculate correct conversion rates, simple regressions without intercept were run for the years 1827 to 1863. The resulting formulas capture about 95 per cent of the variance in the series the gaps of which had to be filled.

In Figure 10.2, data points which could not be used because of missing values are plotted. Since in a distributed lag regression, a single missing value in a regressor (in our case, non-infant deaths) creates a run of values that cannot be used in the analysis, and since births of the preceding year are needed for estimating non-infant deaths, the number of unusable datapoints is higher than the number of missing values in the original data. Since we did not count the births of 1749, all thirty-four parishes have a missing value of non-infant deaths in 1750, which creates a run of unusable datapoints until 1753. Some missing values are clustered in the sixth and seventh decade of the 18th century, with up to eight missing parishes during the Seven Years War. Other gaps in the parish registers occurred in the Napoleonic period of 1810–15, again with up to eight unusable datapoints per year. Excluding the first four years, the number of unusable datapoints is 222, or 5.5 per cent for the entire period of 1754 to 1870.

Figure 10.2 Observations not used in distributed lag regression

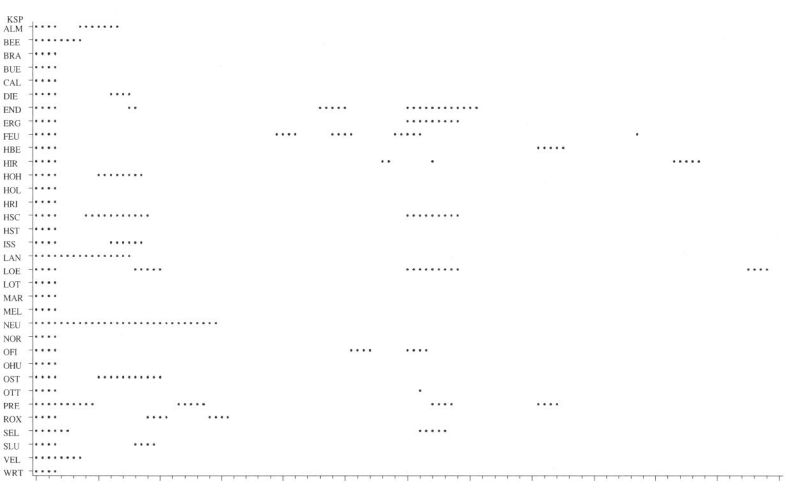

Source: Parish register dataset
Note: Dots represent years with missing values for marriages, lags 0 to 3 of non-infant deaths, or both. Birth data for current and preceding year must be available in order to calculate non-infant deaths. For parish names, see map 1. They have been abbreviated using the first three letters, except for Herbede (HBE), Herringen (HRI), Herscheid (HSC), Herstelle (HST), Oberfischenbach (OFI), Oberhundem (OHU), Schlüsselburg (SLU) and Werther (WRT).

As to the cross-sectional variables, theoretical relevance and availability were both crucial in selecting them. First, it has been argued that marriage behaviour in proto-industrial regions was different from others. Unfortunately, using our sample it is impossible to find out, on a parish level, how large a proportion of the inhabitants was spinning or weaving, and how much that contributed to the household income. Therefore, regional maps produced by Stephanie Reekers were used in order to establish whether a parish belonged to the spinning and weaving zone or not (Reekers, 1993). These maps are mostly based on Prussian district-level statistics from the period around 1800. Second, it can be assumed that household forms influenced the logic of household formation. For example, we might argue that the structural need for remarriage was smaller in those places where a large number of widows and widowers kept their own households, or that patterns of non-neolocal household formation made inheritance less important (Schlumbohm, 1996). For most Catholic regions of Westphalia as well as for one Calvinist territory, 18th-century household lists were evaluated, and each household was classified according to the Cambridge group scheme (see note to Table 10.5). The same household lists also provide proportions of servants. The taxation system was completely different in the 19th century, and so is the character of the sources. Landowners had to pay a tax according to the productivity of the individual parcels they owned, and authorities and landowners made great efforts in order to establish a correct estimate of these values (*Reinerträge*) (Kopsidis, 1996). Therefore, not only is the local acreage of fields, meadows, pastures and so on available, but also is an estimate of their productivity, which is unknown for the 18th century. Moreover, the tax sums of all holders of land entitlements, which could include collective and institutional entitlements, can be evaluated.[5] Thus, for the 19th century, the interaction analysis will focus on issues of wealth and inequality rather than family forms.

[5] For some parishes, these had to be estimated from the individual acreage, using regression equations derived from all suitable observations.

IV. The local and the regional

Figure 10.3 Regression results at different levels of aggregation

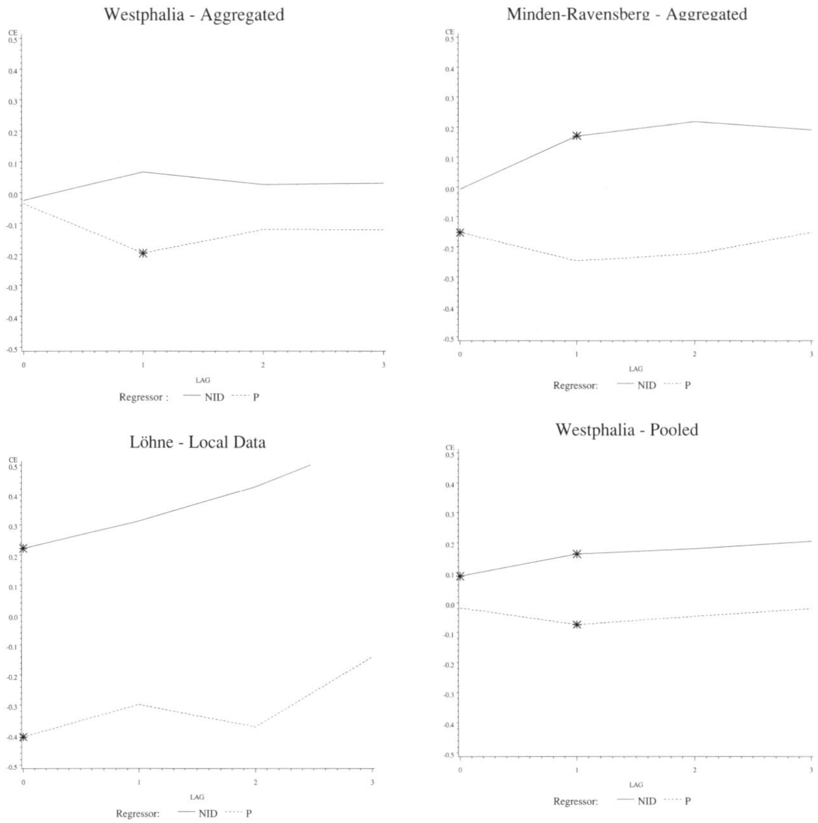

Source: Table 10.1

Since prices are regional but land transmissions are local, aggregating local series can strongly influence the results of the analysis. Moreover, the local marriage and death series are a result of aggregation themselves: they sum up first marriages and remarriages, deaths of single persons and deaths of ever married persons. In Figure 10.3 – based on regressions presented in Table 10.1 the results of a rather simple regression analysis without interactions are presented for four different levels of aggregation. In each graph, the cumulated elasticity CE, that is the lag sum of the regression coefficients, is plotted against lags 0 to 3 for both the longitudinal determinants of marriages investigated here, non-infant deaths (NID) and rye prices (P). A star marks those lags where the t statistic for the regression coefficient is significant at a 5 per cent level. If a regression coefficient at a specific lag is strong, the slope leading to that lag is more steep, and if the coefficient is close to zero, the corresponding line is horizontal (e.g. the rye or P line from lag 2 to lag 3 in the first graph is horizontal, because the regression coefficient for rye at lag 3 is close to zero). For the first graph, only parishes with very few missing values were used, and all demographic variables were summed up for all these parishes.

The results presented in the first graph in Figure 10.3 seem to show that high rye prices had a discouraging effect on marriages at lag 1, and that non-infant mortality was irrelevant. But if we move to smaller aggregates, this picture changes substantially. Aggregating the data for the territory of Minden-Ravensberg only (a largely proto-industrial Lutheran region in the northeast) results in a much stronger and significant impact of non-infant deaths. Taking one parish from that area, Löhne, yields even more extreme results: the cumulated elasticity CE for non-infant deaths even exceeds the area of the graph. Similar graphs for other parishes look wildly different because the coefficients vary greatly. Finally, the results of a pooled regression are presented. In other words, all observations are put into one dataset, so that the first observation (year 1750) for Beelen follows the last observation (year 1870) for the parish of Alme, and so on. The results of the pooled analysis are more stable than the local or micro-regional plots. Beyond the negative impact of high rye prices already noted in the aggregate analysis, they show a marked and significant impact of non-infant deaths.

Table 10.1 Regression results at different levels of aggregation

Level of aggregation	Westphalia aggregated		Minden-Rav. aggregated		Löhne parish		Westphalia pooled	
	b	t	b	t	b	t	b	t
Constant	1.09	6.71**	.97	4.69**	.56	1.37	.82	19.28**
NID_t	-.03	.294	-.01	-.10	.22	2.47*	.09	6.57**
NID_{t-1}	.09	1.16	.18	2.68**	.09	.99	.07	5.59**
NID_{t-2}	-.04	-.54	.05	.71	.11	1.17	.02	1.29
NID_{t-3}	.00	.06	-.03	-.42	.16	1.62	.02	1.95+
P_t	-.03	-.76	-.15	-2.53**	-.41	-2.38	-.02	-.72
P_{t-1}	-.16	-2.80**	-.09	-1.30	.11	.56	-.06	-1.98**
P_{t-2}	.08	1.31	.02	.32	-.07	-.39	.03	.98
P_{t-3}	-.00	-.02	.07	1.16	.23	1.42	.03	1.07
N	70		84		99		3756	

Source: Parish register data set (Schlien, 1993)
Note: OLS estimates were used, except for the pooled series (ML). No adjustment for autocorrelation was employed. All nuptiality series, including each parish series in the pooled regression, were separately tested for first and second order autocorrelation using the Durbin-Watson test; none was found autocorrelated on a 5% test level. The parishes OST, SEL, LAN, ISS, END, ERG, NEU, HOH, BEE, OTT, VEL, ALM, FEU, HSC, HIR have been ignored when calculating the aggregated series for Westphalia in order to minimize the number of missing values. Significance levels: + =10%; * = 5%; ** = 1%

We should interpret these results with caution. They do not indicate that the rhythms of circulation and recombination of goods and factors within the family system were more important for marriage behaviour than the fluctuations on wider and more anonymous markets. We do not know how large a portion of the flows within each system is captured by our indicators. However, these results demonstrate that in Westphalia both kinds of economic contexts for marriage can be observed if we look at the right level of aggregation. This makes our data design a good starting point for investigating the conditions under which both kinds of determinants were stronger and weaker.

However, before we move on to the interaction analysis, marriages and non-infant deaths will be broken down into smaller categories. Does the impact of non-infant deaths reflect a traditional peasant marriage pattern, in which a death in the older generation and a marriage in the younger generation are linked events? Recent scholarship has raised doubts about the existence of such a homeostatic mechanism (Ehmer, 1991). Or does the link between deaths and marriages, as far as it can be observed, reflect the need to reassign roles within peasant households instead? This has been suggested in short-term analysis studies on England and Sweden. In order to better understand the social practice behind the non-infant-death coefficients, we calculate marriage regressions based on family reconstitution data for one parish, Löhne in the region of Minden-Ravensberg. The parish registers for Löhne cover 966 marriages in the period from 1750 to 1870. The family reconstitution, compiled by a local genealogist, covers 1,054 marriages for the same period (that is, 88 more). This discrepancies is due to the fact that the family reconstitutions includes marriage dates for couples who married outside of the parish. Out of the 1,043 marriages, 781 are first marriages (for bride and groom), and 273 are remarriages. With the family reconstitution data, we can also use the annual number of deaths of persons who had been married instead of the rather crude estimate of non-infant deaths. This is appropriate since both modes of niche transfer, inheritance and remarriage, imply that marriages are made more likely by the death of a previously married individual rather than a spinster or bachelor.

Table 10.2 Regression results for different categories of marriages

Dependent Variable	MPR		MFR		RMFR		FMFR	
	b	t	b	t	b	t	b	t
Constant	.22	.89	.56	2.92**	.39	1.05	.71	3.42**
NID_t	.28	3.16**						
NID_{t-1}	.17	1.84+						
NID_{t-2}	.17	1.78+						
NID_{t-3}	.16	1.70+						
EMD_t			.17	2.03*	.18	1.07	.10	1.08
EMD_{t-1}			.08	1.03	.37*	2.36*	-.01	-.13
EMD_{t-2}			.13	1.50	.15	.92	.11	1.16
EMD_{t-3}			.05	.57	-.09	-.54	.08	.82
R^2 adj	.08		.03		.05		-.01	
F	3.04*		1.83		2.19+		.68	
N	99		99		99		99	

Source: Parish registers, Löhne (Schlien, 1993)
Note: OLS estimates were used. MPR: marriages in parish register. MFR: marriages in family reconstitution. RMFR: remarriages in family reconstitution. FMFR: first marriages in family reconstitution. NID: non-infant deaths. EMD: deaths of ever married persons. Significance levels: + =10%; * = 5%; ** = 1%

In order to compare the non-infant deaths influence on marriages with the more precise indicators from the family reconstitutions, regressions were run for all marriages from the parish registers, for all marriages from the family reconstitution, for remarriages from the family reconstitution, and for first marriages from the family reconstitution. As independent variables, only deaths were included – the estimate of non-infant deaths in the first equation, and deaths of ever married individuals in the other equations. OLS estimates were used in order to arrive at R^2 statistics, which were then compared across models. It turns out that the regression of all marriages from family reconstitution data is less exact than from parish register data. This suggests that the migrant marriages additionally included with the family reconstitution were less influenced by local deaths than the local marriages. The model becomes somewhat better when we limit the prediction to remarriages. For first marriages, however, the death of previously married persons seems to be irrelevant. We may conclude that the role of niche transfer through remarriage is corroborated by these data, while the classical niche mechanism linking reproduction to inheritance cannot be detected here.

V. Trends and interactions

The basic assumption in our interaction analysis is that functional relations, for example, between marriage and the economy, are not universal but depend on specific historical and social contexts. Let us first inspect a very basic interaction factor in which historians tend to be most interested: time. In order to explore if the impact of both prices and mortality changed over time, time has been coded as 0 for 1750, 1 for 1870, and corresponding values in between. Figure 10.4, which is based on the coefficients reported in Table 10.3, should be read the same way as the more simple distributed lag plots in Figure 10.3, only now we have two lines for each regressor, non-infant deaths and prices. The two thick lines belong together and describe the impact of rye prices; the two thin lines also should be looked at simultaneously, and refer to non-infant deaths. In both cases, the dashed line gives CE values that are valid when the interaction factor, time, is minimal, that is, for 1750. This first set of CE values is calculated the same way as the CE values reported earlier, that is, as the lag sums of the regression coefficient for the base effects P_t to P_{t-3} and R_t to R_{t-3}. For drawing the solid line, the lag sums interaction effects P_t . *time* to P_{t-3} . *time* and R_t . *time* to R_{t-3} . *time* have been added to this first set of CE values, so that this second set of CE values is valid for time = 1. Stars again mark significant regression coefficients. For the base effects they are placed on the dashed line, and for the interaction effects they are placed on the solid line. When the two thick lines or the two thin lines run far away from each other – as it is the case here at least for the thick lines – we may conclude that a considerable interaction is present; in other words, that the functional relation measured by the distributed lag regression was not the same over the different contexts captured by the interaction factor.

Figure 10.4 Regression results interacted with time

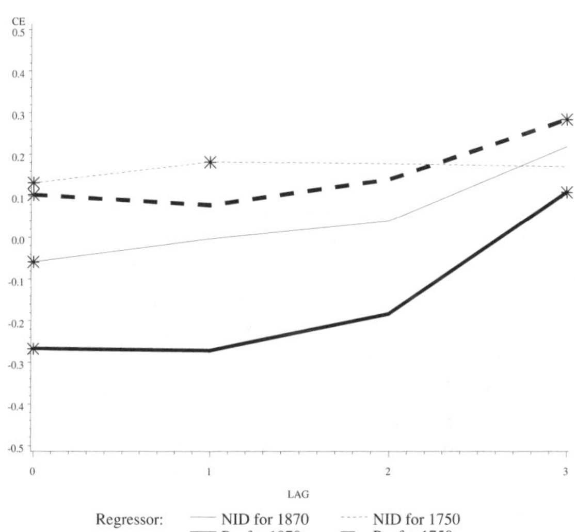

Source: Table 10.3

Table 10.3 Regression results interacted with time

	b	t
Constant	.54	6.86**
NID_t	.13	5.57**
NID_{t-1}	.05	2.18*
NID_{t-2}	.00	-.17
NID_{t-3}	-.01	-.33
P_t	.10	2.17*
P_{t-1}	-.02	-.45
P_{t-2}	.06	1.11
P_{t-3}	.14	2.97**
Time	.54	3.48**
NID_t . Time	-.11	-2.14*
NID_{t-1} . Time	.06	1.20
NID_{t-2} . Time	.05	1.01
NID_{t-3} . Time	.08	1.56
P_t . Time	-.24	-2.85**
P_{t-1} . Time	-.07	-.67
P_{t-2} . Time	-.06	-.57
P_{t-3} . Time	-.24	2.88**
N	3756	

Source: see text
Note: Significance levels: + = 10%; * = 5%; ** = 1%

As can be seen in both Figure 10.4 and Table 10.3, the intercept is .54 around 1750, and it increases by another .54 until the end of the period under study. Around 1750, the impact of mortality was significant at lags 0 and 1. Including all lags, the cumulated elasticity sums up to .17. At the end of our period, the overall impact of mortality may have increased further, but when we look only at the significant effect at lag 0, the trend is negative. In other words, the influence of what we think is remarriage was decreasing. As to the impact of prices, the trend is even more striking. At the beginning of our period, high prices tended to encourage people to marry (CE: .28), while at the end the overall impact of high prices was deterring (CE=.28-.61). This may reflect the fact that Westphalia was a grain-surplus region at the start of our period, but that an increasing part of the population got their income from other sources than grain production as the 19th century went on, and these had to pay more for their living in times of high prices. Taken together, the classic view is corroborated to some degree that in the course of modernization, familial transfers became less important, and people became more dependent upon real wages, terms of trade or other market contexts. Since the effects changed over time and since the available cross-sectional variables refer either to the 18th or the 19th century, in the rest of this chapter separate analyses will be carried out for the first and the second part of the period under study, that is, pre- or post-1810.

Table 10.4 CE values by parish, period and regressor

	1750–1810		1811–1870	
Parish	NID	P	NID	P
ALM	.31	.78	-.40	.07
BEE	.07	.58	.30	-.58
BRA	.39	.13	-.20	.20
BUE	.33	.04	.53	.23
CAL	-.07	.00	.32	-.01
DIE	.46	-.32	.53	.01
END	1.07	.11	.23	-.35
ERG	.48	-.17	-.93	-.04
FEU	.04	.37	-.01	-.24
HBE	.10	.36	.33	-.32
HIR	.03	-.06	.49	.45
HOH	.08	-.48	-.03	.17
HOL	.31	.00	.67	-.17
HRI	.72	-.38	.14	-.21
HSC	-.10	-.34	-.55	.32
HST	.09	.42	-.29	.11
ISS	.25	-.19	.98	-.61
LAN	.32	.11	.76	-.02
LOE	.63	-.04	.34	-.17
LOT	.05	.61	-.02	-.44
MAR	.21	.02	.37	-.46
MEL	.39	-.08	.12	.08
NEU	-.13	.35	.08	.46
NOR	.59	-.37	-.75	-.34
OFI	.61	.09	.16	-.25
OHU	-.21	.44	1.07	.09
OST	-.04	-.25	1.01	.29
OTT	-.14	.59	.26	-.22
PRE	.54	-.01	.18	-.19
ROX	.43	-.02	.61	-.10
SEL	.35	.66	-1.72	.02
SLU	.16	-.16	.15	.06
VEL	.47	-.21	.45	-.32
WRT	.62	.45	.93	-.40

Source: see text
Note: Reported figures are the sums of the regression coefficients over lags 0 to 3 for the independent variables NID, holding all lags of P constant, and *vice versa*. Regressions were run for each parish separately. ML estimated were used. Intercepts were included in the regression analysis. For abbreviations of parish names see Figure 10.1

Apart from varying over time, the elasticities of marriage with regard to non-infant deaths and rye prices also varied across parishes. The elasticities for each parish, cumulated over lags 0 to 3, are reported in Table 10.4. Differences in the strength and even direction of these coefficients are considerable, and some of these differences of course are random. It is also not easy to discern any interpretable regional pattern just by inspecting these cumulative elasticities. For instance, the four parishes from the Paderborn area in our sample (Büren, Hohenwepel, Herstelle and Neuenbeken) with one exception do not display elasticities that are significantly different (t-tests were run) from the eight Münsterländer parishes (Beelen, Diestedde, Holtwick, Nordwalde, Ottenstein, Roxel, Selm and Velen). The exception are the 19th-century rye prices: the Paderborner seemed to benefit and Münsterländer to be harmed by high prices. It is the purpose of the cross-sectional interaction analysis to account for these wildly varying coefficients and to identify the systematic patterns that underlie their variation.

Apart from an attempt to capture the importance of protoindustry, further analysis of 18th-century marriage elasticities will focus on household forms. As Table 10.5 demonstrates, the percentage of the population who lived in nuclear and other households varied considerably: for example in Alme, almost everybody lived in a nuclear household, while in Oberhundem, most people lived in extended households. The same sources allow us to establish the proportions of households that included widows and widowers, or in which they lived on their own, as well as the proportion of servants. Were marriage patterns affected by these varying household structures?

In order to make the results of the interaction analysis more easy to interpret, the same method as employed for the longitudinal interaction factor, *time*, has been used for all the cross-sectional interaction factors, *X*. The variables with which non-infant deaths and rye prices were interacted have all been transformed, so that at the minimum, their value is zero, and at the maximum, unity.

Table 10.5 Cross-sectional variables, family forms and servant rates, 18th century

PARISH	SINGLE	CO-RES.	NUCLEAR	EXTENDED	MULTIPLE	W1	W2	SERVANTS
ALM	.00	.00	99.14	.86	.00	23.45	.00	3.02
BEE	.91	.15	70.98	22.30	5.67	18.75	1.84	13.64
BUE	12.75	.00	87.25	.00	.00	12.14	8.67	5.38
CAL	.69	.00	65.91	25.20	8.20	21.95	1.22	17.27
DIE	.37	.00	62.88	24.91	11.84	8.09	.00	17.92
FEU	.42	.00	50.26	29.76	19.56	20.63	.63	6.64
HIR	4.18	1.10	85.71	9.01	.00	12.05	4.82	13.85
HOH	.13	.26	63.61	22.12	13.87	18.24	.00	5.24
HOL	1.03	.41	49.59	36.24	12.73	17.71	.00	10.73
HST	1.16	.00	86.39	10.78	1.67	17.34	1.73	2.31
MEL	3.05	.00	65.43	26.17	5.34	25.53	1.42	17.23
NEU	.65	.43	70.05	20.43	8.43	19.53	.59	8.43
NOR	.73	.00	73.84	22.20	3.22	17.55	.63	16.42
OHU	.61	.30	41.00	45.69	12.41	26.09	.00	12.86
OST	1.29	.00	90.52	8.19	.00	18.28	1.08	28.02
OTT	2.28	3.42	68.80	17.09	8.40	18.06	1.39	5.13
ROX	.90	.72	77.81	16.17	4.40	17.68	1.52	22.82
SEL	1.98	.19	70.38	23.02	4.43	27.11	1.33	14.46
VEL	.22	.00	54.18	30.26	15.35	22.43	.38	9.93

Source: Alme (1785), Calle (1764), Hirschberg (1785), Mellrich (1755), Oberhundem (1764), Ostinghausen (1775): STAM Hzgt. Westfalen, Landstände; Büren (1787), Herstelle (1787), Hohenwepel (1789), Neuenbeken (1787): STAM Fürstentum Paderborn, Geheimer Rat; Feudingen (1741): Rentkammer Wittgenstein, Viertelsbeschreibungen; Holtwick, Nordwalde Roxel, and Selm (all 1749), and Beelen, Diestedde, Ottenstein, and Velen (all 1750): Bistumsarchiv Münster, Generalvikariat, Handschriften.

Note: All figures are percentages. 'single', 'coresiding', 'nuclear', 'extended' and 'multiple' refer to percentages of the population living in households of the respective type. For definitions of family forms, see Laslett and Wall (1972). W1 are percentages of households in which widows or widowers lived, W2 are percentages of households composed by widows or widowers living alone. 'Servants' are percentages of servants in the population.

Table 10.6 Regression results interacted with cross-sectional variables, 18th century

X =	Proto-industry		Mult. fam. rate		Servant rate		Ext. fam. rate	
	b	t	b	t	b	t	b	t
NID_t	.09	5.01**	.12	3.27**	.06	1.69+	.13	2.82**
NID_{t-1}	.06	3.11**	.11	3.23**	.02	.50	.07	1.58
NID_{t-2}	.01	.72	.01	.34	-.03	-.89	-.02	-.42
NID_{t-3}	.00	.29	.01	.22	.00	-.07	.00	-.10
P_t	.01	.18	.15	1.96+	.29	3.26**	.28	2.68**
P_{t-1}	-.02	-.36	-.04	-.50	-.07	-.74	-.16	-1.42
P_{t-2}	.04	.83	.12	1.44	.05	.52	.17	1.52
P_{t-3}	.05	1.34	-.03	-.39	.08	.85	-.07	-.69
NID_t. X	.08	1.65	-.06	-.81	.12	1.42	-.10	-1.08
NID_{t-1}. X	.05	.99	-.16	-2.39*	.09	1.10	-.08	-.80
NID_{t-2}. X	-.01	-.26	-.05	-.70	.05	.67	.01	.11
NID_{t-3}. X	.05	1.01	.00	.02	.03	.41	.02	.18
P_t.X	.11	1.28	-.21	-1.22	-.56	-2.83**	-.42	-2.13*
P_{t-1}. X	-.10	-1.08	.11	.60	.18	.85	.36	1.67+
P_{t-2}.X	.05	.49	-.29	-1.58	-.10	-.47	-.34	-1.57
P_{t-3}. X	.04	.46	.24	1.46	-.07	-.33	.28	1.41
ALM	.72	8.48	.53	3.70	.60	4.11	.58	3.33
...								
WRT	.49	3.16	.00		.00		.00	
N	1786		996		996		996	

Source: Calculations based on parish register dataset. Rye price series (Gerhard/Kaufhold, 1990). Significance levels: + = 10%; * = 5%; ** =1%
Note: estimates for parish dummies ALM through WRT are not reported.

Figure 10.5 Regression results interacted with cross-sectional variables, 18th century

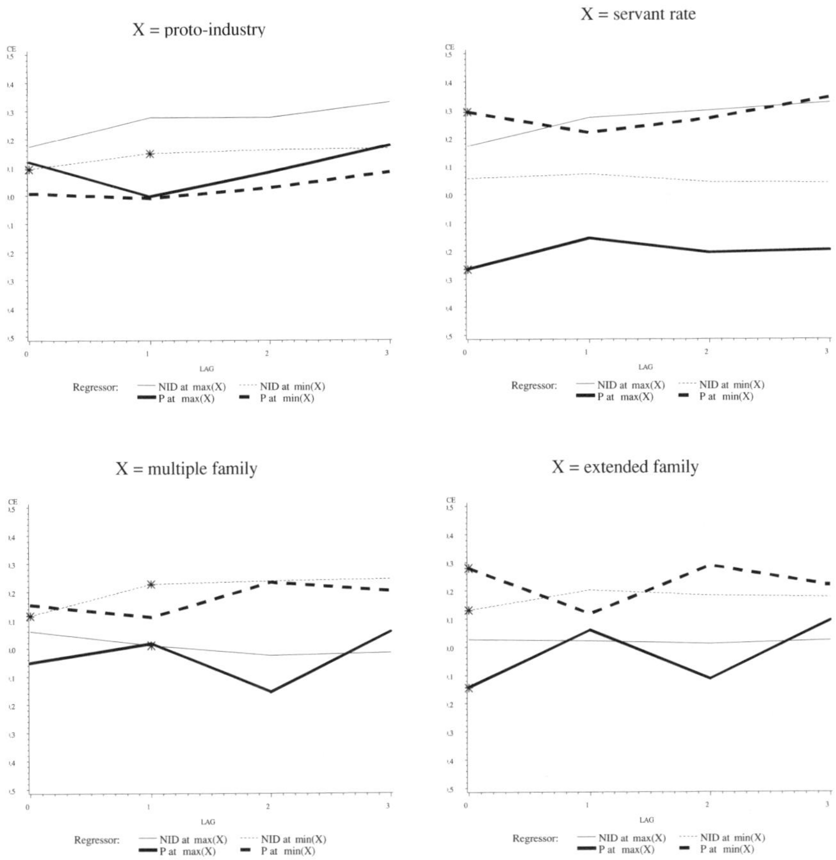

Source: Table 10.6

A question which must obviously be asked is whether marriage behaviour in proto-industrial areas followed a different logic than in other regions. The first graph in Figure 10.5 and the first equation in Table 10.6 present interactions with a dummy variable, *proto-industry*, coded 1 for the parishes of Holtwick, Ottenstein, Lotte, Velen, Isselhorst, Löhne and Werther, and 0 for all other parishes. Analysis is restricted to the period before 1810, since the evidence on proto-industry used refers to the end of the 18th century and also because during the 19th century, parts of the Westphalian countryside underwent a considerable de-industrialization. The regression results do not corroborate the view that proto-industry broke the chain between reproduction and inheritance, or in fact mattered at all. Visually, this becomes clear when we look at the two thick lines and the two thin lines in the graph: both pairs run quite close to each other, and none of the interaction terms is significant. Moreover, the interaction term with the highest t value, nid_t . *proto-industry*, is positive. In other words, if anything, proto-industry led to a higher impact of inheritance or remarriage. It should however be noted that longitudinal indicators of protoindustrial terms of trade are not included with this analysis.

As to family forms, not all the tabulated variables can be expected to have an influence on the way marriage reacted to market fluctuations or to the rhythms of the family economy. For instance, for the logic of marriage and household formation it seems irrelevant how many nuclear families included other relatives. The one arrangement least in accordance with a homeostatic peasant niche model are multiple households, where two couples shared one niche. Recently, Jürgen Schlumbohm, using material from a parish close to the Westphalian border, has pointed out that in times of crises parents and children dropped the rule of neo-local household formation rather than imposing it and putting a brake on reproduction (Schlumbohm, 1996). Indeed, parishes with high proportions of the population living in multiple households are spread all over our sample: there were places such as Velen, Hohenwepel or Feudingen, where quite a number of couples shared households, and others like Alme, Nordwalde or Ostinghausen, where scarcely any household included more than one couple. Looking at the two regions so sharply contrasted by Droste-Hülshoff, we find that family structures were generally not much different in Münsterland and in Paderborn. The only variables for which a significant difference has been found (using t-tests), are the proportion of persons in extended households (24 per cent in Münsterland, and 13 per cent in Paderborn), and the servant rate (14 per cent in Münster, 5 per cent in Paderborn).

The regression results for the second equation, also presented in the third graph in Figure 10.5, show that for the parishes with a minimum of multiple families, the cumulated effect of non-infant deaths was positive (.25), if significant only at lag 1. When we move to the maximum proportion of multiple families, this is weighed up by a negative effect (cumulated elasticity of the interactions: -.27), again significant at lag 1. This supports the view that familial niche transfer, including remarriage, was a decisive factor for marriage behaviour only where the rule of neo-locality was obeyed, a rule which was, in Westphalia, not without exceptions.

Attempts to find interactions with the two widow indicators have failed, and the results of these insignificant regressions are not reported. One the one hand, widows and widowers living alone made up only a small proportion of all households in all parishes. Households including widows and widowers, on the other hand, were pretty widespread everywhere. We might conclude that a household pattern that actually pressed widows and widowers to remarry and thus raised the impact of non-infant deaths on marriage behaviour could not be found in our sample.

The influence of servant rates has also been investigated. In terms of the circulation of family resources, the results are insignificant. However, there seems to be a connection between servant rates and the influence of market fluctuations. The regression results presented in the third equation in Table 10.6 and the second graph in Figure 10.5 reiterate the observation made above that during the earlier period, high prices had a positive impact rather than a deterring one on marriages. This suggests that the selling of grain was an important source of income for a large part of the rural population before 1810. The effect was however reversed in parishes where a large number of servants was employed. It should be noted that the coefficients are significant only at lag 0. Since the rye price series refers to harvest prices, we might be observing an effect of the same year's harvest rather than an effect of the prices proper. We might speculate that in servant areas, there was a beneficial effect of good harvests (and low prices) for the servant population, because a good harvest entailed a high demand for servant labour and better real wages for the servants; it thus became easier for the latter to marry. Intriguingly, very similar results are obtained when we use the rate of persons living in extended families instead of the servant rates. Servant rates and proportions of extended families are virtually uncorrelated across parishes (r=.13), although both are high in Münster and low in Paderborn. Still, people who lived in with their kin might have had a very similar position as servants.

When we move on to the 19th century, the character of the sources used for cross-sectional analysis changes a lot. For this period, we know little about family structures, but much more about property and production. From the cadastral sources evaluated for most parishes, three dimensions of variation can be extracted. First, parishes varied in agrarian productivity and consequently, in agrarian per capita wealth. The latter has been calculated by dividing the local tax sum, as of the 1820s or 1830s, by the overall population number of 1818. Second, in some places the wealthier part of the households owned almost all the land, while in others, the small owners were in a somewhat better position. Third, the overall number of land entitlements per capita varied considerably, depending either on the size of the landless class or on the sizes of landowning households. Table 10.7 gives an overview of these indicators for all parishes.

Table 10.7 Cross-sectional variables, per capita wealth, inequality and entitlement rate, 19th century

PARISH	PCATV	Q1	Q2	Q3	Q4	GINI	TOP25	LOW25	PCAE
ALM	6.58	47	19	28	7	.65	74	1	22
BEE	6.32	8	32	35	24	.66	77	2	16
BRA	15.84								
BUE	8.68	36	27	21	16	.75	84	0	33
CAL	18.53	26	13	21	40	.70	81	0	15
DIE	9.38	11	23	25	40	.73	83	1	
END	8.94	7	28	41	24	.64	75	3	20
ERG	13.90	17	25	21	36	.69	80	1	18
FEU		57	22	17	4	.71	82	1	
HBE	6.76	17	34	26	23	.73	83	1	22
HIR	5.78	25	35	33	7	.55	64	2	33
HOH		39	22	20	19	.75	85	1	28
HOL		26	24	20	29	.78	90	0	
HRI		8	38	22	32	.71	82	2	
HSC	8.19	20	16	29	35	.58	67	1	26
HST		64	24	6	6	.83	90	0	
ISS	4.75	1	15	52	32	.54	67	5	11
LAN		23	39	11	28	.75	91	1	
LOE	6.01	6	10	32	52	.45	55	4	15
LOT	6.14	7	23	41	28	.64	75	2	16
MAR	6.76	10	28	33	29	.66	78	2	22
MEL	15.33	16	30	21	33	.73	84	1	29
NEU		37	19	17	27	.74	86	0	
NOR	13.33	19	16	24	41	.73	84	0	15
OFI	6.00	52	25	18	5	.68	78	1	
OHU	6.82	45	23	16	16	.69	81	1	
OST		17	24	26	34	.74	87	1	
OTT	3.83	31	36	25	7	.65	74	2	31
PRE	10.97	13	23	23	41	.65	75	1	23
ROX	21.65	3	26	24	47	.69	82	1	18
SEL	9.73	27	27	18	27	.78	90	0	20
SLU	12.69	9	20	46	25	.57	67	3	
VEL	5.80	41	15	19	25	.79	88	0	16
WRT									12

Source: Individual entitlements and parish overall tax sums, used for calculation of PCAE, are from Staatsarchiv Detmold (=STAD) M5C; Katasteramt Borken; Katasteramt Ennepe-Ruhr; Katasteramt Warendorf; STAM Katasterbücher Arnsberg; STAM Katasterbücher Münster, STAM Regierung Münster, Katasterverwaltung. Population numbers for 1818 as given in Reekers/Schulz 1952 have been used as a base for the per capita rates, PCATV and PCAE. Overall acreages given in these sources were double-checked with the overall parish acreage in 1885 as given in Königlich Statistisches Bureau (1887), and data for dubious parishes were excluded.

Note: For parish names, see note to Figure 10.2. PCATV: per capita agrarian tax value sum. Q1-Q4: percentage of landowners under tax value of 2.02 Thaler (Q1), between 2.02 and 8.60 Thaler (Q2), between 8.60 and 29.92 (Q3), and over 29.92 Thaler (Q4). These cutoff points were calculated from pooled entitlement data for all parishes, and mark overall quartiles. GINI: Gini coefficient of concentration. TOP25, LOW25: percentage of land owned by wealthiest (TOP25) and poorest (LOW25) 25 % of land owners. PCAE: per capita agrarian entitlements. Land entitlements over 230 *Morgen* are omitted from calculation of Q1-Q4, GINI, TOP25, LOW25, and PCAE. Tax values have been estimated from acreage for some parishes.

Again, we can compare Paderborn and Münsterland and find that the two regions contrasted by Droste were indeed structurally different (t-tests were used for testing the differences). The were less small landowners in Münster (21 per cent as compared to 44 per cent), and the number of entitlements per capita was higher in Paderborn (.30 as opposed to .19). In other words, there seems to be a real background to Droste's observation that the agrarian base for a household could be quite minuscule in Paderborn, in contrast to the Münsterland. As emphasized, the 19th-century sources are from a different domain than the family data studied above. Nevertheless, to some degree they capture the same kind of regional variation as the earlier data. In Table 10.8, the 18th-century family variables are cross-correlated with the 19th-century data on wealth, property and inequality. It turns out that family fragments – single householders such as widows and widowers, or co-residing relatives – were more frequent in the same parishes where the number of small but not minuscule property units was highest, where property was less concentrated with the wealthiest, and where there were many property entitlements per capita. The 19th-century tax data will tell us little about extended or multiple households, or about those where widows and widowers lived together with other family. Eighteenth-century servant areas turn out to be more wealthy in the 19th century, with a high proportion of upper-class households.

Table 10.8 Correlations of cross-sectional variables, 18th and 19th centuries

	N	SINGLE	CORES.	NUCL.	EXT.	MULT.	W1	W2	SERV.
PCATV	13	-.11	-.32	.02	.07	-.11	.10	-.09	.74**
Q1	19	-.01	-.08	-.09	.00	.25	.24	-.04	-.78**
Q2	19	.39+	.59**	.17	-.22	-.29	-.22	.43+	-.01
Q3	19	.06	.24	.30	-.28	-.30	-.31	.17	.36
Q4	19	-.20	-.29	-.11	.23	-.02	-.04	-.24	.77**
GINI	19	-.06	-.42+	-.22	.21	.23	.17	-.20	-.11
TOP25	19	-.12	-.46*	-.27	.29	.26	.23	-.27	.07
LOW25	19	.01	.51*	.19	-.17	-.23	-.18	.18	.03
PCAE	12	.62*	.43	.30	-.51+	-.25	-.43	.56+	-.48

Note: For definitions and source, see Table 10.7. Significance levels: + =10%; * =5%; ** = 1%

Of the cross-sectional variables, per capita wealth was tested first. We might expect that in poorer areas, the circulation of goods within the family was less important simply because there was not much property to circulate, and that people in these areas were more dependent on markets or proletarianized. However, the agrarian per capita wealth level did not turn out to be a decisive factor in terms of interaction analysis for the period after 1810 (insignificant regression results not tabulated). Non-infant deaths increased marriage rates, and high prices diminished marriage rates regardless of the overall level of agrarian wealth. This is in accordance with Galloway's (1993: 103) findings both on a cross-national and on a local level. We might conclude that average agrarian wealth is no good indicator of how many potential couples were in need of familial or market resources, possibly because there were other sources of income not captured in our data, or because the distribution of resources was more important than the average.

Figure 10.6 Regression results interacted with cross-sectional variables; 19th century

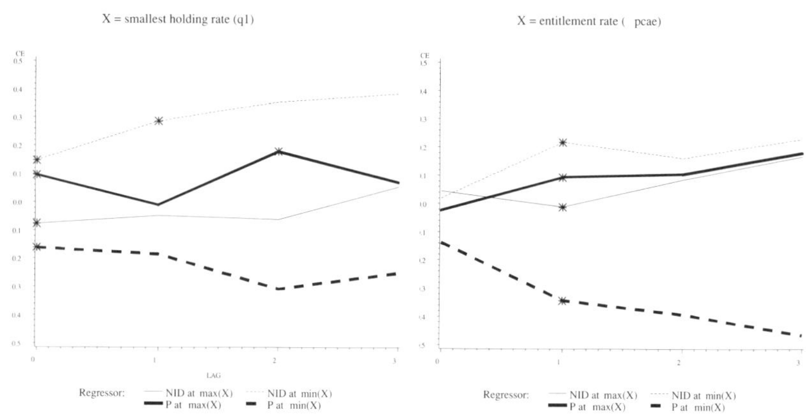

Source: see Table 10.9.

Table 10. 9 Regression results interacted with cross-sectional variables, 19th century

	Q1		PCAE	
	b	t	b	t
NID_t	.15	3.51**	.02	.38
NID_{t-1}	.14	3.33**	.20	3.97**
NID_{t-2}	.07	1.67+	-.06	-1.11
NID_{t-3}	.03	.74	.07	1.37
P_t	-.16	-2.75**	-.14	-1.92+
P_{t-1}	-.02	-.33	-.21	-2.39*
P_{t-2}	-.12	-1.73+	-.05	-.58
P_{t-3}	.06	.97	-.07	-1.02
$NID_t \cdot X$	-.22	-2.42*	.02	.28
$NID_{t-1} \cdot X$	-.11	-1.22	-.25	-2.98**
$NID_{t-2} \cdot X$	-.08	-.89	.15	1.81+
$NID_{t-3} \cdot X$	.09	.93	.01	.16
$P_t \cdot X$	.26	2.00*	.11	.86
$P_{t-1} \cdot X$	-.08	-.53	.32	2.04*
$P_{t-2} \cdot X$	.31	2.02*	.06	.39
$P_{t-3} \cdot X$	-.16	-1.29	.15	1.14
ALM	.87	7.50	.93	11.14
...				
WRT	.00		1.21	8.89
N	1850		1256	

Source: see Table 10.7. Significance levels: + =10%; * = 5%; ** = 1%

Looking at indicators of distribution, the Gini coefficient has also turned out to be insignificant as an interaction factor (insignificant results not tabulated). As has become clear by experimenting with and correlating various indicators of inequality, the Gini coefficient captures the same dimension of variance as the proportion of land owned by the local upper quartile (Top 25). In other words, it tells us how strong the position of the wealthier part of the households was, but not how many poor, middling, or wealthy households were present. The latter is captured by the Q1 to Q4 variables, and here indeed significant interactions were found. The first graph in Figure 10.6 and the first equation in Table 10.9 show that where there was only a minimal number of very small landowners, non-infant deaths had an cumulated impact of CE = .39, and high rye prices deterred people from marrying (CE = -.24). But in areas where the number of small landowners was maximal, these effects were both ironed out (CE for NID interactions: -.32, for P interactions: .33). Analysis for Q4 (not reported) yields reciprocal, if less significant, results. This suggests that in small peasant areas, marriage rhythms were indeed detached from both kinds of economic fluctuations, i.e., on product markets and within family systems. Possibly, self-produced goods were available to a larger fraction of the population in these areas, and people consequently were less harmed by high prices. Also, when small bits and pieces of land are available, we may expect that the land market is more vivid and land transactions frequently occur outside the context of inheritance and remarriage. Similar results are obtained when we look at the rate of land entitlements per person. The second graph in Figure 10.6 and the second equation in Table 10.9 show that where the entitlement rate was minimal, CE for *NID* was .23, and CE for P was -.47. Although the effect of non-infant deaths was not quite ironed out in parishes with a maximal entitlement rate (CE = -.07), the deterrent effect of high rye prices was even reversed in such places (CE = .64).

VI. Conclusion

The purpose of this study has been explorative both in terms of methods and of content. Economic determinants of marriage behaviour can be found both in familial and market systems. Price series have been used as an indicator for market fluctuations, and an estimate of non-infant deaths as an indicator for the reallocation of resources within the family. We should be aware that both indicators are just that, proxies, and that it is impossible to capture all sorts of income available to couples. In addition, by focusing on income indicators, we have restricted the discussion to the costs of marriage and household formation and to the varying ability of couples to cope with these costs. A more complete discussion of marriage and the economy would have to include the benefits of marriage as well, for example, the emotional or material value of children, the value of being one's own master, or the benefits gained from pooling the labour power of a man and a woman. These benefits can also be expected to vary, although typically not in a short term times series fashion, and are certainly worth analysis.

Despite these shortcomings, the results presented here are interpretable. The first set of results is methodological. Marriage is a decision influenced both by regional contexts (here: prices) and local contexts (here: non-infant mortality). Therefore, using a local level of aggregation, but including regional independent variables is appropriate. Moreover, the impact non-infant mortality had on nuptiality can be understood as indicating either a niche transfer mechanism across generations (that is, inheritance) or niche transfer within a generation (that is, remarriage). An inspection of family reconstitution data for one parish has shown that the effect should be understood as mainly due to remarriage. This dovetails with results from other European regions; in fact, there is so far little empirical evidence, be it time series or family reconstitution, that the transfer of niche ownership from fathers to sons has been a decisive determinant of marriage behaviour in any part of Europe. The inheritance model implies a familistic society, in which goods and especially factors - such as land, or the labor of children - circulate not on markets but within the family system. A house, a holding, a man and a women together form the basic unit of such a society, and before a man and a women join together, house and holding have to be present too. The logic of remarriage is but slightly different: house, holding, woman and man still form a functional unit. When the man, or the woman, dies, their labor power is missing. Since factors circulate in the family system, not on factor markets, selling part of the holding or employing a servant of the opposite sex is not an option. The widow or widower will either have to pass the property to a married child, or marry again. Both a niche mechanism and remarriage indicate a pattern in which factor markets are absent and large household units are transferred as a whole. In other words, remarriage is a worthy subject of study in itself, and systematically can be expected to depend on similar social structures as the often-quoted 'chain between reproduction and inheritance'.

The second set of results is provided by the findings of the interaction analysis. Although we may say that on a Westphalian scale, both mortality (and thus the family system), and grain prices (and thus the market) did influence marriage behaviour, this was not true in every period in time and in every place in the same way. In the earlier period, the impact of mortality was clearer, and high prices had a positive influence which was completely reversed until the late 19th century. In other words, marriage behaviour was not drawn into a sphere of market considerations formerly unknown, but the position a large part of the population held within these markets was reversed. Across parishes, sources on 18th century family forms and 19th century land ownership were investigated. Although they were from quite different periods and domains, they seemed to capture similar dimensions of regional variation. One dimension that seemed to influence marriage patterns might be labelled servant regions versus smallholders regions (Mitterauer, 1986). High prices deterred people from marrying in parishes where a lot of servants was employed, or where a large number of people lived in with relatives and presumably worked under similar conditions as servants did. In servant areas, the number of large landowners also tended to be high. A high rate of smallholdings, on the other hand, made people less vulnerable by high rye prices; indeed, Paderborn was among the few parts of Westphalia where high prices encouraged rather than deterred marriages even in the 19th century. Looking at the influence of familial factor transfers or probably remarriages, the small peasant pattern is important again, although not in contrast to servant rates. Where entitlements to land were numerous and holdings small, non-infant mortality mattered little to marriage rhythms. In other words, in regions such as Paderborn nuptiality seems unelastic to both economic contexts, the family and the market. While the importance of smallholding as a structural factor in rural society was quite obvious to contemporary observers – although we would not necessarily agree to the moral judgements given by Droste-Hülshoff – another dimension detected in our data is less self-evident, and it does not seem to be correlated to the question of smallholdings and larger farms. Neo-local household formation was not universal in Westphalia, and there were some places where a considerable minority of the population lived in what we might understand as stem families. In these parishes, familial niche transfers also mattered less.

The aggregate study presented here suggests that there was not just one way in which economic contexts influenced agrarian marriage behaviour. If we want to understand how marriage was embedded into the economy in Westphalia, we will have to investigate several dimensions of rural society. Proto-industry, about which our data have not allowed us to say very much, may be one of them. However, other important topics are the long term shift away from grain production as the primary source of income, the regional variation in land markets and holding patterns, and the varying importance of neo-local household formation. A deeper understanding of rural marriage patterns and their economic contexts will require further investigations of market and familial transactions on the level of individual life courses.

Bibliography

Abel, W. (1935) *Agrarkrisen und Agrarkonjunktur in Mitteleuropa vom 13. bis zum 19 Jahrhundert*, Berlin.

Anonymous [Annette von Droste-Hülshoff] (1996) 'Westphälische Schilderungen. Aus einer Westphälischen Feder', in B. Plachta and W. Woesler (eds), *Sämtliche Werke*, Frankfurt am Main, pp. 63–101.

Ebeling, D. and Klein, P. (1988) 'Das soziale und demographische System der Ravensberger Protoindustrialisierung', in E. Hinrichs and H. van Zon (eds), *Bevölkerungsgeschichte im Vergleich: Studien zu den Niederlanden und Nordwestdeutschland*, pp. 27–48.

Ehmer, J. (1991) *Heiratsverhalten, Sozialstruktur, ökonomischer Wandel. England und Mitteleuropa in der Formationsperiode des Kapitalismus*, Göttingen.

Galloway, P. (1988) 'Basic patterns in annual variations in fertility, nuptiality, mortality, and prices in preindustrial Europe', *Population Studies*, 42, pp. 275–303.

Galloway, P. (1993) 'Population dynamics among rich and poor in European countries, rural Jutland, and urban Rouen', in D. Reher and R. Schofield (eds), *Old and new methods in historical demography*, Oxford, pp. 84–108.

Gehrmann, R. (forthcoming) 'Bevölkerungsgeschichte Norddeutschlands', unpublished manuscript, Berlin.

Gerhard, H.-J. and Kaufhold, K.H. (1990) *Preise im vor- und frühindustriellen Deutschland. Grundnahrungsmittel*, Göttingen.

Göbel, G. (1988) *Bevölkerung und Ökonomie. Historisch-demographische Untersuchung des Kirchspiels Siegen in der Nassau-Oranischen Zeit (1742–1806)*, St. Katharinen.

Hohorst, G. (1977) *Wirtschaftswachstum und Bevölkerungsentwicklung in Preußen 1816–1914*, New York.

Imhof, A.E. (1990) *Lebenserwartungen in Deutschland vom 17. bis 19. Jahrhundert*, Weinheim.

Klein, P. (1993) *Familie und agrarisch-heimgewerbliche Verflechtung. Eine demographische Studie zu Spenge (Ravensberg) 1768–1868*, Bielefeld.

Königlich Statistisches Bureau (1887) *Gemeindelexikon für die Provinz Westfalen. Mit einem Anhang, betreffend die Fürstenthümer Waldeck und Pyrmont. Aufgrund der Materialien der Volkszählung vom 1. Dezember 1885 und anderer amtlicher Quellen*, Berlin.

Krüger, H.-J. (1977) *Die Bevölkerung im Vest Recklinghausen vom Ende des 16. Jahrhunderts bis zum Beginn der Industrialisierung*, Koblenz.

Labrousse, C.-E. (1933) *Esquisse du mouvement des prix et des revenus en France au XVIIIe siècle*, Paris.

Laslett, P. and Wall, R. (eds) (1972) *Household and family in past times*, Cambridge.

Medick, H. (1996) *Weben und Überleben in Laichingen 1650-1900. Lokalgeschichte als Allgemeine Geschichte*, Göttingen.

Mendels, F. (1981) *Industrialization and population pressure in eighteenth-century Flanders*, New York.

Mitterauer, M. (1986) 'Formen ländlicher Familienwirtschaft. Historische Ökotypen und familiale Arbeitsorganisation im österreichischen Raum', in J. Ehmer and M. Mitterauer (eds), *Familienstruktur und Arbeitsorganisation in ländlichen Gesellschaften*, Wien, pp. 185-323.

Reekers, S. (1993) 'Zusammenfassung und Karte der industriellen Gewerbe Westfalens um 1800 (Teil 12)', *Westfälische Forschungen*, 43, pp. 357–513.

Reekers, S. and Schulz, J. (1952) *Die Bevölkerung in den Gemeinden Westfalens 1818–1850*, Dortmund.

Schlien, M. *Familienbuch Löhne. 300 Jahre des Kirchspiels Löhne*, Celle – Klein Hehlen.

Schlumbohm, J. (1996) 'Micro-history and the macro-models of the European demographic system in pre-industrial times: life course patterns in the parish of Belm (northwest Germany), seventeenth to the nineteenth centuries', *The history of the family*, 1, pp. 81–95.

Spree, R. (1977) *Die Wachstumszyklen der deutschen Wirtschaft von 1840 bis 1880*, Berlin.

Tilly, R. and Tilly, C. (1971) 'Agenda for European economic history in the 1970s', *Journal of Economic History*, 31, pp. 184–98.

Weir, D. (1984) 'Life under pressure: France and England, 1670–1870', *Journal of Economic History*, 44, pp. 27–47.

Wrigley, E.A. and Schofield, R.S. (1981) *The population history of England 1541-1871: a reconstruction*, London.

11 The development of regional patterns of nuptiality in 20th-century Europe

Theo ENGELEN, University of Nijmegen

I. Introduction

Within the demographic characteristics of contemporary European populations one finds – on the surface, at least – many similarities with the situation in the 19th century: ages at marriage are high, an important proportion of the population never marries, and there are many one-parent families. We know, on the other hand, that we can not use the classical explanation of these phenomena because traditional marriage restriction no longer functions. These observations lead to the central question in this paper: what happened to Hajnal's European Marriage Pattern in the 20th century?

When John Hajnal introduced the concept of a European Marriage Pattern in 1965[1] (Hajnal, 1965), the ideas were not exactly new. Thomas Malthus already pointed to the contrast between two kinds of demographic regimes. In 'the less civilized parts of the world and in the past', population just grew until it was stopped by the so-called 'positive checks' (poverty, disease, famine and war). Malthus also found an alternative to this grim scenario. In 'the different states of modern Europe', these disastrous results were largely avoided by means of what he called preventive checks, the most important of which was 'delay of the marriage union'. (Malthus, 1978: 205). Still, since 1965 the Hajnal article may well be the most cited article in the historical demographic and family history literature. Its impact on our thinking about marriage, fertility and population control cannot be overestimated. Therefore, we will briefly recapitulate Hajnal's ideas by asking *what* the pattern was said to be like, *where* and *why* it existed, and *when* we can find it.

The characteristics of Hajnal's European marriage pattern are clear and simple. They are (1) a high age at marriage and (2) a high proportion of people who never marry (1965: 101). The exact location of Malthus's 'civilized parts of the world', according to Hajnal is to be found west of the line between Trieste and St Petersburg. Many empirical studies have confirmed the general outline of the European Marriage Pattern. In eastern Europe, couples definitely married younger and the proportion of permanent celibates was much lower than in western Europe. Hajnal's view of the rest of the world is clear-cut: 'Non-European civilizations are like eastern Europe, or more so' (1965: 104).

[1] The pages mentioned here all refer to this article. Also, we follow Hajnal's example by referring to the European instead of the Western European Marriage Pattern.

Why then did western Europe have this particular marriage pattern? When dealing with this question, Hajnal points to the nuclear family system in Europe: 'In Europe it has been necessary for a man to defer marriage until he could establish an independent livelihood adequate to support a family; in other societies the young couple could be incorporated in a larger economic unit, such as a joint family. This, presumably, is more easily achieved and does not require such a long postponement of marriage'(1965: 133). As far as the timing is concerned, Hajnal is convinced that the pattern existed as early as the16th century and persisted until about 1940. After that, it 'seems to be disappearing' (1965: 104).[2] We do not find an explanation for the disappearance of marriage restriction in Hajnal's writings. Still, according to the theory, one would have expected the pattern to disappear much earlier. George Alter, for instance, pointed to this when he edited a special issue of the *Journal of Family History* in which several critical remarks concerning the European Marriage Pattern were made. The problem, Alter writes, is that 'we find low nuptiality in periods, places, and groups where the Malthusian constraints do not seem to apply. Thus, marriage was not earlier in large cities than in rural areas... Nor did members of the bourgeoisie use their wealth to marry their children at earlier ages... Indeed, the very persistence of late marriage throughout nineteenth-century Europe is a challenge to the Hajnal thesis'(Alter, 1991: 2–3).

There are other questions to be answered as well. For instance, does the contrast between continents and countries remain the same when we differentiate after social or occupational sub-populations? Possibly, the differences in the marriage system we find result simply from a structurally different composition of the population. It may well be that the national averages of age at marriage and proportion never married confirm Hajnal's theory, whereas at the same time we will also find similar behaviour for sub-populations with the same characteristics.

Also, is it wise to maintain Hajnal's strict division between western Europe and 'the rest of the world' in the light of more recent information? Outside Europe, we find a much more complicated and differentiated reality than that sketched by Hajnal. In his 1983 article, Hajnal still explicitly treated India, China and eastern Europe as

---

[2] We will not deal with Hajnal's 1983 article (although he himself refers to it as a sequel of the original one) in which the author not simply discusses a marriage pattern anymore, but puts these patterns within the general framework of household formation systems. Again he distinguishes between two clearly different household formation systems: the simple household system and the joint household system. In the northwest European simple household system we recognize aspects of the 1965 argument: relatively late ages at marriage for both sexes and the principle of neo-locality. Areas with a joint household system are characterized by young ages at marriage and the custom for the new couple to start their life together as junior members of an established household. Surprisingly, in 1983 Hajnal does not refer to the 'European' custom of permanent celibacy, although this was a major characteristic of the European Marriage Pattern. On the other hand, Hajnal offers in 'Two kinds of pre-industrial household formation', two new aspects. His section on the uniquely European institution of the circulation of servants (1983: 92–99) is one of them, the splitting of households with several married couples into two or more households in the joint household system is the other (1983: 80–92).

being similar in marriage patterns. Recent publications, however, informed us of a nuptiality valve existing in India (Das Gupta, 1995). The same might be true in other parts of Asia, Africa and Latin America. As for Japan, Osamu Saito concluded that 'the population history before the period of transition can be identified as a regime which was distinct from both the northwest European and the Chinese systems' (Saito, 1996).

Closer to the geographic core of the European marriage pattern, we have also to study the situation in the 'transitional' areas such as southern Europe. In 1983, Laslett tried to enrich Hajnal's ideas by suggesting that Europe has to be subdivided in four regions, West, Central or Middle, Mediterranean and East Mediterranean couples, in his view, differed clearly from their western European counterparts by not (necessarily) forming an independent household immediately after marriage. Also, he argued that female age at marriage was low in southern European countries. As a consequence, there existed a wide age gap between ages at marriage for women and men. There was yet another contrast to western Europe. In Mediterranean countries permanent celibacy, according to Laslett, was low (Laslett, 1983)[3]

In studying the rationale behind the European Marriage Pattern, Hajnal stressed the economic background including the establishing of an independent livelihood. On this issue, Timothy Guinnane made an interesting contribution to the Alter volume in which he stressed the need for a less simplistic economic approach (Guinnane, 1991), whereas in the same volume Katherine Lynch firmly defended Hajnal's position by pointing to the longevity of the European Marriage Pattern as a system of values (Lynch, 1991).

Obviously, many more questions can be added to the ones listed here, but this chapter is just an introduction. It relies heavily on existing studies, and the statistical approach is purely descriptive. Also, because of the fact that national-level data are used, one cannot look into the possible social and regional differences *within* a country. Still, imperfect as they may be, these findings hopefully provide an interesting exploration of the main characteristics of European marriage in the 20th century. First, a description is presented of the development of regional marriage patterns in Europe in the 20th century. Can we trace the Hajnal divide of Europe also after 1900? Do people still marry more and younger in eastern Europe than they do in western Europe? Is Hajnal right when he lets the pattern end around 1940? What is the relative position of Scandinavian and southern European nuptiality? Do these regions belong to the western or to the eastern part of Europe, or do they have special characteristics? To be sure, when one deals with the continent as a whole and one wants to cover a century, details are not to be expected. Although the methodological implications of this approach are clear, the description will be based on national level data only.

---

[3] Kertzer and Hogan (1991) looked into the characteristics of this so-called Mediterranean marriage pattern – although they only used data from one city – and found only the first difference with the northwest European pattern existed. Age at marriage, age gap and celibacy appeared to be consistent with the 'European' marriage pattern.

Once we have located both regional differences and the temporal changes in marital behaviour, this might provide us with a first indication on the background of the marriage patterns. Do these patterns coincide with the well-known differences in economic development or do we have to include value systems? Historians are particularly interested in the 'tenacity of history', the perseverance of behaviour patterns even after the economic rationale for them has disappeared.

II. The development of marriage patterns in 20th-century Europe

Given the nature of the European Marriage Pattern, we have to take fertility into account when studying changes in nuptiality. The Hajnal hypothesis predicts that high levels of nuptiality will result in high levels of fertility. Only when the last phase of the so-called demographic transition reshaped the demographic face of Europe were the two phenomena disconnected. We start by using the indices developed within the Princeton European Fertility Project.[4] Marital fertility is expressed in the index I_g , a measure that controls for age distribution and relates the actual fertility of married women to the maximum fertility possible, found among Hutterite women in North America. The values of I_g range between 0.0 (no births at all) and 1.0 (Hutterite level fertility). The nuptiality index I_m informs us of the proportion of women married between ages 15 and 50, again weighted by the Hutterite fertility rate. A value of 0 means none of these women are married, whereas the theoretical value 1 means all women of that age have entered matrimony. These indices are collected for the years 1900, 1930, 1960 and 1980.

---

[4] This project of the Office of Population Studies of Princeton University was directed by Ansley J. Coale (Coale, 1969) and provided us with a set of monographs on the fertility decline in Portugal, Germany, France, Belgium, Italy, Russia, England and Denmark. See for a comprehensive summary of the project Coale and Watkins (1986).

Figure 11.1 Development of nuptiality and marital fertility, selected European countries, 1900–80

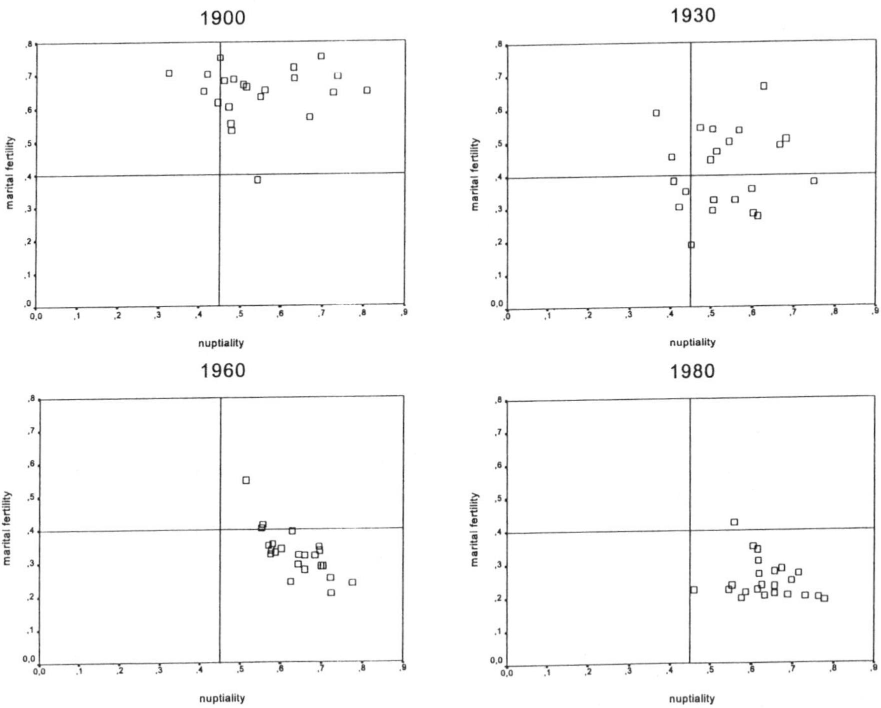

A first impression of 20th-century developments is offered in Figure 11.1. In this figure we plotted nuptiality and fertility against each other for the countries selected.[5] If one compares the scattergrams in the successive years, it is possible to follow the change in reproduction. In 1900, for instance, most values are found in the upper part of the graph because fertility is still relatively high, except for France, the only country below the 0.4 level. The variance in nuptiality levels, on the other hand, is significant, indicating that European reproduction in 1900 is clearly dominated by differences in the prevalence of marriage. Moving on to 1930, fertility levels have declined in every country included, although some still exhibit an I_g of over 0.600. By 1960, the values are more or less concentrated in the lower right corner of the graph. Fertility has declined considerably while nuptiality has increased. This striking convergence of the values is also visible in 1980. In this last year, the (horizontal) differences in nuptiality are more important than the (vertical) variance in fertility that was typical for 1960.

Reproduction in 20th-century Europe clearly moves from a combination of high fertility and low nuptiality towards low fertility and higher nuptiality in the last quarter of the century. On top of that, the relation between the two reproduction components changes. In 1900 we find a correlation of 0.43 between fertility and nuptiality, indicating that fertility rises when nuptiality is high. This is completely in line with Hajnal's theory. By 1930 the correlation has even gained strength, 0.69. After that, however, the neo-Malthusian revolution turns the relationship around. Fertility is low when nuptiality is high in 1960 (-0.753). Twenty years later, as we hope to demonstrate, we are beyond the era that can be described in simple Malthusian concepts (-0.266).

Do we find geographical differences and temporal changes within Europe when we look at nuptiality proper? A first glance at Figure 11.2 shows that for the continent as a whole, the European mean for I_m was almost stable between 1900 and 1930; it decreased only marginally from 0.545 to 0.532. After the Second World War, however, nuptiality increased markedly, not just as a side effect of the new-found peace, but in a structural sense. By 1960 I_m had already reached 0.638, reflecting a much higher proportion of people being married. This trend did not continue until the end of the century: in 1980, European nuptiality had stabilized at a value of 0.636.

[5] The countries are Denmark, Finland, Norway and Sweden (North); Belgium, France, the Netherlands and England and Wales (West); Austria, Germany and Switzerland (Central); Bulgaria, Czechoslovakia, Hungary, Poland, the European part of Russia, Romania and Yugoslavia (East); and Greece, Italy, Portugal and Spain (South). With regard to Germany, until 1945 and since 1989 we obviously deal with one undivided Germany. As we are interested only in the general developments the German Democratic Republic and the Federal Republic of Germany will also be taken together.

Figure 11.2 I_m, 1900–80

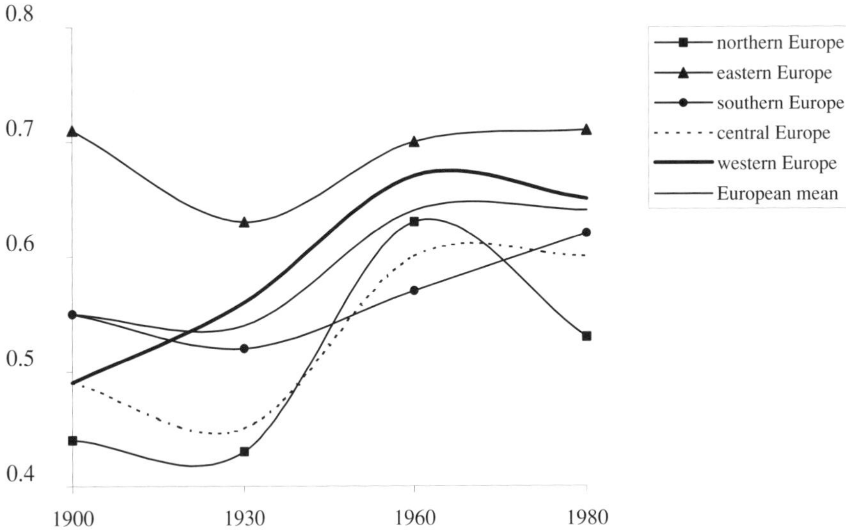

Obviously, this mean hides countries within widely diverging patterns. In Figure 11.2 the nuptiality lines of the regions within Europe are also included in order to aid our interpretation. First of all, we notice that the general development of the graph lines is approximately the same. Whatever it was that influenced the mean marriage rate in Europe as a whole also seems to have determined the development in countries with extraordinarily high or low values. There is a lesson to be learned from this. Although the European continent, especially in the beginning of the century, included countries at quite different stages of modernization, economically as well as culturally, all these countries were apparently responding to the same influences. What we have to explain, then, is the background of the general development shared by all countries, as well as the particular deviations from this trend in selected regions and separate countries.

Table 11.1 Percentage of females single, various ages, selected European countries

		20-24	25-29	45-49
Sweden	1900	80	52	19
	1935	78	49	23
	1970	60	23	8
England and Wales	1900	73	42	15
	1931	74	41	17
	1961	42	—	11
The Netherlands	1900	79	44	14
	1930	75	39	15
	1960	59	20	11
Bulgaria	1900	24	3	1
	1934	35	11	1
	1965	25	7	2
Hungary	1900	36	15	4
	1930	52	24	6
	1970	33	10	6
Romania	1899	20	8	3
	1966	24	8	4

Source: David and McIntyre (1981: 9)

A first observation in this respect is that in every year presented here, the nuptiality level is highest in the countries of eastern Europe. At the beginning of the 20th century, the basic features of the Hajnal pattern can also be found in the proportion of women married at age 20–24 (as an indicator for age at marriage) and at age 45–49 (as an indicator for the celibacy rate) in the European countries.

Table 11.1 presents an example of the results of these diverging patterns. If we look at the values for 1900, the strict dividing line running through Europe is clearly visible. In the western part we find that the great majority of women between age 20 and 24 are unmarried. A comparison with the 25–29 values shows that in this age group, most women have married. Obviously, average age at marriage is to be found in this category. By the time women reached the age of 50, one out of seven had still never been married. In the eastern European countries, on the other hand, nuptiality was much higher. A minority of women aged 20–24 were not yet married and by the time they reached the end of their reproductive years, only approximately 2 per cent were still single.

Although marriage restriction is still clearly visible in 1900 and there are still remnants of the Hajnal marriage pattern in the 1990s, marriage restriction was slowly coming to an end in the 20th century. It is easy to see the limitations of this mechanism of control. In the 19th century, the standard of living in most countries in western Europe rose considerably. Also, medical knowledge and treatment improved greatly. For these reasons, mortality rates declined to historically unprecedented levels. All other things remaining equal, this decrease in mortality alone already caused a substantial population growth. If we take the example of the Swedish population around 1900, it becomes clear that the pre-industrial marriage restriction could not cope with the new mortality standard. Female age at marriage was already 27.5 years, and 18.7 per cent of the population never married. To limit population growth in view of the decreasing mortality would imply that age at marriage would have to rise even more, and that the proportion never married would have to rise even more. However, a further restriction on marriages would be socially unacceptable. For modern observers, it is hard to imagine a society where about one-fifth of the adult population lived celibate lives and when young people postponed sexual activity for more than ten years after reaching sexual maturity. By the end of the 19th century, using the traditional nuptiality valve in the new situation would imply that an even larger part of the population would be temporarily or permanently barred from licit sexual relations.

It certainly is not a coincidence to find the beginning of widespread birth control *within* marriage around the same time. The introduction of contraceptive appliances started around the third quarter of the 19th century, and within a few decades we find marital fertility declining in every country of Europe. At the same time, the inhabitants of western Europe started to marry more and at a younger age.

This takes us back to Figure 11.2. As mentioned before, the first decades of the century witnessed a small decline in nuptiality for the continent as a whole. If we look at the separate regions, we notice that nuptiality decreased in the regions of central, southern and especially eastern Europe. In western Europe, on the other hand, there was at the same time a marked increase. Once contraception within marriage was introduced there, these populations gradually had a lower proportion of people who never married and their brides and grooms were younger than their 19th-century counterparts. In general, one can observe a convergence of marital behaviour in the first six decades of the century. In western European countries, more people married and did so at a younger age. On the other hand, populations in eastern Europe gradually began to postpone marriage to a higher age and more people remained single. Still, even as late as 1960 we can find the outline of the old regimes (see also Table 11.1). Three centuries of marriage restriction were not abandoned at once.

We can only guess what the further structural development would have been without the interruption of the Second World War. As it is, we have to deal with a temporary but strong effect on the process of demographic modernization. The result is obvious in every graph representing marriages: immediately after 1945 there is a peak in nuptiality because delayed marriages were contracted soon after the war ended.

The postwar marriage boom was followed in the 1950s by crude marriage rates which, for Europe in general, were above the level of the 1930s. The end of the war appears to be the beginning of a relatively short period in which marriage was very attractive. Average age at marriage declined throughout northern and western Europe and the proportions ever married increased. The 1960 values in Table 11.1 show the results. Between 1930 and 1960, the proportions of single women aged 20–24 declined by 20–30 per cent. Also in 1960, western European countries harboured fewer single women than ever before.

If one compares the 1960 values with the values of thirty years earlier, there is an increase of nuptiality in every region. The leader in this process was Scandinavia. The mean I_m of Denmark, Finland, Norway and Sweden rose by 0.202. On the other end of the continent, marriage was apparently less popular, or less accessible. Although even the Mediterranean countries witnessed a slight rise in I_m, in 1960 their level of nuptiality clearly was the lowest in Europe. From then on, however, nuptiality rose until in the 1980s the European mean was surpassed.

This relative homogeneity of developments since 1930 came to an end after 1960. Between 1960 and 1980 there were two diverging trends. In eastern Europe and, especially, southern Europe the rise in nuptiality was prolonged, while the two leaders of the earlier rise in nuptiality, i.e. western Europe and northern Europe, now seemed to lead the way to lower proportions of people married. With a dramatic decline of 0.101, Scandinavia was even back at its relative position of 1900 as the region with the lowest nuptiality.

Thus the marriage boom had lasted only a short time. Around the middle of the 1960s, the crude marriage rates in every region of Europe started to decline sharply. The process began in Denmark, Sweden and the German Federal Republic. Norway, England and Wales and Switzerland followed in the early 1070s. Later, the trend emerges in other European countries. This was indeed a powerful process. Within twenty years, the incidence of marriage declined by 30–40 per cent. As a consequence, the proportion of single people in the population rose again after decades of decline. Denmark is an example of this development. In 1971, 47 per cent of the inhabitants aged 20–24 were single; by 1978 this percentage had reached 69 (Festy, 1980: 6). Between 1970 and 1980 the proportion of single Swedish women in the same age rose from 61 per cent to 83 per cent.

To be sure, this was not only the case in Scandinavia. The same development occurred in almost every European country. The percentages for Austria, for instance, were 45 and 57, for England and Wales 41 and 62, for France 45 and 58. In eastern Europe we find the exception to the rule. Here, there was either no decline of the proportion marrying, or the decline was less steep. In general, however, in just ten years (1970–80) young people in Europe seem to have lost their appetite for marriage.

If we look at the age at marriage in the early 1990s, the effects of this attitude is clearly visible. By that time in most parts of Europe, the mean age at first marriage of women was back at the level of the period of rigid marriage restriction, that is, above 25. Brides in Central Europe married on average at 26.0, in Scandinavia at 27.2, and in western Europe at 25.6. Again, the tradition of young marriage in eastern Europe appears to be very strong (average age at marriage was 22.0). Even in the closing decade of the 20th century the Hajnal line divides Europe in a western and an eastern part, with southern Europe as an intermediary (24.9) (Council of Europe, 1994: 35).

Summarizing the development of nuptiality in the 20th century, we can state that around 1900 Europe was divided into two distinct parts. Western European countries had a restrictive marriage regime, whereas in eastern Europe marriage was universal and contracted at a young age. The Mediterranean countries initially had an intermediary position, but for the most part resembled the western pattern. During the first decades of the century marriage restrictions were loosened, and thus the process gained steam after 1945. As a result, in the 1960s marriage patterns in western and eastern Europe were more alike than ever, although the division still remained visible (see among others Coale and Treadway, 1986; Monnier, 1991; Pavlik, 1991). From the middle of the 1960s on, then, all parts of Europe witnessed a change in marriage practices: suddenly, marriage rates started to decline and age at marriage rose once more. Obviously, the attraction of matrimony had faded. We can find a confirmation of this in the concomitant explosive rise in divorce rates (De Guibert-Lantoine and Monnier, 1992: pp. 1022, 1031; Golini, 1987: 703.).

III. Towards an explanation: economic growth or cultural transformation?

Demographic behaviour is guided by two often inter-related factors. In order to change their behaviour, prospective couples have to be economically motivated to do so. Only if and when a new way of handling things offers a rise in income or prospects will they make the change. Still, no matter how promising the economic incentives may be, one also has to take into account the norms and values regulating, for instance, reproduction. In other words, new behaviour has to be culturally or mentally acceptable as well as economically advantageous (Engelen and Hillebrand, 1986; Engelen, 1994, 1997).

To be sure, the revolutionary developments in demographic behaviour are matched by an unprecedented economic growth in the 20th century. In this context, we can also trace a division between the economies of eastern Europe and the other countries. There has also been a reversal of the 'flow of wealth between the generations'. Still, it is difficult to attribute the changes in nuptiality purely to economic influences. It might be plausible to argue that marrying more and younger is a response to the proletarianization of labour. But why, then, did this process not start earlier? What possible economic reason could there be for the reversal of this process from the 1970s on? As far as eastern Europe is concerned, this century witnessed the rise and decline of communist regimes, which introduced severe population policies and planned economies. Through all this, the countries east of the line between St Petersburg and Trieste kept their specific characteristics. This points to structural influences beyond the economic realm.

Therefore, we need to find an alternative explanation. To do this, let us look once again at the development of nuptiality, this time trough the eyes of the participants (Roussel, 1986; Blayo, 1987; Hoffmann-Nowotny, 1987). Beginning around 1900, the options available to young people were not very complicated. In eastern Europe, they had to wait only a short time after reaching sexual maturity before they could marry; and on reaching that age, almost all did marry. For couples in other parts of Europe, especially western and northern Europe, the situation was less easy. Although the era of severe marriage restriction had ended by the time the 20th century started, its remnants still affected the norms and values concerning marriage. Therefore, in most cases young people had to refrain from sexual activities until their mid-twenties and a considerable proportion of them even stayed celibate until they died. In the period 1900–60, this situation changed drastically. Gradually, the restraints against marriage and family building were removed and everyone who wanted to marry could do so. On top of that, the age at marriage declined considerably.

In many countries, this development had already started in the final years of the 19th century. It then accelerated in the first decades of the new century, reaching its climax in the twenty years after the Second World War. Many authors refer to this period as the heyday of the *bourgeois* nuclear family. It was the end of a process of almost 200 years, in which state-controlled marriage sanctioned this family as the normal type of household. By the 1960s, therefore, the proportion of people in Europe who ever married amounted to 95 per cent, and these almost without exception formed classical nuclear families. In doing so they, probably unconsciously, transformed the ideal of many preceding generations into reality.

However, as soon as this 'ideal' situation was reached, there was a radical and rapid change in nuptiality once more. In the 1970s, the proportion married was already back at the level of 1900 and, concomitantly, within a remarkably short time young people could choose from a wide variety of alternative living arrangements. As a result, in the early 1980s the 'classical' nuclear family, consisting of two parents and children, constituted barely 40 percent of the total number of European households. Again, there were regional differences in the velocity of this process, but in every country of Europe the institution of marriage lost its attraction in the last quarter of the century. This can be deduced from the declining proportion ever-married, but also from the rising ages at marriage, the higher divorce rates, one-parent households and one-person households.

Does all this mean that European populations are doing away with the once-cherished family? To answer that question we have to take into account another development. The most important characteristic of European family life in the last decades of the 20th century is the emergence of cohabitation as an accepted and widespread way of forming a household. In pre-industrial and 19th-century Europe, 'consensual unions' did occur mainly, in the lower social classes. The growing number of couples that started cohabitating in the 1970s belonged by contrast to the educated middle classes. Their motives for (temporarily) refusing marriage were in most cases inspired by their desire for independence rather than by the financial problems of their predecessors in earlier centuries. Again the Scandinavian countries seemed to lead the way, successively followed by the other countries, although of all demographic aspects of family life cohabitation showed variance between countries. By 1980, for instance, 15 per cent of all Swedish families consisted of cohabitating couples, whereas in France this was 6 per cent and in Switzerland and Italy only 1 per cent.

The 'new' wave of cohabitation started as a kind of preparation for marriage among young people. In some countries, however, cohabitation very soon became a serious alternative to marriage. In Sweden this process took less than ten years. In southern Europe, on the other hand, even today only a very small minority of couples choose to cohabitate. In general, cohabitation flourishes in those countries where nuptiality is low, and vice versa. Therefore, if one adds the cohabitants to the married couples, the number of people that *de facto* form a 'pair' is very similar in most countries. By implication, one might argue that as long as living together remains as popular as it is today, there is no real threat to the family as such, but only to the institution of marriage. This does not mean that we can treat cohabiting couples as if they were married. Cohabiting couples have significantly fewer children, and in many cases conventional marriage follows cohabitation as soon as the desire to have children emerges. In this respect again, there is an enormous variation among the European countries. In Scandinavia, couples have dissociated fertility from marriage more than in any other part of Europe, but we still find the fertility of cohabiting couples to be significantly below that of married couples.

The acceptance of children born out of wedlock is growing everywhere in Europe to such an extent that the traditional term 'illegitimacy' is increasingly losing its meaning. Almost half of all Swedish children, for instance, are born to parents who are not married. This tendency is typical for all Scandinavian countries, averaging 40.8 per cent. At the other end of the continent, we find the southern European countries where the proportion of extra marital births is very low (8.7 per cent). The other regions have values somewhere in between these two extremes. Still, this variable has – more than the other demographic indicators mentioned – specific deviations from the regional mean. 'Illegitimacy' in Switzerland, Poland, Finland, Portugal and the Netherlands, for instance, clearly differs from the other countries in their respective regions. The link between fertility and marriage obviously has a varying strength (Council of Europe, 1994: 44).[6]

This might also provide a clue for the understanding of the processes described here. From a historical point of view, we do not need to employ economic factors to understand what happened in the closing decades of this century. Recent developments can be interpreted as a prolongation of the modernization and secularization process that started in the wake of the French Revolution, a process which facilitated the emergence of an individualistic approach to life. Obviously, this newfound individualism was difficult to reconcile with the pre-industrial marriage restriction practised in many parts of Europe. As already mentioned, individuals had to pay a high price to keep the population within the limits set by the resources available, by postponing sexual relations or even by lifelong celibacy.

[6] The values refer to the three year average (1990–93) of the proportion of extra-marital births per 100 births.

Until the 20th century, marriage, sexuality and reproduction were an inseparable threesome. Therefore, the introduction of contraceptives implied a revolutionary change. Suddenly, sexuality was disconnected from having children and, consequently, the very reason for the tradition of marriage restriction was gone. As a result, age at marriage declined and marriage rates rose, as was demonstrated in previous pages. But at the same time the connection between sexuality and marriage remained strong, because civil as well as religious authorities allowed sexuality only within marriage. Both developments together explain why the popularity of marriage increased in the first six decades of the century. Marriage was the only possible legitimation for sexuality, and now that sexuality no longer automatically resulted in pregnancies, more people could marry and they did so at a younger age. Figure 11.2 shows that western Europe witnessed the earliest introduction of contraception, and hence in this region nuptiality was already rising between 1900 and 1930.

By the 1960s and especially by 1970, the secularization and individualization which had already facilitated the introduction of contraceptives had gained enough strength to take the next step. Gradually, young people no longer needed the legitimation of marriage to engage in a sexual relationship. Once started, this process was irreversible: within two decades, the connection between marriage and sexuality had disappeared as well.

Finally, in the 1980s and 1990s even the last remnant of the powerful institution of marriage weakened. Its exclusive monopoly over reproduction was questioned by a growing number of couples who decided to raise children without marrying first. From this perspective, the demographic developments in 20th-century Europe originally began during the Reformation and the French Revolution and, therefore, are simply the latest stage of a very long process of change.

The emphasis in this analysis has been on the cultural determinants of the processes described. Secularization, individualization and emancipation can explain the general movement in all European countries, as well as the differences in onset and pace between them. All this, however, does not mean that mental acceptance by itself could have caused such an upheaval in European demography. Economic growth and the concomitant rise in standard of living were the structural conditions for the cultural changes. Only when workers are insured against the uncertainties of life, when women are economically independent from their partners and children from their parents; only then can individuals create the variety of living arrangements that replaced marriage in the past decades. In the end, however, all these individuals are, consciously or unconsciously, heavily influenced by their geographic heritage, because, despite all changes, we still find the regional patterns in Europe that were already described by John Hajnal. However, the findings in this chapter hopefully show that the rationale behind the pattern changed dramatically in the past century.

Bibliography

Alter, G. (1991) 'Introduction', *Journal of Family History*, 16, pp.1-5.

Blayo, C. (1987) 'La fécondité en Europe depuis 1960: convergence ou divergence?,' *Plenaries of the European Population Conference 1987*, pp. 47–112.

Coale, A.J. (1969) 'The decline of fertility in Europe from the French Revolution to World War II', in S.J. Behrman (ed.), *Fertility and family planning: a world view*, Ann Arbor, pp. 3-24.

Coale, A.J. and Watkins, S.C. (1986) *The decline of fertility in Europe: the revised proceedings of a conference on the Princeton European Fertility Project*, Princeton.

Coale, A.J. and Treadway, R. (1986) 'A Summary of the changing distribution of overall fertility, marital fertility, and the proportion married in the provinces of Europe' in A.J. Coale and S.C. Watkins (eds), *The decline of fertility in Europe*, Princeton, pp. 31–79.

Council of Europe (1994) *Recent demographic developments in Europe*, Strasbourg.

Das Gupta, M. (1995) 'Fertility decline in Punjab, India: parallels with historical Europe', *Population Studies*, 49, pp. 481–500.

David, H.P. and McIntyre, R.J. (1981) *Reproductive behavior: Central and Eastern European experience*, New York.

De Guibert-Lantoine, C. and Monnier, A. (1992) 'La conjoncture démographique: l'Europe et les pays développés d'Outre-Mer,' *Population*, 47, pp. 1017–36.

Engelen, T. (1994) 'Family, production and reproduction: on the relationship between economic and demographic processes,' *Economic and Social History in the Netherlands*, 6, pp. 61–82.

Engelen, T. (1997) 'The fertility decline in the Dutch province of Limburg, 1880–1960: on understanding historical actors in a constrained environment,' *The History of the Family*, 2, pp. 405–24.

Engelen, T.L.M. and Hillebrand,. J.H.A. (1986) 'Fertility and nuptiality in the Netherlands 1850–1960,' *Population Studies*, 40, pp. 487–503.

Festy, P. (1980) 'Aspects demographiques de la formation de la famille en Europe Occidentale,' in J.M. Eekelaar and S.N. Katz (eds), *Marriage and cohabitation in contemporary societies: areas of legal, social and ethical change*, Toronto and Boston, pp. 2–15.

Golini, A. (1987) 'Famille et ménage dans l'Italie récente,' *Population*, 42, pp. 699–714.

Guinnane, T. (1991) 'Re-thinking the Western European Marriage Pattern: the decision to marry in Ireland at the turn of the twentieth century,' *Journal of Family History*, 16, pp. 47–64.

Hajnal, J. (1965) 'European marriage patterns in perspective', in D.V. Glass and D.E.C. Eversley (eds), *Population in history: essays in historical demography*, London, pp. 101–46.

Hajnal, J. (1983) 'Two kinds of pre-industrial household formation system', in R.Wall, J. Robin and P. Laslett (eds), *Family forms in historic Europe*, Cambridge, pp. 65–104.

Hoffmann-Nowotny, H.-J. (1987) 'The future of the family,' *Plenaries of the European Population Conference 1987*, pp. 113–200.

Kertzer, D. and Hogan, D. (1991) 'Reflections on the European marriage: sharecropping and proletarianization in Caslecchio, Italy, 1861–1921,' *Journal of Family History*, 16, pp. 31–45.

Laslett, P. (1983) 'Family and household as work group and kin group: areas of traditional Europe compared', in R. Wall, J. Robin and P. Laslett (eds), *Family forms in historic Europe*, Cambridge, pp. 513–64.

Lynch, K.A. (1991) 'The European marriage pattern in the cities: variations on a theme by Hajnal', *Journal of Family History*, 16, pp. 79–96.

Malthus, T.R. (1798) *An essay on the principle of population, as it affects the future improvement of society*, New York, 1960.

Monnier, A. (1991) 'L'Europe de l'Est, différente et diverse', *Population*, 46, pp. 443–62.

Pavlík, Z. (1991) 'Les tendances démographiques longues en Europe de l'Est', *Population*, 46, pp. 463–77.

Roussel, L. (1986) 'Evolution récente de la structure des ménages dans quelques pays industriels,' *Population*, 41, pp. 913–34.

Saito, O. (1996) 'Historical demography: achievements and prospects', *Population Studies*, 50, pp. 537–53.

Conclusions[1]

Michael ANDERSON, University of Edinburgh

The principal objective for the CORN conference of which this book is based, was to understand more about the patterns and causes of variation in European rural marriage patterns between different countries and over time. After two days of discussion, my strongest impression is that we now at least have a clearer grasp of why such questions are so difficult to answer.

A first and very basic point is that answers often depend on what we are trying to measure and the level at which we are trying to measure it. In general, and certainly at a national level, variations in proportions ever-marrying have been much larger than differences in the mean age at marriage. Often, however, we observe large variation within countries on both variables, not only, for example, between urban and rural areas, but also between different rural areas depending on the presence or absence of small towns and, above all, on the extent and nature of different kinds of agricultural and especially non-agricultural activity. Even within agricultural communities, marriage patterns were often very different between those with and those without access to land. These differences within countries were often much larger than differences between countries and differences over time.

This means that we need to be very aware of the danger of ecological fallacy when we compare (and especially when we seek to explain) summary spatial differences without first investigating, as Hendrickx (Chapter 7) and Alter and Oris (Chapter 5), for example, *have* been able to do, whether compositional effects have masked underlying variability to a point where a mean or a median figure is, effectively, meaningless. Especially when writing about whole countries or regions, however, we usually use published data where only summary variables are available. Nevertheless, one important conclusion of the meeting is that to obtain a real understanding of marriage patterns, access to individual data, preferably processed within a life course perspective (Chapter 5), and with a strong awareness of the possibility of structured variability between different groups, is vital wherever possible.

There is also a second, linked point: gender difference must not be ignored, as so often it has been in the past. Changes over time in marriage patterns of males and females can diverge very markedly (as they did, for example, in Scotland in the early 19th century), but often only female figures are computed. This is, in retrospect, strange, if we note that many of the hypotheses which seek to explain variation relate much more to factors affecting men than women; or, as Smith (Chapter 1) and van Poppel (Chapter 6) suggest for very different situations, if the opportunities and con-

---

[1] I am very grateful to George Alter and Liam Kennedy for some helpful comments on a first draft of these remarks - though, since I have not always quite followed their advice, I remain totally responsible for what follows.

straints affecting the marriage behaviour on men and women are very different at any one time.

At least until the rise in cohabitation over the past twenty or so years, the 20th century has seen significant elements of convergence in marriage patterns between different parts of the continent, although some notable differences, many reflecting long-standing variations, remained. But what would Engelen (Chapter 11) have found had he carried his analysis back into the 19th century? I suspect that he would have suggested much more divergent trends, linked to different opportunities for marriage in differently developing economic (and also migration) contexts.

This links to a question that was raised in many different ways: how useful is it to seek to relate the experience of particular regions or places to a model of the 'Western European Marriage Pattern'? This raised the issue of whether the WEMP should be recognised in terms of outcomes (particular profiles of mean ages at marriage and/or percentages never married), or, alternatively, in terms of mechanisms which underpin it (for example, the requirement that newly marrying couples should form an independent household responsible for its own welfare). And, turning from description to explanation, it is clear that while, in different European societies and at different points in time, a range of mechanisms can be observed which regulated the formation of new households, nevertheless different combinations can produce similar outcomes in terms of marriage ages and of the proportions of those who remained in the community who could marry. A variety of such regulatory situations featured in our discussion, including, for example:

(a) direct control over entry to marriage: among examples we noted (see particularly Chapter 8) were control by the church, poor law authorities, the military, gild members, or landlords.

(b) indirect control via regulated access to a necessary fixed resource (for example, the common situation where newly marrying couples needed access to one of a largely unchanging number of parcels of land or occupational slots within the community); where this was the case, surplus children had either to remain unmarried or to move elsewhere, but, depending on the balance that emerged between staying or leaving, the outcome in terms of percentage remaining celibate in the community was very different (Chapter 2).

(c) in other cases, by contrast, the whole context of regulation changed where, for example, there emerged a marked expansion (or, in reverse, a contraction) of opportunities for the establishment of new households, some of which were wholly outside the previous regulatory structures: for example, through taking on full-time income-generating employment (proletarian wage labour as well as proto-industrial activity are relevant here), through opportunities to pioneer settlement of new land, or, where a shortage of housing was the prime constraint on marriage, through changes in access to accommodation suitable for couples and their children. Alternatively, this might simply involve a weakening (or strengthening) of earlier constraints on marriage by the emergence or contraction of situations which allowed additional viable households to be established, for example, through sub-division of property accompanied either by new less land-intensive crops such as the potato (or the reverse when the potato failed), or by changes in access to supplementary incomes. Among the examples we noted were proto-industry, and kelp processing in Scotland.

(d) Finally, in some areas of Finland (Chapter 8), as well as much of the South and the East, household formation was not in many cases a regulatory factor at all, in as far as couples could marry and live with relatives in pre-existing households.

However, while these different and changing constraints clearly influenced the resulting marriage patterns, they did not wholly determine them. Rather they are best seen as opening up or restricting *opportunities* for marriage. Within these contexts, the choices made by individual men and women both whether to marry and when to marry (and the two were not necessarily correlated) depended on a second set of factors. These included:

(a) the costs of, and the time necessary, to assemble the resources (for example, money, domestic or productive capital, influence, or skills) which made marriage and establishing a new household possible.

(b) the couple's view of the medium-term standard of living and other risks of marriage and of largely unregulated childbearing (acceptability of fertility limitation and, to some extent perhaps, access to appropriate means, clearly changed the equation here from the later 19th century in most of Europe). Assessment of these risks was affected in turn by the likely availability in periods of crisis of support from the community through for example, the poor law (the contrast between England and Scotland is of interest here), and by perceived prospects of employment for women and children.

(c) the advantages and disadvantages of alternatives to marriage. Demographers have sometimes implied that marriage was always a desirable state (and Lundh elaborated a particular argument here in Chapter 9), but Guinnane has argued persuasively that this was not necessarily the case in Ireland after the Famine; by contrast, Smith suggested (Chapter 1) that declining employment opportunities for women in 18th century England were a powerful stimulus to marriage, an interesting contrast to some of the older proto-industrialization literature, and one which again stresses the important point that factors affecting choices for men and for women were not always the same.

In turn, these regulatory mechanisms operated within, and choices were made within, varying social, cultural and structural contexts which also often constrained choice or, alternatively, offered new opportunities for marriage. One such factor, widely cited in the literature, is the sex ratio in the marriageable age groups; we in some cases, however, found it to be of rather little significance, probably because it is less relevant where celibacy was high for both sexes so that, even if the sex ratio was severely skewed, there was still a significant supply of potential unmarried partners of both sexes.

A variety of cultural factors seem to have been of much more significance in influencing people's expectations or preferences with respect to marriage. Social pressures, in some cases bolstered by powerful religious (Chapter 7) or legal (Chapter 8) forces, seem often to have influenced opinion on what was an acceptable basis for marriage or an acceptable form of household (for example, with respect to the tolerance shown to the presence of married children in a household, or to cohabitation or prenuptial pregnancy or lone parenthood). The effectiveness of sanctions against deviation from these 'rules' was also a variable (and, in particular, a significant factor influencing the degree of heterogenity of marriage patterns within a society).

This multi-level complex of interacting factors clearly poses considerable difficulty for any attempt to model statistically the causes of different marriage patterns in different places or periods, and they even challenge analyses focused on short and medium term change. Within this context, while changes in interval level variables such as living standards, mortality, and unemployment undoubtedly affected the operation of marriage markets in the short-run (Chapters 5 and 9), medium-term analysis is frequently challenged both by changes in expectations with respect to living standards (Chapters 3 and 6) and by major structural changes which introduced, for example, new forms of employment to supplement agricultural incomes (or, conversely, which in quite a short timespan removed them). Frequently, moreover, these structural disjunctions were often the results of actions taken by individuals who were not directly part of the affected local or regional marriage market or the social structures which on a day-to-day basis controlled it. In particular, changing policies of elites, both as landlords and as providers of employment, were often key exogenous agents in nuptiality change.

But there is also a much more important way in which marriage behaviour can be influenced by factors external to its immediate context. In almost every society or community that we discussed, external migration acted as a safety valve, balancing numbers of men and women to each other and/or to resources, and, in particular reducing levels of permanent celibacy. But, in some societies, out-migration became not the residual but the preferred option for some sections of the population, and in these cases marriage patterns could be much more radically affected, notably by changes in the perceived attractiveness of external migration destinations.

One overall conclusion might be that attempts at both generalisation and quantitative analysis of marriage behaviour need to be undertaken in ways which are extremely sensitive to contextual factors both at a point in time and over time. Thus may suggest that in-depth, targeted, comparative studies, with a significant qualitative component, are at the present time likely to be more productive in terms of understanding than aggregate statistical modelling of regional or national nuptiality change, except across rather short periods of time. There are still more questions than answers, but at least we are now rather clearer as to what some of the more productive questions are likely to be.